Lukaszewski
on CRISIS COMMUNICATION:
WHAT YOUR CEO NEEDS TO KNOW ABOUT REPUTATION RISK AND CRISIS MANAGEMENT

by
James E. Lukaszewski
(loo-ka-SHEV-skee)

Kristen Noakes-Fry, Editor

ISBN 978-1-931332-57-6 (Perfect Bound)
ISBN 978-1-931332-64-4 (eBook)
ISBN 978-1-931332-66-8 (Hard Cover)

Rothstein Associates Inc., Publisher
Brookfield, Connecticut USA
www.rothstein.com

ISBN 978-1-931332-57-6 (Perfect Bound)
ISBN 978-1-931332-64-4 (eBook)
ISBN 978-1-931332-66-8 (Hard Cover)

Library of Congress Control Number
2012953013

PUBLISHER:
Philip Jan Rothstein, FBCI
Rothstein Associates Inc.
The Rothstein Catalog on Disaster Recovery
4 Arapaho Rd.
Brookfield, Connecticut 06804-3104 USA
203.740.7444 • 203.740.7401 fax
info@rothstein.com
www.rothstein.com

Keep informed of the latest crisis communication, crisis management
and business continuity news.
Sign up for Business Survival™ Weblog: Business Continuity for Key Decision-Makers
from Rothstein Associates at www.rothstein.com/blog

Dedication

Chester A. Burger

1921-2011

A Special Dedication to Chester A. Burger:
Goodbye, Chet.
The Remembrance of a Remarkable Man
appears later in this book.

Acknowledgments

I would like to thank Philip Jan Rothstein, FBCI, my publisher, and Kristen Noakes-Fry, my editor. Their patience, perseverance, prodding, and occasional provoking are what brought this book into the world.

Preface

"A Word with Your Boss, Please..."

If I could speak to the chief executive of your company or organization about the importance of communications in your preparation for crisis or emergency, we would discuss just a few career preserving subjects, and the conversation would take only a few minutes. In short, we would discuss:

1. How responding quickly in the first 60-120 minutes of an emergency or disaster can save assets, markets, and reputations – and avoid or delay career-defining moments, his or hers.

2. How managing victims immediately, humanely, with compassion will de-escalate the visibility that poorly handled victims always causes.

3. The reputational toxicity of silence.

4. How well-handled and perfectly managed crises that are poorly communicated will always be remembered as poorly handled crises.

5. If you fail to manage your own destiny from the start, there is always someone out there waiting and willing to do it for you.

6. Speed beats smart every time. Waiting to execute the perfect response will cost you your reputation, and likely your job, and you will still fail.

7. Bad news always ripens badly. Bad news brings bad stories. Mistakes will be made and the media will make things up. Fifty percent of your energy and 25% of your resources will go to fixing yesterday's mistakes, yours and the media's.

8. Effective crisis communication involves simple, sensible, sincere, constructive, positive, and ethical approaches applied from the start.

9. How to overcome the abusive, intrusive, and coercive behavior of new media bloviators, bellyachers, back-bench bitchers, activists, and critics (and the media).

The unplanned visibility that a crisis creates builds expectations of your honorable behavior among your most critical audiences and stakeholders including your own employees, the community, the government, and the victims. Are you ready?

Managing this unplanned visibility, combined with a real sense of unconventional wisdom, is precisely what this book is about. Most managers and leaders consider themselves to be truly excellent communicators. This book will help you move these critical people, as well as your constituencies, to new levels of understanding and more prompt response when crisis strikes. This book is about going beyond the conventional wisdom. It's about doing things that matter, now. When you get what there is to do and say, done and said during that first golden hour of response opportunity, the victims will thank you and the media will leave you alone.

James E. Lukaszewski
Bloomington, Minnesota, USA
January, 2013

Foreword

"The Pragmatist"

I first met Jim Lukaszewski at a lecture more than 20 years ago, at a Public Relations Society of America (PRSA) national event. I was then setting up a Crisis Communications Group for a national PR firm, Ruder Finn, and thought I'd find out what I could learn from someone who was already a recognized expert in the field of crisis communications. We never met again, in person. But we started to become "email buddies" in 1994, after I launched my own consultancy and an email newsletter, *Crisis Manager*. I still recall Jim periodically sending me kindly worded missives, critiquing some of the ideas I espoused in my newsletter. Eventually, he agreed to become one of my guest authors.

The industry has come a long way since Jim and I had to explain what we meant by "crisis management." History made our job easier and more essential, following the explosion of Internet-centered communication from the early 1990s onward, covering crises ranging from Brookstone-Firestone's killer tires, to the demise of Enron and Arthur Andersen, to 9/11 and Katrina. Along the way, these incidents were complicated by "from the scene" reporting at every major natural and man-made disaster by individuals whose only claim to journalism talent was ownership of a portable device capable of recording and sending photos and video.

One of the things that makes Jim's new book unique, even in a field that itself is still relatively unique, is Jim's practical instruction on the intelligent and sensitive treatment of victims, which can lessen negative publicity for an organization in crisis and its brand, shorten the period of time the crisis remains in the public eye, and reduce the severity of any legal repercussions arising from the crisis. Jim also tells how to cope with the awesome power of the emergence of the "citizen journalist" – Internet-connected device-owning people able to report what they consider to be important news the moment it happens, 24/7.

And Jim, also, has been in the trenches battling crisis fires side by side with the lawyers, who sometimes, if you don't know how to work with them constructively, can actually make the crisis worse by focusing on courts of law versus courts of public opinion. The latter, as Jim explains, is what puts you out of business the fastest!

In this book, you will:

- have information on hand that, in my opinion, is worth hundreds of thousands of dollars, because it reflects the accumulated, multi-decade insights of one of the world's leading crisis communicators;
- learn more than you are likely to hear in 95% of the college courses that even begin to touch on the subject of crisis communications;
- significantly enhance your value to any employer and/or to clients if you are a consultant; and,
- have on hand, at all times, instructions that guide you through all aspects of the crisis communications process, from planning through tactics and beyond.

At this point in both our careers, Jim and I have the privilege of being considered "elder statesmen" in the field of crisis management. When I am asked, as frequently happens, what a PR professional or student should read to improve his or her skills in the area of crisis communications, I always say, "Buy anything by Jim Lukaszewski."

In my almost three decades as a crisis management consultant, author and editor, I have encountered few authors whose material is a must-read. Jim is one of them, and *Lukaszewski on Crisis Communications* may be his finest work.

Jonathan Bernstein
President of Bernstein Crisis Management Inc.
and author of *Manager's Guide to Crisis Management* and *Keeping the Wolves at Bay*
Los Angeles, California, USA
November, 2012

Foreword

"The Teacher/Counselor"

I've known Jim Lukaszewski for about half of his career. I've read his writings and attended dozens of his presentations. He is one of the most knowledgeable people on Earth when it comes to issues of crisis management. For the past four decades, Jim has been an international thought leader in the area of crisis communications. His counsel on dealing with crises has saved the reputation of corporation after corporation, individual after individual, and in *Lukaszewski on Crisis Communication: What Your CEO Needs to Know About Reputation Risk and Crisis Management* he shares his thoughts, wisdom and experiences with us.

This authoritative treatise is for everyone who may ever deal with a crisis – public relations practitioners, professors, attorneys, and public relations students. It is a crisis management book about crisis communication planning, focusing on many of the areas that most plans and planning omit, ignore, treat with disdain, or deal with superficially. It is filled with how-to tips, charts, forms, checklists, and sensible approaches. He provides a simple, practical, and constructive process for preventing crises; and when they hit, he tells how to manage them in the best interest of the organization.

In addition to advice on planning for and dealing with managing crises, *Lukaszewski on Crisis Communication: What Your CEO Needs to Know About Reputation Risk and Crisis Management* contains instructions for dealing with *all* aspects of a crisis. For example, one chapter focuses on understanding and overcoming management's reluctance to participate in the crisis management process, especially before a crisis occurs. He also gives wise advice for how the practitioner can gain the credibility needed to keep and maintain management's attention, and what should be the role of leaders and their leadership during the crisis, as well as after the crisis has been concluded.

Very importantly, the book emphasizes the victims of the crisis. Lukaszewski demonstrates how victims drive the crisis more than any other factor. Jim has spent his career talking to managers about the victim issue and how victims can redefine reputations, products, services, and top management careers. His sage advice on this topic has saved the career of more than one major corporate CEO, and now he is passing this advice along to others.

No book on crisis communication would be complete without chapters on media relations, both legacy media and new media. However, this is not the traditional how-to-create-a-favorable-news-release information. Rather, Jim addresses the tough, ethical issues of media relations during a crisis. A unique contribution to this book is an exploration of the role of the Internet, the World Wide Web, and social media in the crisis management process. More than one organization or individual has been the subject of a major crisis because of something a disgruntled employee or unhappy customer posted. In these pages, Jim outlines how to monitor these new media to forecast potential crises, and how to use them to prevent and help solve crises. In his discussion of the ethics of crisis management, Jim applies what he has learned as a member of the Public Relations Society of America's Board of Ethics and Professional Standards, and from his participation in re-creating PRSA's Code of Ethics.

Finally, Lukaszewski addresses the legal aspects of crisis communication – dealing with attorneys, legal issues, and how to move away from the typically defensive PR posture when attorneys are in the room. Traditionally, in a crisis, the views of legal counselors often seem diametrically opposed to those of the PR counselor. The lawyers maintain that "anything we say can and will be used against us." In this section of the book, Jim provides unique insights into how lawyers think, the function of the legal process, and how the PR practitioners can thoughtfully and persuasively urge attorneys to help the CEO to "tell it all, tell the truth, and tell it faster." The legal risks escalate dramatically when the strategy is to stall, delay, and maintain silence. Wait till you read his section on apology! Lukaszewski teaches the PR counselor and company executives how to accommodate and strategically redirect the resistance offered by legal counsel.

Lukaszewski on Crisis Communication: What Your CEO Needs to Know About Reputation Risk and Crisis Management is one of those books that is appropriate for both the teacher and the practitioner. Each chapter begins with introductory questions and learning points and ends with review points and questions about the chapter. Read this book, and *read it now*, before the crisis occurs; this work may help you to prevent the crisis, and it certainly will help you plan and manage it.

There are two types of organizations: those who have a crisis, and those who will. This book may just help you save your organization when it's time for your crisis, or at the very least, help you choose the kind of organization you'd rather be.

Jay Rayburn

Jay Rayburn, APR, CPRC, Ph.D., Fellow PRSA
Division Director, Advertising and Public Relations
School of Communication, Florida State University
Tallahassee, Florida, USA
November, 2012

Foreword

"The Game Changer"

Last year I celebrated my 30th year at Lee Hecht Harrison, the world's leading career management and talent development consulting company, with 300 offices in more than 65 countries. Currently, I serve as Chairman of the company. About halfway through my tenure, I met Jim Lukaszewski, and the timing couldn't have been better. Our acquisition by a large Swiss-based corporation seven years earlier had given us the resources to expand domestically and globally – and expand we did!

As the leadership team and I regularly took stock of our development, the questions were inevitable: Is the pace of our growth appropriate? How can we be sure that our professional preeminence would not be compromised in our quest for industry leadership? How can we be sure that our cultural integrity would not be adversely impacted by this growth? How do we sustain our commitment to our long-standing ethical mantra: *Never compromise our ethical standards for commercial gain*? And with our broader reach, how do we maintain our commitment to communicate authentically and transparently with our various publics, starting with our own colleagues?

There were frequent conversations on these issues among our leadership team, key employees, and select clients. And, at the suggestion of our PR firm, we had a conversation with Jim Lukaszewski. Jim has a long and successful history of being thrust into the business lives of C-Suite leaders, some of whom were paying the price of a ready-fire-aim business track with too few "pit-stops" and too little cultural re-tooling. Lou Gerstner once said, "Culture isn't one thing a leader does... it's everything." With his extensive experience, Jim's voice was valuable as we moved forward.

With Jim's guidance, we created the industry's first business ethics guidebook, specific to our unique services and business practices. In 2004, I took on the assignment of Interim Chief Compliance Officer for our parent company. Jim demystified the issues and introduced us to major thought leaders in the field of business ethics. Jim also served as an invaluable sounding board in the development of my 2007 book, *The Manager's Book of Decencies: How Small Gestures Build Great Companies* (McGraw-Hill, 2007).

Most of us have had a select few individuals during the course of our lives who have been real game-changers – high-impact contributors to our personal or career development. Throughout my own personal development and career path, I have had my share as well, sometimes coming from unexpected places. Jim Lukaszewski is one of those.

Jim's main contribution has been that of an educator, communicator, and motivator, teaching that decency matters, transparency matters, authenticity matters, listening matters, accessibility matters, living our published values matters, and in the event of an ethical lapse, a speedy, constructive, and genuine response matters.

In his new book, *Lukaszewski on Crisis Communication: What Your CEO Needs to Know About Reputation Risk and Crisis Management*, Jim gives the leader of the future a priceless tool developed by a trusted, strategic, and passionate advisor. As with Jim Lukaszewski's lectures, podcasts, and publications, in this his latest work, the task of crisis-response emerges as more than a to-do list – it is a true, learnable art. As important, even *more* important, the book's final and critical chapter cautions against CEO myopia, or, worse-yet, ethics fatigue. It is, at the end of the day, all about *leadership*, the ability to galvanize diverse talent and resources toward a common goal. It is also the fine art of achieving this goal while avoiding the ethical pitfalls, land mines, and pot holes that can be the undoing of even the best-intended leadership visions. Jim's book should be compulsory reading for leaders, aspiring leaders, and students of the business game.

Steve Harrison

Steve Harrison, Non-Executive Chairman, Lee Hecht Harrison
Former member, Adecco Worldwide Executive Committee.
International speaker on ethics, leadership, and corporate culture.
Board Member, JAG (Jobs for American Graduates)
Author, *The Manager's Book of Decencies:
How Small Gestures Build Great Businesses*
Woodcliff Lake, New Jersey, USA
November, 2012

Contents

Chapter 4: Creating the Crisis Communication Plan: Components and Models 97

Introduction

Common Sense at Lightning Speed

While others may be credited for inventing the discipline of *crisis communication*, Jim Lukaszewski is one of the field's most influential innovators and practitioners. He has and continues to effectively counsel countless CEOs, executives, and management and communication leadership teams in public and private companies and NGOs. He also is one of the foremost *teachers* of crisis communication strategy and tactics, informing and motivating thousands of managers, communicators, educators and students in person and online.

Why is this new book, *Lukaszewski on Crisis Communication: What Your CEO Needs to Know About Reputation Risk and Crisis Management,* so effective? Jim's common-sense approach stands out because it helps guide people to respond and communicate effectively, cutting through the fog and confusion typical of the onset of a crisis.

I tested Jim's definition of a *crisis* with a class of MBA students recently. I quoted Jim as saying: "A crisis is a show-stopping, people-stopping, product-stopping, reputation-defining, trust-busting event that creates *victims* and/or explosive visibility..." I went on to explain that potential victims could include employees, customers, or the public; that the crisis may close your business, disrupt operations, cause physical or environmental damage, or threaten the firm's financial standing or public image.

Suddenly the lights went on in 27 heads. Crises "create victims," have "explosive visibility," can "close your business," "threaten financial standing and reputation." For the MBA students, Jim's insightful definition instantly brought to mind a wide-ranging pantheon of recent crises and how they were handled – unintended acceleration, celebrity infidelity, an oil well explosion and catastrophic spill, racist internet pranks, an earthquake/tsunami, and the list goes on. It made the possibility of a crisis personal for the students, all of whom were middle managers – "It could happen to my organization – so we've got to be prepared."

This new book tells the experienced and inexperienced how and why to respond in the crisis situations they are most likely to face. In a crisis, Jim recommends five approaches: "Be positive; be compassionate; be transparent; apologize sincerely, and with meaning; and settle quickly." These simple tenets are the most complex to execute because they run counter to many management cultures. They all were eye-openers for the MBA class and – with Jim's positive-outcome orientation – provide incrementally achievable goals for all managers and communicators who want to be well-equipped to prepare for and respond to crises of every type. Consider how implementing these five tenets would have improved outcomes and reputations for many contemporary crises.

Most of us need templates and checklists to develop customized crisis plans and communication materials. This book supplements discussion topics by including comprehensive "how-to" lists and templates. For example, to help readers implement Jim's insightful advice to always use positive, declarative language and to eradicate the use of negative words, the handbook lists scores of positive words and phrases and translates frequently used, negative examples into positive equivalents. It categorizes scores of crises by risk. It lists the causes of victimization. In three highly-detailed and actionable chapters, this book describes media behavior and attitudes and details social and digital media tactics. Most important, it offers a step-by-step guide to crisis readiness – how to prepare and train your organization before a crisis.

Lukaszewski is passionate that unless crisis communication preparation is well-planned and specific, it will fail to be helpful – in fact, lack of focused planning causes confusion, delay, hesitation, even management timidity in most crisis response situations. He's equally clear on the role of the professional communicator in a crisis: for communicators, the most important lesson of all is to say things that matter, do things that matter, and be prepared to give useful information and advice on the spot. Here's a walkthrough of Lukaszewski's step-by-step approach to understanding, preparing for, managing, and recovering from crises:

Chapter 1:
Defining Crisis: It's All About Victims

There are many ways to define a *crisis*. Lukaszewski's definition starts with the extraordinary 24/7 communication cycle and the reputational threats this new environment can stimulate, and focuses on the significance and power of *the victim dimension* to dislocate, distort, and even destroy the credibility of even the most competent response and readiness processes. Chapter 1 then illustrates how *a crisis,* which he defines as "the sudden, unexpected creation of victims, accompanied by unplanned visibility for an organization," occurs, providing a case study example, followed by lessons learned.

Chapter 2:
Crisis Communication: Building Leadership Ready for Crisis

Lukaszewski contends that the prudent organization studies its vulnerabilities, identifies those that present the greatest risk, and gets ready with what it must do and say to respond quickly and effectively in the face of a crisis. Why? "Crisis management is the exercise of common sense at lightning speed" – a skill set lacking in most management teams. However, these skills can and should be learned. His fundamental insight for CEOs: All crises are management problems first. Preplanning executive actions can avoid career-defining moments, and leadership that shows compassion, community sensitivity, and sensible, ethical approaches can move companies to victory and out of harm's way. He concludes by establishing the need for powerful verbal communications on the part of the CEO when an organization is in crisis or preparing to handle one. The leader must become a *verbal visionary,* and *the crisis communicator must help him or her become one.*

Chapter 3:
Crisis Communication: Preparing the Organization for Crisis

The process of readiness preparation begins with what Lukaszewski calls *visibility analysis* – examining the possible sources of crises and their planned and unplanned potential for visibility. This is an important learning experience for the communicator, revealing an often surprisingly wide variety of activities and situations about the organization which pose great risks. With checklists and an ingenious "Audience and Stakeholder Analysis" chart, the chapter details how to systematically conduct stakeholder analysis, issues analysis, and threat identification for your organization. Then, he walks you through establishing the most likely risk categories for your organization, and creating the response strategies and priorities based on the most likely scenarios your organization can face. Last, you learn how to create policies and set responsibilities based on likely scenarios, so the organization's leaders know precisely what to do and who will do it in a crisis.

Chapter 4:
Creating the Crisis Communication Plan: Components and Models
Very few books on crisis management offer instruction on how to build a crisis plan. In this highly utilitarian chapter, Lukaszewski takes you through the process with plenty of detail and rationale along the way. His premise: Any crisis plan, especially for communications, must focus on achieving pre-established objectives during the critical first few hours of a crisis. After that, the crisis degenerates into a management problem ground down by the organization until resolved. He takes the reader through scenario-based planning; the necessity and rewards of involving the boss in the process; and assembling, publishing and maintaining – keeping current the elements of your plan. He includes scenario-based message development, which arms the team with quickly updatable content to communicate in the first few hours of the crisis, as well as explaining how to create an effective scenario to test and fine-tune your plan.

Chapter 5:
Crisis Communication Plan in Action: Media Relations
Since dealing with the media in a crisis is perhaps the single most challenging undertaking for organizations, Lukaszewski devotes three chapters to the topic. He shares lessons learned from four decades of dealing with the media, outlining how to achieve great results by employing novel, powerful, positive emergency media responses. He argues that effective media relations begins by defining media policy, designating spokespersons and what they should be doing, and the importance of *always* setting the record straight if you make a mistake. For success with the media, communicators and organizational leadership must understand and anticipate the nature and predilections of the media, including the investigative news magazine shows. This chapter provides 14 lessons for how to deal with the *60 Minutes* of the world. The final three highly insightful discussions in this chapter enable readers to assess the validity and believability of news stories; to assess the damage and deal with bad news; and to understand just where journalists are coming from in order to deal with them on an equal footing.

Chapter 6:
Crisis Communication Plan in Action: The Crisis News Conference
When the crisis situation warrants it – and only then – the news conference can be highly effective in getting key messages out. Knowing when to hold a news conference, the various types of conferences professionals employ, and how to make them most effective are the central topics of this chapter. Lukaszewski explains the rationale for media conferences and provides checklists to keep communicators on track with planning, tactics, and all of the

myriad details. Strategic and accurate messages are fundamental to news conference success. He offers advice on what types of questions to expect and how to anticipate them in advance, using tactics ranging from audience analysis to Google searches. Lukaszewski's list of "killer questions," the attributes of a good answer, and his list of negative terms and positive words to eradicate them are must-reads for CEOs and communicators alike. He concludes this chapter with the three important ingredients of answers: a direct answer to the question followed by your scripted messages and then – via the technique he calls bridging – an answer to the question you *wish* they had asked.

Chapter 7:
Crisis Communication Plan in Action: Social Media
Companies and their crisis teams have to stay ahead of this global communication revolution, both by monitoring news via alerts and feeds and pushing out their own online news updates through new media platforms. Chapter 7 explores the difference between legacy, new and social media; why organizations need to know how to deal effectively with all media; how to use new media tools to monitor your company's issues, risks and reputation; and how to neutralize an Internet crisis. In a case study, readers learn about "Surviving a Personal Blog Attack – or Not." In addition, you learn why the basic rules of media relations still apply, whether dealing with traditional or social media. Audience analysis, communications strategy, expressed through thoughtful, accurate content should fill the communication channels, digital or legacy. Moreover, organizations can protect their interests by developing a strategy to address the risks of social media usage that focuses on user behavior – that of employees, the business and constituents – via published policies, training, and awareness programs that cover digital and social media use.

Chapter 8:
Crisis Communication Plan in Action: The Activist Challenge
Why devote a chapter to the challenges presented by activists? Today's activists have the power to muster public sentiment with very little capital and thereby negate corporate strategies, change laws, create new laws and, well, make organizations look silly or worse. Today's activists are emotionally committed to opposing and targeting traditional corporate behavior. Lukaszewski advises that to win these jousts in the area of public opinion, large organizations have to be as committed to victory as their critics are committed to defeating them. Fortunately, understanding the patterns of activist tactics puts organizations and their leadership in a position to communicate effectively, sometimes even successfully. Lukaszewski delineates the most common activist allegations, offering counterintuitive approaches to neutralizing them while avoiding the most common preparation errors. His

"Seven Guidelines for Communication when Under Attack" should be committed to memory – including a favorite: "Your silence is toxic to your cause." Always emphasizing the positive, Lukaszewski concludes this discussion of largely bad behavior with a manifesto of "principles, policies, or intentions for addressing contentious public circumstances and situations, and behaving with integrity, honesty, and even good humor."

Chapter 9:
Crisis Communication Plan in Action: Litigation and Legal Issues

Thanks to the author's extensive experience working with attorneys in high-visibility litigations, this chapter may be the most common-sense, pragmatic approach to these contentious relationships. In Lukaszewski's words, "Trust me... you want to avoid the criminal justice system at all costs... Lawsuits and indictments against your company are guaranteed to result in a level of visibility that you want to avoid." His salient advice includes the due diligence process; litigation volume reduction; understanding the differences between civil and criminal litigation (including two detailed infographic maps of criminal and civil procedures); as well as how to prepare for litigation. He also provides insight into attorneys' motivations and strategies, tips on working well with them, and advice for lawyers in dealing with the media. In addition, he offers tips on designing litigation strategy, managing visibility during litigation, and ways to regain public credibility following damaging situations and highly visible threats to reputation. And, as he writes, "I always recommend to clients involved in potential or actual litigation that they propose settlement talks immediately." Lukaszewski is *passionate* about apologies, and his apologia for the necessity of making apologies sincerely and credibly ends this section.

Chapter 10:
Crisis Communication: Looking Ahead

Successful crisis and reputation management depend on forecasting future risks and opportunities. Only organizations that are forward-looking flourish. Only organizations that are prepared to face a crisis succeed.

Lukaszewski wraps up this thought-provoking, commonsense volume with answers to some basic questions organizational representatives always ask him. He concludes that: "It is the perpetrators themselves – especially over-confident leaders – who sabotage the competence of responses in crises."

Final Observations

How many times in the last few years have we observed this remarkably damaging phenomenon, with CEOs blurting out insensitive, thoughtless quips that undermine the best efforts of the organization to make amends in a crisis? The greatest single weakness in crisis response and readiness among communicators and other staff functions is failing to be ready to help leaders lead, even when these leaders' own careers may be on the line. Here is Jim's summary of the importance of crisis communication:

Crisis Communication Matters Because It:

1. *Can avoid career-defining moments for the boss and perhaps other senior managers.*
2. *Moderates and minimizes damage to reputation and employee morale.*
3. *Enhances a company's ability to recover from financial losses, regulatory fines, loss of market share, damages to equipment or products, or business interruption.*
4. *Reduces potential exposure to civil or criminal liability.*
5. *Should eliminate at least one or two substantial crisis risks.*
6. *May reduce your insurance premiums.*
7. *Provides an opportunity for management to demonstrate an ability to deal with difficult circumstances and lead the organization out of trouble.*
8. *Appears to be the most crucial factor for recovery – when it is effective.*
9. *Reduces the production of new critics and complainers.*
10. *Is the "right" thing to do.*

To all of the CEOs and executives for whom what you say and do in the first moments of a crisis is an instant test of your leadership, this book will prepare you to step up to the challenge of crisis communication.

To all the managers and communication leaders of public and private organizations who are responsible for preparing and guiding crisis management and communications, this book will prepare you to have more influence, give better advice, and become a more trusted strategic adviser during a crisis.

To all the communication professors and their students, this book contains the valuable insight and advice you need to learn how to be prepared to meet crisis communication challenges of the future, set forth in engaging, memorable and inspiring style.

Ken Koprowski

Ken Koprowski, M.A.
Crisis Communication Consultant and Professor
President, Westchester/Fairfield County Chapter of PRSA
and PRSA Tristate District Chair
New York City, New York, USA
November, 2012

1

Defining Crisis:
It's All About Victims

Keywords: crisis, problem, readiness, disaster, operational, non-operational, victim, testosterosis, apology, victim recovery cycle

A s we walk together through the crisis preparation and readiness process, it would seem useful to agree on or, at least, to have in mind a working definition of crisis. Typically, crises are defined in general terms with the specificity coming as a part of the readiness-and-response planning process. To get your thinking started, I prefer to define crisis with focus on victims, a concept rarely dealt with in crisis communication and operational response planning. Victims and how they are treated will determine just how much of your crisis response will be carried out successfully.

This chapter will help you to:

➢ Define a *crisis* and what differentiates it from other problems and business interruptions that an organization can experience.

➢ Recognize the importance of being prepared (*readiness*) in advance to communicate effectively with employees, *victims*, and the press in the event of a crisis.

➢ Understand what makes a person or group a victim and how the presence of victims relates to what defines an event as a crisis.

➢ See how to manage the victims in a crisis with the compassion, fairness, and honesty that will bring the situation under control and help the public image of your organization, while preserving, protecting, and defining your organization's reputation.

1.1 Crisis Management and Readiness Defined

1.1.1 Crisis and Components of Crisis

> Simply put, *crisis* is the sudden, unexpected creation of victims.

With today's focus on extraordinarily rapid communication and the reputational threats this new environment can stimulate, it is wise to consider the significance and power of the victim dimension to dislocate, distort, and even destroy the credibility of even the most competent response and readiness processes. Simply put, **crisis is the sudden, unexpected creation of victims, accompanied by unplanned visibility for an organization.**

So let's begin at the beginning with some working definitions of crisis and the components of crisis.

1. Show-stopping, people-stopping, product-stopping, or reputation-defining, trust-busting event that creates victims and/or explosive visibility. Victims can be people, animals, living systems, i.e. forests, the atmosphere, somebody's backyard.

Causes of Victimization:

Abuse	Confrontation	Fear
Arrogance	Cotention	Lies
Assault	Deception	Negligence
Bullying	Discrediting	Omission
Callousness	Dismissiveness	Sarcasm
Carelessness	Disparagement	Shame
Commission	Embarrassment	Surprise

2. Any unplanned event that may cause death or significant injury to employees, customers, the public, or animals; or one that can close your business, disrupt operations, cause physical or environmental damage, or threaten the firm's financial standing or public image.

1.1.2 Nature of Crisis

From my experience, my estimated metrics for crisis management are pretty straightforward:

- 95% of all crises are the result of daily operations and present low-level threats to reputation.
- 5% of crises are non-operational in nature, highly emotional, victim producing, and represent significant threats to reputation, operations, and value.

- Berserk employee
- Bomb threats
- Business loss
- Congressional action
- Crimes in progress
- Criminal behavior
- Decapitation
- Demonstrations / protests
- Disgruntled employee
- Embezzlement
- Employee violence
- Ethics problems
- Extortion
- Kidnapping
- Litigation
- Major allegations
- Major business decisions
- Major crimes
- Major theft
- Obscene / coercive telephone calls
- Sabotage
- Scandal
- Sexual harassment
- Stock price drop
- Terrorist actions
- Web attacks
- Whistle-blowers
- Workplace violence

Case Study: Restaurant Food Poisoning

Of the many critical situations that can befall a business, food contamination or other health threats are among the most publicly visible and important public issues. Victims are being created by the actual circumstances of the problem, and additional victims, through the intense and often explosive visibility of the situations are being created as well. For a chain of restaurants, potential victims could include customers who ate at any of the restaurant locations earlier in the day or in the previous few days.

The Company

Dave's Diner, a regionally famous family-owned chain of full-service restaurants is located in 13 Midwestern US states. For the first time in the family's history, the last three new restaurants were franchisees in St. Louis, Memphis, and Oklahoma City.

The Crisis

The first incidents involved two private parties at their flagship Dave's Diner in Des Moines. Reports of ill customers reached the restaurant as local emergency rooms began taking in seriously and suddenly ill patients of all kinds – children, older adults, a cross-section of individuals from the community. A local radio station, apparently tipped off by an ER worker, sent a local freelance reporter to several emergency rooms in the area to interview both staff and victims. The reporter, almost immediately, began doing live broadcast interviews with victims and their families.

The Complexities

Before long, more than a dozen victims were reported to be in critical condition, two of them on life support equipment. The vast majority of victims were suffering symptoms ranging from explosive diarrhea to upset stomach.

As with any such situation, Dave's Diner was required to make certain notifications immediately, thus involving government agencies and other civil authorities.

With very little information to go on, the owners of Dave's Diner organization were almost immediately facing very serious public questions, most requiring some affirmative action, now. They were required to take actions and make decisions with very little information; meanwhile, negative visibility was growing by the minute. For a family company which had built up decades of goodwill, this was a very stressful situation.

Although it appeared that only the store in Des Moines was involved, media coverage seemed to be uncovering individuals with health issues who ate at other stores in the chain in the past few days. Almost immediately, customer victims began calling their local restaurant to find out who was going to pay for trips to the doctor and other situations in which these individuals and families found themselves. As news of the situation spread across the media, restaurants in other locations and states were beginning to receive calls from local news outlets.

The questions came fast and furious: How many victims are there? What are their conditions? How many hospitals are they being treated in? Is there any sense of the cause? What is the company doing about victim care, determining the causes, working with health authorities? How many stores will the company close until the mystery is resolved? Will the company take financial responsibility for the victims? How difficult is it going to be for victims to be compensated and taken care of?

Needless to say, the Dave's Diner corporate offices were navigating a gigantic legal minefield for which the company was completely unprepared.

The Approach

The company chose to take a "moderately proactive" approach, which, in the long run, damaged the reputation of the company:

- All calls from victims and the media were referred to the corporate headquarters. Local store managers were not briefed on the situation and were prohibited from commenting in response to calls.
- The statement from the company was delayed. Although the company promised a statement, it took a couple of hours before anything meaningful was said.
- The company appeared to step away from taking responsibility.
- While the initial response was empathetic, seeming to recognize that there were problems, they only promised to promptly "look into" the situation.
- A spokesman for the chain, one of the members of the founding family, said the organization was evaluating "whether or not it was appropriate for the company to reimburse those making claims."
- The company professed to be cooperating with all public authorities, and urged calm as the source of the contamination or causative agents were investigated.

▶ The company announced that it had closed the party and convention facility, which was the location of the original outbreak of illness, along with its special kitchen, in order to find the cause.

▶ The company never took complete responsibility, promising that it would take, "appropriate responsibility, depending on the circumstances and what the various investigations would show."

The Culmination

▶ Countermanding the company's decision to keep all restaurants open during the investigation, local health authorities ordered the immediate closure and quarantine of the two restaurants in Des Moines, even though victims were only coming from the banquet facilities at the older flagship store.

▶ By late evening of the first day, victims' families were holding large meetings organized by the news media and local health activist organizations.

▶ A local union (which had been trying to unionize restaurant workers for several years) seized the opportunity to establish a hotline to anonymously report operating infractions by the company, any circumstances where the restaurant was forcing its employees to cut safety corners, and any other relevant information that public authorities should consider as well as be known by the public.

Lessons Learned

▶ Management's *failure to act* with extreme promptness and selfless responsibility corroded what had been for decades a most positive reputation. Dave's Diner was fortunate that there were no deaths in this particular case. However, there were extraordinary legal consequences and community suspicion.

▶ It took the executives of Dave's Diner almost seven days to apologize. Thus, the chain was deprived of the good will and support of many employees and loyal customers. Even public officials who wanted to support this really good local business in its time of need were prohibited from acting by the company's behavior.

▶ The long-range result for the Dave's Diner chain included lawsuits, loss of business, closure of some of its smaller locations, difficulty in signing up new franchisees, and significant delay in carrying out its intended business plan.

The Conclusions

▶ Situations involving public health and safety require dramatic, comprehensive and conclusive responses, decisions, and actions from the very beginning.

> ▶ Every hesitation, marginal or confused response will energize victims, survivors, critics, public authorities, folks with their own agendas, and increasingly trigger social media activity, although such was not the case in this example.
>
> ▶ Victims, whether people, animals, or living systems, must be dealt with as promptly as possible.
>
> ▶ The general strategy for crisis response involves five powerful steps, each activated as quickly as possible, preferably within an hour (the golden hour) of recognition that the crisis has occurred or is occurring:
>
>   1. Stop the production of victims. In this case, close those restaurants immediately.
>   2. Manage the victim dimension. Step up, arrange for handling victim expenses, family disruptions, and fears.
>   3. Communicate internally first, recognizing that such communication becomes public almost instantly. Failure to speak promptly triggers enormous uninformed communication by employees.
>   4. Organize and initiate regular public communication quickly. Deal with those who opt in on their own, the news media, bloggers, and bloviators.
>   5. Notify those indirectly affected who require notification or would expect notification.

1.2 All Crises Are Problems – Not All Problems Are Crises

The vast majority of issues and problems (operationally and otherwise) faced on a day-to-day basis are not truly crises, but rather problems and issues the organization must learn to anticipate, face, remediate, and resolve. Recognizing the nature of a true crisis means you must define carefully those situations that could become crises before including them as part of your organization's crisis readiness process and, ultimately, crisis communication strategy.

Very few problems are crises. For example, these examples are probably *not crises:*

▶ A long-term issue, which occasionally flares up and embarrasses us.

▶ A routine or predictably irritating high-profile problem.

▶ A disruption in an otherwise "normal" environment.

> These serious crises often have highly emotional components and are rarely studied, much less mentioned, in business management schools.

If every adverse incident is labeled a crisis, then management will say, correctly, "Since it is not possible to prepare for everything, and we can't predict exactly what will happen, we will rely on our skills and ability to handle situations as they arise." If this is the attitude of your management, we suggest that you severely redefine and redescribe your crisis scenario candidates to be able to convince operating executives to prepare for real crises.

However your organization happens to be structured – corporate sector, government, military, not-for-profit – in general, two distinct functions exist:

- The *line* function is the operating area of the organization. It's where leadership resides, decisions are made, vision and mission are developed, revenue is generated, and major contact with the public occurs.
- *Staff* functions, conversely, are those that generally support all line functions, or provide key services such as communications, finance, human resources, law, security, and administration. Staff functions are strictly expense items and rarely, if ever, attract or generate revenue or contribute directly to the bottom line.

1.2.1 Operational and Non-Operational Crises

Another way to look at an organization is to, again, divide it into two parts: operations and non-operations. The definitions are fairly similar for line versus staff; however, looking at an organization from an emergency, disaster, or crisis perspective, it is safe to estimate that 95% of all crises occur as a result of the day-to-day operations of an organization. This fact leads to two realities. First, there is substantial resident expertise to deal with these types of situations. Second, the level of confidence in a solution is high among operating management because these situations are often daily facts of life and the subject of ongoing experience building for managers and leaders.

While my estimate is that only 5% of serious problems, crises, or disasters occur in the non-operating areas of the organization, these are generally the most difficult to manage and most damaging to trust and reputation. These serious crises often have highly emotional components and are rarely studied, much less mentioned, in business management schools. Most management knowledge of non-operating events is provided by management consultants, the direct experiences of employees, or available professional back-channels.

It is also essential to define what is being dealt with and to classify problems and situations in ways that make sense and for which, therefore, preparation is desirable and achievable.

> The principal ingredient of any crisis is the creation of victims… Avoiding responsibility and shifting blame can become significant barriers for the organization and its leadership.

1.2.2 Crises and Disasters

In the context of the victim dimension, it's helpful to recall the differences between a crisis and a disaster. Crises are caused by human beings through commission, omission, accidents, negligence, or ignorance. On the other hand, larger forces, generally natural events, usually cause disasters – tsunamis, earthquakes, hurricanes, tornadoes, and incredibly powerful storms. Disasters can produce victims, but unless responders act negatively, or behave carelessly or callously, a disaster brings with it far less potential for blame, bad news, and the mindless victimization through timid or hesitant responses that so often occur in a crisis.

The principal ingredient of a crisis is the creation of victims. It is the presence of victims and how they are managed that creates a crisis. Virtually every post-mortem on crisis communication decisions, management decisions, and government decision-making and response processes highlights the victim aspect as the driving, emotionally energizing force. Bad news of any consequence is about victims, victimization, or the potential for both. There are three types: people can be victims; animals can be victims; and living systems can be victims. Avoiding responsibility and shifting blame can become significant barriers for the organization and its leadership.

Disasters are large-scale situations that also may result in victims, but for which placing blame can be more difficult. Disasters are often caused by nature or other entities that are entirely beyond the control of an organization, government, or business. Disasters tend to be more operational in nature, but many do have non-operating and emotional aspects. Disasters become crises when they are badly handled or poorly responded to, or when the victims are mishandled or left to suffer.

The crisis component of any serious situation is explosive and generally very brief, sometimes lasting only a devastating instant. The recovery aspect, including the resumption of business operations, occurs incrementally over a much longer span of time. Practically speaking, the crisis management aspects of these situations are very short lived, and the major components of responding to these situations are disaster recovery, reputation repair, and occasionally business continuation.

Clearly, much communication is required in the very early phases of a crisis when information about victims, survivors, causes, and remedies is needed most urgently. As the need to blame is replaced by effective, empathetic understanding and action, the news value – as well as the communication required – tends to decline. As the process moves into recovery and resumption activities, public communication often is significantly and mistakenly reduced.

1.2.3 Disaster Examples
Disasters almost always have major operating impacts, disruptions, and other consequences. Even though they can often be quite urgent and significant situations, they, too, can be prepared for in advance and generally responded to at a lower level of emotion. Disasters caused by bombings and sabotage

will increase intervention by police or government authorities. These agencies tend to usurp early response and communications. However, it is in your best interest to let these outside authorities take control over response and communications, and even encourage it.

Organizations should plan for these threats and disasters:

▶ Bomb threats and incidents
▶ Crimes in progress
▶ Demonstrations/protests
▶ Disgruntled/violent employees
▶ Earthquake
▶ Evacuation
▶ Explosion/fire/flames
▶ Flooding/torrential rain/winter storms/hurricanes
▶ General disruptions/threats
▶ Hazardous materials/chemical spills/gas leaks/toxic fumes
▶ Major accidents
▶ Major storms
▶ Negative embarrassing news coverage
▶ Noxious odors
▶ Obscene telephone calls
▶ Power outages
▶ Ruptured water pipes/falling water/sewer backups
▶ Sabotage/threats of sabotage
▶ Smoke/burning odors
▶ Tornadoes

In many organizations, especially those with security functions, disaster response is assigned to security, another staff function, rather than to corporate communications or the legal department. Thus, it is important that you start today to build constructive relationships with all staff functions around readiness.

Crisis Category Examples

We have identified five general categories of crisis. Managers can rank all of these categories in terms of their potential severity and likelihood. Crises with the highest probabilities and highest potential impact require a crisis response plan.

1. **Local events,** which would draw attention to your organization as a whole, could include:
   ▸ Activist action
   ▸ Any item from the *Call Headquarters If* list
   ▸ Arrest of plant manager or other senior executive
   ▸ Bomb threat
   ▸ Boycott by contractors
   ▸ Community confrontation
   ▸ Customer complaints
   ▸ Drug activity or drug raid
   ▸ Employee complaints
   ▸ Employee violence
   ▸ Indictment of local employees and managers
   ▸ Job actions
   ▸ Local labor problem gaining national attention
   ▸ Major accident or disaster
   ▸ Major negative news stories
   ▸ Outage situations
   ▸ Rumors
   ▸ Violence in the workplace
   ▸ Whistle-blowers

2. **Operating crises,** which would draw attention to your organization as a whole, could include:
   ▸ Adverse international event
   ▸ Billing, bookkeeping, or collection errors (massive)
   ▸ Business loss (Wall Street is surprised and issues a "sell" recommendation)
   ▸ Civil or criminal litigation
   ▸ Competitor allegations
   ▸ Computer and data theft
   ▸ Computer failure
   ▸ Computer security breach
   ▸ Computer virus affecting your organization's data processing or manufacturing capabilities
   ▸ Congressional action

- Continuous deterioration of the business
- Decapitation (sudden loss of key executives, usually through accident or conflict)
- Ethics problem
- Extended loss of production capacity
- Extortion
- Financial issues
- Government investigations
- Hazardous material team activation
- Hostile takeovers
- Incident or disaster that gains substantial government attention
- Major chemical explosion or leak
- Major fire
- Major operations interruption
- Major power outage
- Mergers and acquisitions
- Product contamination
- Reorganizations
- Rumors that disrupt the business
- Sabotage or acts of vandalism
- Sarbanes-Oxley, Dodd-Frank, DOJ, or SEC investigations
- Serious accident or incident involving the death of employee on the job or people in the vicinity
- Subpoenas or class action suits
- Sudden death of or injury to one or more of the company's senior executives
- Sudden drop in stock price
- Transportation emergency involving a chemical leak or major health and safety threat
- Transportation emergency involving imported products
- Wall Street surprises
- Whistle-blowers

3. **Non-operating crises**, which would draw attention to your organization as a whole, often elicit extreme emotions and are the most dangerous and difficult to address. Examples include:
   - Activist action or threats

- Alleged liability or negligence implicating a company employee
- Berserk employee acting alone against the company
- Bomb threat/bombing
- Chronic safety and environmental problems
- Civil and criminal investigations
- Confrontation
- Customers
- Deranged employee taking action against other employees, or the company
- Disgruntled employees
- Emergence of credible information challenging the safety or efficacy of a company product, service, or practice
- Environmental spills, accidents, fears
- Facility closings and employee layoffs
- Government actions
- Health loss/prevention
- Incapacitation of many employees
- Industrial accidents
- Investigation or indictment of the company, its employees, or former employees for alleged improprieties on or off the job
- Kidnapping
- Labor relations
- Litigation
- Major crimes
- Major negative business decisions
- Major negative criminal or civil allegations
- Major theft
- Malevolence
- Malfeasance
- Market shifts
- Organzied Opposition
- Outsider intervention
- Product failures
- Public attacks
- Recycling/environmental issues
- Regulation

- Rumors
- Scandal
- Sexual harassment
- Terrorist actions
- Whistle-blowers
- Wildcat strikes
- Workplace violence

4. **Operating/non-operating combination events,** which typically produce apparent victims and draw attention to your organization as a whole, could include:

- Arson
- Bomb threat
- Boycott by vendors
- Boycott of contractors
- Competitor allegations
- Congressional action
- Contamination affecting major sections of the nation or populations
- Coordinated terrorist action
- Financial dislocations
- Incident or disaster that gains substantial government attention
- Labor relations
- Potential for government action
- Reorganizations
- Subpoenas or class action suits
- Toxic substance release under the U.S. and other national and local laws, rules, or regulations

5. **Web-based attacks and competitive targeting,** which would draw attention to your organization as a whole, could include:

- Activist opposition
- Angry customers
- Attack sites
- Boycotts
- CEO and senior executive targeting
- Data theft or misuse
- Distortions
- Email attacks

- Extortion
- Lies
- Organized opposition
- Personal attacks
- Product attacks
- Rumors
- Sexual harassment
- Short sales
- Single product targets
- Spamming
- "Sucks" sites
- Terrorism
- Video attacks

Creating victims is what makes a crisis a crisis.

1.3 Crisis Is About Victims

A crisis is a major operations disruption, which poses a significant threat to employees or customers, user safety and wellbeing, or to the company's reputation, that can or will cause explosive, unplanned visibility and victims. Practically speaking, a true crisis situation is a people-stopper, product-stopper, show-stopper, reputation-definer, or some combination of all four – and it produces victims (people, animals, living systems). Creating victims is what makes a crisis a crisis.

The greatest barriers to appropriate victim management are denial, the lack of leadership, and a fear of liability, fostered by advice given to management by well-meaning counsel. However, any credible way to reduce or mitigate this fear is essential to better behavior, reputation management, and litigation reduction.

One lawyer interviewed for "Risk Management: Extreme Honesty May be the Best Policy" (Kraman, 1999) put it this way, "In over 25 years of representing both physicians and patients, it became apparent that a large percentage of patient dissatisfaction was generated by physician attitude and denial, rather than the negligence itself. In fact, my experience has been that close to half of malpractice cases could have been avoided through disclosure or apology but instead were relegated to litigation. What the majority of patients really wanted was simply an honest explanation of what happened, and if appropriate, an apology. Unfortunately, when they were not only offered neither but were rejected as well, they felt doubly wronged and then sought legal counsel." (**Note:** *Litigation issues are covered in depth in Chapter 9 of this book.*)

Because the concept of victim management is essential to crisis communication, the topic will be touched upon in just about every chapter of this book. In the section below we cover the basics of defining victims and their needs, concepts that will be discussed from different aspects in the following chapters.

1.3.1 Leadership Is About Victims

Crisis-created internal and external victims are the greatest threat to the organization. A key role for senior management, as well as other managers, is making certain that the needs of victims are tended to immediately, fully and compassionately. The most significant causes of litigation and lousy visibility during crises are the ignored or discredited needs of victims, victims' families, and survivors – and the failure of leadership to aggressively manage the victim dimension.

Leadership's focus on victims sets the tone for the entire response effort. Management should be supportive, break down barriers, act like brothers and sisters, mothers and fathers, grandmothers and grandfathers to those who are injured or are suffering as a result of what is going on. They should be at the hospital, in the homes of affected families, and meeting with groups of those affected – sharing comfort and understanding.

When the damage involves animals and living systems as well as people, bold, visible action needs to be taken by organizational leaders and sustained.

> **The highest priority and most crucial aspect of managing crises is the victim dimension.**

Management should motivate employees and responders by being present where it's dangerous or difficult – to encourage, help build understanding and appropriate concern, and to help employees through what often are difficult, psychologically stressful, and emotional times. A pat on the back and a positive word from the boss have enormous emotional power.

The highest priority and most crucial aspect of managing crises is the victim dimension. Victims provide explosive emotional drive, resulting in high visibility, high liability, and high anxiety. Yet, when it comes to management issues and training, dealing with victims is among the sloppiest, most mysterious, and most poorly handled of all crisis response activities.

1.3.2 Why Management Has Difficulty With Victims

We can identify five powerful reasons to account for the difficulty management has in dealing with victims:

1. Management perceives victim behavior as irrational.
2. Management is reluctant to assume blame or responsibility promptly.

3. Management's obsession with results forces them to be anti-victim and emotionless.

4. Management training in ethics and in managing emotional circumstances is minimal, both in business schools and in business life.

5. Peers often criticize or belittle as "sissies" executives who act ethically or with sensitivity.

One lesson learned while becoming a manager is training in repressing personal emotions. Simply put, if it can't be easily measured, if it's difficult to quantify, or if it can't be metricized in some way, it's not important. On top of this, managers are trained to discount, disregard, and disrespect virtually every kind of circumstance that might be or is emotional.

Peers, shareholders, and the business community expect managers to tough it out and avoid looking like sissies, at least at first. As a result, management response to crisis often comes across as callous, arrogant, cold, and heartless.

Going one step further, many business people are taught a kind of decision-making ritual – one in which even the most crucial decisions are made through a process of conflict, confrontation, and aggressive intellectual and verbal combat. This kind of behavior is completely predictable – be ready for it.

> **An ethical management and crisis response strategy is a victim-reducing, litigation-reducing strategy.**

In crises, one crucial responsibility of the communicator is to forge an alliance with both the Legal Department and Human Resources to help management avoid both the collateral damage and the devastating consequences of mismanaging the victim dimension. In addition, this alliance will clarify for management the significant benefits to reputation, public trust, and legal liability reduction to be achieved by managing the victim dimension promptly, ethically, and empathetically. Let me put it very clearly: *An ethical management and crisis response strategy is a victim-reducing, litigation-reducing strategy.*

1.3.3 What Does It Mean to Be a Victim?

Victimhood is a self-designated state. Whether there are wounds, bullet holes, or any other visible or invisible damage, human beings have the capacity to choose to feel victimized. They can also choose to be victimized on behalf of others.

Victimhood is self-sustaining and highly emotional. Being a victim is a self-perpetuating, self-energizing state. That is, the individual chooses how long he or she will remain in a situation or state of mind that makes him or her feel victimized. And while they choose to act on their victimness, they do it 24/7.

Victimhood is self-terminating. It ends when the victims, by themselves, determine to let go of what is adversely affecting them and get on with the rest of their lives.

No matter how damaging an event, only a small number of individuals will actually feel victimized – even in mass casualty situations. While many may be injured, or disadvantaged, or require extraordinary assistance, very few view themselves as hopeless, helpless, demoralized, frustrated, and victimized.

Victimhood is suffering alone. Being a victim is an individual state. Even in mass casualty circumstances with many injured or wounded at the same time, each person suffers alone. Even the phrase "mass casualties" is a serious, potentially devastating misnomer. Every person suffers differently, experiences pain differently, and needs to be treated individually. Otherwise the victimization with its sense of frustration, helplessness, and being misunderstood will persist. Victims are emotionally energized.

Victims become intellectually deaf. Dealing with victims becomes difficult because they instantly become self-absorbed and self-focused on the problems and afflictions of being a victim. They hear little. Their inner voice continuously rehearses their problems and circumstances. When they use their outer voice, it is to complain, whine, and warn. They notice little, mostly the negatives, and they are stimulated primarily by additional negative circumstances, stories, denials, and demeaning descriptions of their situation. Victims constantly ask questions, but rarely actually hear the responses. This is what is so frustrating for responders and perpetrators alike. Attempts to help are often interpreted as efforts to control and to minimize responsibility.

1.3.4 How Poor Communication Prolongs Victimization

Overcoming intellectual deafness requires focus and empathetic communication. At first, this approach may appear to be deceptively ineffective and slow – or even to have the potential to trigger even more anger, fear, and antagonism. However, experience proves that *simple, sincere,* and *positive* approaches, sensible to a fault, are the most successful. Actions, communications, and behaviors that fail to meet these three challenging standards will fail and prolong the victimization.

Victimization is triggered or prolonged by the behavior of the perpetrator, and even by the response of society to attempts by the victims to resolve the issues or to repair or eliminate whatever caused them to become victims in the first place. Victim-causing, victimizing, or victim-stimulating behavior is identifiable. Here are seven victim-causing perpetrator behaviors:

▶ **Denial:** Refusal to accept that something bad has happened, that there may be victims or others directly affected that require prompt public acknowledgement. Denial can include refusing to acknowledge that the crisis is serious; that the media or public have any real stake or interest in whatever the problem happens to be; that the situation should take anyone's time in the organization except those in top management specifically tasked to deal with it; and that the problem is of any particular consequence to the organization provided no one talks about it except those directly involved. Denial responses can include:

❒ "Let's not over-react."

❒ "Let's keep it to ourselves."

❒ "We don't need to tell the people in PR just yet. They'll just blab it all over."

❒ "If we don't talk, no one will know."

▶ **Victim confusion:** When reporters, employees, angry neighbors, and victims' families call asking for help, information, explanation, or apology, company representatives become defensive. They respond, "Hey! We're victims too." Symptoms of victim confusion include time-wasting explanations of how we've been such good corporate citizens, how we've contributed to the opera, the little league, or the shelter program: "We don't deserve to be treated this badly;" "Mistakes can happen, even to the best of companies;" "We're only human."

When these behaviors fail to pass the community, media, or victim straight-face test, or are criticized or laughed at, a stream of further defensive responses may follow:

❒ "If the government enforces this regulation, it will destroy our competitiveness."

❒ "If we have to close this plant, it's their fault."

❒ "It's the only decision we can make."

❒ "If this decision stands, many will suffer needlessly."

❒ "If we didn't do this, someone else would."

❒ "Our institute can be permanently damaged if we overreact."

▶ **Testosterosis:** The need to lash out first, to look for ways to hit back rather than to deal with the problem, refuse to give in, and refuse to respect those who may have a difference of opinion or a legitimate issue.

▶ **Arrogance:** Arrogance is contempt for adversaries, sometimes even for victims, and almost always for the news media. It takes the form of reluctance to apologize, to express concern or empathy, or to take appropriate responsibility because: "If we do that, we'll be liable," or, "We'll look like sissies," or, "We'll set bad precedents," or, "There'll be copycats," or, "We'll legitimize bad actions or people." Arrogance is also making decisions for others without their consent or participation.

▶ **Blame shifting/search for the guilty:** They will dig into the organization or community to look for traitors, turncoats, troublemakers, seeking those who push back or remain unconvinced in order to shift the blame to them.

▶ **Fear of exposure:** As the bad news coverage and employee animosity piles up, the media and victims begin asking, "What did you know and when did you know it?," or "What have you done, and when did you do it?" along with other humiliating, embarrassing, and damaging questions. Angry, callous responses create even more victims, or harden the attitudes of existing victims.

▶ **Management by whining around:** When the decision is made to finally move forward, the organization talks only about its own pain, expense, and inconvenience, statements which make victims, employees, neighbors, and the government angrier and the media more aggressively negative. Whining is not strategic. It is self-deceptive.

1.3.5 What Do Victims Need?

Victims have four powerful needs. If these four needs are provided promptly – preferably by the perpetrator – victims can more easily move through their state of victimization and be less likely to need, or to call or respond to attorneys, the media, or even to call attention to themselves. The reality is that if the perpetrator fails to meet these victim needs or does so only partially, victims will find ways to provide them for themselves, often at the perpetrator's expense and humiliation.

> **Victims rarely sue because they are angry...
> Generally, victims sue because their situation is
> not acknowledged and their feelings are
> ignored, belittled, discredited, or trivialized.**

▶ **Validation,** that they are indeed victims. This recognition is best rendered by the perpetrator; if not, public groups, government, or the news media will do it.

▶ **Visibility,** a platform from which to describe their pain and warn others. Preferably, again, the platform should come from the perpetrator. If the perpetrator is unresponsive, the victims will find a way to talk about their suffering and to warn others to avoid their fate.

▶ **Vindication,** the need victims have to take credit for any action by the perpetrator to ensure that whatever happened to the victims will be prevented from happening to others. Victims rarely sue because they are angry, their life has been changed dramatically, or because lots of plaintiff's attorneys are chasing them around. Generally, victims sue because their situation is not acknowledged and their feelings are ignored, belittled, or trivialized. If they are prevented from publicly discussing what happened to them in meaningful ways, and no one is taking prompt constructive action to prevent similarly situated individuals, animals, or living systems from suffering the same fate, victims will be looking to take more aggressive action.

▶ **Apology,** directly and promptly tends to dramatically reduce victimization and virtually eliminate litigation. While the lawyers may strongly advise against any form of apology because, under law, an apology is an admission, there is a growing body of evidence and data to demonstrate that apologies, promptly and sincerely delivered, virtually eliminate the potential for litigation. This means that while the lawyer's advice needs to be listened to, if the victim refuses to sue, it may be time to reassign the lawyer to negotiating an effective settlement rather than pursuing a futile effort to deny what the victim needs most. (*For more about the legal aspects of apology, see Chapter 9.*)

1.3.6 Psychological Effects of Crises and Disasters on Victims

Crises and disasters can take a toll on the psychological well-being of victims. In your planning for crisis communications, you need to be aware of these important considerations.

Psychological problems always result from disaster experiences.

Source: National Center for Post Traumatic Stress Disorder, White River Junction, Vermont

Employees experience a range of psychological and physiological symptoms after a traumatic workplace incident. Helping workers recognize potential reactions can assist the recovery process.

Most survivors of natural disasters experience normal stress reactions for several days, such as:

▶ **Emotional reactions:** Temporary feelings (i.e., for several days to a couple of weeks) of shock, fear, grief, anger, resentment, guilt, shame, helplessness, hopelessness, emotional numbness (difficulty feeling love and intimacy, or in taking interest and pleasure in day-to-day activities).

> ▶ **Cognitive reactions:** Confusion, disorientation, indecisiveness, worry, shortened attention span, difficulty concentrating, memory loss, unwanted memories, self-blame.

> ▶ **Physical reactions:** Tension, fatigue, edginess, difficulty sleeping, bodily aches or pain, being startled easily, racing heartbeat, nausea, change in appetite.

> ▶ **Interpersonal reactions** in relationships at work, in friendships, marriage, or as a parent, such as: distrust, irritability, conflict, withdrawal, isolation, feeling rejected or abandoned, being distant, judgmental, or over controlling.

Most disaster survivors only experience mild, normal stress reactions, and disaster experiences may even promote personal growth and strengthen relationships. However, as many as one in three disaster survivors experience some or all of the following severe stress symptoms, which may lead to lasting post-traumatic stress disorder, anxiety disorders, or depression:

> ▶ Dissociation (feeling completely unreal or outside yourself, like in a dream; having "blank" periods of time you cannot remember).

> ▶ Intrusive re-experiencing (terrifying memories, nightmares, or flashbacks).

> ▶ Extreme attempts to avoid disturbing memories (such as through substance abuse).

> ▶ Extreme emotional numbing (completely unable to feel emotion, as if utterly empty).

> ▶ Hyper arousal (panic attacks, rage, extreme irritability, intense agitation).

> ▶ Severe anxiety (paralyzing worry, extreme helplessness, compulsions, or obsessions).

> ▶ Severe depression (complete loss of hope, self-worth, motivation, or purpose in life).

What can disaster survivors do to reduce the risk of negative psychological consequences and to best recover from disaster stress?

> ▶ **Protect:** Find a safe haven that provides shelter, food and liquids, sanitation, privacy, and chances to sit quietly, relax, and sleep at least briefly.

> ▶ **Direct:** Begin setting and working on immediate personal priorities to enable you to preserve or regain a sense of hope, purpose, and self-esteem.

> ▶ **Connect:** Maintain or re-establish communication with family, peers, and counselors in order to talk about your experiences. Take any chance to "tell your story" and to be a listener to others as they tell theirs, so that you and they can release the stress a little bit at a time.

> ▶ **Select:** Identify key resources such as FEMA, the American Red Cross, the Salvation Army, or the local and state health departments for basic emergency assistance.

Preplanning Efforts

Source: Daniel Paulk, Ph.D., psychologist, Crisis Management International, Atlanta, Georgia

Crisis counseling and concern for employees should be incorporated into corporate contingency plans. When preparing the plan, consider:

- Do we have an organized, structured protocol to deal with the human element?
- What are the tasks we will need to do immediately with employees?
- How will we find employees and provide for their safety after an event?
- How will we contain employees after an event?
- What have we rehearsed that would help us to respond?
- How will we communicate with employees?
- What will we communicate to employees?
- What will we say to employees? Who should say it?
- How do we get employees back to the site the next day? What issues will need to be addressed?

1.3.7 Understanding the Victim Recovery Cycle

The Victim Recovery Cycle offers a perspective to help those who create victims better understand what people are going through, or what those people will care about - such as animals and the environment.

Cycle I: Victims' Feelings

- Anger
- Concern over lack of response
- Disbelief, dread
- Expectation of help
- Internalization, agony
- Frustration at "intentional delays"
- Fearful curiosity

Cycle II: Seeking Retribution

- Feeling that help received is inadequate, late, and insincere
- Hitting back
- Pooling anger with other victims
- Search for the obviously guilty
- Turn to plaintiff's bar and other activists to get retribution, if possible
- Victims seek their own solutions

Cycle III: The Search for Healing

- Growing sense of helplessness, "Nobody understands what I'm going through"
- "They" could have done more, faster
- Severely distorted recollection with a permanent sense of endless anger

Cycle IV: Victims' Needs

- Closure
- Compassion
- Empathy/apology
- Expressions of regret
- Forum
- Information
- Involvement
- Recognition
- Reasons/rationale
- Someone to blame
- Validation
- Vindication
- Visibility

Chapter 1 - Questions for Study and Discussion

1. The author contends that a problem becomes a crisis due to the presence of a "victim." Did this assertion surprise you? Why is it important to recognize this relationship? How would you explain the relationship between "victim" and "crisis" to someone else?

2. List three highly publicized corporate crises that have been in the news or in the courts recently. How has the presence of a victim or victims made the situation more difficult for all the parties involved to handle? If you had been in charge of corporate communications at the company, how would you have handled the situation differently?

References, Chapter 1

Kraman S.S., Hamm, G. (1999). Risk management: extreme honesty may be the best policy. *Annals of Internal Medicine*, 131: 963-967.

2

Crisis Communication:
Getting Leadership Ready for Crisis

Keywords: crisis management, vulnerability, leadership, readiness, organizational barriers, verbal visionary

*C**risis management*** may be defined as the *exercise of common sense at lightning speed.* Importantly, the effectiveness of crisis *communication* during the hours, days, and weeks it takes to resolve and recover from an event will prove essential to preserving the reputation, credibility, and morale of your organization. My years of experience and observation of crisis response have made it abundantly clear that every business and organization is vulnerable to mistakes, mishaps, surprise events, and human error. *We are all vulnerable!* However, experience also demonstrates that it is a prudent organization that has studied its vulnerabilities, identified those that present the greatest risk, and gets ready with what it must do and say to respond quickly and effectively in the face of a crisis.

This chapter will help you to:

➤ Identify the words and actions on the part of management that can significantly worsen a crisis situation and, conversely, the ones that can move the situation toward a more satisfactory resolution.

➤ Overcome management objections to crisis communication readiness.

➤ Master the skills required to be a *verbal visionary* and valued counselor in an organization.

Each year I have the privilege of working with many senior and chief executives across the full spectrum of leadership activity: the corporate sector, government, military, non-profit organizations, and others. One powerful leadership aspiration that comes through in each of these settings is the leader's gut-level desire to transform the organization, or to transform how the organization thinks; or to transform the attitudes of a group of individuals or a customer base. Personal, top executive leadership is the transformational force that energizes people and organizations to achieve big goals. Readiness success depends on this same leadership energy. Leadership confusion, timidity, or hesitation can cause responses to fail in many respects.

Two key concepts about crisis management:

1. All crises happen explosively and instantly. All crises, however, are remediated incrementally, often over long periods of time.

2. *Crisis management* is a communicator's phrase and image. *Readiness* is a management word and is something managers and leaders can understand and work toward. Generally, executives move away from the concept of crisis management, believing a crisis will never happen to them and, if it does, their competence, inherent skill, and experience will allow them to manage the situation very easily and very well. Work to replace the concept of crisis management with the term *readiness*.

How prepared is *your* organization for:

▶ Angry constituents, including employees?
▶ Catastrophic events?
▶ Cyber attack?
▶ Data breach?
▶ Employee violence?
▶ Epidemic?
▶ Financial meltdown?
▶ Long-term external agitation?
▶ Major criminal act?
▶ Mismanagement?
▶ Persistent attacks and bad news?
▶ Security breaches or leaks?
▶ Significant media or reputational crisis?
▶ Victimization of others?
▶ Weather-related disaster?

2.1 Leadership Patterns That Influence Readiness

A gradual acceleration of management change at the very senior levels of most organizations began in the mid-1990s, attributable to three major factors:

1. Global ownership through technology is able to put more pressure on those at the top of organizations to produce more effectively or be replaced.

2. In response to these pressures, more and more companies increased their demands on their leaders, rather than their organizations. The resulting acceleration and turnover, coincidentally, has produced a related lowering in the average age of chief executives worldwide.

3. Each decade tends to produce its own collection of corporate-level scandals, misbehavior, and poor responses leading to extraordinarily negative public perceptions of business leaders and businesses in general.

2.1.1 General Readiness Success Principles

When we analyze the most important components of readiness, based on preparedness and response analysis, we get a snapshot of what it takes to be ready.

Readiness Equation:	
Accurate contact information	75% of readiness
▶ Always knowing the where-abouts of key decision makers	
Pre-authorization	15% of readiness
▶ Decisions made in advance to expedite action	
Extensive scenario preparation and testing	8% of readiness
▶ Actual practice and preparation exercises	
Surprise	2% unexpected
	100%

When readiness is a part of company policy and culture, a handful of really powerful principles seem to be at work:

▶ From the beginning, the CEO and senior executives endorse and participate in readiness.

▶ Plan success requires support throughout the entire organization.

▶ Successful plans and readiness include all key functions of the organization.

- The factors that cause strategic efforts to fail are detected, deterred, prevented, or eliminated.
- One crucial goal is to identify and eliminate risks.
- Failure to eliminate risks by identifying vulnerabilities actually raises risk levels.

2.1.2 Overcoming Management Objections to Readiness Activities

Nine Reasons Crisis Management Matters

1. Helps avoid career-defining moments for the boss.
2. Moderates and minimizes damage to reputation and employee morale.
3. Enhances a company's ability to recover from financial losses, regulatory fines, loss of market share, damages to equipment or products, or business interruption.
4. Reduces potential exposure to civil or criminal liability.
5. May reduce your insurance premiums.
6. Provides an opportunity for management to demonstrate an ability to deal with difficult circumstances.
7. Appears to be the most crucial factor for recovery - when it is effective.
8. Reduces the production of new critics and complainers.
9. Is the "right" thing to do.

Typical Organizational Barriers

Organizational barriers can be forecast and must be anticipated, detected, and overcome. An audit of potential organizational or process disruptions needs to be completed early in the readiness process. Look for:

- Organizational over-confidence.
- Resistance to procedures that automatically trigger corporate notification, i.e., a *Call Headquarters If* list.
- Competing response priorities between divisions, functions, and product lines.
- Other existing crisis plans, such as plans developed by others or required by government regulations.
- Relationship between corporate and division/branch/field operations.
- Response confusion and turf issues.
- Existing management response plans.
- A sense of arrogance and self-sufficiency.

▌ Challenging the idea of readiness and those who propose it.
▌ Resistance from sales and marketing as interference with sales success.

Case Study: Blown to Bits

Most academic medical centers receive cadavers as gifts from families and individuals to further scientific study at the discretion of the recipient institutions. When there is a surplus of cadavers, there are brokers who take these bodies off the hands of medical institutions and providers to sell them to other research organizations and companies.

The Company

The medical school at Southwestern State, a university in the U.S. with a very favorable reputation among academic institutions in its class, found itself in the odd situation of having a surplus of cadavers. Southwestern turned over a dozen or so gift cadavers to a broker who, in turn, sold them to a munitions manufacturer that needed to study the explosive impacts of some of its products on human subjects.

The Crisis

The problem arose when the Kendall family, who had contributed a cadaver, decided they wanted the body returned following whatever scientific use to which it was put. It didn't take long to make some inquiries and discover that their loved one's body had been provided to the munitions manufacturer and blown to bits. Upon being told, the family immediately hired an attorney, who filed suit for recovery of the body.

The Complexities

The Kendall family and their attorney launched their media campaign with a very tearful and well-attended press conference, which caused an immediate and extraordinary public uproar. In fact, the uproar was felt throughout the academic medical community. Philanthropic journals carried stories warning potential future donors. More gruesome details became available courtesy of an employee of the explosives company. More families began to come forward inquiring about what had become of the bodies of their loved ones.

At this point, the plight of the grieving Kendall family, the reputations of all those involved, the regulatory environment, and the goodwill of Southwestern State Medical Center became the focus of high-profile analysis and investigation. The questions are really quite predictable:

1. Why weren't the families notified and given the choice of deciding how their gift was to be utilized?

2. Whose idea was this and why wasn't there better oversight by the medical school and the University?

3. How could this gruesome practice of trading in cadavers be kept hidden from the donors, the university, and the people of the state?

4. Why aren't there laws against these grave robbing activities?

5. Who would compensate the families for this extraordinary double loss of a loved one?

6. Could any remains be recovered and reinterred?

The Approach

The institution immediately issued a public apology, though there was an extraordinary internal struggle among the attorneys, medical personnel, and the university administration over doing this so quickly. The lawyers counseled against such a dramatic admission so early in the event.

A particularly skillful forensic pathologist was asked by the university to become the spokesperson for all questions on these matters. His instructions were simple and straightforward: be candid, be empathetic, be disclosive, explain, teach, elaborate, be apologetic, and answer every question.

The university established a process whereby the attorneys of other families who had come forward could receive instructions on the most direct methods for filing lawsuits. At the same time, the university retained a law firm specializing in settlements, despite the protestations of their defense counsel.

The Kendalls and other families were invited to help plan a permanent memorial honoring the memory of those who died "a second time."

The Culmination

The outcome of this approach is pretty easy to forecast:

▶ All litigation was settled out-of-court within a few months.

▶ The initial visibility in connection with the story evaporated pretty quickly.

▶ Southwestern State University Medical School received an unexpected substantial gift from one family.

▶ All cadaver donors received explicit instructions about how loved ones would be treated. In addition, every donor was allowed to request the right to provide permission for the ultimate scientific use of their loved one's remains.

▶ A tracking system was put in place so that, at any given time, family members could know the location and the condition of the loved ones.

Lessons Learned

By responding promptly with compassion to needs of the family, the university established a sound precedent for dealing with this kind of crisis. In addition, the university learned that there are always more options to consider beyond what the lawyers propose.

The Conclusions

▶ Candor builds trust even when the news is horrible or horrifying.

▶ Apology is perhaps the most powerful behavior to detoxify explosively negative situations.

▶ Apologies expedite settlement and deter litigation.

▶ Victim and survivor participation in the resolution of suffering, fear, abuse, and mistakes helps everyone recover more quickly.

▶ Perpetrator engagement with the victims and survivors changes the tone in a very positive, respectful way that leads to mitigation and resolution.

2.2 The New Top Executive Agenda

In 2013, it can be estimated that the typical CEO will spend 40% or more of his or her time on non-operating issues such as globalization, adverse legislation, anti-corporate activism, and compensation controversy, to name a few. These interruptions seem soft and distractive, often requiring moral rather than monetary or business judgment. These non-operating problems do cause powerful, time consuming and potentially career-defining risks for the CEO.

The severe recession of 2008-2010 and the scandalous behavior by banks, insurance companies, real estate organizations, credit card distributors, and Wall Street have forced a renewed focus on even more non-operating, regulatory measures and on the morality of senior executive behavior. With the rise of social networking and 24/7 Web activism, more individuals than ever are watching, counting, and publicizing whether what bosses do and say matches what they have done and said. This trend seems clear in North America and in Europe, even in Asia and China: career-defining risks for CEOs and senior executives are increasing.

> It would seem logical if you are addressing or advising senior leaders and CEO to be somewhat familiar with what they do, what they know, how they think, and where they come from.

2.2.1 Inside the Mind of the CEO

Worrying and whining about who and what the CEO is listening to – in place of or in addition to us – is one of the age-old traditions of those in staff work.

It is the source of much teeth-gnashing among other staff functions, such as communications, law, finance, accounting, human resources, security, marketing, and even strategic planning.

The odd thing, of course, is virtually none of the employees serving in these functions knows anything about being a CEO, becoming a CEO, or what the challenges of the CEO's job happen to be. It would seem logical if you are addressing or advising senior leaders and CEOs to be somewhat familiar with what they do, what they know, how they think, and where they come from. As a method of getting there, let's do a reality check on the business of being a CEO.

The position of CEO is less and less like it used to be:

▶ Today's CEO tends to be younger, to be getting to the job earlier, and even getting out of the job way before retirement, all of which means that CEOs will be doing other significant jobs in their lives rather than simply rising professionally to become the CEO of one company.
▶ Huge compensation packages allow CEOs to drop out before they are fired or forced out. Even when they are forced out or fired, they get a large compensation package as well.
▶ More and more non-business issues (e.g., globalization, adverse legislation, anti-corporate activism, employee violence, and angry neighbors and customers) are intruding upon management and leadership time. These interruptions seem soft and distractive, often requiring moral rather than monetary or business judgment.
▶ CEOs have yet to be formally measured on their morality or belief systems.
▶ Particularly in the U.S. and in Europe, career-defining risks for CEOs are increasing.

2.2.2 The Five Main Tasks of the CEO

Believe it or not, no true school for CEOs really exists anywhere. No educational organization can teach the next CEO of Coca-Cola how to do that job. Acquiring the skills to be a CEO tends to be mostly an on-the-job training experience. There is only one such position in any organization and each is completely unique. To understand the CEO's environment, one has to recognize the five general divisions of tasks the CEO faces daily, and faces alone: soft intrusions, hard obstacles, nagging problems, career-defining moments, and strategic vision for the future.

▶ **Soft intrusions** include negotiations with employees or major customers; anti-corporate government action; poor sales; nagging negative news; personal, professional, corporate embarrassment; and constant negative social media.

- **Hard obstacles** are situations with objectively measurable impact, such as a 50% stock price drop in less than a week; job actions and walkouts; major product market loss; product failure; and embarrassing cyber attacks.

- **Nagging problems** include consistent negative activist attacks on individual executives and board members; rumors; leaks, unfounded and founded allegations; mergers, takeovers, and cutbacks; and chatter about executive behavior, compensation, and mistakes.

- **Career-defining moments** include persistent non-performance of stock; criminal indictment; serious people failure; serious, high-profile product failure; continuing bad product performance; embarrassing, needless, obviously stupid events, and well-formed, persistent, high-profile nagging.

- **A vision of the future and a strategy to get there.**

2.2.3 Four Kinds of Information the CEO Needs

The CEO is completely dependent on his/her organization for success. To build followership and achieve a vision, the enlightened CEO expects feedback from those in staff positions. Whether he or she is coping with a crisis or operations crucial to success, the CEO needs essentially four kinds of information continuously.

1. **Data:**

   - A sense of the market: A sense of the acceptability of the organization's goods and services.

   - Temperament of investors: What are they feeling? What are they saying? What are they telling other investors and analysts?

   - Emotional state of the organization: What are people saying? How are they behaving? Are we a "happy" ship? Is anyone having fun? Or is there a feeling of dread, of doom, or simply a sense of mindlessly rearranging the deck chairs on a daily basis?

   - Candid assessment of the existing situation: What options for action do we have based on the data? Do the issues to be faced and the situations in which we find ourselves fit known patterns that we can plan against or leverage ahead?

   - Candid assessment of the people in positions of responsibility to achieve their missions and reach these destinations.

2. **Perception issues:** The more senior the manager, the more isolated he or she become.

⟩ What is the wake being left behind by our actions?

⟩ What are we learning? How can we benefit from those learnings? Who can benefit most?

⟩ What are the perceptions which need the most prompt correction, clarification, or comment?

3. **Responses to be executed in real time:** Building or rebuilding confidence and trust requires real-time, face-to-face communication between top executives and key constituencies.

4. **What to do next:** What is the next step? What is going to happen next? What are the barriers to success? What might be some unintended consequences of our actions?

Intel co-founder Gordon E. Moore (1965) identified a long-term trend that the capabilities of digital electronic devices would continue to improve exponentially for at least 10 years. His prediction – which proved valid with the trend continuing until this day – became known as *Moore's Law*. In the case of the CEO's communication burden, however, the inverse of Moore's Law would seem to apply and could be stated: "The more sensitive, the more damaging, the more victims a situation creates, the less time is allowed before the public expects massive communication from the boss." Verbal communication and the communication of leadership ideas today must be faster than timely, faster than promptly, they must be done now.

> Faced with a crisis, management may spend a lot of time in denial, covering bases that don't immediately matter, such as embarrassment, avoidance, self-forgiveness, searching for the guilty, or just self-talk.

2.2.4 Needed: A Defined Role for the Boss During Crises

Probably the greatest deficit in response planning for emergency situations is the lack of scenario-specific instructions for what the bosses need to be doing, and when they should be doing it. Why does this matter? A crisis or emergency situation gives top executives something important to do – immediately – together or separately. Bosses dive in willingly, eager to apply all of their intellectual power, experience, and intuition. One consequence of management enthusiasm is that all of your conscientious planning, preparation, rehearsal, and simulation may be sidetracked, since top management will start from the very beginning and spend hours trying to figure out what they and everyone else should be doing. Faced with a crisis, management may spend a lot of time covering bases that don't immediately matter, such as embarrassment-avoidance, self-forgiveness, searching for the guilty, or just self-talk. Meanwhile, the situation continues to leak, foam, stink, burn, and, perhaps, even kill or maim.

2.2.5 Needed: The Definitive Management Response Strategy

There is a proven step-by-step approach to crisis response that establishes a very constructive leadership mindset.

Step one: Stop the production of victims.

Step two: Manage the victim dimension.

Step three: Initiate employee and critical stakeholder communications.

Step four: Notify those indirectly affected, those who, while not necessarily victims, have a problem because you have a problem.

Step five: Deal with the self-anointed and self-appointed. These are the various news media, bloviators, belly-achers, back-bench complainers, everyone and anyone who opts in on their own in time of crisis.

2.3 Crisis Realities

2.3.1 Crisis Reality No. 1: Crisis Management Always Causes Managers to Be in Crisis Themselves

Immediately following the tsunami that hit Japan in January of 2011, with more than 10,000 deaths and two nuclear plants disabled, Japanese authorities were reluctant at first to act for fear of damaging their expensive nuclear equipment and causing wider harm than had already occurred. In fact this is how almost all corporate crisis responses begin. Remember the BP oil spill of 2010? Toyota? The banking crisis? The home loan crisis? The stock market collapse? The credit card crunch? Enron? Johnson & Johnson took nearly 10 days to decide to remove Tylenol from store shelves in the famous 1982 case in which its drug was contaminated with cyanide and seven people died. In just about every corporate and public disaster situation within my memory, a certain pattern of leadership behavior has prevailed. In the beginning:

1. **Denial:** that the situation is as serious as outside sources (and some inside sources), especially the news media, tend to declare, "Let's not overreact."

2. **Resistance:** the claim that interference or intervention by outside sources and forces would simply complicate, stall, and perhaps prevent a speedier resolution. All the while, the perpetrating company or organization takes only the smallest steps. Managers are fighting the cost of the crisis being assigned to their budgets, and worrying more about the condition of their equipment and

assets than the damage being done, and about victims being created through the crisis itself.

3. **Bewilderment:** the executives are huddling behind closed doors, trying to figure out what exactly happened, who is responsible, how the blame may be shifted away from them, how to minimize what is said about the situation itself, and how to maximize what is said about the company's former good works.

4. **Self-deception:** intentional minimizing, understating, and withholding crucial information from the employees, the public, and the victims, hoping that the situation can be remedied privately, easily, and perhaps even heroically.

5. **Self-talk:** usually takes the form of complaining about news media coverage, government interference, regulation, and unknowledgeable or inexperienced oversight; and about people without credentials getting too much power and visibility.

6. **Victim confusion/self forgiveness:** talk about how much the company itself is suffering, that despite its wonderful history of corporate social responsibility, it has now become a victim of overzealous politicians, activists, opportunistic reporters, and unqualified people trying to extort compensation. No credit for all the past good deeds.

7. **Management by whining around:** BP's former CEO Tony Hayward is the all-time champ with the quote, "We're sorry for the massive disruption it's caused their lives. There's no one who wants this over more than I do. I would like my life back." The stress, tension, constant mistakes and outside pressure is very wearing on executives in charge of responding. Unfortunately, in today's nanosecond-deadline media environment, even a sincere expression of frustration and anguish can be interpreted just as Mr. Hayward's was. It turned out to be a career-defining moment for him.

This sequence of events or one closely resembling it is repeated in nearly every major and minor disaster and catastrophic situation. This is the pattern of management in crisis. The blunt reality is, however, that because all crises and their creation of victims happen so explosively and the resolution of these extraordinary problems and challenges can take place only incrementally, the odds of any crisis being handled promptly and appropriately are relatively small, especially as the complexity of the situation grows.

Eventually, as gaffs, bad decisions, willful delays, and economic and asset protection decisions dominate over victim management, decisions gets exposed and events begin dragging management in the direction they should have been going from the start.

> **Those who talk will control the destiny of those who remain silent.**

Those who manage crisis, those who communicate about crisis, and those from management who will be paralyzed by crisis need to understand three powerful crisis realities:

- **All crisis responses are mistake-prone:** they are riddled with errors, and underestimate the intensity or seriousness of the situation. *Lesson:* It is always better to overstate the issues, understate the preparation and capacity, and overreact from the very beginning.

- **Crisis management always causes management to be in a crisis:** these situations should be discussed far more openly, and far more quickly, probably as they are occurring. Shortcomings, what isn't known, and what needs to be learned need to be exposed, disclosed, and discussed continuously. *Lesson:* If the perpetrator fails to talk about the true situation, someone else almost certainly *will* talk. And those who talk will control the destiny of those who remain silent.

- **Heads often roll in crisis situations:** because those who lead, manage, and talk are put under extraordinary strain and pressure by their own behavior, mistakes, and attempts to minimize the situation. *Lesson:* Put someone in charge immediately who knows what to do. Give that person a checkbook and an army – and then get out of the way.

In virtually every one of these crisis situations, right along with the screaming headlines and the agitating journalists, far too many public relations practitioners are right in there criticizing, pandering, and puffing. From a management perspective, these PR comments are simply uninformed staff level jibber-jabber which fail to address the critical operating issues and questions that crisis always creates. And they don't help management get back on track faster.

Is it any wonder that management refuses to talk to its communicators, hides information from them, and keeps them in the dark and away from the table? For communicators, the most important lesson of all is to say things that matter, do things that matter, and be prepared to give useful information and advice on the spot. The communicator should suggest operational actions that matter, and focus on helping management resolve their internal crises and anguish by recommending important, constructive next-step operating options.

> **For communicators, the most important lesson of all is to say things that matter, do things that matter, and be prepared to give useful information and advice on the spot.**

2.3.2 Crisis Reality No. 2: Involve Management Early On

For effective response to a crisis, emergency, or other big issue, the boss or someone the boss deeply trusts must be involved from the very beginning.

Many crisis response processes fail because the crisis may be the first time the boss finds out that there is a plan and people whose job it is to take action. When crises occur the bosses tend go to the same room and "clump." Since they're all in one clump, response processes, especially communication, will be frozen until they decide to decide, or decide not to decide. The events that most attract management attention meet our earlier definition of crisis, that is, they are *show-stopping, people-stopping, product-stopping, reputation-defining events that create victims and/or explosive visibility and career defining moments.*

2.3.3 Crisis Reality No. 3: Establish the Right
Response Trigger Mechanism

All crises are management problems. Very few problems are crises. It takes wisdom and sensibility to tell the difference. Communication and other staff-related functions may play a role, but, initially and ultimately, crises are management problems first. An effective management response depends on the ability of management to pre-organize, pre-authorize, and pre-determine decisions and behavior.

2.3.4 Crisis Reality No. 4: Define and Execute Key Management Roles

Management has three key roles in crisis: leadership, pre-authorization, and facilitation.

Pre-authorization. In the ideal readiness model, most decisions about crises are made well in advance of the need to actually respond. The key to effective crisis response is pre-authorization, making the important decisions ahead of time so that those empowered to respond are also empowered to decide and act. Senior executives hanging around the Command Center slow down or freeze activity.

Leadership. One of the more powerful weaknesses in crisis response is the lack of specific roles and assignments for top management. The result of this crucial gap in crisis management planning is the mismanagement, lack of management, or paralysis that afflicts crisis response efforts. This defect occurs all too frequently in plans I review, responses I analyze, and scenarios I explore with client companies.

In the course of directing a client's crisis response, analyzing past responses to crisis, or developing powerful response strategies, it's clear to me that crisis response promptness and effectiveness depends on having five essential leadership responsibilities spelled out carefully in your crisis plans for the CEO (or surviving leaders):

1. *Assert the moral authority expected of ethical leadership.* No matter how devastating or catastrophic the crisis is, in most cultures, forgiveness is possible provided the organization, through its early behaviors and leadership, takes appropriate and expected steps to learn from and deal with the issues. The behaviors briefly and in order, are:

   ▌ Candor and disclosure (acknowledgement that something adverse has happened or is happening).

   ▌ Explanation and revelation about the nature of the problem (some early analysis).

   ▌ Commitment to communicate throughout the process (even if there are lots of critics).

   ▌ Empathy (intentional acts of helpfulness, kindness, and compassion).

   ▌ Oversight (inviting outsiders, even victims, to look over your shoulders).

   ▌ Commitment to zero (finding ways to prevent similar events from occurring again).

   ▌ Restitution or penance (paying the price - generally doing more than would be expected, asked for, or required).

2. *Take responsibility for the care of victims.* The single most crucial element in any crisis, aside from ending the victim-causing event, is managing the victim dimension. There are only three kinds of victims: people, animals, and living systems. It's top management's responsibility to see that appropriate steps are taken to care for victims' needs. This is both a reputation-preservation and a litigation-reduction activity. Most devastating responses to crises occur when victims are left to their own devices, when victims' needs go unfulfilled, or for whatever reasons (usually legal), the organization that created the victims refuses to take even the simplest of humane steps to ease the pain, suffering, and victimization of those afflicted. Out of all of the CEO's essential

responsibilities, taking a personal interest and an active role in the care of victims is the most important. Maintain a positive, constructive pressure to get victim issues resolved promptly.

3. *Set the appropriate tone for the organizational response.* Tone refers to the internal management behavior that helps the organization meet the expectations triggered by a crucial, critical, or catastrophic situation. If senior management takes on the posture of being attacked or victimized, the entire organization will react the same way. Very rarely are large organizations and institutions considered victims. They're generally considered to be the perpetrators, at worst, or arrogant bystanders, at best. It's the most senior executives who need to set a constructive tone that encourages positive attitudes, language, and prompt responses. This approach protects the organization's relationships with various constituents during the response and recovery period, shows respect for victims, and reduces the threat of trust or reputation damage.

4. *Set the organization's voice.* Put a face and a voice on the organization or institution as it moves through the crisis. This action is directed towards the external world – how we describe ourselves, what we're doing, how the response is going, what responsibilities we're taking, and what outside scrutiny we're inviting.

5. *Commit acts of leadership at every level.* Leaders acting like leaders has significance during urgent situations. Literally walk around and talk to people. Encourage, suggest, knock down barriers, and help everyone stay focused on the ultimate response process goals. Random acts of leadership are always welcome in any environment, but especially during crisis. Rather than huddling in their executive offices trying to determine what steps should be taken to resolve the situation, 90% of senior executive activities should have executives out and about being leaders, motivators, and instigators of empathy.

Of all these, it's the prevention of similar occurrences that will help victims come to closure and provide sufficient evidence that enough lessons have been learned to avoid the need for litigation and other forms of public embarrassment and humiliation.

All crises are management problems first. Preplanning executive actions can avoid career-defining moments. Include specific executive instructions in all plans.

Facilitation. Every crisis response reaches points of serious delay, disruption, or dislocation. This is when the executive swings into action and breaks down barriers, leases that jet to fly needed supplies from San Francisco to Tampa, hops in the chopper to go to the governor's mansion to go eyeball-to-eyeball with public officials to break down barriers and get things done. Motivate employees and responders by being present where it's dangerous or difficult – to encourage, to help build understanding and appropriate concern, and to be a good supervisor helping employees through what often are difficult, psychologically stressful, and emotional times. A pat on the back and a positive word from the boss have enormous emotional power.

What About Your Boss?
In my experience, senior executives have a simple set of questions when bad things occur:

- What am I supposed to know?
- What am I supposed to do?
- When am I supposed to do it?
- What am I supposed to say?
- When am I supposed to say it?
- When can I get back to work and let you do what I'm paying you to do?

What are *your* answers to these questions?

2.4 Avoiding Destructive Management Behavior
When we analyze those things that cause management programs to implode, explode, derail, self-destruct, slide into the ditch, or fall significantly short of expectations, we find identifiable, negative communication behaviors and activities that precede or predict disaster and cause negative collateral damage. Many of these negative behaviors are identified below. If any of the destructive behaviors, attitudes, and approaches on this list can be recognized as a routine part of your management's communication behaviors, you can use this knowledge to identify the reasons for many past failures and to forecast the potential for future failures.

One useful way to bring unhelpful behaviors and attitudes to the attention of management is to label the behaviors, describe them, and then distribute these descriptions widely so that others can recognize, point out, and discourage these negative behaviors as they occur. Since there are some important caveats to overcoming management's destructive communication behaviors, keep these five precautions in mind.

2.4.1 Five Precautions to Keep in Mind

1. **Remember who's driving the bus:** It is, after all, the prerogative of management to move the organization in the direction it wishes, with the tools and methodologies it chooses.

2. **Staff functions have limitations:** Public relations, law, finance, human resources, and other support services are staff functions. Quite often, how much behavior change a staff function can actually foster is severely limited. After all, the function of staff members is to help those who run the organization run it better rather than to substitute their own operational judgments.

3. **Change the changeable, do the doable, know the knowable:** Many times even an interesting list, like the one below, won't really be all that much help. Be prepared to move incrementally and as directly as possible. Work with the most problem-plagued executives, but first coach and train those around them. Manage the issue up.

4. **Understand the limitations of leadership:** The CEO's position is often the loneliest one in the organization. When it comes to serious management and leadership problems, the CEO may have only one or two people to talk to, and sometimes no one. Most very senior people operate at an altitude where the air is extremely rarified and politicized, and the politics are titanic. Senior people may have little opportunity or incentive to change. Sometimes senior executives tend to measure one another by the kinds of negative behaviors, mistaking them for signs of toughness or strength.

5. **Develop a sensible behavior change strategy:** Quite often, poor CEO/senior executive behavior can be altered only when one or more of the executives' peers can have some interaction or talk with those executives about their negative behavior. Because of the potential for loss of face, such peer confrontations may be difficult for staff to arrange, but possible. The most sensible strategy of all is to develop relationships with the one or two people the boss really trusts and to enlist them in helping moderate, modify, or remediate destructive management communication behavior. Bringing about these behavior changes is a risky process, but the slim chance of success makes it worth the effort.

2.4.2 A Sampling of Behaviors that Need to be Changed or Avoided

> Making the situation overly complex is the foggy, fuzzy hiding place of the guilty, complicit, or negligent... If a 13-year-old has trouble understanding your explanation, someone may ultimately go to jail as a result.

For the organization to make progress and have some sense of harmony in its operations, the number of occurrences and the intensity of these management behaviors need to be **reduced**.

1. **Arrogance:** The arrogant manager takes action without consulting those directly or indirectly affected, demonstrating that he or she does not care and does not want to care. In contrast, the empathetic manager or leader can put himself or herself into the shoes of an employee, advisor, or critic, examine the situation, and then speak from that perspective first. Almost every decision made by a decision maker helps 50% of those affected, and hurts or diminishes the remaining half. Always remember to look at the decisions through the eyes of the executive who made those decisions.

2. **Backbiting:** It is a mistake to assume that because the doorways of the executive offices are close together, communication is going on – it is only in times of trouble that the true lack of communication reveals itself. Backbiting invariably occurs when there is almost zero cross-communication on the fundamentals of achieving goals and objectives; thus, it becomes easier to bitch and bellyache than to engage in constructive conversation. Some executives believe that progress is achieved better through conflicting agendas and competition among senior managers.

3. **Bickering:** When resources are slim, politics takes center stage. Bickering can be management's way of injecting organizational politics with negativity in the hope of gaining more resources or attention from top management.

4. **Cold logic:** An organization without empathy, without a tear or a kind word for victims, is an organization without a heart. In such an organization, management attempts to unemotionally and amorally make decisions that affect the emotions of workers, neighbors, critics, and others connected to the organization. When this logic is applied to health and safety questions, environmental threat questions, and quality of life questions, executives tend to look, sound, and act heartless. The result of cold logic is an

organization that will fail without any friends and will eventually get punished.

5. **Complexity:** Making the situation overly complex is the foggy, fuzzy hiding place of the guilty, complicit, or negligent. Just remember the oil industry executives who when talking about their trading activities, which destroyed a major portion of the U.S. economy, arrogantly described these activities as "rocket science," saying, in effect, "You can't understand this stuff because it's too complicated, only a few are smart enough." The unavoidable fact to remember here is that if a 13-year-old has trouble understanding your explanation, someone may ultimately go to jail as a result. True communication involves having open, plain-language conversations about specific topics with various audiences. Understandability is crucial to relationships, public confidence, and trust.

> Always remember that victims, enemies, and critics accumulate. They never go away, and they never stop bleeding on you.

6. **Discrediting:** When challenged, organizations waste valuable time determining how to discredit the source or sources, rather than seeking to answer the questions and build understanding. Discrediting is bad strategy under every circumstance. It always backfires. Sometimes lawyers suggest this approach to create combat; sometimes the boss just wants to stick it in someone's eye. Always remember that victims, enemies, and critics accumulate. They never go away, and they never stop bleeding on you. If the mistakes don't get you, attempting to harm the reputation of some person or some group, for any reason, probably will.

7. **Double negative defensiveness:** Management's defensiveness shows the moment the following kinds of statements are made: "We didn't know so we couldn't have resolved the issue," "It wasn't supposed to be that way; therefore, we couldn't anticipate it," "We are never negative," "He didn't understand that we weren't going to help," or "It wasn't our fault; we never got enough information to proceed." Put to the proof, such statements reveal themselves as inaccurate, uninformative, and untrue.

8. **Evil management needs to be eradicated.** The combination of arrogance, deception, and remorseless, wicked, corrupt behavior results in what can only be called evil. Involved in this evil will be bad people, executives, workers, and managers. If evil exists in your organization, and management sanctions such behaviors, opt

out. Evil is impossible to eradicate once it has become an accepted behavior by management. Evil management needs to be eradicated. Or just leave.

9. **Favoritism:** The misperception that the boss is giving more resources, attention, or focus to a competing staff function is often an erroneous observation, stemming primarily from what the priorities of the boss appear to be. If you want to be the boss's favorite, suggest and do things that support the boss's goals. Suggest, recommend, and do things that support the organization's goals.

10. **Hitting back:** See #18, Testosterosis.

11. **Hot rhetoric:** War-like talk, behavior, and preparations almost always assure that war will occur. In turn, this behavior guarantees the perpetrator's own incineration – legally, rhetorically, publicly, and emotionally. Most organizations and companies can't withstand the blast-back caused by intensely wronged individuals and victims. Keep the rhetoric cool. Wage peace at all times. Once the smoldering starts, there's no telling when or where an emotional explosion will occur.

12. **Mindless verbiage:** Usually self-congratulatory or self-forgiving rhetoric is the beginning of stonewalling. We all recognize it as an indicator of guilt, duplicity, or stupidity: "It's just an isolated incident," "It's far less serious than the media is making it out to be," "It's being blown way out of proportion," "We are victims, too," "The allegations are untrue," "We never did it that way," or "We categorically deny the allegations."

13. **Negative language:** Negativity always causes confusion, is erroneous, destructive, and in some respect contains lies. Examples: "They are wrong," "You are a liar," "They don't meet the threshold of response to our situation," "They're not competent to make the judgments being made," or "They just don't understand."

> **Unethical behavior, if permitted and tolerated, when combined with evil intent, often leads to illegal behavior and more crises.**

14. **No comment:** Refusing to respond is rarely a constructive communications technique, which guarantees that 7 out of 10 believe you are guilty of something. Worse, this approach causes doubt, uncertainty, and sometimes fear in those individuals who are well aware of what would be admitted were comment to occur.

15. **Omission/withholding the full truth:** Failure to mention important negative facts or significant positive facts that could affect outcomes from the perspectives of other groups or individuals is a high-risk strategy that eventually backfires to burn reputations and careers. It usually becomes a problem when significant aspects of the "truth" are told only from our perspective without acknowledgement of victim legitimacy or the need to address the concerns of victims and critics.

16. **Reciprocitosis:** Often, a highly visible individual (or group) has participated greatly in the life of an organization or community or made substantial contributions, and, thus, expects support and assistance when things go wrong. The fact here is that while it's possible to build a reservoir of good will on many ordinary issues in an organization, it's virtually impossible to build a reservoir of goodwill on critical issues like health- and safety-related problems, pollution accusations, ethical behavior, criminal behavior, reputational problems caused by evil management, and just plain bad decisions.

17. **Silence:** Silence is a toxic strategy. Silence almost always implies guilt, complicity, stupidity, or negligence. "If they won't answer the easy questions, what else are they hiding?" The longer it takes to acknowledge obvious problems, issues, and situations, the greater the implied guilt; the more complex it becomes to explain what actually happened; the larger and more burdenson the fines, settlements, and remediated solutions become. Honorable organizations can talk about and address any issue or concern promptly. Silence is always toxic to the perpetrator. Silence is a toxic strategy.

18. **Testosterosis:** Aggressive "smash them in the mouth" behavior brings with it the refusal to move ahead or to put petty, silly, meaningless issues and problems behind us. While it is mostly a guy thing, women executives experience and act this way as well. When it takes the form of attacks on victims, these attacks only create additional victims along with the potential for litigation and, sometimes, explosive, corrosive visibility. These attacks often backfire against the executive in charge. Former friends and allies will distance themselves, standing back to see how bad the situation is going to get.

19. **Verbal vegetables:** Sometimes there is language that we just know we're going to eat, or be forced to take back as situations unfold: "No one told us," "It isn't our fault," "We have been unfairly accused," "It wasn't as though we didn't understand," "We are victims, too," "We are not a crooked company or people," or "I did not have sexual relations with that woman."

Destructive management communication behavior will lead to similar behavior at various levels within an organization. These negative behaviors foster stress within the organization that can prompt unethical behaviors to appease aggressive managers. *Unethical behavior, if permitted and tolerated, when combined with evil intent, often leads to illegal behavior and more crises.* Ask any prosecutor.

Add your own local favorites to this list; then attack them, expose them, rout them out, inhibit them, and stop them. The repair cost in reputation, credibility, trust, and lost talent is enormous.

2.5 Lukaszewski's 12 Axioms of Crisis Survival for Leaders

> Leadership that shows compassion, community sensitivity, and sensible, ethical approaches moves companies to victory and out of harm's way.

Managing emergencies, crises, and disasters successfully means recognizing the patterns of success, failure, and defeat. Understanding these patterns enables us to coach and prepare management's actions, emotions, and expectations before and during emergency situations.

1. Defeat is almost always the work of over-optimistic bosses, uninformed co-workers and associates, well-meaning friends, or dysfunction within the organization. Neither the media, nor your toughest critics, nor your opponents, nor the government - the entities commonly blamed for failure - know enough to defeat you.

2. Act promptly. It is better to make mistakes and overreact today rather than wait until tomorrow and have to explain what you knew and when you knew it, what you did and when you did it, and why you waited while more victims were created.

3. Keep the issues and focus tight and small to help you solve your problems and move forward. Neither your "industry," outsiders, nor the media can solve your problems (they don't care), and you cannot solve theirs. You must solve your own.

4. Disasters and problems rarely kill products or companies unless you let them. It is your own negative communication and attitude that cause tough questions, bad stories, and real damage.

5. Colorful, emotional, and memorable language creates headlines that are impossible to live down.

6. In emergencies, 25% of your resources and 50% of your energy go toward fixing yesterday's mistakes. This is the cost of rebuilding trust.

7. Positive, aggressive, assertive communication limits follow-up questions, focuses on the most important aspects of the problem, and moves the entire process forward to resolution, even in the face of a negative environment or antagonistic news media. Actions always speak louder than words.

8. No question you are asked about your situation will surprise you. You may become irritated, agitated, or even humiliated because a really tough or touchy subject is raised, but you won't be surprised. Just remember, every question is a platform to get your messages out.

9. Preparation, rehearsal, and a certain amount of luck will keep you going and help you win.

10. Luck is limited.

11. The general public does not care about your problems until you make them care.

   ▶ 50% of the general public has no reason to care.

   ▶ 25% of the general public probably has troubles worse than yours, from their perspective, anyway.

   ▶ If you get the attention of those remaining, they are probably glad you have the trouble you have.

   ▶ Be very careful making more people care. You may rue that day.

12. Leadership that shows compassion, community sensitivity, and sensible, ethical approaches moves companies to victory and out of harm's way. Timidity, hesitation, arrogance, and whining bring defeat. Keep the pressure on to win.

> **Leaders are people of tomorrow. They work outside of the box. Their main job is to see over the horizon, identify new destinations, and then lead us to them.**

2.6 The Leader as Verbal Visionary

The need for powerful verbal communications is more apparent than ever when an organization is in crisis or preparing to handle one. A much higher level of leadership and communications is called for, a level beyond the ordinary. The work of the leader, then, is the work of a **verbal visionary**.

2.6.1 Managers and Leaders: The Difference

   ▶ The role of the **manager** in any organization is to meet expectations, meet established goals or objectives, and help others to do so within the scope of a plan or operational activity.

- **Leadership,** on the other hand, depends on verbal skill and personal example. Leaders are people of tomorrow. They work outside of the box. Their main job is to see over the horizon, identify new destinations, and then lead us to them. The leader then returns to tell, show, or verbally illustrate the various elements and destinations of the journey and the priorities for moving the organization forward. Leaders lead through inspiration, motivation, verbalizing strategic vision, conducting strategic evaluations and questioning, and solving people problems.

For executives or managers as well as for the staff members who coach or strategize with them, preparation for career-defining crisis entails enhanced leadership thinking and decision-making. One type of preparation is improved personal communication skills that will allow everyone involved in handling crisis communication to have a more positive influence on the outcome of the situation.

Today, the dominant force in decision-making is verbal power – speaking and writing. In virtually every culture – especially in the United States, Canada, the Americas, and Europe – the world moves at verbal speed. Thus, the real power in many situations lies in the ability to move people to action through the power of one's words.

2.6.2 Principles of a Verbal Visionary

As a verbal visionary, your principles are:

Sensitivity to core values – you understand people and what they value, what they are concerned about, want to protect, want protection from. You know that personal core values are almost impossible to change because they serve as such a powerful personal protective mechanism.

Trust/credibility – you are trustworthy and have credibility conferred upon you by others based on their perception of your past actions, as they see your past actions as predictors of your future behavior.

Integrity – you also have integrity, the uncompromising adherence to a code of moral principles, utter sincerity, honesty, and candor.

Are you a Verbal Visionary?

Those who will come to rely on you as a verbal visionary will expect you to be able to express and discuss your principles, your aspirations, the foundation of your beliefs, the source of your thinking, and your own internal destination. Being a verbal visionary means understanding your self-concepts and being able to share those understandings with others.

One of the most satisfying and powerful aspects of being a verbal visionary is knowing that the advice you offer and your ability to explore important ideas are genuinely helpful to the other person's goals and objectives, personal beliefs and motivations, sense of reality, and priority of ideas.

What Does a Verbal Visionary Do?

Whatever your job title or responsibility in an organization – whether you are an executive, a member of the management team, or an outside consultant – as a verbal visionary, your role, first of all, is that of *counselor*. You are a pragmatist, a truth seeker, a Dutch uncle, a storyteller, an inspiration, and a motivator to others. You can think of yourself as a truth coach – someone who avoids the trap of believing in narrow truths that ultimately satisfy no one. A Dutch uncle is defined as a "severe mentor" – in other words, someone who loves you enough to tell you the absolute truth, all the time. As a story-teller, a counselor conveys important verbal information through effective storytelling. The storytelling skill is important because we all relate to stories more easily than to most other forms of communication. As motivators, counselors work on behaviors, model skills, and share what they say in ways that are motivational and inspirational.

A verbal visionary is *wise*. This wisdom is expressed by using verbal contrasts to analyze a situation and then to verbally describe a dramatic contrast between good and bad, between bland and colorful, between emotional and factual. Wise people also ask good questions. Their questions help build understanding, and do not attack, demean, diminish, or minimize. Wise people are constructively doubtful. When they encounter an absence of obviously conclusive evidence, they demonstrate that ideas and purposes can be constructively analyzed, usefully dissected, thoughtfully examined and discussed. Wise people can render complex ideas and concepts understandable through dramatic and positive simplification. Wisdom is information that snaps on a little light in your brain.

A verbal visionary is also candid. Candor is truth with an attitude. It's truth with meaning, truth with insight. It's truth with that pragmatic touch. That's why we appreciate candor more than truth.

A verbal visionary is ethical and principled, and lives by a set of rules and personal behaviors we all recognize as predominantly in the interest of others. A verbal visionary is an advocate for honorable action, an individual who is morally assertive without religious fervor. Verbal visionaries are also teachers, coaches, and mentors.

2.6.3 How Will You Know If You Have Become a Verbal Visionary?

Assuming you are in the process of becoming a verbal visionary, here's a quiz you can take to assess your progress.

▶ Do you act and speak in other people's best interests all the time?

- Are you quoted by those you respect and those who seek your help?

- Do people take action based on what you say? Do people tell you or talk about you as being a person of vision? Or as being a person of extraordinarily positive help?

- Do you feel like a verbal visionary? Can you tell when you're actually moving people to action and helping them find the emotional energy to benefit themselves?

- Can you describe your own sense of destiny, your principles, your beliefs, and your limits?

- Can you systematically go after the truth first? Are you a pragmatist?

The more "yes" answers, the more likely it is that you're well on your way to becoming a verbal visionary. The more "yes" answers, the closer you are to being a visionary person.

2.7 Preparing Executives – Becoming a Valued Communications Advisor on the Team

2.7.1 What Executives Need

Top executives need and want:

1. **People who listen.** Not people who can barely wait to talk, but people who can listen, hear, and react, reflecting back ideas from the perspective of management, while evaluating the broader human and perception impacts as well.

2. **People who have intuition** to advance ideas and interpret events. Too often we retreat to the language, philosophies and assumptions of our profession. When management learns to expect that behavior, our value is lost.

3. **People who have guts.** Communicators must overcome the fear of doing or saying something that might appear offensive. Unfortunately, communicators spend too much time trying to be inoffensive. In reality, inoffensiveness lowers your credibility and builds management frustration. Military strategists will tell you that the two greatest enemies of victory are timidity and hesitation. They only lead to frustrations and confusion.

4. **People who give two kinds of feedback:**

   - *Data feedback:* What the situation is; what the statistics of the situation are.

▶ *Feeling feedback:* Executives want to know they are being heard, even if the counselor's interpretation moves in directions the executive finds uncomfortable. The executive wants a signal that the counselor understands the management mentality. *Feeling feedback* means listening beyond the words. Successful counselors are those who hear the executive's unsaid feelings speaking even louder than words.

5. **People who inspire.** Often inspiration boils down to carefully applying common sense and recognizing pragmatic ideas, actions, and relationships.

6. **People who are trusted.** To most executives being trusted means keeping your mouth shut. But, it also means communicating with extraordinary candor (by understanding who the boss is, telling it like it is, and interpreting what the boss wants effectively.

7. **People who have insight.** This is the power to recognize patterns of behavior, patterns of attitude, patterns of organizational activity and response – and to notice the differences, contrasts and revelations that lie at the heart of developing new strategies, tactical approaches and solutions to management problems.

8. **People who are complete thinkers.** A complete thinker is a counselor who always offers options for action when citing problems. The complete thinker is able to identify it, analyze it, forecast outcomes, recommend a range of ideas, and then test specific options.

9. **People who are pragmatists.** Top executives want advice that is positive, yet down-to-earth and immediately useful, i.e. how to do the doable.

10. **People who understand the dollar value of time.** These people exhibit the ability to forecast impacts, make recommendations quickly and carefully, and turn questions into answers and good ideas into better ones – virtually on the spot and without being asked.

From the point of view of the CEO, the job of management is often to deal with paradox, contradiction, confusion, confrontation, and conflict rather than to predict challenges. CEOs often question themselves and their work and, once in a while, look back over their shoulders to see whether anyone is following. But when you are at the top, you do have an unobstructed view plus a perception of the level of leadership necessary. Creating leaders requires that we seek to understand and accept the executive perception of what leadership means.

2.7.2 Discovering and Choosing Truth

Those of you reading this book are interested in managing the communication aspects of crises. All crises are matters of substance, involve important questions, and in some cases take lives or put people's lives at risk. The biggest daily choice you face is discovering and choosing truth.

> **Two of the most powerful lessons I've learned in my career are that bad news and poor judgment ripen badly - they never get better with age.**

Let me share with you one of the most interesting and powerful realities of handling communications: *the power of what you say and how you say it.* The people who are doing an effective job for their companies have excellent verbal skills and are what earlier in this chapter we called "verbal visionaries." They have come to realize the most fundamental reality of communication in virtually any culture. The world moves at verbal speed. In the English language, that's 150 words per minute.

We believe that a successful, important, meaningful corporate communications career requires self-examination, self-reflection, and a core set of beliefs to guide this constant stream of choices:

- To choose honorable action over something less.
- To choose candor over something less.
- To choose disclosure over something less.
- To choose responsiveness over something less.
- To choose openness over something less.
- To choose what matters over something less.
- To choose the truth no matter what.

Successful communicators focus on substantive matters, specifically on what is really important. They can be called "verbal visionaries" because they are able to share insight on the spot or tell a revealing story with a major lesson or truth. They have impact. They are driven by and make their choices based on a simple set of guiding principles.

2.7.3 Guiding Principles

1. **Choose the truth**. The truly tough issue is how one gets to the truth. To get to the truth you must understand who you are, think through what you believe, write those things down, say them out loud, and perfect them. Then, you must act on those beliefs, test your beliefs, check your assumptions, and test them again.

2. **Quantify what you want to accomplish.** Write it down. Say it out loud. Work on it until you can say it effectively and powerfully to others, until what you want to accomplish is powerful enough to move others to action.

3. **Project who you want to be.** Identify those circumstances in which you want to find yourself. Begin to identify the parameters of these personal goals. Then, act on your assumptions.

4. **Plan to have significant impact.** Impact is about influencing others to act, believe, or respond from their own perspective.

Two of the most powerful lessons I've learned in my career are that bad news and poor judgment ripen badly – they never get better with age. And, if you start each day with small truths and work daily in a relentlessly positive, incremental way, you will arrive at larger truths faster.

Be Focused On the Crucial 5%

Remember that organizational change is incremental. What leaders have to do is to focus on the crucial 5% of what is truly essential to move the organization forward. That leaves 95% of the brains, smarts, strategic planning, and execution to the rest of the organization.

Years ago when I was just beginning my career in public relations, I did a marketing study for a Minnesota-based Fortune 500 company that specialized in high technology switching equipment. The marketing study was extensive, expensive, and one of the most interesting projects I'd worked on at that time in my career. When I made my presentation to the assembled executives and their staffs, the response was clearly enthusiastic. When I asked the CEO about moving forward, he said that the majority of the things I talked about were things the organization needed to do and would be enormously helpful.

When I asked him how many of my recommendations we could begin implementing, his response astounded me. "Oh," he said, "I think we can manage about 4% of what you recommended." I was stunned. Virtually everything in my report seemed to be useful, successful, and implementable. Everyone was enthusiastic. So in my naive but brazen way, I asked directly if I had made a mistake. Had I misunderstood what happened just an hour earlier?

The CEO's response was, "No, Jim, you didn't make a mistake. But the fact is that this is a 5,000-employee organization. I am only the CEO. The reality is: those who show up to work every day run this company. Some days we do really well. Some days key people don't show, or are here but don't get much done. I'm 57 years old, which means I'll be the CEO of this organization for probably the next six-to-eight years maximum. If I can shift this organization's focus or center of direction 4-5% each year I'll be doing extraordinarily well, and that's considering our competitive environment and how our business changes from month-to-month. This means that in the entire term of my tenure as chairman, if I can turn this organization 35-40%, I'll be doing extremely well, absent a catastrophe like a hostile takeover, which could turn this ship 90 degrees or 125 degrees in an afternoon."

The lessons for me were these: first, the absolute need to focus on that 5% of what is truly, truly important; and second, the limitations of leadership. Even the most dynamic, exciting, and amazing individual is unlikely to make radical changes in an organization overnight. Organizational change is incremental.

(The 95/5 concept was inspired by Price Pritchett (2002), who noted the mission-critical approach to culture integration and culture change. Organizational change is incremental.)

Chapter 2 – Questions for Study and Discussion:

1. For a CEO, how does his or her age, background, career track, experience, and length of time in office influence his or her ability to handle a crisis effectively? What are some common mistakes? How might they be avoided?

2. What is the difference between a "manager" and a "leader?" Why, when an organization is involved in a crisis, does it desperately need leaders? What are three key areas of growth for a manager that can improve the perception that he or she is actually a leader? How will the manager know that he or she is now being perceived as a leader? What difference will that make in immediate results?

3. What does it take to become a "verbal visionary" who can take on the role of being an effective counselor and advisor to management in a crisis? If you aspire to such a role for yourself, what are three things you could do differently at work on Monday morning? If you are currently seeking or applying for a position that requires those skills, what would be your first step in preparing yourself for such a job? What training might it require?

References, Chapter 2

Moore, G.E. (1965, April 19). Cramming more components into integrated circuits. *Electronics*, 38(8), 4.

Pritchett, P. (2002). *The employee handbook for shaping corporate culture.* Dallas, TX: Pritchett, LP.

3

Crisis Communication:
Preparing for Crisis and Visibility

Keywords: threat identification, planned visibility, unplanned visibility, vulnerabilities, community core values, audience analysis, Incident Response Team, Call Headquarters If

As your organization improves its readiness for a possible crisis, you, as a communicator, will take on the role of being a strategic, thoughtful, prepared, and candid consultant and counselor. Much of your credibility will depend on your systematic, knowledgeable approaches to developing the kind of information that managers need to make critical operating decisions when emergencies occur.

This chapter will help you to:

> ➤ Conduct a vulnerability analysis, identifying threats that could leave your organization open to exposure.

> ➤ Identify the key issues that can lead to "unplanned visibility" for your organization, a challenge requiring communication activity.

> ➤ Communicate effectively with employees, victims, community, suppliers, and the community in time of crisis.

> ➤ Recognize which problems require a corporate response and which do not.

3.1 Threat Identification and Visibility Analysis

Readiness preparation for a possible crisis begins with *visibility analysis*, examining the possible sources of crises, their planned visibility and their unplanned visibility. In the process of completing this analysis, you will discover many things about your organization that may surprise you. Among the things you will discover is the extraordinary diversity of activities in which employees and the company are involved. Then, in the vulnerability portion of your analysis, you'll discover a wide variety of activities and situations about which you may have been completely unaware, over which you have little control, which present great risk.

As you conduct your visibility analysis, especially as you interview senior executives and location managers, you'll gain a deeper insight into the operating concerns of the business. Remember that this is the real reason we do visibility analysis and crisis planning – to gain the understanding necessary to appropriately guide and coach managers and leaders through the crisis.

Stay focused on the task, which is to help those who operate the business get through very difficult situations, even when they may think at first that such events will never happen to them, and if crises occur, management is bright, young and smart enough to deal with them.

3.1.1 Step 1: Planned Visibility Analysis: The Community Involvement Audit

The first phase in the analysis of your organization's planned visibility is to conduct a community involvement audit or visibility audit at the corporate level. The community involvement audit identifies those activities in which your organization is involved each month of the year in six major categories. These categories reflect the visible actions of the company in your community and your environment. The six categories might be: Girl Scouts; Emergency Medical response squads; holding significant public office, elective or appointed; heading a significant NPO; being a church elder; or, sponsoring local sports competitions.

A good method for gathering this information is to put small groups of supervisors and active employees together to do the analysis for each geographic location where your business operates. You'll be pleasantly surprised at the level and volume of participation by those involved. In fact, one of the by-products of the community involvement audit is a much better understanding of the exposure of your business in the communities in which it operates.

> **One of the by-products of the community involvement audit is a much better understanding of your organization'exposure in the communities in which it operates.**

Once you have identified your community involvement or your corporate exposure, it's time to look at your operation from another perspective – that of your vulnerabilities.

3.1.2 Step 2: Unplanned Visibility: Vulnerability Analysis

The second type of exposure your organization is subject to is unplanned visibility. Explosively visible and highly emotional situations create victims caused by unexpected outcomes to routine, day-to-day operating processes, and circumstances beyond your control being imposed on you and your organization. We refer to them as *vulnerabilities*. Vulnerability analysis is also a small group process, usually done by managers and supervisors. Completing vulnerability analysis in large numbers of small groups helps educate the organization and sensitize the business to the concepts of vulnerability and emergency preparation.

A vulnerability analysis has two parts:

- The first part is to identify vulnerabilities. For most organizations or businesses, vulnerabilities tend to come from seven discrete areas: 1) your own people, 2) other people, 3) the environment, 4) technology, 5) government, 6) the economy, and 7) vendors.
- The second part is to make simultaneous qualitative judgments about the impact, likelihood of occurrence, and collateral damage caused by a specific vulnerability.

It is as critical that you rate these vulnerabilities as it is for you to identify them. The whole purpose of this process is to move toward identifying those key issues that could genuinely harm the organization and for which you absolutely must prepare. A complete vulnerability analysis involves both identification and quantification of the most serious risks and events that could occur.

Field Site Interviews

While these first two steps in the visibility analysis process can be performed at headquarters, truly competent crisis planning involves going on site, working through the same processes there, and preparing a comprehensive site profile.

Site interviews are generally carried out with local managers and key supervisors. The process is highly structured so that time is conserved in conducting the analysis, and consistent information is gathered across the entire company. This approach tends to identify unique individual vulnerabilities for each site during the interview process.

Resist the urge to mail the survey to supervisors. For best results, face-to-face interviewing is the rule here. Trained, observant interviewers will obtain much greater knowledge and insight into the vulnerabilities and potential problem areas for local sites.

3.1.3 Step 3: Senior Executive Reflection Studies

The toughest part of visibility analysis is interviewing senior executives to gain their insights, observations, knowledge, and sensitivities. The successful technique requires a different sort of approach.

Note first that the focus of the interview is either some important recent or high-profile problem the company suffered, or a hypothetical high-profile event that could happen to the organization, but has probably happened to someone else. Because senior operating executives rarely work in a world of hypothetical situations and speculation, it's often difficult for them to give serious attention to scenarios that have yet to occur. Remember, the goal in interviewing senior executives is more to gain insight into how they will help manage the situation once it arises than it is to test their specific knowledge of unique vulnerabilities the organization might face.

Anecdotal information gathered from senior executives will help to drive the training and installation process once you have developed an approach to crisis management and planning.

As you move toward identifying the most important issues the organization faces, it is important that the visibility information gained through your analysis be aggregated effectively. We suggest gathering and consolidating the community involvement audit information in two formats:

1. Monthly compilations simply listing all January activities, all February activities, all March activities, etc. through the end of the year.

2. A multi-element calendar – which is really six calendars, one for each of the major planned visibility activity areas – that is organized by calendar month. So your first calendar would involve *City/Regional/National/International Events* – all January responses aggregated, all February response aggregated, etc. Then do one for *Civic/Philanthropic Organization Participation* and so on.

All vulnerabilities should be aggregated by threat source and arranged within each category by the highest sensible priority, rather than the highest emotional priority score.

Next, tabulate the data generated from your senior executive reflection studies and your site surveys. You're looking here for the most unusual, the most threatening circumstances, not necessarily all the data, although the data may be of interest to others in the organization. Remember that what the boss fears the most is what you prepare for first.

Once you have completed this information-organizing step, you are ready for the crucial next step of *identifying those specific vulnerabilities or issues that require extensive preparation.*

> **The greatest problem with emergencies and disasters is surprise. One of the major goals of readiness for surviving emergencies is to reduce the level of surprise.**

How Am I Vulnerable?

The greatest problem with emergencies and disasters is surprise. One of the major goals of readiness for surviving emergencies is to reduce the surprise factor. This preparation, in turn, reduces, even forecasts, mistakes, which means there will be fewer situations to repair later on.

Fortunately, emergencies follow recognizable patterns. For example:

- No time to think or make decisions.
- Unanticipated serious consequences.
- Incomplete, inaccurate or conflicting information.
- Uncertainty.
- Stress and fatigue.
- Bureaucratic resistance.
- Threats today that will need to be repaired tomorrow.

Just as you can predict these recognizable patterns, you can also identify the source(s) of your organization's vulnerabilities. Generally, organizational vulnerabilities are the result of actions that make you visible within our own community. Analyzing your visibility is key to controlling emergencies.

As vulnerability and visibility are examined and identified, it's important to couple the knowledge gained with what we already know about emergency situations. Emergencies seem to take on lives of their own especially if:

▶ The media make mistakes, suspect dishonesty or cover-up, or perceive larger issues.

▶ Emotionalism is allowed to overshadow reality.

▶ The issue or problem is simply managed poorly.

▶ The organization's actions or policies are at odds with what is being communicated.

▶ The organization appears disorganized or unprepared.

▶ Victims are being ignored, demeaned or discredited.

When we create victims, the nature of our exposure intensifies.

3.2 Visibility and Victims Make Us Vulnerable

There are two types of visibility: planned and unplanned. The vast majority of corporate visibility is planned and comes from those activities carried out routinely. We explored the importance of victims and their treatment in Chapter 1. *When we create victims, the nature of our exposure intensifies.*

3.2.1 Planned Visibility

We've categorized planned visibility as being city/regional/national/international events, civic/philanthropic organization participation, company-sponsored events and participation, governmental interaction, products/service/promotion and delivery, and schools and education participation.

As the opportunity for unplanned visibility exists with planned events, it is important to periodically assess the planned level of corporate visibility for the purpose of preparing to respond in the event of unplanned visibility.

3.2.2 Unplanned Visibility

Unplanned visibility is the result of some unintended operating process outcome that affects people, animals, or the environment and attracts the attention of the news media, specific groups, or government. Analyzing vulnerabilities takes three important factors into account:

▶ Impact.

▶ Chance of occurrence.

▶ Collateral damage.

Impact means the number of people affected, the number of telephones that failed, the number of deaths, etc. The larger the impact an issue has, the more the environment, technology, vendors, and/or people will be affected and involved.

Chance of occurrence is a subjective rating of the likelihood of an event taking place.

Impact and chance of occurrence are useful planning and training techniques for analyzing potential unplanned visibility threats (people, technology, environment, government, economics, and vendors). The process of quantifying vulnerabilities helps you focus on a limited number of key issues for which the organization will actually carry out some level of preparation.

Collateral damage acknowledges the reality that when exposure problems occur, there is a lot more damage, spread over a larger area, than originally thought or assumed. Collateral damage can mean the feelings of fear created by the circumstances absent any visible physical injury. Loss of reputation is often a collateral damage situation. Loss of trust, confidence, or market share are all examples of very tangible and important damage losses.

Before you complete this portion of this book you will have established a lexicon of vulnerabilities for your organization. Use the extensive list of problems, crises, bad news, and adverse visibility situations listed here to get a start on this *dark-side* thinking process and begin an assessment of the kinds of operational problems your organization could experience.

3.3 Threat Identification - Key Issues Prioritization and Worksheet

> Most organizations have only a dozen or so truly key issues at any given time. While some are extremely basic and remain the same, they still require extensive preparation.

3.3.1 What Is a Key Issue?

Most organizations have only a dozen or so truly key issues at any given time. While some are extremely basic and remain the same, they still require extensive preparation – tornados, hurricanes, earthquakes, other natural disaster situations, and explosions. These are genuine key issues and, as you will see in the next section, developing scenarios for them is critical to your preparation process.

Additional key issues come from community involvement analyses, vulnerability analyses, site interviews, and senior executive reflection studies.

After you have identified most sources of unplanned visibility, resource limitations will only allow so much preparation. Therefore, in addition to those critical, naturally-occurring organizational threats, you must choose those vulnerabilities and activities with the highest impact and greatest potential for damage, injury, or harm should they occur.

The priority column of the completed vulnerability analysis worksheets is one indication of the level of threat each particular unplanned visibility could pose. The higher the rating number, the higher the priority for consideration as a key issue.

In addition to the rating number, use your intuition to determine which situations truly meet the criteria for a key issue. Those seven criteria are:

1. It could be a show-stopper.
2. It could be a people-stopper.
3. It could be a product-stopper.
4. It could be a community-stopper.
5. Large numbers of community audiences will be affected.
6. It intuitively presents substantial vulnerability even though the likelihood of actual occurrence might be quite small.
7 There will be victims and seriously negative visibility.

Identifying key issues also involves another evaluation process, one even more powerful than the criteria just listed – the potential impact on *community core values*.

3.3.2 The Human Factor: Community Core Values (Why people get angry in the first place)

Through analysis and interaction during crises, it has become very evident that communities in every culture live by a set of values so basic and universal that they are the core of what citizens want and expect. Every element of your crisis communication plan must take into account six core community values. The actions we take, the words we use, and the way we think when executing a crisis response must be compatible with and reflect our understanding of the community's powerful and controlling values. A community core value I define as a personal protective belief, meaning circumstances and situations in the community which may not be altered, changed, or even casually manipulated without the permission and participation of the citizens affected. Think of core values from the community's perspective. If you act in opposition to any of these deeply held values – or even appear to be considering it – without the direct, obvious, and open permission of the community, people will be instantly angry and will, in fact, often take to the streets to get your attention and help you change what you intend to do. These powerful, personal protective beliefs are:

▶ Healthy and safe communities.
▶ Protecting the value of possessions and property.
▶ Environmental threats.
▶ The assurance of a quality of life:

- ❑ Peace of mind
- ❑ Pride in community
- ❑ Absence of conflict/freedom from fear
- ◗ Peer concern (pressure)/when my neighbor is concerned, I am concerned.
- ◗ Economic security.

It is essential that your threat analysis and key issue identification activities consider honestly and carefully the ways in which your plan, messages, and actions will affect core community values. You must consider the following questions.

Will our plans and actions to mitigate, remediate, or respond to emergencies affect:

- ◗ The *health and safety* of individuals or families?
- ◗ The *economic security* of families, individuals, or the community as a whole?
- ◗ The ability of individuals, families, and businesses to preserve the *value of their property*?
- ◗ People's *pride in their homes and community*?
- ◗ The level of *conflict* in people's lives - does it create or intensify?
- ◗ The *peace of mind* of large numbers of people?

If the answer to some or all of the above questions is "yes," that should serve as a powerful signal that inept, uncaring, or insensitive communication and action strategies will not only irritate the community but may also create genuine community outrage. Perhaps the best advice when planning emergency response action is to put yourself in the shoes of the community members from every perspective. Putting yourself in their shoes may mean holding meetings with people who represent all aspects of the community as you develop your plan to make certain that the things you might include as corporate actions and responses are compatible with community values. If you fail to take these positive steps early on, you may find that long-term and powerful resentments emerge following the resolution of an emergency – even if you have handled the emergency well.

As you look at your responses from a community perspective – analyzing the questions from victims, neighbors, public officials, your own employees, and ultimately the media – you'll see that feedback tends to focus on the six core community values above.

As you assess the nature of each threat, those threats that infringe upon core community values will automatically become more critical than most others.

3.3.3 Community Audience Analysis

In addition to core community values, another powerful factor for determining which vulnerabilities ultimately reach your key issue list is the number of community audiences affected by any potential threat. One important test for each potential threat is your analysis and actual identification of those audiences likely to be affected by that the potential threat.

> **For every potential key issue scenario you can estimate accurately the exact audience to be affected and develop appropriate response plans.**

Most emergencies affect only a few audiences at the same time. The rest remain oblivious to any problem unless there is substantial media coverage, grapevine activity, or word-of-mouth, neighbor-to-neighbor comment. For every potential key issue scenario, you can estimate accurately the exact audiences to be affected and develop appropriate response plans.

In addition, audience reaction and priority of response need to be built into your scenario for the purpose of simulation and practice. *The Community Environment* chart in the figure below allows a quick analysis of the various audiences that make up most community communications environments. Work with this chart to identify the audiences that will be most concerned in crisis situations.

As you analyze just which groups in the community will be affected by problems and emergencies in your organization, keep in mind that only portions of any audience category will have an interest, and that, except in the most unusual circumstances, many audiences may be affected at different times. As a general rule, throughout our preparation for managing communication during emergencies, a knowledge of community core values and victimization allows us to forecast the level of audience interest and determine in advance the kinds of messages and actions each audience will look for when bad things happen.

The Community Environment Chart
The Environment of Audience and Stakeholder Analysis
Copyright© 2013, The Lukaszewski Group Inc.

Key Issue Identification Process

Step 1: Using a blank copy of the Key Issues Worksheet below, *list potential key issues, the nature of the threat, and the audiences affected.* Circulate the results among key individuals in your organization for additional ranking, comment, and analysis.

Ask the raters to choose the most important dozen. Then ask the raters to rank them in order of potential severity to the organization (1 being the greatest threat, 12 the lowest threat).

Step 2: *Create a timeline* that allows approximately three weeks each for development of individual scenarios for use in crisis communications management coaching and training. These scenarios will ultimately reside in your crisis management plan for quick referral should those situations arise.

Step 3: *Schedule annual reviews* of key issues and scenarios for timeliness and relevance.

The Key Issues Worksheet (Completed Example)
Copyright© 2013, The Lukaszewski Group Inc.

Instructions for Use:

Utilize the **Key Issues Worksheet** to organize and clarify those high priority vulnerabilities your organization currently faces.

Step 1.   Refer to the Vulnerability Analysis to determine which visibility threats are or will become key issues:

▶ Visibility threats with high priorities

▶ Threats or issues which intuitively present substantial vulnerability

Step 2.   List and describe in more detail each key issue.

Key Issue: **Leaking or ruptured fuel tank**

> **Nature of Threat**: *Ground water contamination; decline in property values; potential lawsuit_____*
>
> _____
> _____
> _____
> _____
> _____
> _____
> _____
>
> **Audiences Affected**: *Well owners, property owners, community-at-large*

Key Issue: **CRT exposure**

> **Nature of Threat**: *Secretaries/engineers/call center operators at risk* _____
>
>
>
> **Audiences Affected**: *Employees, local labor union*

Key Issue: **Vendor threats/product flaws**

> **Nature of Threat**: *Part, component, or ingredient quality* _____
>
>
>
> **Audiences Affected**: *Customers, prospects, government regulators*

Key Issue: **Delivery problems**

> **Nature of Threat:** *Could shut the plant down or stop work temporarily* __
>
>
>
> **Audiences Affected:** *Employees, vendors, customers*

3.4 Incident Response Categories

3.4.1 Crucial Incident-Specific Response Categories

The fastest response approach to control, contain, counteract, or accommodate especially threatening crisis situations is achieved through the creation of **Incident Response Teams** (IRTs), based on the most likely destructive threat scenarios. Every pre-selected crisis scenario becomes the responsibility of a specific Incident Response Manager (IRM), and his/her support structure. In smaller organizations, the IRTs train to handle as many scenarios as they can.

In large organizations, IRTs can be formed to respond to specific crisis situations. Key crisis situations for which Incident-Specific Response Teams (ISRTs) should be pre-organized, trained, and pre-authorized include:

> Bomb threat/kidnap/extortion.
> Catastrophic occurrences.
> Legal scenarios/litigation (civil, criminal, product liability, personal injury, class action).
> Police action (locally or at Headquarters).
> Suicide.
> Public policy and high-profile negative problems.
> Regulatory/legislative/Congressional action.
> Scandal.
> Sensational reputation threats.
> Shareholder (material) events.
> Suspicious substance.
> Terrorist attack.
> Unplanned, highly negative financial visibility.
> Workplace violence.
> Other unique and crucial scenarios reflecting serious threats to your organization and readiness.

Very little is actually learned about emergencies and crises at the time they occur.

3.4.2 Getting the Facts: Conducting Investigations

The operative reality of crisis is that 50% of our energy and 25% of our resources today will go to and be focused on resolving the mistakes we made yesterday – even if based on poor, incorrect, or erroneous information. Improving readiness is essential to crisis prevention. Getting the facts and verifying them is essential throughout the crisis response process and afterwards.

Very little is actually learned about emergencies and crises at the time they occur. The desire to get back to business, minimize costs, and even prevent or inhibit litigation can serve as incentives to avoid any thorough study of crisis situations.

At the same time, media reporting and colorful commentary come in such copious amounts during the usual early blizzard of media coverage that you have to wonder where it all comes from. Unfortunately, this information is mostly fabricated by reporters and bloggers. They talk to people, or people talk to them, and then the reporters and bloggers manufacture the rest of the information. For the crisis-afflicted organization, reputation preservation and recovery is going to depend on facts or reliable information, continuously provided. Keeping the record straight is essential to helping victims recover faster as well as giving you some control over the destiny of your organization.

Among the items to be managed are action/decision logs, keeping information in sequence, and creating a record as incidents and responses proceed. Getting the facts requires a managed and organized effort that is systematic, professional, and can stand the test of outside scrutiny.

Internal investigations are generally placed under the umbrella of Global Counsel, in collaboration with outside counsel of the Chief of Finance. The purpose of this particular area of information is simply to outline the facets of an internal investigation conducted for a global company. Corporate Security may also play a role, if appropriate.

3.5 Setting Crisis Response Communication Strategies and Priorities

Effective decisions and actions must precede communication. The reality is that once the instant of crisis has occurred, the process of recovery has begun. Recovery can be quite complicated and lengthy. The operational response goal is to put the focus truly on the first 1-3 hours of the scenario to assure that tone, tempo, scope, and intent are established powerfully and constructively. Emergency communication response priorities must address appropriate operational action and match the expectations of all potential audiences who could be affected or afflicted by your actions or who have been affected or afflicted by the crisis situation.

Emergencies will require almost simultaneous communication activity in all priority response areas. Effective execution is a primary concern precisely because time is limited. The more promptly actions are taken in response, the more quickly recovery can occur and production of victims can cease.

This five-level sensible strategy makes communication a process that management can understand, relate to, and, most importantly, buy into. Sensible response strategies lead to sensible communication actions. Such a set of priorities:

- Is the most effective way to contain, control, and reduce the visibility impact of emergent situations and any resulting reputational damage;
- Tends to reduce the ability of the media to alter the outcomes of crisis situations because those affected hear from us directly, thus avoiding the filtration, inaccuracy, or emotionalism news reporters bring to high-profile situations; and,
- Is, most importantly, the way our mothers, employees, neighbors, and the victims expect us to relay critical information.

> **Speed of action beats smart actions every time. Nothing is sillier and more damaging than a bunch of smart people trying to explain why they failed or refused to act promptly.**

Speed of communications is essential. Be slow, be inconsistent, be hesitant, be timid, be defensive, hold back – and even if your response is operationally flawless – it will be perceived always as slow, sloppy, inconsistent... you get the picture. Speed of action beats smart actions every time. Nothing is sillier and more damaging than a bunch of smart people trying to explain why they failed or refused to act promptly.

3.5.1 Priority # 1: Stop the Production of Victims

Ending the production of victims is the most powerful way to get control of a crisis. Yes, if it is leaking, foaming, stinking, burning, flaming, or exploding, the very first priority is to get the emergent situation under control, stabilized, or eliminated, but this is precisely because it will stop victim production. Our concern about the media finding out and other related communication activity is clearly of secondary importance in the face of an emergency that is yet to be brought under control or well managed.

Management expects those who give advice in these situations to have a sense of the optimal priority order or sequence of decisions and actions to make or support response recommendations that make sense in view of current circumstances.

3.5.2 Priority #2: Manage the Victim Dimension and Those Most Directly Affected

What we say and what we do for those most directly affected (the victims) – humanely and quickly – are our most important strategic objectives. Effective communication with victims and their families reduces media interest and coverage while building the trust of the community, public and regulatory officials, and those we most care about – our own employees.

The most important steps any organization can take during any emergency or crisis are to:

- Take conclusive action to quickly resolve or stabilize victim issues, problems, or situations being caused by the crisis.

- Act quickly and soundly to address the needs of victims, their immediate families, and relatives; to deal with continuing threats to those on-site or nearby; and to begin repairs or remediation of destroyed or damaged physical plant and property as soon as possible.

- Communicate and behave with empathy and sympathy constantly.

Assign responsibility for monitoring the medical and health progress of victims to a senior representative of the company. This responsibility will include on-site monitoring at hospitals. In cases of serious injury or death, the families will decide what information is released publicly, if any. The Health Insurance Portability and Accountability Act of 1996 (HIPAA) Privacy and Security Rules (http://www.hhs.gov/ocr/privacy/) establishes patient privacy guidelines that must be followed and in most cases prohibit disclosing patient names and information without patient consent.

3.5.3 Priority #3: Communicate With Employees

After survivors, employees are the crucial audience for crisis communication. Employees need to know their roles during a crisis, particularly if they have crisis-related duties. If they are to continue doing their regular jobs during a crisis, they need to know what is expected of them and how normal operations will be altered for the duration of the crisis. They will want to know what the organization is doing to return to normal conditions, how it will do that, and what "returning to normal" means.

> To employees, it seems natural to give the "inside scoop" to families, friends, neighbors, and others in the community. This type of information frequently becomes public.

We recommend the *75-word Rule of Communication*. This rule means providing frequent 75-word bursts of information. Studies of information retention indicate that information conveyed in writing or orally that is up to 75 words can be retained by individuals and often repeated almost verbatim, even during sensitive or urgent times. Use the format of a statement and attribute it to someone important in the company, and use these brief, quotable-sized statements before employees and other key audiences.

Seventy-five words is approximately 30 seconds speaking time (in English-speaking cultures). This approach will quickly begin to script your employees and anyone else coming into contact with the information, which will enable you to maintain control of a story appropriately as events unfold. Remember, employees rarely want to know every detail (or even many of the details); they just want to know that the people leading the organization are on top of the situation and are willing to talk about what is going on, meaning that employees don't have to make something up when someone asks them.

Even though employees may not talk directly to the media, they are often sources of information for people outside the company. To employees, it seems natural to give the "inside scoop" to families, friends, neighbors, and others in the community. This type of information frequently becomes public.

Employees also need to know the key themes, messages, and examples the company is using to respond to wider audiences. This knowledge helps keep non-media audiences accurately informed.

When talking with employees, emphasize the necessity of referring all media inquiries to the designated spokesperson. Emphasize that they need to be courteous if called or approached. The best employee response to a media inquiry is: "I'll refer you to a company spokesperson who will have the most up-to-date information."

Good Employee Communication Practices

- **Brief employees on the situation as soon as possible,** preferably before or at the same time as responding to the media. For companywide crises, the Manager of Employee Communications, if you have one, should coordinate employee communication activities.
- **Keep internal and external messages consistent.** Internal news should be as factual and as thorough as the news distributed to the media and other external audiences. In short, both must tell the same story.
- **Give all employees the same information.**
- **Emphasize that all inquiries are to be referred to the spokesperson.** At the same time, advise employees to be courteous to the media if they are approached or called. Advise them simply to refer questions to the spokesperson, who will have the most up-to-date information.
- **Use face-to-face communication for employee briefings.** The nature and urgency of the crisis will determine the feasibility of top management personally addressing employees. However, some personal contact – for example, by supervisors – is far more credible and effective than a memorandum tacked to a bulletin board.

▶ **Remember that personal discussions promote two-way communication** and reduce the "grapevine effect," which often distorts or misrepresents the facts surrounding events.

▶ **Help employees to be comfortable resuming business as usual, if possible.** This may not be possible in some situations, but any employee not involved directly in handling the emergency should be encouraged to return to normal tasks. Getting back to business as usual may be especially important in the aftermath of a crisis when a disruption in work schedules will not only have an economic impact, but may also result in unfavorable media coverage.

▶ **Be sensitive to employee emotions** when co-workers are threatened, injured, or killed. Establish a toll-free, confidential employee assistance hotline and refer all employees with questions or concerns. In certain situations, such as multiple employee deaths or mass casualties, make provisions for group intervention counseling by experts and interaction with spiritual leaders.

▶ **Recognize employee contributions** to managing the crisis. Acknowledge the participation of team members and others who help during a crisis, thanking them in public and through internal statements.

▶ **Establish a sense of continuity over the long haul** to signal employees and key constituencies that recovery remains in progress and is still being accomplished. Avoid the management tendency to stop communicating at the earliest possible time, an attitude that causes fear and loss of trust. It's a good practice to establish a rhythm for periodic employee updates.

▶ **Keep a significant individual in charge** of the problem until resolved. Sometimes the hardest aspect of a crisis to resolve is the collateral damage also caused at the time the crisis occurred. A recognizable person of stature or substance remaining in charge can be essential to maintaining the trust rebuilding when crises occur.

Injury and Fatality Communication

Delivering the bad news is never easy, not even for people who must do this routinely as part of their jobs. We recommend profiting from the experience of law enforcement professionals, who offer extensive and excellent advice on this topic (see footnote on the Iowa Department of Justice, 2008).

▶ **What to Say if Someone Is Hurt**

  ❑ When an employee is injured, the employee's supervisor should follow authorized notification procedures.

❏ All information regarding identity, nature, and extent of injuries or cause of death is to be held strictly confidential until the Vice President of PR/Corporate Communications (or other suitable individual) authorizes release.

❏ If the victim violated safety rules, it may be more appropriate for this information to be made public by the U.S. Occupational Safety and Health Administration (OSHA), or police and fire authorities. For the company to call attention to the negligence of someone who has just been hurt is callous and arrogant.

❏ The Local Emergency Team will assign someone to maintain an updated list of all employees who are not accounted for. The Vice President of PR/Corporate Communications will be kept informed of this list, including the status of injured employees, and death notifications.

3.5.4 Priority #4: Communicate With Those Affected Indirectly

> If media coverage of the event is nationwide, the company should be in touch with key elected state and federal officials and regulatory agencies.

Persons affected *indirectly* include survivors, neighbors, government officials and regulators, community leaders, customers, suppliers, shareholders, allies, partners, collaborators, and co-inventers or co-marketers.

Many crisis situations will mandate contact with government officials at various levels. If media coverage of the event is nationwide, the company should be in touch with key elected state and federal officials and regulatory agencies to ensure that they have accurate and prompt information to be prepared for possible media questions. The type of crisis will dictate the extent of such notifications.

▶ Corporate Relations will coordinate the regulatory reporting process.

▶ Government Relations will notify elected officials.

▶ Locally the Facility/Plant Manager, if available, (otherwise his or her backup) will coordinate with the Community Relations Manager in deciding which local officials to contact.

▶ The regions will coordinate with the Community Relations Officer in deciding which local officials to contact.

▶ Establish a priority and process for keeping all indirectly affected audiences, groups, and individuals informed.,

Neighbors and Community Leaders

Cooperation and communication with neighbors and local community leaders can help resolve and mitigate any lingering negative effects. The type of crisis dictates the extent of notification.

» In local/regional emergencies, the PR Manager or Regional Communication Contact is responsible for notifying community leaders.

» Depending on the nature of the emergency, the regional communications contact also advises corporate relations.

Customers and Suppliers

Communicating with customers and suppliers, while not at the top of the agenda during the early stages of a crisis, should move toward the top of the list once the immediate needs of the crisis are met. Customers and suppliers, like employees, should learn of a crisis situation directly from the company, particularly if the crisis is expected to affect the relationship between them.

> To accommodate the extraordinary demands of many publics when crises occur, it is crucial to establish a crisis communication policy.

Best Practices for Government Communication

» *Take the initiative!*

» *Contact local officials before they contact you.*

» *Contact legislators who represent the district in which the emergency has occurred.* The local or government official who believes in the organization's efforts to resolve the crisis can be an important third party advocate if contacted by the media.

» *Share media statements, news releases, and related communications directly with government and regulatory officials.* In the early stages of a crisis, there may be no time for drafting separate communication documents. A news release or fact sheet, for example, will suffice to demonstrate the company's prompt response.

» *Distribute appropriate information on the company's safety, environmental, and community relations records.* Local officials may need to be reminded of the ways in which the company has contributed to the community. They should also be informed about the company's policies to safeguard its employees and neighbors. Fact sheets highlighting community involvement, as well as the company's commitment to environmental safety, should be made available.

» *Be open to officials and regulators visiting a crisis site quickly. Make it a safe visit.*

Communication Guidelines for Dealing with Customers and Suppliers

Customers and suppliers often become some of the news media's preferred, but unwitting sources during crisis situations. The mistaken belief of these friends is that they are helping to tell the "right story." They assume that we are too busy dealing with the situation to explain it ourselves adequately. So, in the absence of information from us, they make something up.

The most important information to communicate to customers and suppliers is where they should refer the media for accurate, up-to-date information.

Be aware that the most persistent reporters who go after suppliers and vendors are those with the trade publications that serve your industry. There is a mistaken belief that trade publications are "on our side." The reality is quite different. The trade press are among the most aggressive, negative, and competitive in terms of disclosing or revealing adverse industry information. They now compete with hundreds of blogs, Twitter sources, and traditional media. It may not seem that way on the surface, particularly because trade journalists speak our language and seem knowledgeably sympathetic to our situation, but trade publications are very often the source of leaks, mistakes, and silly assumptions.

▶ The Customer Service and Purchasing departments should coordinate communications to customers and suppliers.

▶ Messages to customers and suppliers should be consistent with those given to the media and employees. Keep customers' interests and needs in mind.

▶ Communicate personally whenever possible. When the numbers are manageable, marketing managers or sales representatives should make telephone calls to regular customer contacts.

▶ Launch your dark website to provide readily available information, accessible with convenience to anyone who is interested. Such information would include providing an outline of the problem, the company's position, information on how the crisis will affect the customer, frequent updates on the site, and notifications of customers and others. Drive everyone potentially affected to your Website. You will become the information source of choice for everyone, including the media.

3.5.5 Priority #5: Communicate With the Media, Other Self-Appointed External Individuals, and Communications Organizations

Terrible events will be followed by terrible stories. How you behave and how responsive you can be will determine the tone and quality of media coverage your organization receives. An empathetic, prompt, professional approach will help to ensure the best possible coverage under the circumstances.

To prepare for and be ready to accommodate the extraordinary demands of many publics when crises occur, it is crucial to establish a crisis communication policy, as the impact of social media and traditional media relations requirements have become very similar. However, some fundamental rules remain obvious and should be applied:

1. All crises are local and, therefore, local media, audiences, victims, and those directly affected must take precedence over all other interests, including national media.

2. The web is the greatest and most powerful tool for dealing with mass media response situations. The impact of the web is powerful, immediate, 24/7, and can help manage the messages.

3. Finding the truth is extremely difficult. The truth itself is about 15% facts and data and 85% emotion and point of reference. The truth is unique for each receiver of information. In crises, facts and data, as well as emotions and point of reference, change very rapidly, therefore truth winds up being a moving target for everyone involved and affected. In the early moments of crisis, even early hours of the crisis, so little is actually known by anybody that finding the truth is extraordinarily difficult. Communicators need to be ready to constantly and continuously update the information they're receiving to accommodate both the search for truth and the interim satisfaction of every stakeholder group, victim, affected bystander, and government official.

> In the scenario response process, as scenarios are developed, it is determined, step-by-step and minute-by-minute, where decisions will likely occur and need to be made.

3.6 Management Responsibility in a Crisis

Probably the greatest lack in response planning for emergency situations is having scenario-specific, situation-focused, pre-approved, and understood instructions for what management needs to be doing, and when they should be doing it. As we said in Chapter 1, a crisis or emergency situation gives top executives something important to do immediately – either together or separately. To focus their responses, senior management and the top corporate functions need definitive role definitions and tasks in crisis situations.

3.6.1 Crisis Communication Roles by Corporate Function

Depending on the corporate response strategy selected, crisis communication responsibilities are determined by position. It is the position that provides the administrative power to break down barriers and get things done quickly. Quickness of action is generally the most important reputational decider when major problems must be resolved.

Key corporate actors or functions will have specific roles and responsibilities when crises occur. These roles and responsibilities must be customized to each crisis scenario included in the corporate crisis communication plan.

The roles, responsibilities, and actions described here are the minimums required of these individuals and functions to ensure that the plan process will work as developed.

1. **Regional Communication Contact (RCC)**
    The typical position having this responsibility could be a regional manager, regional vice president, or the senior corporate communicator responsible for the region where an incident occurs. This person:

    ▶ Is the point person and often the chief area spokesperson during a regional or local crisis.

    ▶ Decides if Corporate should be called.

    ▶ Contacts Corporate Crisis Communication Response Officer (CCCRO) or Corporate Emergency Response Team (CERT).

2. **Emergency Communication Response Partners (ECRP)**

    These are the departments and divisions within various parts of the corporation that can be called upon to:

    ▶ Provide knowledge, expertise, assistance, and advice.

    ▶ Activate additional help from within their department or division.

    ▶ Help assess the impact of the crisis.

    ▶ Serve on the Emergency Communication Team.

3. **CCCRO**

    The CCCRO has four options:

    1. Activate or not activate an emergency response.

    2. Involve senior officers.

    3. Activate one or more ISRTs.

    4. Let local CERTs handle the matter.

The local CERT:

▶ Maintains whereabouts process for regional, branch, or facility offices (participants voluntarily providing their locations 24/7 to a central location).

▶ Decides whether to activate broader crisis response. If yes:

    ❐ Contacts appropriate senior officers.

    ❐ Notifies, if appropriate, Crisis Communications Command Center staff (CCCCS), standby resources, and subject matter experts.

    ❐ Assesses need for senior management involvement.

    ❐ Activates on-site or off-site crisis center.

▶ Approves overall strategic approach.

▶ Approves drafts of news releases, statements, and news wires.

▶ Pre-authorizes actions and statements to reduce delays.

▶ Decides how much senior officer involvement is necessary, and

▶ Contacts appropriate senior officers.

▶ Decides whether Incident-Specific Response Teams (ISRTs) should be activated.

    ❐ Initiates team contact.

    ❐ Activates Incident Response Manager (IRM).

    ❐ Delegates responsibilities to IRM.

▶ Decides whether a CERT should be created to handle the crisis. If yes:

    ❐ Initiates team formation.

    ❐ Delegates responsibility.

4. **CCCCS**

▶ Open, activate, and staff the designated on-site or off-site facility (CCCC).

▶ Form small task groups to handle anticipated tasks.

▶ Assess the scope and impact of the crisis.

▶ Obtain input from Subject Matter Experts (SMEs).

▶ Develop communication and operations response approaches.

▶ Activate standby resources.

5. **Subject Matter Experts (SMEs)**

▶ Are available as long as the CCCC remains operational.

▶ Post briefing material, and other data.

6. **Standby Resources (SRs)**

  ▶ Organize resources needed to operate the CCCC.

  ▶ Facilitate access to buildings, supplies, equipment, and food.

  ▶ Coordinate standby people and physical resources.

7. **Corporate Relations Department (CRD)**

  ▶ Establishes crisis communication policies, procedures, and plans; disseminates them and provides local/regional guidance.

  ▶ Conducts ongoing exposure management and crisis prevention programs.

  ▶ Assesses the scope of potential incidents/crises and recommends appropriate response options quickly.

  ▶ Develops lists of internal and third-party experts who can be called on for information and/or advice in potential crisis situations.

  ▶ Coordinates tests of the corporate crisis communication plan at Headquarters.

  ▶ Directs communication with national media, key regulatory and legislative officials, customers, employees, and others when a Headquarters response is appropriate.

  ▶ Authorizes opinion research to measure the effects of a crisis and the perceptions of key audiences.

  ▶ Maintains contact with all IRMs and SMEs and their backups.

8. **Top Management Responsibilities**

  The Chief Executive Officer (CEO), Chief Operating Officer (COO), Chief Financial Officer (CFO), Chief Information Officer (CIO), and members of the Board of Directors have one, some, or all of four general responsibilities when crises occur:

  ▶ Energize and motivate those who are charged with responding.

  ▶ Execute scenario-specific activities or decision-making.

  ▶ Authorize action decisions, resource allocation, and policy exceptions that facilitate active, aggressive response.

  ▶ Lead and support notification efforts in event of death, injury, disaster, or serious threat to reputation.

Special Roles

1. The CEO

The CEO's principal responsibility is setting the tone and empathetic attitudes for the response. Being visible and empathetic toward those who are managing the crisis and those who are most directly affected by it is essential. According to pre-determined triggers and company policies, the CEO may visit those injured or otherwise incapacitated or inconvenienced by the emergency, the scene of the problem, or the site(s) where – because of the emergency – large numbers of individuals have gathered.

The CEO will rally employee spirit, action, and attitudes, especially when the effects of the crisis are very serious and emotionally charged. The CEO will be visible by meeting and helping manage relationships with high-profile individuals (i.e., state governors, Members of Congress, other public policy makers, and very angry or emotional opponents). The CEO will demonstrate the company's concern and moderate potential damage to its reputation.

In very catastrophic situations, the CEO should consider leading the response effort. What else is more important? What else does the CEO have to do?

2. The CFO and CIO

The CFO and CIO have the power to lift the barricades of corporate policy and brush aside the barriers that exist in all crisis situations. They will shoulder the responsibility for looking ahead, clearing the way, and helping facilitate aggressive, responsive reaction.

3. The Board of Directors

While the Board may not have a specific role in these matters, there may be circumstances in which enormous resources will be necessary, swift approval and authorization secured, and coalitions of companies formed to manage very serious industry or geographic problems. The Board's Emergency Management Liaison Committee (EMLC) will facilitate policy change and policy making at the highest levels in the most expeditious fashion. The EMLC will also participate in all preparations for corporate crisis situations, including:

▶ Identify who informs the Board and under what circumstances.

▶ Execute scenario-specific activities or decision-making.

▶ Include Board notification and activities expected in the response elements to scenarios you hypothesize when planning.

▶ Identify the level of seriousness required to trigger Board notification.

4. **Corporate PR Team**

The Corporate PR Team is responsible for:

▶ Determining the scope of potential incidents that could occur. Incidents include: on-site (at a field operation or manufacturing plant) or off-site (e.g., transportation or customer use of domestic or imported products for which the group is responsible).

▶ Recommending appropriate response options quickly.

▶ Providing on-the-spot initial or refresher training for individuals who have response duties.

▶ Coordinating the testing and institutionalization of crisis communication plans at Headquarters and all field operations or manufacturing plants.

▶ Developing a current list of internal and/or external (third party) technical experts who can be called upon for information regarding company products or use applications that are potential candidates for a crisis situation.

▶ Directing communication with national media, key regulatory and legislative officials, customers, employees, and other constituencies when a response from Headquarters is appropriate.

▶ Coaching spokesperson(s); mobilizing necessary resources.

▶ Authorizing opinion research after crises have ended to assess the effects of the crises.

> One of the most difficult problems to resolve in crisis response is tying field operations and responses together with the concerns and controls required by corporate headquarters.

3.6.2 Coordination Between Field and Headquarters: The "Call Headquarters If" Process

One of the most difficult problems to resolve in crisis response is tying field operations and responses together with the concerns and controls required by corporate headquarters. Effective planning always coordinates field responses with corporate headquarters' needs. One of the easier techniques to accomplish this is the use of a *Call Headquarters If* list. The *Call Headquarters If* process simply pre-identifies specific situations that Headquarters feels it must be informed about promptly. Most branch operations operate successfully because they have autonomy and distance from Headquarters. However, there are threats to reputation and other situations in which it would be a serious mistake for the branch to respond without corporate assistance or at least potential extensive corporate involvement. Therefore, as a part of the planning process, crucial scenarios are designated in advance as requiring notification from the field should they occur.

If any of the situations, circumstances, or incidents included on the *Call Headquarters If* list occurs in any region, branch, or facility, they should be reported immediately to the appropriate crisis response unit within the corporate structure.

This policy applies to everyone. Even the substantial expectation that one of the incidents on the *Call Headquarters If* list could occur must be reported immediately.

The "Call Headquarters If" List

The list below is a compilation of entries from many different kinds of companies. Technically, the *Call Headquarters If* list for most organizations is relatively short, a dozen or fewer entries, and the contents are extraordinarily important. Remember, branch or field operations must have the autonomy and authority to respond promptly to the vast majority of issues and problems that occur.

Inclusion on the *Call Headquarters If* list means that a response process is in place and ready to go at corporate Headquarters, or that there is a crisis action response group or support available through the Help Desk — whichever methodology the organization chooses to use for emergency response.

Call Headquarters in the event of:

- activist demonstration
- adverse legislation
- arson
- bomb threat
- boycotts by contractors
- community confrontation
- cyber attack
- disaster that affects local facilities
- disclosure of:
  - accidental employee death
  - activist action
  - activation of local Emergency Communication Team
  - alert from manager/employee
  - berserk employee
  - business loss
  - decapitation (loss of corporate leadership)
  - ethics violations
  - homicide
  - internal investigations
  - lawsuit/class action
  - legal fact-finding
  - major accidents
  - major operations interruption
  - malfeasance
  - natural disaster
  - rumors
  - sabotage
  - scandal
  - suicide
  - terrorist action
- disgruntled employee
- drugs/marijuana farms /methamphetamine labs
- employee arrest for serious crime
- employee violence incident
- evacuation of local facilities or environs

- face-to-face confrontations with outside opposition groups
- government inquiry
- HAZMAT (hazardous material) team activation
- kidnapping/extortion threats
- law enforcement action
- major crimes
- major power outage
- major theft
- major wild fires
- media call
- media inquiries about substances identified under SARA
- organized opposition
- permit violations
- pesticide spill
- picketing
- potential for high visibility
- potential to trigger government action
- release of substance identified under SARA
- reputation or credibility damage
- rumors
- serious injury/death
- significant business interruption
- significant customer impact
- social media or blogging controversies
- strikes
- substantial loss of wildlife
- sudden stock drop
- suspicious substance
- terrorist threat or rumors
- threat beyond local facility's boundary
- threatened work stoppage
- whistle-blower
- work stoppage by contractors
- work stoppage by employee

3.6.3 When to Send the Boss

To be successful, every crisis response process requires a planned response element devoted exclusively to senior management roles and responsibilities. In a crisis, five specific top management-related operating concerns are:

1. Setting the tone of the response, any response.
2. Defining specific responsibilities:
   - Be available; be helpful.
   - What to do; when to do it.
   - What to say; when to say it.
   - What to delegate and to whom.
   - Leading the recovery when it's over.
3. Establishing a policy base for crisis response inside the organization.
4. Avoiding negative behaviors, language, and decisions that only slow response down, distract those with response assignments, and endanger the reputation of the organization and careers of the executives.
5. When to send the boss.

> The issue of if and when to send the boss is one of the most strategic decisions made in crisis response situations.

It is important to have scenario-driven policies for determining the circumstances under which the boss will be put in front of the cameras, the public, and the victims. This is the crucial question that confronts every crisis response planner and advisor. Decide in advance, scenario by scenario. Talk the scenario through with the boss and get his or her agreement.

When there are many victims and great threat to constituent relationships, sending the boss can be a powerful signal and symbol. Thus, the issue of if and when to send the boss is one of the most strategic decisions made in crisis response situations.

There are several schools of thought. The first is to send the boss every time. The second is to pick selected situations in which the boss would be expected to be out front. The third is that the boss only goes out when he/she wants to go out.

Here are eight examples of situations that absolutely require the presence of the boss. Remember also, the smaller the market, the fewer fatalities it takes to require senior management presence.

1. Human injury or death of some magnitude (massive casualties).

2. Unusual death or threat situation, explosive visibility, negligence, significant collateral victim generation (people, animals, living systems).

3. Major environmental accident or health and safety threat situations.

4. Massive animal kill, injury, or threat to their well-being.

5. Significant accident or incident involving employees.

6. Serious, emotionally disruptive, or dramatic situations, e.g., layoffs, shut downs, significant job actions, community upset, demonstrations, highly emotional outpouring of negative (or positive) public sentiment.

7. Employee suicide or dangerous or violent threatening situation.

8. Extremely negative reputation-defining situation, such as an indictment, significant product failure, tampering, or negligence.

My personal approach is, first and foremost, to determine how the CEO actually feels about public involvement in crisis situations. Usually a far better result is achieved if the CEO already displays an inclination up front to speak or to be visible. I ask three questions: 1) Is this top person willing to be coached, either by internal resources or external consultants as a part of preparation and response process? 2) Will the boss absorb and implement the coaching he or she receives? 3) Will the boss participate in drills and exercises as a part of the readiness process?

Chapter 3 – Questions for Study and Discussion

1. What is the difference between "unplanned visibility" and "planned visibility"? Why is it important?

2. How can an emergency actually benefit your organization as a learning experience?

3. What is the importance of a "vulnerability analysis"? What does such an analysis entail? How is it important in creating your crisis communications plan?

4. Why are "scenarios" important? What are the most effective scenarios? How can you select a scenario that will get the best cooperation from upper management?

References, Chapter 3

Iowa Department of Justice, Crime Victim Assistance Division (2008). *In person, in time: recommended procedures for death notification.* Retrieved from http://www.iowa.gov/government/ag/helping_victims/contents/In_Person _In_Time_2008.pdf

4

Creating the Crisis Communication Plan: Components and Models

Keywords: crisis communication management plan, golden hour, dark site construction and maintenance, scenario building, pre-authorization, crisis communications exercise

Essential to effective crisis management and communication is the ability to manage, control, and respond in the first few minutes or hours of a problem. In the world of emergency medicine, this window of time is often called the *golden hour* because of the belief that the highest survivability results from rapid intervention during these early moments following traumatic injury. Similarly, any crisis plan, especially for communications, must focus on achieving stated objectives during these first few golden hours..

This chapter will help you to:

➢ Prepare a crisis communication plan.

➢ Coordinate the various crisis plans and policies that may already be in existence in the organization.

➢ Build a "dark site" to make current, accurate news available to the media and others seeking up-to-date information about the event.

➢ Maintain readiness by conducting regular exercises, tests, and scenarios to ensure that plans are up-to-date and workable.

➢ Involve upper management actively in all phases of planning and testing, especially the beginning.

Most organizations assume confidently that they can instantaneously execute competent and expeditious management of problems – even when intelligence, education, logic, experience, and daily observation would indicate otherwise. If you are not ready to handle a *crisis situation* and, as a result, make things worse, then the visibility you generate will be all negative. Managing the unplanned visibility that occurs as part of an emergency or crisis situation requires understanding, preparation, cooperation, and communication at every level of your organization.

4.1 Preparing to Do the Right Thing

When bad things happen to good organizations, the people in charge often stall, delay and deny doing everything except those very actions that most people would recognize as the "right" thing to do. By considering the behaviors with the most potential to affect the organization directly, we can identify a list of weaknesses that those in trouble tend to exhibit before, during, and after a crisis occurs. The list is important in preparing for a crisis because it is those reputation-defining behaviors for which you must be prepared and for which those in your organization must be trained to help management overcome.

1. Lack of empathy (meaning arrogance).
2. Communication delay caused by management timidity or hesitation, and the lack of legal or administrative preparation.
3. Failure to anticipate a problem or the failure to anticipate the degree of angry community response.
4. Lack of coordination among groups within the organization and between the organization and its outside agencies and resources.
5. Lack of clarity about the respective roles key decision-makers are expected to play.
6. Failure to communicate quickly and directly with those most affected, especially employees.
7. Inconsistent messages or no messages.
8. Failure to forecast changes in situations or outcomes.
9. Overestimate readiness.
10. Underestimate community or government concern or unwillingness to cooperate.
11. Lack of training and familiarity with established procedures and techniques for handling these emotional challenges, circumstances like embarrassment, humiliation, angry neighbors, or defeat.
12. Insufficient commitment and on-site leadership to respond quickly, compassionately, and conclusively.

4.1.1 Crisis Communication Plan Development

As you begin to develop your crisis communication management plan, it is important to coordinate all response planning. Emerging contingency planning methodology must accommodate crisis communication strategies. This is crucial to response performance effectiveness. Virtually every after-action report and lessons-learned document we see in serious circumstances mentions very early on, if not first, that a "lack of communication" or "communication breakdown" was responsible for much of the confusion and consternation early in the response process. We believe that *crisis communication* must drive the two other aspects of contingency planning – *business continuity management* and *disaster recovery*. Too often, these three disciplines carry out their planning separately in isolation, only to watch their efforts collide to the detriment and embarrassment of the organization when a crisis occurs. A crucial part of the planning process involves cataloging, analyzing, cross-referencing, and coordinating all response requirements. For organizations of more than 50 employees, federal law and local and state rules and regulations may require communications and public response strategies for dozens of potential operating and non-operating scenarios.

> **We believe that crisis communication must drive the two other aspects of contingency planning – business continuity management and disaster recovery.**

Your corporate-level preparation should focus on four broad areas:

- Non-operating problems which can be managed effectively only at the corporate level, such as those affecting reputation, integrity, credibility, shareholders, or which may have government impact.

- Umbrella guidance, coaching, and training that send the unmistakable signal to the division, branch, or field that this work is crucial and that operating people are expected to be involved.

- Development of useful scenarios and models to reduce the time necessary for division, branch, or field operations to be involved in planning and testing their responses.

- Prior authorization for those actions and decisions that can facilitate coordination, reduce bureaucracy, and move the response process forward with greater speed.

Bureaucracy forces timidity and hesitation, the two key ingredients in operational failure. An effective plan focuses intensely on the problems and operates temporarily with the prior authorization or in spite of the bureaucracy. The development process can be carried out entirely in-house or with the assistance of outside consultants. In either case, the same basic tasks will be required to construct the plan. Involving as many people as possible will reap long-term rewards. Remember that the most powerful benefit of crisis planning and readiness comes from the lessons people learn from participating in the process, lessons that often prove more valuable than the documents produced. We have divided the plan development process into five specific tasks:

4.1.2 Plan Development Tasks

Task I: Existing Plan Assessment and Refinement:
Review and assess existing communication plans and notification processes to determine crisis response capability and readiness. Work with division operations and communications representatives to develop a uniform, easy-to-use framework and cross reference to existing plans that will guide division managers through the communication response process in the first hours of a crisis and will help to coordinate actions and decisions with headquarters appropriately.

Task II: Corporate Crisis Plan Development:
Based on executive interviews, identify and prioritize existing and potential operational and communication threats. (*For information on assessing threats and vulnerabilities, see Chapter 2 of this book.*) The resulting response system will include several complete corporate crisis scenario response procedures to be used as the basis for testing actual response readiness and perfecting communication tactics and strategies.

Recommended elements for the plan include:

- Contact data and whereabouts process;
- Coordination strategies between division and headquarters, including a *Call Headquarters If* process;
- Corporate crisis communication policy;
- Incident control/crisis communication management process;
- Post-crisis updating/follow-up procedures;
- Process for establishing a corporate crisis command center;
- Recommendations for response contact technology, i.e., mobile telephones, special high-volume call services, email notification processes, automated emergency notification systems, and the increasing use of the use of social media tools like Twitter;
- Recommendations for specific tools (crisis telephone kit, wallet cards, smart phone apps, etc.); and,
- Specific scenario-based response procedures.

Task III: Communication Guidance for Divisions, Branches, Remote Facilities, and Franchise Owners:
Knowledge and information developed through this project will be of critical importance to division, branch, and remote facility managers; franchise owners; and center operators.

Specifically, this task will develop guidance and model approaches in the areas of:

▶ Managing the four or five most critical high-profile local scenarios;

▶ Identifying vulnerabilities and assessing their potential; and

▶ Developing local approaches to mitigate damage to the firm's reputation in the event problems occur.

Task IV: Communications Coaching and Training:
Senior executives and appropriate division and local managers most likely to be involved in key crisis scenarios should be coached on the corporate approach, processes, and policies to follow during crises, as well as the lessons to be learned from crisis communication management. Mock interviews and intense role-play will solidify understanding and knowledge of the process and recognition of individual/team responsibilities.

Task V: Installation/Simulation, Ongoing Readiness Training:
Untested plans fail in most respects. Scenario-based installation/simulation training will be needed for appropriate managers, supervisors, and interested franchise owners on specific response procedures and notification approaches.

Training on crisis communication response issues should plan to achieve the following objectives:

▶ Brief and teach corporate crisis response approach;

▶ Demonstrate technologies to be implemented;

▶ Identify division issues and questions;

▶ Introduce *Call Headquarters If* list of critical vulnerabilities that require corporate notification; and

▶ Plan for future crisis response cooperation.

This effort will identify specific processes and procedures to help ensure that the company is appropriately and adequately prepared to manage communication related to predetermined division and corporate crisis situations.

4.2 Scenario Development in Crisis Communication Planning

Throughout this book, you will find that much of your work will be scenario-driven. Along the way, you will be constructing and practicing with *scenarios*, some based on events at fictional companies, others based on hypothetical incidents that could occur in your own organizations. Earlier in this book, you were invited to conduct a *vulnerability analysis* and review past serious problems in your organization (and similar organizations) as well as problems that could easily happen in your organization.

Successful crisis plans are scenario based.

Successful crisis plans are scenario based. You will use scenarios throughout the research and planning process, and after your plan is complete, you will use scenarios as part of keeping the plan current and all your processes in a state of readiness. You will want to retain all these scenarios, whatever their original purpose, gather them together along with annotations and notes to be filed, reviewed, and updated regularly.

Scenario preparation is the crucial ingredient in effective emergency and crisis response. General crisis planning simply fails to work. Just as a plan must be tested periodically to identify capabilities and weaknesses and revise response approaches, the scenario process is truly the most helpful to the organization and its management in the planning stages.

4.2.1 Involving the Boss

In my experience, participation by the boss in drills and exercises is important for three powerful reasons:

▶ Surprise reduction for the boss. Reducing surprise reveals leadership opportunities more quickly.

▶ Participation sends the most powerful signal possible to others playing readiness roles that this is important to the boss and, therefore, should be important to them.

▶ The organization does a far better job of responding when the boss takes a leadership role.

Of the possible approaches to sending the boss in a crisis situation, I prefer one which is essentially scenario-based: pick selected situations in which the boss would be expected to be out front. Identify the scenarios that could be the most damaging, or the most victim-creating, or that might create a more persistent situation that creates long-term bad news and embarrassment. Develop response plans in which the CEO has important communication options. I recommend this process:

1. Select three really tough, embarrassing, victim-producing or explosive visibility scenarios.

2. Run the scenarios by the boss and explain that these are situations in which it could be expected that the most senior person in the organization (assuming that person survives or is not too severely injured) would be expected to be out front making statements and highly visible.

3. Always ask if the boss can identify, from his or her perspective, more important scenarios in which he or she should be visible. You might be surprised. The boss may have two or three that you haven't thought of or that you hadn't thought were as important as they actually turn out to be.

4. Start with whichever scenario the boss feels most concerned about. Develop response scripts and a sequence of actions, behaviors, and decisions the CEO will need to make and carry out as a part of those scenarios.

5. Walk and talk the senior executive and perhaps one or two other senior people through the scenarios to make certain that these individuals understand their roles and can be prepared for what they must do when called upon. Give these senior people the opportunity to react to what you propose and to offer suggestions and comments. Allow them to practice what they would be doing in a future exercise or real situation.

6. Ask again if there are other problems in addition to the ones you talked through that may be more important and should be prepared for. If the answer is "yes" and new scenarios are mentioned, get those ready as well. Prioritize them from both your perspective and that of the senior executives.

> **When bad things happen, they are managed by the people who survive and the people who show up.**

Avoid planning roles for the CEO in scenarios which indicate little need for executive leadership. If you do, the CEO will likely find a reason to skip the exercise or simply take over and do whatever he or she thinks matters. Even if you disagree with the CEO's choices for visibility and participation, it is his or her ship, watch, reputation, and career. The CEO has the power to decide, get on the team, and to have you work it through with him or her.

Certain scenarios require specialists in response and communication. When you need special experts, very likely there will be contingency funds available. Securing contingency budgets for these added elements in your readiness plans will allow you to get the budget supplements you'll need very promptly. If you're preparing for the boss's scenario, what the boss wants and needs is usually what the boss gets.

Also remember that the views of the boss's backup individual(s) need to be solicited as well. Consider possible scenarios in which the boss is completely unavailable, injured, or incapacitated (for example, in an elevator that is stuck between floors when the power goes out, in a plane somewhere over the Pacific Ocean, off with a girlfriend, etc.). Given that possibility, the number two's wishes in terms of preparation for readiness will need to be considered in your planning, rehearsal, and scenario development processes.

When bad things happen, they are managed by the people who survive and the people who show up. The essence of readiness is to have a core team or specialist teams ready to go when a crisis occurs. Making these decisions from the very beginning about what to do with the top executives is crucial to having an effective, prompt first response and to setting the tone and direction of other responders as well.

4.2.2 Using Scenarios to Identify Problem Areas

While it is easy to forecast potential problem areas, the use of scenarios allows you to think through what would happen minute-by-minute and thereby gauge your current level of understanding and determine what that level of understanding needs to be. Through scenario story development, you can determine:

- What resources will be needed?
- Who will be affected?
- What questions will have to be answered?
- What collateral damage can be forecast?
- What outside help may be needed as part of the response process?
- What weaknesses are there in your readiness process?

> Developing scenarios is among the most powerful team-building and team-unifying activities that leaders and responders can undergo.

This process also protects you from applying yesterday's error-prone response reactions to a present circumstance, an approach that serves only to tie up management, paralyze the process, and render executive decision-making irrelevant, especially in the early going. Past-based planning mode results in too many people rehashing yesterday's misunderstandings and defending yesterday's decisions and actions. Readiness is always about being successfully prepared.

The scenario approach allows you to work in a future-thinking mode, thereby averting most arguments about the past. It fosters clear thinking about alternative strategies and options going forward. In fact, developing scenarios is among the most powerful team-building and team-unifying activities that leaders and responders can undergo.

Your two best starting points for scenario development are your *vulnerability analysis*, as well as an analysis of past serious problems within your organization, and events that happened to others that could possibly happen to you. We encourage you to engage in a number of scenarios in order to identify comprehensively the full ramifications of situations, events, actions, and problems presented in each scenario. Once you have carried out the thinking, analysis, and testing process with each scenario, the scenario can be reduced to simpler form and included in the crisis plan.

A good place to start is with creating operational response timelines for days one and two of some typical crisis situations.

4.2.3 Model Scenario Workup Summary
Situation Analysis:
> Briefly describe the situation, potential vulnerabilities, issues, and concerns.

> What are four or five absolutely critical issues, questions, people, or problems the company needs to anticipate and think about?

> ▶ List the facts of the situation as you understand them.

> ▶ List the critical, reputation-defining issues raised by the situation.

> ▶ Identify those people, groups, and organizations directly and indirectly affected by the situation.

> ▶ What facts, circumstances, rumors, information, and reports need explanation or clarification?

> ▶ What information needs to be collected?

Strategic Considerations:
> ▶ What issues, concerns, and problems does the situation raise?

> ▶ What critical management decisions need to be made quickly?

> ▶ What are the potential consequences/implications of the decisions made?

> ▶ Who does what?

Response Team:
> Who does what, when? Identify the roster of operators, responders, and communicators.

Operational Response/ Action Steps:
> List the essential operational steps the company needs to take to correct the problem, to bring the situation under control.

Communication Response/Action Steps:
> List the essential communication-focused action steps necessary to inform, alert, educate, and train the appropriate constituents.

- Who speaks for the company? Why?
- Will the company talk to the media? Why or why not?
- How will you communicate to the public?
- How will you communicate with employees?
- What is being done to help the victims?
- What essential response steps need to be taken to understand and communicate about the situation adequately?

> **List the key themes and specific messages the company should use in communication with all audiences — internally and externally, but especially employees and victims.**

Key Themes/ Specific Messages:
List the key themes and specific messages the company should use in communication with all audiences – internally and externally, but especially employees and victims.

Holding Statements:
A holding statement is a brief comment, usually around 75 words, designed to provide useful information without subjecting the spokesperson to questions. What are the elements of a statement for the company to use with key audiences?

Q & A:
List and develop answers to the most likely, challenging, and difficult questions that may be asked about the situation. Also, begin developing questions you would love to respond to if only someone would ask you.

4.3 Assemble the Documents for Your Crisis Communication Plan

We generally recommend that initial plan documents be kept extremely simple and straightforward. The materials for the plan can be gathered and maintained electronically, in a smart phone or in an Ipad, or they can be printed out and kept in a three-ring binder. If the materials were assembled in a three-ring binder, what follows is how the sections might look; however, based on the needs and concerns of your organization and the type and complexity you have gathered, you may have more tabs, fewer tabs, or tabs with different labels. These will get you started:

- **Tab 1** Contains crucial *contact lists* you developed during your research and testing of specific scenarios.

▶ **Tab 2** contains *scenarios* that, in their most useful form, are *annotated flowcharts* that also contain questions and answers, specific media contact tips, and other information to help resolve the emergent situation by providing as much useful knowledge as possible in pictorial form.

▶ **Tab 3** holds *standby statements* related to the scenarios developed. Standby statements have spaces in which the specific information and data a particular emergency generates can be filled in.

▶ **Tab 4** contains key *scenario-related questions and answers* along with a briefing document related to each scenario. Even though one may use statements as a means of communicating effectively and in a controlled way during an emergency, ultimately reporters, the public, government regulators, customers, vendors, and employees will be asking questions. Virtually all of the questions any scenario might create can be predicted. These questions and answers will be essential for use as briefing and response tools for all audiences.

▶ **Tab 5** holds emergency *media relations tips* and special media guidance based on your organization's *communications policy*. These tips help guide all spokespersons and others in releasing information appropriately, including what clearances are needed, what other permissions are needed, and who the other spokespeople are. This section may include information on conducting news conferences or other special media relations, and social media techniques.

4.3.1 Your Published Crisis Plan

The final corporate crisis management and communication manual might have a table of contents that would look something like this:

SAMPLE TABLE OF CONTENTS

4.3.2 Select the Most Appropriate Activation Process

> The most important element in any crisis response process is the continuous availability of a response group that regularly assesses preparation for a wide variety of scenarios

Prompt response requires relentless *readiness*, which embodies all aspects of crisis plan preparation and maintenance. The most important element in any crisis response process is the continuous availability of a response group that regularly prepares for a wide variety of scenarios, even highly improbable ones. It is this group that will *execute the first response*, allowing others in the organization time to fully implement a remediation plan. Five basic types of response activation approaches are in use today:

▶ **Special Response Unit (SRU) approach:** In this model, a single group with backups is set up to assure prompt response to any incidents that might occur. It is self-activating and empowered to work anywhere within the organization. It can allocate resources, resolve disputes, and act fast to make important decisions. The SRU reports to the Crisis Management Team (CMT), which is generally composed of the most senior executives of the company.

▶ **Crisis czar (Officer of the Day) approach:** One person, or a small group of individuals on a rotation schedule throughout the year, trusted by senior management, is given the power to decide if and when to activate the crisis response plan and mobilize the organization. This is a very effective approach to crisis management. It allows the highest degree of *pre-authorization* and a close personal relationship with top management. This engenders a level of confidence and support that promotes prompt response and activation of resources. There is less push-back and second-guessing.

▶ **Command Center approach:** This model vests crisis management decision making at a fairly low level within the organization but offers some very distinct advantages. Someone within the command center structure has the responsibility to think about, prepare for, and monitor corporate vulnerabilities on a routine basis. When reports of problems occur, this unit is the central repository for all questions, concerns, and incident reports. The group has the power to activate appropriate crisis response, marshal resources, and, most importantly, respond very, very promptly. The command center approach combines detection/deterrence and ongoing readiness into one area within the legal department, corporate security, or risk management.

▶ **Incident response approach:** While this may be the most cumbersome structure, it does involve more people in the response and preparation process to handle and manage emergencies. The CMT, consisting of top management, has the overall charge. A crisis management committee consisting of an appropriate array of key second- and third-level executives advises it. This second group does the actual assessment and activation of crisis response. The response itself is carried out through the use of Incident-specific Response Teams (IRTs). Each IRT has a specific focus, such as environment, human resources, non-operational issues, kidnap/extortion, shareholder/investor relations/U.S. Security and Exchange Commission.

▶ **The Help Line:** This technique is indeed the easiest way for employees to report adverse or suspicious activity of any kind. It involves establishing a central phone number which is manned by someone, probably from the security department, who has in front of him or her a console or large reference document with every kind of adverse situation imaginable indexed there, from airborne odors to x-ray exposure. From this single point of contact, the individual manning this position is able to alert appropriate authorities and those within the company, and to initiate appropriate response activity on their own, and immediately. All calls are taken and responded to, including anonymous tips. Surprisingly, where help lines are used, most callers identify themselves and are carrying out part of their employee or participant responsibility by reporting circumstances and events.

4.4 Maintaining and Keeping Plans Current

The overall goal of readiness is to prevent, detect, deter, and identify the most threatening circumstances in advance and to prepare to manage or otherwise resolve the circumstance on a crisis basis. The readiness concept also introduces into crisis communication management the responsibility to link the more operational kinds of threats – those that can be forecast simply by looking at what the organization does every day – with non-operating circumstances, especially those involving highly emotional and provocative circumstances and ethical behavior and those subject to codes of conduct, compliance programs, or those that are the focus of integrity processes and laws such as Sarbanes-Oxley.

> **Readiness is a state of mind. Prevention activities are those that focus on eliminating threats and potential disasters.**

Maintaining readiness is an extraordinary challenge, primarily because executives are virtually never measured or compensated on their ability to prevent, detect, deter, or manage crisis situations. In fact, some managers consider readiness – except that required by law – to be something of a nuisance. The more senior the manager, the more likely it is that he or she will rely on inherent skill, knowledge, and ability to get through trouble spots, even those with serious consequences, and to successfully survive.

Readiness is a state of mind. Prevention activities are those that focus on reducing risk and on eliminating threats and potential disasters. Readiness confirmation and planning ought to identify at least one current serious threat and eliminate it from consideration, either by dealing with it directly or by getting rid of it.

The useful life of any plan is three years. Experience demonstrates that even when plans are kept rigorously up-to-date by using some or all of the techniques described in this section, a full-blown review and restructuring is probably warranted every three years. An organization is most prepared and ready for crisis response at the time the plan itself is initially introduced. After that, even with regular, consistent updating and periodic refreshing of plans and crisis preparations, response and readiness degrade.

Many readiness and preparation activities are possible, including planning, and it is important to consider their relative value. Keep this empirical assessment of the importance of readiness activities in mind:

Activity	Value of the Activity to Readiness
1 Keeping all responder/decision maker contact lists current	75 %
2. Simulations/ongoing evaluations, lessons learned from current activities	15 %
3. Ongoing preemptive and preventive analysis of threats and vulnerabilities	5 %
4. Distributing revised materials on a "destroy by" date basis	1 %
5. Development of new scenarios as appropriate	2 %
6. Ongoing response plan revisions	1 %
7. Planning additional exercises	1 %

4.4.1 The Reality of Keeping Plans Current

Crisis prevention, crisis preparation planning, and readiness confirmation are complementary concepts. They revolve around identifying the people-stopping, product-stopping, and show-stopping issues or incidents that, by their very definition, can shut down all or part of the business. Crisis preparation includes crisis prevention when show-stopping problems are examined, and potential crisis problems are resolved so that the opportunity for a substantial disruption is remediated or removed. The preparation process also pre-empts those behaviors and needs commonly generated by a crisis.

Organizations can be better prepared, but only if they are willing to pay attention to readiness and the benefits that ongoing preparation provide. Prevention means working to stay ready for those vulnerabilities and key issues that, though remote, would have substantial impact were they to occur. It should become part of the corporate culture. Crisis prevention and readiness begin with recognizing the seven realities of crisis planning.

1. **The useful life of a crisis plan is limited.** Personnel changes, business restructuring, and re-direction usually overtake even the best updating process – 36 months is about the useful life of most plans.

2. **Spokespeople change; corporate leaders change.** This means their replacements often require additional help to get up to speed, which is the most important reason we suggest intensive, approximately annual simulations. This technique brings newcomers up to speed in a matter of hours and helps reinforce the knowledge of more seasoned employees.

3. **The greatest single weakness of most crisis plans is the lack of defined roles for top management (and those individuals trusted by management).** Plans designed by low-level insiders without the input of the boss will not be implemented if the reputations, careers, or futures of high-level insiders will be defined by the crisis at hand. If the boss fails to buy it or has not bought in, the boss and those he or she trusts will do something else when problems occur. Build in appropriate management actions and decisionmaking.

4. **The fallacy of the single spokesperson.** What happens if your single spokesperson doesn't survive the incident? What happens if your single spokesperson has the flu? What happens if your single spokesperson knows virtually nothing about the problem or issue causing the crisis? What if your single spokesperson is among those indicted or incarcerated? What if events dictated a different approach?

   More current theory says that while there may be a chief spokesperson, there should also be backups, subject matter experts (SMEs), and most importantly, incident management specialists (IMSs) conversant with specific organizational threats such as kidnapping, extortion, natural disasters, sabotage, and employee violence. The IMSs are empowered and ready to respond or to direct the response with special expertise, credibility, and the necessary resources.

5. **Crisis prevention is the most challenging aspect of crisis planning.** While it's relatively easy to identify and plan for events that can logically disrupt the organization, it is very difficult to generate interest in planning for things that are unlikely to occur. Good crisis prevention involves exposure management techniques that

spot problems early on and trigger preparations to respond and actions to eliminate or manage new threats before they occur.

Remember, untested plans will fail, in most respects.

6. **Being ready requires seven important crisis communication plan management updating procedures:**

   ▶ Ongoing preparation with roughly annual simulations.

   ▶ Sharing critical crisis communication experience case studies.

   ▶ Useful right way/wrong way video-based, situation-specific refresher programs.

   ▶ Interpreting, and packaging as case studies, crises experienced by other organizations in terms of how your organization might respond if faced with a similar difficulty.

   ▶ Crisis prevention/exposure management processes as an ongoing threat reduction activity.

   ▶ Dark website preparation and updating.

   ▶ Website assessment for crisis response readiness.

   Remember, untested plans will fail, in most respects. The above updating process is structured to be distributed relatively evenly across a three-to four-year time track. Two are ongoing. All are absolutely useful, worthy of senior management's time and interest, and will encourage a mentality of readiness within your organization.

7. **Issues, questions, and coverage can develop on the web, through e-mail and increasingly in social media.** These threats are real and potentially more damaging than anything the media may cause. The risk is that these cyber attacks and social media attacks spread quickly to mainstream media and seriously complicate your response strategy.

4.4.2 The Six Revitalization Tracks

Maintaining readiness requires that procedures are established to ensure regular plan updating. The updating process is divided into six tracks.

Track 1: Annual Readiness / Training / Task Review
Ongoing preparation and training each year. The elements include:

   ▶ Simulations/ongoing evaluation/lessons learned

   ▶ Response plan revisions

   ▶ Development of new scenarios

   ▶ Planning additional exercises

   ▶ Updating the emergency media kit

   ▶ Distributing the revised emergency media kit

*Track 2: **Sharing Critical Crisis Communication Experience***
Experience-sharing through brief case studies:
- New threat examples
- New cases
- Distribution to key managers and team members on a regular basis

*Track 3: **Useful Tools – 20-Minute Right-Way/Wrong-Way Videos***
Describes the development of useful tools:
- Right-way/wrong-way videos (with emphasis on handling problems the right way)
- Web-based interactive exercises
- Seminars by outside consultants or peer companies based on your plans and scenarios

*Track 4: **Planning Additional Exercises***
Involves formatting useful current situations taken from news stories about your organization, or similar circumstances of a competitor or peer organization, and turning them into teaching tools:
- Identifying useful video news clips, radio stories, or other incidents
- Developing learning points or lessons
- Packaging for distribution to appropriate target audiences

*Track 5: **Exposure Surveillance and Forecasting Process***
Ongoing exposure surveillance and forecasting program designed to alert management at the earliest possible time to potentially damaging scenarios. It involves four phases:
- Monitoring and assessing potential exposures
- Forecasting the impact of the those potential exposures
- Periodic issuance of confidential issue reports
- Quarterly exposure review meetings with senior management (more frequently, if necessary)

Exposure Surveillance and Forecasting is the purposeful monitoring of key corporate exposure sources, opportunities, issues, and questions. Jerr Boschee and Scott Meyer developed this approach while they were at the Control Data Corporation. They called it "Exposure Reporting." The goals of exposure surveillance and forecasting are to:
- Apprise management of possible threats and opportunities
- Anticipate planned and unplanned visibility
- Prepare management to act promptly, conclusively, pragmatically

- Mitigate problems and threats, early in the process
- Estimate the potential organizational impact and exposure from threats, opportunities and circumstances

The information rarely exceeds two pages and is so valuable and vital to company security that its distribution should be limited only to very senior management.

Remember that news is about yesterday. Exposure management is a strategic risk reduction process about tomorrow.

Exposure surveillance and forecasting generates acceptance because it fills a key void in management information needs. The approach is helpful, positive, insightful, early, and relevant. Remember that news is about yesterday. Exposure management is a strategic risk reduction process about tomorrow.

Track 6: Dark Site Construction and Maintenance/Website and Social Media Readiness Assessment

This activity involves the creation and ongoing maintenance of pre-structured websites, by scenario, that reside on a server until a specific scenario arises.

When a crisis or seriously negative event occurs in today's world, everyone heads to a website before they look for anything else. Failing to have a website in place and ready to go is what often leads to mistaken stories, stories based on erroneous assumptions. Things get made up very quickly, including by reporters.

There is a mistaken belief that putting things on the web actually spreads information across the web. In practice, websites are destinations where people go intentionally. Those expecting to benefit from websites need to lead or herd people to their sites. This is one of the great benefits of a website. It is electronic. You can urge and herd people to your site when important information resides there; you can gain information and valuable data from their visits, as well as get a sense of what interests people most. Or, if you have wisely gathered their contact information beforehand, you can simply push a keystroke and put the entire content of your messages, and work, faster than a speeding headline, rumor, or Twitter chatter, information that is critical to those stakeholders you care about most.

(**Note:** *For more information about what should be on your Crisis or Dark Website, see Chapter 5.*)

If you have a crisis website or are planning to establish one, here is an initial review and analysis of website readiness to handle a serious situation. Examine your site for, among other things, the following:

1. Language use.
2. Current structure vs. ideal structure for exploring and dealing with

the problems at hand.

3. Where a crisis page may ideally fit within your site structure, or whether a whole different site might be appropriate.

4. How your site compares to other crisis or urgent information type websites.

5. The placement on the homepage for ease of location.

6. Overall ease of navigation throughout the entire site.

7. Presence of tracking metrics.

As you analyze these questions, here are some insights into what I would recommend in view of the circumstances the clients find themselves.

Some general rules I tend to follow:

1. Crisis websites generally have little production value. Production values tend to reduce credibility and trust. Their appearance and their information must meet the test of being "simple, sensible."

2. General tone of the site needs to be positive and constructive, basically any and all comments need to be relatively brief so that the visitor can read the materials, absorb them, and easily use them.

3. Use lists to rebuild information.

4. Avoid using any negative language or phrases. This approach causes confusion and more questions.

Optional/Additional Analysis

These techniques can significantly increase the effectiveness of your crisis site.

1. SEO assessment, ongoing analysis.

2. Preemptive social media opportunities and vulnerabilities.

3. Chill out – What goes on the web stays on the web, forever. If you are angry, defensive, offended by something, chill out before you post. Today's angry, unmoderated response issues or criticism will come back to dog you essentially forever.

Use the Power of the Web to:

▶ **Manage media coverage:** During emergencies, it is unlikely that many news stories will be about you (unless you are the direct target), but many stories may include you. Make the inclusion of accurate information possible by recognizing that virtually all reporters nowadays consult the web as they develop their stories.

▶ **Reduce media calls:** While reducing such calls may at first seem inadvisable, in emergencies only a fraction of media calls are about actually doing any kind of a story. The vast majority of calls are to confirm information, such as the spelling of people's names, titles, and the company's location. In our experience, having a promptly illuminated dark site with appropriate and timely information can reduce 90% of media relations telephone call pressure.

> In our experience, having a promptly illuminated dark site with appropriate and timely information can reduce 90% of media relations telephone call pressure.

▶ **Provide information 24/7:** The web does provide a powerful "at your convenience" component to reporters. No matter where they are located or what their deadline, they can access your information when it suits them. The web counterparts of the traditional media now break so many major stories that having 24-hour access to accurate information is increasingly essential, especially in crisis situations.

▶ **Script everybody:** This may be the most powerful benefit of this entire approach. It's on the record and, if done appropriately, becomes the absolute fact base for reporting. Even if you are under attack by competitors, activists, critics, or others, your website content will have the effect of setting the tone and the record for whatever public discussion ensues, providing a consistent message that it is positive, declarative, and constructive. You can use your Corrections and Clarifications section to straighten out any reporting errors, misunderstandings, or manufactured information.

▶ **Set and manage the record:** An important and powerful benefit of having a fully functioning dark site available when emergencies occur is that when you manage the record, you establish future interpretation as events are unfolding. During crises, the record of your behaviors, responses, and activities is being created in various places. The authoritative voice, however, will be your own if you adopt this approach and have an emergency dark site ready to make operational when a crisis occurs.

Dark sites help keep fast-breaking events and information in perspective. The site can, in fact, keep your story straight.

4.5 Message Development

Getting useful, effective messages out is the goal of emergency communi-cation management. What we say in emergencies will become the perception of what we do, especially early on because we may actually be doing very little, at first. Positive, simple, sensible communications will limit follow-up questions and focus on the most important aspects of crisis response, moving the entire process forward.

The very last time you want to be developing messages is during an emergency when pressures and distractions are enormous. Some pressures you will encounter include:

▶ Confusing, conflicting, fragmentary information; changing information, including rumors and fake facts.

▶ Unreliable communication up and down the organization.

▶ Preoccupation with only a portion of the problem.

▶ Collateral damage caused by poor judgment, even with the best of intentions and quick action.

> **Using language that communicates concern and sensitivity is important. A people-sensitive vocabulary is a must as you construct your comments and your answers to questions.**

In Chapter 2, you identified your organization's key issues. Once you know your issues and have planned the actions you will need to take, you need to know what to say.

The greatest challenge in emergencies and the pre-preparation of messages is remembering the critical sensitivities of dealing with core community values and the need to be candid, forthright, and honest in terms of what employees, victims, neighbors, customers, vendors, shareholders, and the media expect. It is important that the language you use both achieves your communications objectives and maintains the truthful perception of a situation.

Using language that communicates concern and sensitivity is important. A people-sensitive vocabulary is a must as you construct your comments and your answers to questions. Because you can identify in advance the topic areas in which you will be most likely to receive questions from people affected by any event, you can be prepared to anticipate the gut-level concerns of audiences. When you address these concerns, audiences will feel better about you and you will show up better in the media coverage. Once you have selected your approach and your vocabulary, structure the thoughts in your message around the following:

▶ Be simple, specific, and positive.

▶ Speak in community-oriented terms.

▶ Talk only about what you know.

▶ Talk only about what you do.

▶ Take the initiative. Anticipate the questions.

▶ Be ready at the onset to answer the questions you wish they would ask.

4.5.1 The Process of Message Development

Message development is a straightforward, multi-step process to develop scripts that serve as the basis for answering questions and making statements when emergencies occur. Creating these messages is essential to success of your organization in reacting effectively during the "golden time" in the first hours of the crisis, in which you demonstrate your readiness and competent communication in the face of a split-second emergency. Message development needs to be part of every phase of planning, scenario drills, and exercises.

Step 1   **Identify those situations and emergencies about which questions will be asked.** Simply make a list of the topic areas you could be asked about, depending on what scenario you are using.

Step 2   **Under each scenario begin listing the kinds of questions reporters, neighbors, employees, employees' families, victims and survivors, or other audiences might ask.** (See the Scenario Question Development Worksheet in the supplemental materials.) Each major event you have identified will probably generate questions. Therefore, as you develop scenarios, it should be fairly easy to create the kinds of questions you'll need to respond to should those events actually occur.

Step 3:   **Develop communications objectives related to each situation you have described.** These communications objectives have two parts:

▶ **Plain language communications statement:** the exact words a spokesperson would use to answer a question, make a statement, etc. This plain language statement would have two or three subjects, topics, or points, which could be elaborated on further.

> During emergencies there is very little time to translate from technical language to simple language.

▶ **Messages:** These are explanations and stories that illustrate the important elements of your plain language statement.

Step 4: Develop plain language communications statements for each scenario. Include the words you would actually use. During emergencies there is very little time to translate from technical language to simple language. Do as much translation as you can during this answer construction phase.

Step 5 Develop messages. Messages take the topic components of your plain language statements and illustrate them with appropriate descriptions and stories or examples. A story or example is the most crucial part of the message. That's where the real communication lies. A plain language statement needs specifics or it is just an example of a wandering generality that will raise more questions. It's often these wandering generalities that make spokespersons seem so cold, unfeeling, and uncaring from the perspective of the audience.

> By saying these objectives out loud when you're developing the messages, you will be able to edit them, correct them, and make them truly responsive to the issues and situations they are meant to address.

Step 6: Say communications objectives out loud. The last time you want to actually say these statements and messages out loud for the first time is when an emergency actually occurs. By saying these objectives out loud when you're developing the messages, you will be able to edit them, correct them, and make them truly responsive to the issues and situations they are meant to address.

4.6 Model Crisis Communication Exercise

A *tabletop exercise* is often used as a starting point for crisis response planning and as a precursor to a full-blown crisis simulation exercise. A typical tabletop involves five steps:

1. Identify and develop a particularly difficult and convincing scenario against which to execute the tabletop exercise.

2. Identify all individuals who would have an important role to play in resolving the scenario selected.

3. Using a facilitator and a useful discussion outline, conduct a discussion of the problem following the sequence of events that would in all likelihood occur.

4. Identify major areas of response concern, events as they unfold, key players, and the decisions made.

5. Follow a template, or model of analysis, that allows each suggested response to be fleshed out in terms of what would actually happen.

4.6.1 Create an Effective Scenario Response

Create an effective scenario response from which everyone can learn. The goal is to be able to proactively put in place and to pre-authorize as many aspects of the response as possible.

A good scenario is a tool that will help you:

- Examine the probable chronology of events.
- Analyze hypothetical situations.
- Identify options for dealing with the crisis.
- Make recommendations based on those options.
- Forecast unintended consequences.
- Identify key contacts and needed corporate resources.

4.6.2 Restructure Your Thinking About Drills and Exercises

Let's reshape your thinking about this crucial aspect of crisis preparation by restructuring your thoughts about why drills and exercises are important and how they should be done.

The purpose of all exercises and simulations is to confirm the readiness of participants. All exercises should be planned and announced in advance. There should be adequate time to study and review materials and response activities. The exercise should be scheduled and conducted regardless of who is in attendance, since emergencies never happen when the entire team is in place and ready to go.

Because most drills focus on finding fault, CEOs or senior executives rarely enjoy participating and often avoid them. To them it often seems that the process is designed to make them look stupid or foolish. A better strategy is to help the CEO and other senior executives know as much as possible about what they will be doing so that the drill will be a truly successful activity under their leadership.

The smart money says make the boss look like a leader and a hero. This means preparing the CEO for the exercise and giving him/her the ability to lead when it takes place.

> Rather than conduct an exercise with lots of negative criticism... catalogue those things that are done competently and well.

Rather than conduct an exercise with lots of negative criticism, which only results in defensiveness, pushback, and an unwillingness to fix problems or move ahead, catalogue those things that are done competently and well. This permits the development of a collateral list of crucial action items – things that need to be improved, re-installed, or replaced to improve readiness.

Prepare Participants in Advance

Simulations consume an enormous amount of time and resources. To be worth the investment, participants need to prepare for the exercise. This six-step process will ensure a successful outcome.

Step 1   Provide participants with the most up-to-date version of your crisis response plan for review before participating.

Step 2   As an early part of the simulation exercise, the existing crisis response plan should be reviewed and discussed with all participants.

Step 3   Specific lessons that will be learned as a part of the simulation exercise should be outlined before the exercise begins.

Step 4   Those monitoring the exercise should be looking as much for excellence of performance and readiness as for deficiencies, mistakes, and problems.

Step 5   Monitors and participants, upon evaluation, should look for the most critical areas for improvement, which usually involve:

> ▶ Whereabouts of key people.

> ▶ Communications efficiency and effectiveness.

> ▶ Pre-authorization of crucial decisions.

> ▶ Collateral damage.

> ▶ Predictable shortcomings due to arrogance, overestimating readiness, or underestimating the scope of difficulties that problems present.

> ▶ Prompt decision making.

> ▶ An effective plan for senior management involvement.

> ▶ Unexpected behavior by friends, co-workers, and people we thought were "on our side."

Step 6   To be effective, everything that is said is a part of the simulation, and any evaluation of the simulation must be constructive, positive, and helpful.

Remember, lists of negatives which embarrass and fail to result in process or readiness improvement, make senior executives reluctant to participate again. Help executives be heroes and leaders, and they will return. Make leaders look like fools, and they will resent your approach and will stay away. Worse, when a crisis does occur, they won't call you, and they will invent their own solutions, whatever the cost, whatever the damage.

4.7 When You Need to Obtain Public Forgiveness

When you are planning, take into account that some damaging event or situation could occur to cause harm to organizational reputation and public confidence. Be prepared with a recognizable sequence of actions and remedial steps that will help alleviate the victim pain and rebuild relationships and community trust. The survival of your company, your reputation, your career and livelihood may be at stake here. This is the pathway forward. Do every step or your problems will persist.

Step 1:   **Candor.** Promptly verbalize public acknowledgment that people or groups of people, the environment, or the public trust are affected; and that something will be done to remediate the situation.

Step 2:   **Extreme Empathy/Apology.** Deliver a verbalized or written statement of personal regret, remorse, and sorry, acknowledging personal responsibility for having injured, insulted, failed, or wronged another, humbly asking for forgiveness in exchange for more appropriate future behavior and to make amends in return.

Step 3:   **Explanation.** No matter how silly, stupid, or embarrassing the problem-causing error was, explain promptly and briefly why the problem occurred and the known underlying reasons or behaviors that led to the situation.

Step 4.   **Affirmation.** Talk about what you've learned from the situation and how it will influence your future behavior. Unconditionally commit to regularly report additional information until it is all out or until no public interest remains.

Step 5:   **Declaration.** Conduct a public commitment and discussion of specific, positive steps to be taken to conclusively address the issues and resolve the situation.

Step 6:   **Contrition.** Continue to verbalize your regret, empathy, sympathy, and even embarrassment. Take appropriate responsibility for having allowed the situation to occur in the first place, whether by omission, commission, accident, or negligence.

Step 7:   **Consultation.** Promptly ask for help and counsel from "victims," government, and the community of origin affected – even from your opponents. Directly involve and request the participation of those affected most directly to help develop more permanent solutions, more acceptable behaviors, and to design principles and approaches that will preclude similar problems from re-occurring.

Step 8: **Commitment.** Publicly set your goals at zero. Zero errors, zero defects, zero dumb decisions, and zero problems. Promise publicly that to the best of your ability situations like this will be prevented from occurring again. To the best of your ability, situations like this will never occur again.

Step 9: **Restitution.** Find a way to quickly pay the price. Make or require restitution. Go beyond community and victim expectations and what would be required under normal circumstances to remediate the problem.

> **Publicly set your goals at zero. Zero errors, zero defects, zero dumb decisions, zero problems.**

In most adverse reputational situations, the troubled company will be forced to take each of these steps eventually – often very publicly and with great humiliation. Experience demonstrates that extraordinary reputational damage is within the controlling power of the troubled organization, but only if the leadership of that organization chooses to behave and speak appropriately and promptly. The crucial issue is the desire of the organization to take conclusive action quickly, taking advantage of the golden hour.

Chapter 4 – Questions for Study and Discussion

1. Why do CEOs and upper management avoid participating in drills and exercises? What steps would you take to make sure they willingly participated in scenarios and provided valuable input into all phases of the planning process?

2. What are the advantages of a tabletop exercise? Why is it useful to conduct a tabletop exercise before initiating a full-blown crisis simulation exercise?

3. Explain how the web can be useful to you in crisis communication. How would you explain the value of a "dark site" to the executive who will be approving the budget for its construction?

4. What is the greatest single weakness in most crisis plans? What can be built into a plan to strengthen this area?

5

Crisis Communication Plan in Action: Media Relations

Keywords: crisis website, media relations policy, dark site, color words, power words, news magazine shows

Media relations during emergencies are crucial – not just for your company but for media organizations as well. The crisis is important to the media because it has the potential to create big business for the news media. Thus, developing a news media relations strategy for your company is crucial because the public depends on traditional media in crisis for its insight and, though declining, its credibility. A media relations strategy is a communications tool that provides great exposure, great risk, and great opportunity for real-time surprises.

This chapter will help you to:

➢ Achieve novel, powerful, positive emergency media responses.

➢ Develop media relations policies, procedures, and plans.

➢ Deal with network news programs.

➢ Understand the requirements of being a good spokesperson.

➢ See the crisis from the point of view of the reporter or editor.

➢ Create and deliver the message that best represents your organization.

➢ Manage victims and their needs.

5.1 The Crisis Media Relations Policy

5.1.1 Sample Crisis Media Relations Policy

The first step in managing relations with the social and traditional media is to establish a sensible, professional crisis media relations policy. Here is a seven-point sample approach.

1. *Regional managers and Headquarters Media Relations employees are the designated spokespersons for XYZ Company, its parent, and subsidiaries.*

2. *All other employees must secure prior approval from Headquarters Media Relations for any outside publication, speech, interview, discussion, or other communication with or to the media if it involves XYZ Company or can have an impact on the Company.*

3. *Media calls from national and international media should be directed to Headquarters Media Relations.*

4. *Calls for financial information or overall (rather than regional) company information should be directed to Headquarters Media Relations.*

5. *The Headquarters Media Relations team will answer calls from financial analysts either by using information in the public domain or by referring calls to Investor Relations.*

6. *Local media calls are to be handled by local managers when regional regulatory activity, local employee information, or regulatory questions are involved.*

7. *Local issues may be discussed with the media if the information is public or if it is not material. Material information is that which would influence a reasonable investor to buy, sell, or hold stock. It is important that questions about this type of information be directed to Headquarters Media Relations and Investor Relations.*

> **Organizational messages, regardless of who conveys them, must always be internally and externally consistent.**

5.1.2 Guidelines for Designated Spokespersons

Organizational messages, regardless of who conveys them, must always be internally and externally consistent. Always use or obtain approved language. Model guidelines could include:

1. Predictions about strategy, earnings, sales, value of the company, industry trends, and the like must be avoided. Widely known existing strategies can be discussed as long as they are expected to remain the same.

2. Under regulation FD (Full Disclosure), the United States Securities and Exchange Commission (SEC) considers that all company spokespersons, regardless of title or level, equal XYZ Company representatives. In fact, under FD, all audiences are to receive equal treatment at the risk of penalties and sanctions that the SEC has become quite accustomed to imposing.

3. In 2002, the United States Congress passed the Sarbanes-Oxley Act, a law that initially imposed very strict regulations on accounting and disclosure. The passage of this law affects most publicly held companies regardless of where they operate in the world. Recent amendments to Sarbanes-Oxley adopted and initiated in 2004 set even more stringent requirements in terms of ethics and the behavior of corporate leaders, and the punishment they can experience should corporate governance laws be violated. The Sarbanes-Oxley laws have been subsequently amended and remain controversial.

5.1.3 Good Spokesperson Practices

In situations of crisis or catastrophe, the importance of competent, compassionate, careful spokespeople is crucial. After reading this section, one could argue that these techniques and practices are those of any good spokesperson. That would be true. However, in times of crisis and catastrophe, bad things happen faster and control is lost much more quickly. It is the spokesperson who sets the tone, tempo, and expectations of those paying attention or relaying on the spokesperson for information.

▶ **Remain calm.** Crisis and catastrophe communication require the highest levels of professionalism from spokespersons. Whether the spokesperson is the most senior executive in the organization or someone else, that person's job is to reassure people, exhibit confidence and competence, and use his or her words and writings to help focus on resolving the issues at hand and reducing the production of victims and collateral damage.

▶ **Coordinate all comments with the crisis website.** Since most real news covers adverse situations, reporters tend to be quite experienced in covering crises. Therefore, they have a natural suspicion of information handed out by paid representatives, causing reporters to look for discrepancies rather than story lines. Make certain that whatever is said from a lectern, live, is identical to or compatible with whatever is being posted on your website.

▶ **Use positive language.** Distortions, lies, misunderstandings, and conflicting information are generally caused by the use of negative characterizations and responses. A spokesperson's goal in writing and in speaking is to answer questions and provide information in completely positive and declarative language.

▶ **Avoid all negative words, phrases, and descriptions.** Negative language causes confusion and additional questions. Negative language is, essentially, non-communication. Negative language is almost always misinterpreted, leading to further negative questions regarding whatever the misinterpretation happens to be. Every negative response, phrase, characterization, or description causes additional questions, many of which are very difficult to answer. Some negative circumstances are considered to be outright lies from the start. Almost any answer or statement that uses the word "can't" is considered a lie right off the bat.

▶ **Disclose some facts immediately and continuously,** even if the news is bad. Information delayed is considered information withheld. In addition, piecemeal disclosure can result in prolonged coverage. The spokesperson must quickly begin to collect the facts and initiate information flow to various audiences and the media.

▶ **Devote a dedicated website to the controversies at hand.** On this site should reside a growing repository of useful, current, and generally helpful information, including studies, laws, rules and regulations, questions and answers, and corrections and clarifications of information already provided.

▶ **Act quickly.** The first hour or two is critical to getting the organization's story out. Once a story is out, it may be difficult to change the perceptions that result.

▶ **Treat the media professionally and with equality.** Show respect and distance. Say what you mean to say, and then say good-bye. You may also indicate when you will speak again, if ever.

▶ **Treat all inquiries fairly and promptly.** Refer all inquiries to the website initially so everyone has access to the same basic information. This approach can reduce media calls and inquiries by significant amounts, sometimes as much as 90%. In crises, most reporters are not calling to do an original story but to verify information or validate other stories they have read, seen, or heard. A visit to your website can often satisfy those concerns, and reporters will move on to other things.

▶ **Stick to the facts.** Talk about what you know to be true. When asked a question or situation for which the spokesperson does not have an answer, the spokesperson's response should be positive and declarative. For example, the spokesperson could say, "My knowledge of that is limited. I know a couple of things." The spokesperson then says what he or she knows and asks if the inquirer would like additional information beyond that given. In 90% of the cases, this response will satisfy whoever is asking the question. If the inquirer needs more information and says so, the spokesperson can respond appropriately.

▶ **Avoid "I don't know."** Far too often, if the answer is, "I don't know," the positive, declarative approach is much better and avoids wild goose chases looking for information that was never really sought after in the first place.

▶ **Avoid guessing and speculation.** Questions that begin with, "Suppose..." "Couldn't...?" "Shouldn't...?" or "What if...?" or "How bad could it have been?" require speculative responses or guesses. Talk only about what you know. Ironically, guessing forces the reporter to keep speculating, causing even more distortion.

▶ **Avoid making estimates.** Many will be attempting to estimate the costs of catastrophe and damage. Be ready for it. Either have appropriate estimates available, a forecast for when such estimates will be available, or a reasonable and truthful explanation as to why such estimates are not available and may never be. Crisis and catastrophe provide visibility for many organizations, many businesses, and many points of view. Damage estimates are very controversial, and these are questions you can anticipate. (Remember the problems BP had with the daily changes in estimating the scope of the oil spill.)

> It is possible to respond in a positive way to even the most negative, challenging, harsh, or intimidating question. Use positive, declarative language.

▶ **Avoid flatly refusing to provide information.** The use of phrases such as "no comment" needs to be avoided. These phrases automatically establish a negative environment, with the spokesperson being the target of doubts, distrust, and even becoming discredited. There are some excellent response options when a request for information has either yet to surface or must be withheld: "I'll need more information before I can answer that question," "That information is being withheld at the present time for _____ reasons, but we hope to release it soon," "The answer to that question will become available as the situation unfolds," "When we have reliable information in response to that question, we will provide it," and "The answer to that question (or series of questions) is proprietary and will remain confidential." As you can see by these responses, it is possible to respond in a positive way to even the most negative, challenging, harsh, or intimidating question. Use positive, declarative language.

▶ **Release information** about victims only after families have been notified, and with the permission of the families – or let the families do it.

▶ **Express genuine regret if there are fatalities or injuries to report.** Being empathetic is expected. Responsibility is a matter for the company's officers and legal counsel, and possibly the courts, to determine. "Responsibility will be determined some time in the future, our concern now are helping the victims, cleaning up, talking with neighbors, etc." Empathy and sympathy may actually reduce exposure to litigation. (**Note:** *See Chapter 3 for more information about communicating information about injuries and fatalities.*)

▶ **Only tell reporters what you would be comfortable having your mother see in print or hear on television or radio.**

▶ **Think before you respond.** Whenever you talk to a reporter, you are being interviewed. Period. Use approved messages and statements.

▶ **Provide the media with useful, positive information,** such as facility/plant safety statistics and other information relevant to news coverage. However, remember that bad problems will cause bad stories. Too many safety statistics will stimulate even more emotionally charged responses from victims and survivors.

▶ Control the interview:
  ❑ Avoid all negative words and phrases.
  ❑ Be brief and positive.
  ❑ Bundle your main points into groups of three or four.
  ❑ Choose the setting for safety and message value.
  ❑ Establish ground rules.

- ❏ Help reporters make their deadlines.
- ❏ Make available photographs and broadcast-quality video footage.
- ❏ Repeat key information several times.
- ❏ Set starting times and ending times for media interviews or press conferences.
- ❏ Stay calm.
- ❏ Tell the reporter what is important.
- ❏ Use appropriate and approved statements and messages.

▶ **Have a media access plan where possible and reasonable.** Designate a single media entrance, staffed by security guards. All other entrances should be posted with signs directing media to the appropriate location. Only reporters or photographers with approved identification should be given access, and then only with approval of the spokesperson or designee of the Crisis Communication Team. Media should be escorted while on the premises.

▶ **Monitor media coverage, correct and clarify.** Monitoring media coverage matters, because mistakes occur. Therefore, your organization must have an ongoing strategy for correcting and clarifying mistakes that has little reliance on the media. Corrections in either new media or traditional media are rare and need to be substantial. Establish a "Corrections and Clarifications" area on your website (see section 5.2 below for a description of this technique). Rather than asking the media for a correction and clarification, direct the reporter and others to your website. The one exception is the wire services, which should be monitored closely. Wire services are the major way media outside the local area where the crisis is occurring get their news and information. Wire services are better than most at making corrections.

▶ **Anticipate likely questions.** The media will always want to know:

- ❏ **What happened?** Describe the incident with as much detail and as little technical jargon as possible. Be ready to comment on the nature of the emergency, whether there was a fire or explosion, and if there were any injuries.
- ❏ **When did it happen?** Reporters like precise detail, but it is reasonable to approximate to the nearest half-hour.

❑ **Who was involved?** Withhold names until families have been notified. In the event of injuries or deaths, confirm to the reporter that the injured were taken to a hospital. Also, this question provides the opportunity to comment briefly on the employees instrumental in rescue or clean-up attempts. Advise the reporter of the company's emergency plans and other procedural safeguards in place.

❑ **Where did it happen?** Identify the location of the emergency. Also indicate the effect or lack of effect of the accident on the rest of the facility or the communities adjacent to the site, if any.

❑ **Why did the accident occur?** Until more complete information is available, indicate that an investigation is under way and the cause has not yet been determined.

▶ **Prepare answers for the most likely questions.** Test them, say them out loud, and fix them so they work. Keep them to about 75 words, about 30 seconds speaking time.

▶ **Speak with compassion.** Always show concern, empathy, sympathy, remorse, or contrition, and use compassionate language:

Alarmed	Empathetic/empathize	Sorrowful/sorry
Appalled	Failed/failure	Sympathize/sympathetic
Ashamed	Humiliated	Tragic
Concerned	Let you down	Unfortunate
Devastated	Mortified	Unhappy
Disappointed	Regret/regrettable	Unintended/unintentional
Disheartened	Sad/saddened	Unnecessary
Embarrassed	Shocked/surprised	Unsatisfactory

▶ **Stay out of the "bunker."** When *60 Minutes* calls, tell employees and ask for their help. Remember that the media, like prosecutors, rely on the paralysis caused by bad stories to divide and isolate, which allows the media to create only their version of the truth.

(**Note:** *For more about handling media questions, see news conference information in Chapter 6.*)

Case Study: The Accidental Spokesperson

The Company

LightChem North is a branch plant of a large chemical company, located in upstate New York. This company's 350-employee workforce is engaged in recycling and recovering used metal parts from various industries. They chemically degrease, electrolytically remove plating substances as well as recover them, and selectively rehabilitate certain metal parts for reuse in mechanical devices.

The Crisis

During what was meant to be a routine change in solvents — in which used and contaminated solvent is replaced with clean, fresh solvent — a glitch in the transfer crane operation caused approximately 250-300 gallons of this hot, organic liquid to spill out of the container from about twelve feet in the air. Upon hitting the floor, the chemical splashed onto two to three dozen workers, all of whom were immediately burned and partially asphyxiated. The substance was Compound 2, 4, 9, Trichloroethylene, a degreasing solvent with heavy vapors that rest close to the ground. This chlorinated hydrocarbon is listed by the EPA as a known carcinogen and health hazard that, when inhaled, causes nervous system depression, and, externally, can irritate and burn skin and eyes.

The Complexities

Personnel at the LightChem plant had practiced for similar emergencies a number of times, and those workers in the nearby area who were able to function began to respond, but the fumes were extraordinarily powerful. As it happens, all of the showers intended for decontamination purposes were located in an area opposite where the spill had occurred and were essentially blocked from use, at least temporarily. The nearest fire rescue station was approximately seven miles down the road in town, and four of the plant's seven-day shift EMTs were victims.

The Choices

1. Call headquarters. Report the incident and await instructions.

2. Take immediate action to deal with the situation as it was developing in the plant itself and contacting 9-1-1.

3. Evacuate the plant and as many personnel as possible to prevent them from being overcome by fumes and let the three functioning EMTs handle most of the response.

The Culmination

As the sound of sirens could be heard nearing the plant, Charles Westerfield, the plant manager, a 12-year veteran of this facility, reflexively closed the gates around the plant. He quickly posted his two security guards near the front gate to allow the fire trucks in when they arrived and keep anybody else out. About a mile ahead of the fire trucks were two local television station vans and, in the distance, Charles could see and hear what must have been a news helicopter flying in from one of the major news centers in the state.

As the news cars stopped near the gate, cameramen and reporters jumped out of the vehicles and came running to the now-closed front gate. Charles walked out to greet them and as the reporters ran up with their cameras rolling and microphones out, they were asking for a quick explanation of what was going on inside the plant. Charles was well known to the media people as as being one of the more important employers in the region and, being very friendly and approachable, he knew the reporters by name. The most insistent reporter from Channel 4 was also the most excited in asking her questions.

Charles looked through the chain link fence at the cameras and said, quite simply, "Mary, calm down, calm down, calm down. We've been spilling this stuff and burning people with it for years. This is no big deal." He then said some other things that were important to know and valuable to hear. However, his single "sound bite" ricocheted onto every news outlet in the local region and beyond. The result was embarrassment for LightChem North as well as unwelcome attention for Charles Westerfield, whose words reached the ears of executives at the chemical company headquarters. Up until this incident, Charles and his work as plant manager had been highly regarded by his superiors at the company.

As required by law, LightChem North regularly conducted quarterly drills in the plant to prepare workers to react appropriately and promptly to spills of these toxic organic chemicals used in the remanufacturing process. This training permitted the workers to handle this emergency and its complications just as they had in the quarterly drills. However, in the company's very detailed emergency plans, no one apparently anticipated that a good natured, friendly plant manager, one willing to speak to the press, would cause the level of trouble that he did.

The Conclusions

Every day we see *Lukaszewski's First Rule of Crisis Survival* reasserted and revalidated. This axiom is: Neither the media, your critics, the government, your toughest competitor, or your angriest neighbor can take you down. Crises and bad news are almost always caused by internal denial, over-confident management and executives, lack of readiness, well-meaning friends, or relatives.

As obvious as this scenario is in its readiness lessons, it bears repeating that an appropriate spokesperson and a back-up spokesperson need to be selected and ready for events of this nature. Had the plant manager been a victim, for example, having someone else ready to step out and communicate effectively and promptly would have been very much in the plant's interest. The time to pick spokespersons is during your readiness preparations and exercise — and part of their preparation needs to include what to say and not say to the media.

5.1.4 Setting the Record Straight if You Make a Mistake

Sufficient resources need to be allocated to the task of keeping the record straight and anticipating future errors. Errors are inevitable, but good record keeping not only keeps the record straight but also prevents the appearance – at some time in the future – of poor planning, poor execution, or intentional mistakes. What if we make a mistake in handling a crisis? Here are some guidelines for setting the record straight:

- **Act quickly to correct data errors, misstatements, and bad information.**
- **Use discretion when requesting corrections on air or in print.** The media may be willing, but the result is often a whole new series of stories.
- **In any event, make certain the reporter knows what the errors were.** The editor should know, too.
- **Apologize quickly if you lose your cool.**
- **Document the corrective action taken.** The media may not use the information, but the goal is to keep the record straight.
- **Get your corrections into databases.** Contact the Associated Press, UPI, Nexis, AOL, and other databases with "story error corrections." Look in these databases, find the errors, and be aggressive correcting them. Bad news lives forever in a database if not fixed.
- **Establish a "Corrections and Clarifications" section on your website.** Whatever documents or records need correcting, put those up on the site, in total, on the left side of the screen. On the right side, place your positively and declaratively stated corrections or clarifications across from the erroneous or otherwise offensive or misleading material. Use positive, declarative language.

> **Reporters consult the web and social media on stories of all kinds, including emergencies and fast-breaking situations.**

5.2 The Crisis Website (*or "Dark Site"*) in Media Relations Strategy

Because the web has become such an important element in effective and comprehensive response to crisis situations, more and more companies are establishing template sites, sometimes called *dark* or *stealth sites*, which are pre-organized and populated with pre-authorized information. They are set up to respond immediately to the general nature of crises and to specific scenarios, and are used to get ahead of the negativity often caused by delays in responding to situations of public interest.

These dark sites reside on a server. As information is developed, various portions of these sites are reviewed, authorized, and go live as circumstances warrant. It's also possible to have automatic e-mail notifications sent to those who have pre-registered to have access to the site during an emergency, as well as to those whose interest has been pre-identified as a way to help them stay current as new or revised information becomes available. This approach can head off misinformation or the outright fabrication of information that the pressure of crisis events often causes.

These sites feature a "fill-in-the-blank" architecture in which key information can be easily inserted and promptly made widely available, especially to employees and the news media. The vast majority of media calls in crises are inquiries for basic information. The most frequently requested information is the location of the emergency, exact time of the event, victim identifications, if any, and potential damage to the product, reputation, facility, or business. Responding to these inquiries takes enormous amounts of time and generally yields very simple stories that acknowledge the event's basic nature. Having a website with basic information immediately available can reduce media relations calls by up to 90%.

Recent studies show that reporters, by overwhelming percentages, consult the Web and social media on stories of all kinds, including emergencies and fast-breaking situations. The risk in fielding all media questions personally is that dealing directly with reporters often creates many more stories than would otherwise be the case. Additional questions get asked, and a different kind of story gets written or broadcast. (**Note:** *For more about handling issues around social media, see Chapter 7.*)

5.2.1 Creating a Crisis or Dark Website

A dark website can be opened from the primary website's home page. The following interior pages can then be accessed through individual buttons on the dark site's home page:

- **Archives:** Accessible location where information older than 72 hours resides.

- **Accurate Stories:** A sampling of stories that have already run on the situation.

- **Company Profile:** Useful information about the company or organization, such as the number of employees, square footage of the affected location, products manufactured, position in the marketplace, and other relevant facts that help the reporter correctly characterize your company or organization and what it does in relation to the problem at hand.

- **Contact Us Now:** A format where site visitors can e-mail questions, comments, and observations, either for response, for information, or to speak out anonymously. Allow a window with approximately 1,500 characters so that ample space is available for messages. Do not permit attachments.

▌ **Corrections and Clarifications:** Post articles, news coverage, and quotes that need immediate correction or clarification. Stories or item content are loaded into the left-hand side of the page. Corrective statements and clarifications are inserted on the right-hand side of the page directly across from the inaccurate information on the left-hand side of the page.

▌ **Critics' and Opponents' Commentary:** The views and observations of those who criticize us. Also link to Corrections and Clarifications section of the site so your side gets a chance to respond.

▌ **Current Statements:** Useful quotes from one or two key people.

▌ **Dashboards:** Real-time readings of changes in data that might matter to victims, their families, employees, the public as a whole, and especially news media and other monitors of your crisis response.

▌ **Dear So and So:** A way to contact very senior people in the organization directly to obtain personal responses.

▌ **Downloads and Tools:** Special documents or functions that might help the website user learn more or to explore more within the site.

▌ **Key People:** Key contact names and telephone numbers.

▌ **Latest Information:** Summary of information updates, the time when additional information will be available, and from whom it can be expected.

▌ **Links:** Other informative or useful sites for those concerned or interested.

▌ **Links to Share Information through New Media and Social Media Sites.**

▌ **Photos:** E-mail-ready still photographs of the facilities or site prior to the incident.

▌ **Press Releases.**

▌ **Questions and Answers:** Five to ten crucial questions and answers regarding the situation.

▌ **Quick Links:** For frequently sought after information, a single point of use linkage.

- **Register for Updates:** A location where individuals can sign up to be notified promptly by e-mail as new content is added to the website. Additionally, you may want to contact key reporters, and others likely to cover emergencies and fast-breaking situations, to request permission to include their e-mail addresses on dark site notification lists to avoid delay in providing the latest available information.

- **Recent Updates:** A listing of those things just added to the site or with other sources, with links.

- **RSS Feeds:** Response contacts, a mini telephone/e-mail directory for key functions in the company connected to crisis response from the executive officers down to on-scene operational locations.

- **Situation:** Basic statement of the situation – the who, what, when, where, why, and how.

- **Twitter Link:** Statements from the organization on various facets of the crisis and response.

- **Useful links:** Quick connections to information and questions that you would love people to have the information about, but they might not know to ask.

- **Video and Audio:** Downloadable clips relevant to the situation or scenario.

> Those who worry about hackers and curious or disgruntled current or former employees ... should consider storing dark site information on a DVD, which can be on a "need to know" basis.

Remember, these sites are lit up only after something happens. Once they are brought online, they will probably need to stay up for some time. These sites also become repositories of useful information, which can become a resource for reporters and, again, reduce interview time by pre-answering the easy, common sense questions reporters are going to ask. Within your own industry, you might consider doing a brief survey to determine which peer companies have prepared dark sites, and which ones have actually used them. Ask to see them to get a better idea of how this concept works. (**Note:** *Crisis or Dark websites are also discussed in Chapter 4 of this book.*)

Data Security: Those who worry about hackers and curious or disgruntled current or former employees discovering and tampering with corporate preparation for disasters, divestures, lay-offs, and other difficult problems should consider storing dark site information on a DVD, which can be provided on a "need to know" basis. At a minimum, this material should be password protected and reviewed for relevance on a regular basis, and kept in a secure (locked) location.

5.2.2 Basic Media Relations Strategy

Media relations skill, strategy, and execution often help control and moderate explosive visibility in a crisis by adopting a more managed approach. An advance commitment of people, dollars, and mental energy is all that stands between being ready when a crisis occurs and being at the mercy of events and the media. This section will help you achieve effective emergency media relations preparation.

To deal effectively with the media element of the emergency management equation, you need to be prepared to act quickly, making decisions with respect to the news media that will let you manage them and get ahead of the curve – once they call or if they have already called.

Consider these critical strategies:

▶ Should we make a concerted effort either to downplay the newsworthiness of the event or to encourage media coverage?

▶ Should we prepare a basic media statement for use in response to media questions?

▶ Should we prepare a Q&A summary for use in response to media questions?

▶ Should we confine our media comments to our statements and Q&A or attempt to be more responsive?

▶ If the media ask for documents, should we provide them? If so, which documents?

▶ How forthcoming should we be in responding to media questions about specific issues?

▶ What are the two or three fundamental messages/themes we would like to communicate most via the news media?

▶ What can/should we say about victims?

▶ How much public interest will there be? Why?

▶ How much does the public need to know?

▶ Is/will/would/should there be a role for the media in this emergency?

▶ What happens if we do nothing?

▶ How quickly do we get information up on our website?

▶ Do we preempt the reporter to call by posting large quantities of information on the web early?

▶ Do we have a handle on the social media chatter?

5.3 Understanding the Nature of News

To understand what the reporter is thinking, it helps to understand what news is from the reporter's perspective. An analysis of reporter behavior supports this general definition:

News is about the unusual, how the unusual affects people, animals, and living systems, and what the effects of the unusual are.

> Keep in mind that news is always about yesterday... In crisis, stick to what you know. Walking into the future is always troublesome when it is done by the news media or by a willing spokesperson.

5.3.1 The Attributes of News

News has some or all of these 14 attributes:

1. **Unusual:** News is about what is different, about unusual results or surprising outcomes.

2. **Affect:** News has emotional appeal. When news is about people, animals, or living systems it is generally far more interesting than news about the malfunction of some machine or other inanimate object – unless, of course, human victims are involved.

3. **Effect:** News centers on results or outcomes – death, injury, homelessness, personal harm, shame, failure, anger, disaster, stupidity, etc.

4. **Change:** Most change can become newsworthy very easily. The media tends to automatically view change primarily as mistake repair – somebody screwed up and someone is responsible. If the change is revolutionary, the question asked is, "Why did it take so long?" If it is improved, who is responsible for continuing to mock the previously ineffective or inadequate product? If some procedure, product, process, or operation is changed for reasons that are less than clear, the reporter will ask, "What did you know and when did you know it? What did you do and when did you do it?"

5. **Conflict:** Drama, like news, is usually about conflict and contention. Conflict can arise from one or more of four sources:

    a. From **insiders,** i.e., whistle-blowers, disgruntled employees, or dissatisfied contractors;

    b. From **outsiders,** i.e., competitors, competing interests, or government;

    c. From **organized** opposition, i.e., customers, neighbors, retirees, or politicians;

    d. From **confrontation**, i.e., intentionally baiting and bullying. Today's audiences, for whatever reason, want cause and effect, often with no time or care about how one caused the other. The more your story lends itself to extremes, the more newsworthy it will be – a small vendor taking on a huge company, alleging unfair practices; a town taking on a proposed new big box store; or parents angry at a school district. All of these examples can be stated very simply, directly, and confrontationally. These will be good stories even if the information essential to understanding the circumstances gets left out, as it so often does.

6. **Danger:** News is often driven by the perception of danger, such as some residual threat that exists to the community, human beings, animals, or the environment.

7. **Extremes:** If your story lends itself to extremes, it is going to be more newsworthy.

8. **Failure:** Ideas, products, and programs are expected to succeed; that's the American Way. *Therefore, failure is automatically news.*

9. **Mistakes:** Business, large institutions, and famous people are expected to function perfectly at all times. When these entities make errors and mistakes, the story becomes inherently newsworthy. The bigger the mistake, the more likely it will be re-covered by the media for six months to a year, sometimes every year for a period of time. The media love mistakes. No matter how good a good company is, if it makes a mistake, that mistake will be reported as an integral part of every "good" news story for some time in the future. (*See* "4. Change.")

10. **Reporter's perspective:** News is more worthy if it hits close to home. Reporters' experiences are essential to the way they cover news stories; for example, if a reporter's nephew works in your plant that just burned down or if the reporter worked there while in college, that makes for a much better story from a reporter's perspective.

11. **Secrecy:** News is about whatever you want to hide. The media loves secrets, but it just can't and won't keep them for you.

12. **Vulnerabilities:** News often occurs when something you should have known could go wrong did go wrong, but you weren't prepared. You were vulnerable. You were exposed. These vulnerabilities and exposures add to the news value of a story about you.

13. **Weaknesses:** Newsworthy perceptions of weakness often arise merely from the observations of uninformed outsiders, including the reporter. If something you are doing or might do appears to be weak or wrongheaded, it can enhance the news value of a story.

14. **Editor's perspective:** Finally, the rule that supersedes all other rules is that news is what the editor thinks it is. If the editor thinks you have a problem, you do!

Keep in mind that news is always about yesterday. One of the reasons media are so prone to spread the alarm carelessly, needlessly, and explosively is because reporters don't know; thus, they feel the obligation to speculate about everything in an attempt to help the audience get a head-start on tomorrow. This is one of the least endearing qualities of the news media. In crisis, stick to what you know. Walking into the future is always troublesome when it is done by the news media or by a willing spokesperson.

News Is an Emotional Business

Reporters are paid to ask questions effectively, but they have found that using words of high emotion – I call them *color words* – elicit more colorful, often surprising answers because they tend to grab the guts of the spokesperson, the editor, and the audience. Expect this and recognize its effect on spokespersons. Reporters are increasingly taking on the roles of interpreters, alarmists, forecasters, and speculators. Emergencies provide the perfect environment for interpretation by reporters because of the combination of limited time, an urgent need for story material, and a shortage of space for words. Emotionalizing the story can be very powerful and compelling, especially when spokespersons of the "perpetrating" organization are caught off guard and appear embarrassed, defensive, or wrong.

For the media, as a business, crisis stories are exercises in marketing and gaining market share, and advertising dollars. As a result, reporters are under enormous pressure to get something fast, something different, something first, and to keep it coming as long as effective stories can be fabricated from whatever is available.

> **You can provide an interesting array of tools to assist all reporters, regardless of media, helping them to convey your story, its impact, and perhaps some of the potential outcome.**

5.3.2 Tools to Assist the Media: Fact Sheets

You can provide an interesting array of tools to assist all reporters, regardless of media, helping them to convey your story, its impact, and perhaps some of the potential outcome. Each scenario may have some or all of these tools, but keep in mind they are being designed primarily for use by reporters. These tools will help you with all audiences, since every one of these devices will be placed on your crisis website.

Facts are important, and are often the source of highly emotional stories. Use fact sheets to get critical, correct information on your website promptly. They will be appreciated because they help save time by providing answers for reporters' questions about the company and its operations. In addition, the fact sheets are useful for you because they help manage the reputation being created by news reporters and victims' stories. Since most of the components of fact sheets are available on a website, the formats allow them to be downloaded easily by the reporter and other visitors to your site. Here are some of the more useful ingredients that fact sheets can contain as free-standing information resources on your website:

1. **Data:** All pertinent information such as site acreage, number of employees, products and major uses, mill/plant square footage, number of storage tanks, location of waste disposal sites and types of waste produced, number of years at location, etc. The most effective and important data is that which is updated on a 24/7 basis. When you provide information (e.g., readings from various gauges, counts of various items of circumstances, or just ongoing monitoring), each of these data sources becomes what is called a dashboard. As on a car dashboard, the gauges move to register various important values, indicating the status of various operating systems and circumstances. Reporters have come to rely on dashboards as important ongoing sources of current information.

2. **Maps** of the general area with the facility designated and reference distances from the nearest towns, company offices, etc.

3. **Location information** for residences within the area (one-to-two mile radius) in case of toxic chemical releases or should evacuation become necessary.

4. **Drawings** (construction prints or maps) of the structure or area involved.

5. **Layouts** of the production equipment and safety system at the site.

6. **Schematic drawings** of the surface and sub-surface safety and monitoring equipment.

7. **Photographs** of the facility prior to the disaster and then sequential shots of the same views (one picture each from the north, south, east, and west) taken day-to-day as operations progress.

5.4 Preparing for Reporters

5.4.1 What to Do Before Reporters Call

If the crisis faced by your organization is the result of a physical site disaster, you will need to deal with reporters who are determined to be on the scene viewing the situation in person and speaking to you, your employees, the victims, the witnesses, etc. Much of the advice in this section is offered in the context of media relations in a physical site disaster; however, the information is equally applicable to any other kind of crisis that captures the imagination of the media.

The media often learn about an emergency by monitoring police and fire radio transmissions. Another common source for reporters is direct contact from victims; eyewitnesses; iReport submissions to local, national, or global news websites; and even by the perpetrators of the problem. Or, the news tip may be from a passerby, neighbor, or one of your own employees who alerts the local radio or television station, thus assuring some news media attention. If your emergency is newsworthy, following these simple steps will help you to be ready when the telephone rings:

1. **Communicate local media relations procedure to everyone who needs reminding.**

2. **Get ready. You are going to be very busy. Train someone to answer the telephone and gather the following information:**

   ▶ Reporter's name.

   ▶ Name of media outlet.

   ▶ Reporter's office, after-hours, and home telephone numbers.

   ▶ Subject of reporter's call.

   ▶ Potential questions the reporter wants answered.

   ▶ Deadline for the information needed.

   ▶ Whom the call was referred to (e.g., to Corporate Public Affairs).

   ▶ Any follow-up needed.

3. **Use well-designed Media Contact Information Sheet and Emergency Media Call Log forms.**

4. **To manage huge phone call volume from reporters, get your dark website up as quickly as possible and refer all callers to the website first.** Interestingly enough, in crisis situations, many reporters are calling to find out what is going on. If a reporter has a conversation with a spokesperson, it is much more likely to lead to an original story with a lot of interpretations and conclusions than if a useful series of Web pages, dashboards, and other crucial information is available on the Web. While there may still be an early story, it is more likely to be accurate because the information for the story came from your website.

5. **Build a database of reporters and stakeholders, those who request information, so you can get back to them very quickly when there is new information to provide.**

5.4.2 What to Do When Reporters Call

Six actions should be performed when reporters call:

1. **Ask each reporter for their deadline.** Give yourself some time to prepare to get the right answers and/or the right spokesperson(s) to answer the questions that might be asked. Ask by what time the reporter must truly have the requested information.

2. **Ask each reporter why they are calling.** The reporter may not be calling about your emergency. While reporters are often unwilling to share the specific questions, you have the right to know the subject of the story the reporter is developing and the reporter's attitude about the subject or the nature of their editorial assignment. Ask for specific information.

3. **Ask each reporter who else he or she will be interviewing.** The reporter may say "no one," or may share specific names. It's always helpful to know who else the reporter is talking to. Is it a competitor, disgruntled employee, organized opposition group, and/or public official? To know, you have to ask. Being informed helps you prepare better answers to reporter questions and, therefore, to be more comfortable.

4. **Ask each reporter if they have any special needs.** Television requires space, access, plus the opportunity to capture dramatic images of something that is leaking, foaming, or burning – and, of course, victims.

5　**Tell each reporter when or if you will call them back,** and when you will decide whether to do or not do any interviews.

6. **Set appropriate ground rules at the time you agree to respond or do an interview** – the time, location, length of the interview, and topics you will talk about. Consider ways to reduce the media crush, perhaps by suggesting an interview by telephone.

7. **Refer reporters to your website every time new information is available.**

5.4.3 What to Do Before Reporters Arrive

> **Because employees can get ignored in crisis situations, they are likely to make up things... because they have no other information. Posting transcripts on the web is highly informative and extremely helpful.**

Once you have scheduled to meet with reporters, take these steps before the news media arrive:

1. **Select an appropriate location for interviews.** Unless it specifically suits your communication objective, choose a place where you can sit down, preferably a neutral area, like a conference room or office in an area that is away from the emergency. Look behind you. Always keep the background in mind. The background should be as neutral as possible.

2. **Develop strategic communications objectives, specific statements, messages, and stories.**

3. **Brief communications staff, executives, and employees about who is coming and why.** Prepare a brief memo or e-mail about what you plan to say and do. Remind your staff of their roles, if any, while the media are present, particularly if that role is to be quiet.

4. **Share your communications objectives and messages widely within your organization.** Post internal transcripts on your website for all crucial interviews. Posting interview transcripts on the web is highly informative and extremely helpful. When everyone in the organization is in on the story, you will get better results and better performance. In addition, the spokesperson is also likely to read the same transcripts, which will allow the spokesperson to be more consistent in future interviews as well as to be able to correct the record promptly when something is misstated or misspoken.

5.4.4 What to Do While Reporters Are With You

While the media are there:

1. **Stick to the script.** Communicate your messages using your communication objectives.

2. **Stick to a time schedule and schedule briefings, as necessary.** Be professional; start and end promptly. When bad things happen, reporters expect to be told and involved. Hold group briefings that enable all reporters to hear the same thing at the same time. Get key ingredients of your story on your website as promptly as possible, whether or not you have interviews scheduled with reporters.

3. **Establish a place where reporters may gather as they arrive,** such as a conference room, trailer, or special roped-off area. Having a place set aside for media will help reporters to do their jobs better while giving you the breathing room you need to handle the emergency itself calmly.

5.4.5 When Can the Media Visit the Site?

If the crisis involves a physical disaster, media representatives, photographers, and television camerapersons expect to view the disaster site and damaged property, as well as to interview witnesses and victims. They will be insistent, and you must be patient in dealing with this request – otherwise, they will simply find a way to get there anyway. Here's a process to help formulate the best reaction:

▶ Is there any personal danger from escaping gas, hot embers, radioactivity, unstable walls or roofs, etc.?

▶ Could a visitor inadvertently disturb evidence that would hamper official investigations by safety, police, and fire officials or by insurance investigators?

▶ Assuming the area is safe and that all investigations are complete, are you able to escort the media personally on a tour of the damaged facility? If conditions warrant, remember to warn writers and photographers that certain electronic equipment cannot be used due to concentrations of combustible materials.

▶ Is there an alternative to a tour, such as a media briefing using photographic blow-ups or a floor plan drawing of the facility, which will fully explain what happened and where? Can these be made available electronically via the Web, e-mail, or CD-ROM?

▶ Can you assemble the people who performed heroic or very useful acts, so that the media can interview them? Making all employees and potential interviewees aware of the facts of their situations reduces discrepancies between your carefully considered statements and comments by others who may not have correct information.

A site visit or visits will take place at some point in the crisis. For the most part, when and how the site visit occurs is up to you, but you have no control over airborne camerapersons and photographers, or of access to sites adjacent to corporate property. However, you do have the obligation to know how these kinds of shots will look when broadcast or printed; thus, you need to be prepared for the questions these visuals will raise.

5.4.6 What to Do as the Media Come and Go

Reporters rarely all leave at one time. The greater the emergency, the more likely it is that you will be dealing with teams made up of rotating reporters.

1. **Debrief constantly.** Ask common sense questions about how well you are handling interviews. Evaluate whether your communications objectives were being achieved.

2. **Jot down key information about all interviews. Share interview results with others.** Your local Emergency Communication Team and the Corporate Emergency Communication Team should be briefed routinely on media contacts during emergency situations.

This information will allow these teams to help prepare you for future interviews. In addition, they may spot errors or inappropriate stories that need correction or follow-up.

3. **Follow up with the media only if appropriate or strategically important.** In most cases, it is not necessary to follow up with the news media. Doing your job during the interview is all that is needed. However, in some circumstances you will want to follow up. The most common situations are:

   ▶ Correction of reports based on information given during the interview.

   ▶ New data.

   ▶ New angle or previously unknown information.

   ▶ Correction of information poorly or incorrectly reported.

   ▶ Helpful information based on the story reported.

   ▶ Newly recognized strategic communications objectives.

4. **Manage mistakes.** Let mistakes pass unless there is a material victim- or litigation-related reason for contacting the news media to correct them. Discuss the mistakes with Public Affairs.

5.5 Surviving *60 Minutes* and the Other News Magazine Shows

Some national magazine-type news shows are revenue-producers for the networks and in syndication. There are many, many others locally produced.

5.5.1 Fourteen Lessons for Handling News Magazine Shows

> **Ignoring news magazine programs won't make them go away and may, in fact, actually stimulate more coverage.**

The broadcast news magazine format is well-established, and its impact on network news is demonstrated daily as "regular" news broadcasts become more tabloid-like in their feature stories as they compete for audiences having dozens of news source choices and formats (including their smart phones) each day.

Lesson 1: **Ignoring news magazine programs won't make them go away** and may, in fact, actually stimulate more coverage. These programs are big money-makers for the networks and command first use of resources and the best talent.

Lesson 2: **Some of these programs have enormous market power.** For example, *60 Minutes* has been one of the top five programs on television since it began more than 30 years ago.

Lesson 3:   **Some of these programs have no market power.** Therefore, avoid wasting time on those that can't or won't hurt you. Ask for a sample video of the program, or view it on the Web.

Lesson 4:   **Audiences, if they can, often act on the information they see.**

Lesson 5:   **People in all walks of life (including your employees) will be attracted by the flattering attention and talk to the producers or talent for such a show,** even if they realize that, ultimately, they could be harmed by the story. Why? The ego in each of us needs an audience from time to time.

Lesson 6:   **If a segment producer wants an interview with you, they will find a way.** Producers have been known to hire detective agencies and others to scout out story targets for ambush interviews. Make it easy for them – or, at the very least, rehearse for the ambush.

Lesson 7:   **If the subject is complex or the network needs litigation protection, the paid advisors to the producer may include the most highly respected outside consultants and university faculty.** Networks hire former insiders (even former insiders who have been tried and convicted for their crimes) as consultants to segment producers to assure the quality of the questions and the accuracy of the knowledge base. Everyone wants to be a news consultant, even if only once.

Lesson 8:   **The most damaging information or story points will come from individuals who work with you** or who have worked for you, from documents that never should have been written or studies that should never have been done, from hand-written notes in the margins of otherwise innocuous documents, or from the stupid, colorful, attention-getting words and statements the spokesperson just couldn't resist using.

Lesson 9:   **Be prepared to aggressively research, correct, clarify and comment on each area of inquiry.** Sometimes adequate proof can eliminate whole areas of questioning – but don't count on it.

Lesson 10: **New information or your righting of a wrong may not be persuasive enough to get the wrong information and subsequent damage to your reputation out of a segment.**

Lesson 11: **Someone always knows the truth of the allegations.** Find the truth no matter who knows it.

Lesson 12: **If bad news does air on one of these programs, get ready for more.** As unhappy former employees, customers, vendors, or others become aware of the story, they may come forward with "new information" they think the media should know. Someone in your organization knows who these unhappy people are. Locate these people, and be ready to counter their stories with the truth.

Lesson 13:   **Relentlessly manage the interview and preparation process:** Record, track, transcribe, respond, provide balance, and engage the producer.

Lesson 14:   **Sometimes these lessons work, sometimes they don't.**

> **For news magazine content... each story idea is evaluated against a formula that guarantees its audience.**

5.5.2 Six Key Tests for a News Magazine Show Story Concept

News magazine content sources are not the same as general news stories. Most general news stories come from the police blotter and other public sources, news sources, or reporters assigned to cover certain beats. For news magazine content, on the other hand, each story idea is evaluated against a formula that guarantees its audience. Before a story concept can advance into production, it must pass six key tests:

Test 1:   **Focus** – A black and white issue, easily identified philosophically or factually by the audience, i.e., right versus wrong, ethical versus unethical, etc.

Test 2:   **Viewpoint** – Pick a side that is clear, understandable, and stands for something the audience will care about. This means a clear, predetermined story outcome that the producer can go on to prove.

Test 3:   **Colorful characters** – Victims, individuals, and families, good and bad, whom the audience will want to hear about.

Test 4:   **Ambush opportunity** – Drama or at least the likelihood that someone in a position to add a dramatic component to the story can be "captured" in an exciting, embarrassing, humiliating, or at least dramatic situation.

Test 5:   **Trap questions** – These questions cause people to stop in their tracks and sweat, on-camera, close-up. Fear is a critical element in many news magazine shows.

Test 6:   **High level of emotional tension** – This tension is created through depicting conflict, controversy, confrontation, anger, sadness, or frustration that clearly come through to, or directly involve or threaten, the viewer.

5.5.3 Story Sources

Litigation is one of the most dynamic sources of material for news magazine shows. In some cases, the attorney for the plaintiff wants to get the story of a client or prospective client on the air, simply to bring pressure on the defendant(s) they are suing or intend to sue. In addition, the goal may well be to uncover other affected individuals who, in turn, could potentially become part of a much larger legal action, even a class action lawsuit. Today it's the uncontrollable, unedited, free-for-all Internet that has emerged as an excellent source of story ideas and sources.

5.5.4 Our Approach to News Magazine Shows

> Always express an interest in cooperating, but maintain a very realistic sense of skepticism based primarily on how news magazine shows "do in" their targets.

1. **Negotiate – get something for everything given.**

   Quite often, a fair amount of room exists to negotiate various issues, topics, even some of the questions that will be asked, especially true if you're the target of the story and the news magazine really needs your participation to make the story work. For example, if the producer needs certain information, ask for the request in writing along with a list of any other subjects he/she might want to talk about.

2. **Cooperative, but reluctant.**

   Always express an interest in cooperating, but maintain a very realistic sense of skepticism based primarily on how news magazine shows "do in" their targets. Ask to see recent segments produced by the same individual who is assigned to your story, preferably one segment that is a "positive" story and another that is a "negative" story.

3. **Rigorous, but circumspect.**

   Listen to representatives of the news magazine shows very carefully. Remember that they are not on a mission to help you or your organization. Instead, they are on a mission to prevent or protect victims, to detect or deter bad situations, to support and protect underdogs, and to entertain an audience already saturated by news shows.

   Keep good records. Log who calls, what is said, questions asked, and your responses. Pay very close attention; and write everything down. Record all interviews and conversations. Respond to all questions. Provide your own timeline for events.

4. Professional, but concerned.

Targets of news magazine coverage are often tempted to respond to information requests by developing voluminous amounts of background material and data and providing it in huge, tabbed, three-ring binders. Resist this urge. It is never about data; it is always about emotion and answering specific questions.

Put very little in writing. Verbalize most of your responses. Not only will your attorneys like this approach, but you will stay much more in control of the information that is flowing from you and your organization to the news magazine program.

> **Preparation is a surprise-reduction process.**

5. Message driven, but alert for more data.

Determine as quickly as possible the two or three critical messages or concepts you would like to get across repeatedly as a part of responding to the news magazine's specific area of inquiry. Be as pragmatic as you can in choosing your message topics. Clearly, if you've injured people or threatened their health and safety, no one will care about the basic goodness of your company or the number of awards it has won.

Address the issue raised or the area of concern as directly, positively, but humanely as possible. Put yourself in the viewer's shoes.

Be ready for the "surprise" fact or victim. There should be no question or issue that will truly surprise you or your organization. Yes, you can be embarrassed. Yes, you can be humiliated. Yes, you can get angry. But none of these situations are really surprises. You simply failed to prepare. Preparation is a surprise-reduction process.

6. Be alert.

These shows practice a very blatant ongoing deception with story subjects and targets. It is both obvious and subtle. Listen. When producers say they have talked to someone – which they rarely do – ask questions about the supposed interview. Find out what was learned or if they even reached the person they said they called. Often information will be purposely omitted to see what your response will be; your response can then be challenged based on the producer's fuller knowledge. Keeping you from knowing what they know is the most common form of deception. This treatment reflects what they really feel about you – not trustworthy, not honorable, anti-people, and probably guilty of something. It's the way they live, the way it is. Ask questions. Check out allegations. Respond appropriately, promptly. In reality, producers know very little.

7. Maintain perspective.

Remember that the news magazine show produces programs every week, day in and day out. Its employees are on a gut-level mission to save the world from something. This week it's you. Resist the urge to take anything about it personally – not the questions, not the situation, not the show's manner of handling them. That it is not personal is a very difficult concept to understand, but you must understand and believe it. They don't really care about what they are doing to you. It's just another story, another audience. It's what they do.

Maintaining perspective allows you to act professionally with some distance, and to stay focused on getting through the situation in the best possible fashion.

If your situation is bad, clumsy, stupid, careless, or criminal, the story will be bad. Your goal has to be to move through the process, suffering little, if any, additional damage and, with some luck, demonstrating how good an organization you have or how good an individual you are in the face of this incredibly difficult, highly visible situation.

> **Remember, contacting a reporter again brings with it very serious risks. Better techniques include corrections, clarification, and commentary.**

When You Are Asked for a Written Response...

In the wake of a series of very costly and depressing lawsuits, an eager young ABC producer – on the advice of counsel – wrote a letter to a target company that provided some specific questions, spelling out in advance each of the areas in which the show was interested, and asking for a written response.

Seeking to be responsive, the target company took the letter from the producer, analyzed it, and farmed out every part of it to the appropriate department, manager, and boss. From this input was assembled a multi-tabbed notebook containing responses and data that was then promptly sent back to the producer.

Needless to say, the producer was overwhelmed. He never expected to receive such a treasure trove of areas to investigate, substantiate, and cross-reference. The target company had opened up whole new areas of investigation and, as a result, a much tougher segment was produced – all because the target behaved in its normal, helpful way.

This story provides two lessons:

> ▶ The first is that while you need to develop information thoroughly, carefully, and completely for yourself, the frustrating challenge is to boil it all down into a very few words to be shared with the inquiring producer.

> ▶ The second is that the media does not know what you do not want to talk about until you tell them. It is the typical, enormous corporate data dump that provides unwanted questions and conflicts.

Corollary: Once you tell them what you do not want to talk about, that will be all they will want to talk about.

5.6 Assessing the Validity of News Stories

Journalism today is relentlessly competitive, amoral, aggressive, and negative. Survey after survey demonstrates the public's belief that reporters use deception and practice reckless destruction of reputation. News subjects need the criteria to judge the validity and believability of their news interview experience, the resulting stories, and of the behavior of the reporters who question them. Remember, contacting a reporter again brings with it very serious risks. Better techniques include corrections, clarification, and commentary, which is described later in this section.

Management is always looking for ways to validate or challenge what the news media is doing and needs the means to evaluate the validity and believability of stories as well as the professional behavior of reporters. Insight into and control over reporter behavior is an integral part of what spokespersons and interviewees provide. Reporter behavior often reflects the nature, character, volatility, and value of information received from spokespeople.

5.6.1 Lukaszewski's Validity/Believability Index Test Questions

The higher the score, the lower the believability and the probable validity of the news story, while a lower score would indicate a high degree of truthfulness. A score above 11 indicates the decreasing believability of a news story. Question reporters directly to test their believability and credibility and, therefore, the probability of the truthfulness of a story.

Lukaszewski's Validity/Believability Index Test

<u>Score</u>

		Yes	No
1.	Did the reporter personally witness what he/she is reporting about?	1　2　3	4　5

		Yes	No
2.	Did the reporter have any specific knowledge about the Topic prior to reporting about it?	1　2　3	4　5

		Yes	No
3.	Is the description and dialog of opposing views balanced, equal, and fair?	1　2　3	4　5

		Fair Biased	Unbal.
4.	Is the story clearly biased, unbalanced, or unfair?	1　2　3	4　5

		Few	Many
5.	How many emotionally charged, inflammatory, and negative words, phrases, or concepts are used?	1　2　3	4　5

		Truthful	Deceptive
6.	How do story content, direction, and perception square with what the reporter told interviewees?	1　2　3	4　5

		Some Too	Much
7.	How much "surprise" material was used during interviews?	1　2　3	4　5

			None
8.	How do the observations of others present at the same news event compare with and support the reporter's version?	1　2　3	4　5

		Few	Many
9.	How many anonymous sources are used?	1　2　3	4　5

		Respectful	Disrespectful
10.	Was the reporter insulting, overly suspicious or disrespectful?	1　2　3	4　5

		Yes	No
11.	Does the headline or promotion appropriately reflect the content of the story?	1　2　3	4　5

Truth is never the result of deception, disrespect, or insulting, aggressive reporter behavior even when your lack of preparation or unrealistic assessment of the situation seems to force the reporter to behave inappropriately. Insist on polite, courteous, professional behavior. Keep your temper in check.

5.6.2 Bad News: Assessing the Damage

If you determine that the company or spokesperson or topic has been wronged in a news story, you must decide what to do about it. Your decision should be based on the answers to the following questions:

▶ Is it important enough to correct or would a correction amount to nit picking?

▶ Just how damaging is the charge, criticism, or error?

▶ Will a correction simply give greater visibility to an opposite point of view?

▶ Is a correction worth a restatement of the entire situation, including the error, to new audiences?

▶ Is it possible to reach the identical audience originally exposed to the error?

▶ Did you respond promptly and accurately to the media inquiries that led to the story?

If after considering these elements, you decide to seek correction, clarification, or retraction, please remember the risks. The safest technique is always the Correction, Clarification, and Commentary approach.

Making Bad News Worse

Five sure-fire ways to make bad news even worse are to:

1. Lose your temper.

2. Phone or e-mail the offending medium and demand a meeting with management at which you threaten everything from withholding advertising to bodily harm.

3. Call the reporter and demand a retraction.

4. Attack the medium on your website.

5. Bring a lawsuit. However, remember the possible fallout – if you sue one medium, you have essentially sued them all.

5.6.3 What to Do and Avoid in Emergency Communication (Including Interviews)

DO	AVOID
▶ Maintain your composure.	▶ Speculating about anything.
▶ Provide information to authorities and the media as quickly as facts can be verified.	▶ Guessing at the cause.
	▶ Placing blame for the emergency.
▶ Be prompt with information about rescue and recovery operations.	▶ Guessing at people's injuries.
	▶ Attempting to estimate the dollar damage. (You are not the expert – work with local authorities on this.)
▶ Tell the truth.	
▶ When you don't know an answer, admit it. Then promise to get the information as quickly as possible and get it.	▶ Arguing with a reporter.
	▶ Saying: "No comment," "I'm not allowed to talk," "I can't tell you anything," "I don't have time to talk to you."
▶ Take the initiative in getting your information out.	
▶ Accompany media when they are on site.	▶ Playing favorites with reporters or between electronic vs. print media.
▶ Recognize media deadlines.	▶ Discussing anything "off-the-record."
▶ Use non-technical language.	
▶ Give all reporters covering an event equal access to facts and subject matter experts.	▶ Asking to see the reporter's story.
	▶ Expecting the community's trust. You must earn it.
▶ Set ground rules for reporters and enforce them.	
▶ Check back frequently with reporters to help them keep the facts straight.	
▶ Correct inaccuracies quickly.	
▶ Express sympathy.	
▶ Emphasize the positive while being candid about the negative.	

5.7 Understanding Journalists
A Cautionary Tale

According to Janet Malcolm (1990):

"Every journalist who is not too stupid or too full of himself to notice what is going on knows that what he does is morally indefensible. He is a kind of confidence man, preying on people's vanity, ignorance, or loneliness, gaining their trust and betraying them without remorse... On reading the article or book in question, [the source] has to face the fact that the journalist – who seemed so friendly and sympathetic, so keen to understand him fully, so remarkably attuned to his vision of things – never had the slightest intention of collaborating with him on his story but always intended to write a story of his own. The disparity between what seems to be the intention of an interview as it is taking place and what it actually turns out to have been in aid of always comes as a shock to the subject"(pp. 3-4).

5.7.1 Where Reporters Come From

It is important to have a positive but pragmatic understanding of who reporters are and where they come from. These insights help improve the media relations skills of the professional communicator as well as the knowledge of those whom he or she advises. Reporters are indeed unique individuals. Here, from a variety of perspectives, are some useful insights into who they are, how they work, and why they do what they do.

The Philosophic Spectrum

> The reporter is always looking for a story about something living. Most business people...give reports, summaries of data, and statistical analysis... The result is often needless miscommunication that produces poor stories and even worse, poor perceptions.

Reporters belong on the people side of the philosophic spectrum. The reporter is concerned about issues, problems, and situations that affect people, animals, and living systems. Many interview subjects come from the other side, the economic side, of the philosophic spectrum. This is the data/fact side. For reporters, it is always about the story, something with a plot, and a lesson, often at your expense. For business people, it is typically about the facts related to reports, sales, earnings and moving the merchandise. The power of this insight is to remember that the reporter is always looking for a story about something living. Most business people, when asked to provide information, give reports, summaries of data, and statistical analysis. These are dramatically different languages and approaches. The result is often needless miscommunication that produces poor stories and even worse, poor perceptions.

The difficulty is, of course, that few reporters care about the complexities of business. They are always interested in what is happening to people, animals, and living systems. The lesson for the spokesperson is that to be an effective communicator through the news media to the publics you wish to reach, verbal skills and habits must change. It is the spokesperson who must refine, refocus, redefine, and more carefully describe those things that are important to communicate. If the translation is left to the reporter, you may not be pleased with the results. What is printed in the newspaper and what appears on television or in other news media is the responsibility of the spokesperson. The reporter is fundamentally a gatherer of information for the medium that he/she represents. That raw material is then re-engineered, redesigned, and edited to fit both the medium's format and the news approach of a given organization. Keep in mind that this post-production is usually done by people who didn't attend your interview.

5.7.2 Establishing a Professional Relationship With Reporters

> Recognize that dealing with reporters is a fact of life and that the goal is to achieve communications objectives by getting the messages out as well as by being responsive to reporters.

Let's talk frankly about how we relate to reporters when they want to interview us. While several schools of thought exist, only the third truly serves our purposes and the public interest:

1. **One Way:** Tell it all; tell it fast; let the media figure it out.
2. **Another Way:** Try to be buddies; try to be friendly; try to build a relationship; try to appear as though you like reporters.
3. **The Best Way:** Establish a professional relationship; recognize that dealing with reporters is a fact of life and that the goal is to achieve communication objectives by getting newsworthy messages out and by being responsive to reporters.

The Five Caveats

What should be the nature of your relationship with reporters? The answer is simple. It should be professional based on five basic caveats:

1. Set objectives (have a reason for dealing with reporters).
2. Do your homework on reporters.
3. Do your homework on their medium.
4. Understand the nature of the relationship (you are always a story).
5. Establish your own internal ground rules and stick to them.

5.7.3 How Reporters Create Emotional Responses From Spokespersons

In analyzing hundreds of interviews over the last 30 years, I have catalogued the kinds of behaviors that reporters learn to use in interviews to trigger emotional quotes from spokespersons.

Learn to spot, overcome or ignore these reporter tactics:

- Accuse the interviewee of "anti-consumer" action (bias, exorbitant profits, neglect of handicapped and aged, hiding the truth, destroying the competition, bribery, etc.).
- Ask about some specific company failure.
- Ask for disagreement.
- Ask the interviewee for an opinion of competitor products or services.
- Ask the interviewee for a personal opinion on a controversial company policy.
- Ask the interviewee to respond to controversial or critical statements made by others in or out of the interviewee's organization.
- Attribute imaginary facts or data.
- Claim not to understand a technical or "company" answer.
- Confirm an answer, then misinterpret or misquote it.
- Demand an answer to questions the interviewee cannot or should not answer.
- Go on to another subject before interviewee is able to make a complete or positive reply to the first.
- Interrupt.
- On one subject, use several increasingly probing follow-up questions.
- Pose a tough, complex question for quick response.
- Put words into interviewee's mouth.
- Seek condemnation of another person's position.
- Shoot rapid-fire, hostile-sounding questions – pressing the interviewee's pace of answering.
- Solicit candid comments "off-the-record."
- State a non-truth or distortion as fact or inside information in order to get a reaction.

5.7.4 Assessing the Validity of News Stories
Executive Attitudes About the Media

Negative reporter behaviors – all of which we observe in the news media each day – shape executive attitudes about the news media and reporters and affects their willingness to do interviews. I've monitored and studied these attitudes over the years through formal surveys and ongoing coaching of executives. My research shows executives are generally suspicious of the media. This is how they characterize reporters:

▶ Anti-business.
▶ Avoiding common sense.
▶ Cover only bad news.
▶ Fail to do homework.
▶ Fail to follow up.
▶ Fail to repair the damage they do.
▶ Ignorant about business and technology.
▶ Inaccurate.
▶ Intentionally hurt people.
▶ Intimidate people.
▶ Invade people's privacy.
▶ Oversimplify.
▶ Report events differently than other eyewitnesses.
▶ Sensationalize just about everything.
▶ Sometimes display unpatriotic attitudes.

Media Attitudes about Executives and Business People

Fair is fair. Interestingly enough, the media have attitudes of their own. When I talk to reporters about business people they respond candidly, making five specific criticisms of executives. Reporters think executives are:

1. Dull.
2. Inaccessible.
3. Late.
4. Not understandable.
5. Callous, uncaring about people.

Three powerful forces shape the attitude of the media about business and business people:

1. Their interaction with executives through the interview process.
2. Their interaction with business organizations through public relations and communication representatives who serve as spokespersons.
3. The enormous disparity in power, influence, and wealth between business and the remainder of the community and victims.

Reporters have an internal sense about business people. That feeling tells them that business people:

▶ Are arrogant and self-serving.

- Are hostile to reporters and their questions.
- Don't care about people very much.
- Don't know that reporters don't write headlines or have complete control of the length or content of their stories.
- Don't know what news is.
- Don't permit free access.
- Don't trust the media.
- Don't understand that the culture of the newsroom conditions which cause reporters to have little use for colleagues whose copy flatters the people they write about.
- Don't want to accept the fact that embarrassment and conflict are almost always newsworthy.
- Expect reporters to know how businesses operate.
- Refuse to accept that, though possibly unfair, the media has complete power to set the agenda and define what news is.
- Refuse to understand that if the reporter thinks there is trouble, there is trouble.

These insights are important because they help us know what news really is and how we can be more newsworthy.

5.7.5 Reporters Need to Emotionalize
Color Words

> **How reporters emotionalize stories boils down to a specific collection of emotionally charged words... to generate what, for the purposes of their stories, are better, more colorful answers.**

Perhaps the greatest reason that interaction with reporters requires so much caution and preparation is the relentless, negative emotionalism that reporters build into their questions, as they attempt to create news which can survive the competition in an increasingly negative marketplace. Analysis of how reporters emotionalize stories boils down to a specific collection of emotionally charged words reporters have learned to use in order to generate what, for the purposes of their stories, are better, more colorful answers. I call them *color words*, and they are the reporter's secret weapons. Over the years I've collected this list of color words from actual interviews. As you read them, you'll get that belly-twisting feeling:

Color Words

Afraid	Defective	Harassed	Rotten
Aggravate	Demean	Harmful	Sabotage
Alarmed	Deny	Hateful	Sad
Alleged	Despair	Hopeless	Sarcastic
Anger	Desperation	Hostile	Scared
Angry	Despicable	Humiliated	Scum
Anguish	Destroy	Hurt	Self-pity
Antagonize	Destructive	Idiot	Selfish
Anxious	Deteriorate	Ignorant	Sham
Apathetic	Disappointed	Immature	Shame
Appalled	Disarray	Incompetent	Shameful
Apprehensive	Discontented	Inept	Shatter
Argue	Discouraged	Investigate	Sick
Arrogant	Disdain	Inappropriate	Silly
Ashamed	Disgusted	Irritated	Skunk
Assassinate	Dismiss	Litigate	Slander
Attack	Disrespect	Mad	Slash
Awful	Distorted	Mangled	Sloppy
Bad	Distraught	Mangy	Stampede
Betrayed	Disturbed	Manipulate	Struggle
Blame	Doubt	Mean	Stupid
Blasted	Duplicity	Meek	Surrender
Bombs	Ecotage	Messy	Tampering
Bored	Embarrassed	Minimize	Tarnish
Botched	Embattled	Miserable	Tense
Brainwashed	Endanger	Monopoly	Terrible
Bungled	Enraged	Nag	Terrified
Buried	Evil	Negligent	Terror-stricken
Catastrophic	Eviscerate	Out-of-touch	Terrorized
Collusion	Excessive	Overwhelmed	Threatened
Conceal	Exaggerate	Outrageous	Toxic
Confused	Exposed	Painful	Tragic
Contempt	Fascinating	Panicky	Traitor
Corrosive	Face-saving	Petrified	Tumultuous
Cover-up	Fearful	Pitiful	Ugly
Cringe	Fight	Poisonous	Unbelievable
Critical	Foolish	Profiteering	Underhanded
Crooked	Frightened	Questionable	Undermine
Curious	Frustrating	Regret	Uneasy
Damaging	Furious	Repudiate	Unhappy
Danger	Gratuitous	Resentful	Unsure
Deadly	Greed	Resigned	Weird
Defeated	Guilty	Rip-off	Worried

Power Words: The Antidote to Color Words and Mistakes

For the spokesperson, the antidote to color words is power words. These are words with attention-getting power that, when verbalized, focus the listener on what you want to talk about minus the emotional belly-grabbing capacity of color words. These power words are control techniques to use whenever confronted by reporters using color words or emotionally charged phrases.

Power Words			
Critical	Exciting	Legitimize	Tense
Crucial	Fascinating	New	Tough
Different	Great	Normal	Unique
Emphasize	Helpful	Powerful	Unusual
Empathize	Hopeful	Prioritize	Urgent
Energize	Important	Strong	Useful
Enthusiastic	Interesting	Surprised	Valuable

5.7.6 How Reporters Probe for Information

Each reporter's style is different. In addition to using emotion-laden words to develop very frightening questions, reporters have learned to ask simple, direct questions. These questions, when written down, don't seem all that difficult, but when they are spoken during an interview, they have the tendency to be threatening and destabilizing. I call it *probing for information*. Here's how reporters do it.

They ask for clarification:

▶ "Can you be more specific?"

▶ "Exactly what do you mean?"

▶ "What else?"

▶ "What do you mean by that?"

They ask for justification:

▶ "How did you get to that?"

▶ "Why do you have to do it at all?"

▶ "Is that all there is to it?"

▶ "What if it were your husband, wife, or child?"

▶ "What would your critics say?"

They refocus the question:

▶ "If I said _____ what would you say?"

▶ "If I know that (name) said _____, what would you say?"

▶ "If that's so, what about...?"

▶ "How would you relate that to this...?"

They translate you:

- "So, if you say that, then what you mean is...Right?"
- "I thought you'd really be angrier about..."

They put words in your mouth:

- "You sound frustrated. Why?"
- "This must really disturb you, how much?"
- "I hear a lot of anger in your voice, at whom?"

The Most Common Mistakes Reporters Make (Intentionally)

> Saving the world from something every day is not the recipe for personal happiness because it is a goal that is basically unachievable.

1. **Lack of preparation.** It's only in such programs as *Frontline, 60 Minutes, I-team Investigations*, and the like that reporters do substantial amounts of homework, or have staff assistance before they get to do stories.

2. **Failing to understand the business.** Since the typical reporter may be working on two or more stories a day, which may equate to as many as a thousand stories a year, it's pretty tough for the reporter to understand anyone's business in any depth at all.

3. **Apply the "Rule of 298."** An example of this would be if your business already services 298 out of 300 possible customers, the story would not be how successful you were in marketing your service, but the problems you were having in securing those last two customers.

4. **Suspect everyone.** Yes, and they're always basically unhappy and unsatisfied as well. Saving the world from something every day is the recipe for personal unhappiness because world-saving is a goal that is rarely achievable. This level of motivation means they are also always working, lurking, and watching for news to occur.

5. **Deceive to bully and surprise.** Spokespersons are often surprised by questions in interviews. Spokespersons take the questions at face value and make assumptions about the truthfulness of the reporter. For example, when the reporter says they've talked to someone, the spokesperson assumes they've had a robust conversation. Usually it means they reached them on the phone briefly and got transferred somewhere else. Or they'll say so-and-so, someone you know, told them to speak with you. Again, the assumption is made that there were instructions and that what the reporter is asking about has some relationship to the person just named. It rarely does. And, the old bully technique of getting angry with a spokesperson if answers seem too evasive or nonresponsive.

Be Very Cautious About Becoming a News Source.

There is a critical misnomer among communicators which tends to mislead those we work for. This is the notion of building relationships with reporters. For those of you who are former reporters, and many communicators do come from journalism, if you think back to your journalism days, I would be very surprised if you felt that you had "relationships" with PR people or any potential source of news. In fact, you treated those who were your sources as just that, sources. In our zealotry to convince our bosses that we can offer something extra in the communication exchange, that extra being a reporter relationship, we are perhaps, inadvertently misleading them.

Becoming a news source is a very serious decision. You have to know what you're doing. The most important fact being *once a source, always a source.* Attorneys generally have the greatest misunderstanding and reporters play off of their love of speaking about the law to get information from them as a news source. The lawyer tends to think that they have special treatment because they "have a relationship" with a reporter. Be candid with those you advise so that they know what their options are. The best advice of all is to simply be on-the-record with what you intend to say. For those things you never intend to say, remain silent.

5.8 Bad News: How to Recognize and Deal with It

The worst thing about bad news is that it ripens badly. And bad news generally leads to bad stories. A variety of techniques we've talked about already, and will talk about in the succeeding chapters, can help you more promptly get your information out and challenge, correct or clarify the bad news that crises tend to create. Increasingly significant bad news will redefine the career or careers of those in charge.

There are four crucial reasons for aggressively dealing with bad news, including talking about it yourself even before it becomes the subject of media coverage and analysis:

1. Being the first to tell those who need to know about your situation, before they hear it from others, is a trust builder. If there's one thing we know about the damage of crisis situations, our silence makes them trust-busters.

2. Since reporters generally cover crises situations in ways that are completely predictable, your early announcements combined with a strategic analysis of the implications and circumstances (see Correction, Clarification and Commentary) allows you to manage the story from the very beginning rather than waiting to see what the journalist might pick out as key points to focus on. The techniques we talk about throughout this book are ways to help you manage your destiny. And if there's one thing we know for sure, if you fail to manage your own destiny, there is someone out

there, a journalist, a bloviator, a blogger, an angry employee or neighbor, to manage your destiny for you.

3. These early and helpful information sharing strategies tend to detoxify even the worst of stories, if done sensibly, sincerely, in positive language, offering constructive, useful information.

4. The most powerful communication you will be doing in crisis is that which takes place between you and your constituencies and stakeholders, directly. The strategic use of a website and the powerful and speedy access your web-based responses provide, will begin to script all audiences, including the media. The reason is simple: in crisis, nobody – not even the perpetrator – knows really what's happening for some time. It is the early information that tends to dominate future coverage and future commentary.

Balance and Accuracy, the YoYo Factor

In 30 years, I have seen only one satisfactory correction by a news outlet, and that was because the reporter was arrested and jailed for hacking an executive's e-mail. If you want a satisfactory correction, remember the yo-yo factor... you're on your own.

When it comes to balance and accuracy, you're on your own (the yo-yo factor). I generally advise avoiding asking for corrections, letters to the editor, or even op-ed pieces or special blog commentaries. If you act preemptively when you know you have bad news, as we spoke of in the last section, coupled with an aggressive, web-based correction, clarification and commentary strategy on your website, combined with preemptively distributed messages to your constituencies, employees, stakeholders and others, you are going to find yourself in much more control of the story, and much more in control of the interpretation of the coverage.

In journalism today you have zero recourse for forcing corrections or clarifications. There are still one or two operating News Councils in the United States, but they really will not help you. The bottom line recommendation they make is to find a sympathetic reporter and do a news story about your concerns or your umbrage or your dissatisfaction. Clearly, this is a pretty lame approach, but reflects all media's reluctance to correct mistakes, or to apologize. Even when the media is operating at their worst, which usually involves mass casualty situations, there is never an apology, never a concern for their impact on the lives of others. The *New York Times* is the classic example. Early in this century, they hired a consultant to analyze their databases to determine the level of errors, mistakes and wrong information. It was significant. There is a report available through their website. However, after a very brief period, less than a day, they decided that rather than clean their database, it was more important to leave the errors in place, apparently so that they would never miss an opportunity to pummel some unsuspecting news subject. When your job is saving the world, and in America you have a

Constitutional Amendment that essentially says journalists can do this without many, if any, restrictions, rules or regulations, the responsibility for balance and accuracy is yours rather than the reporter's. One of the most important ingredients of your media relations strategy in crisis is preparing from the very beginning to maintain the balance, accuracy and credibility of your behavior and actions with your constituencies directly, rather than through traditional or new media channels.

To Sue or Not to Sue

I always recommend against clients suing a news medium. If you sue one, you wind up having every other media outlet acting as though they too are being sued. Filing a really aggressive, provocational, angry complaint gets you or your client about fifteen minutes of relief, and comfort. The blowback, which is inevitable, will cost someone high up in the organization their career, make you look truly foolish to those people who expect better of you, and generally makes your bad news exponentially worse.

National Consumer Center
Federal Communications Commission
445 Twelfth Street, S.W.
Washington, D.C. 20554
(888) 225-5322

Chapter 5 – Questions for Study and Discussion

1 What would you say are the three most important things to include in a media relations policy? Why?

2 How does a good spokesperson handle an error – that is, incorrect information that was given out to the press?

3 What is a "dark site"? Why have one? What is the best time to set one up?

4 Since news is supposedly factual, why is the emotional side important? How can this emotional side hurt the coverage of your organization's story? How can a spokesperson cooperate with the press in filling this need without sacrificing accuracy?

5 When your company has been wronged in a news story, what is the best way to set the record straight (without making things worse)?

References, Chapter 5

Malcolm, J. (1990). *The journalist and the murderer* (pp. 3-4). New York: Vintage Books.

6

Crisis Communication Plan in Action: The Crisis News Conference

Keywords::news briefing, news backgrounder, off the record, on the record, killer questions, bridging, complexity-to-process, pyramid-like answers

The news conference remains an effective way to communicate when a crisis occurs; you must especially manage many reporters and a great deal of often-conflicting information. The successful crisis news conference requires planning and preparation, even when there is little time. This section provides useful, checklist approaches to the process of executing successful crisis-related news conferences.

This chapter will help you to:

> Determine whether you need a news conference at a particular point in the crisis.

> Choose the medium for the conference.

> Plan every detail of managing the conference.

> Prepare to give good answers to any kind of questions.

6.1 Preparing For the Crisis News Conference

6.1.1 When to Hold a News Conference

Successful news conferences have similar and important components. This checklist will help you decide whether a news conference is a useful approach for your crisis, even it satisfies the press only temporarily.

A news conference should be held when:

▶ Your situation is absolutely newsworthy.

▶ Your situation or issue would be time-consuming to explain to reporters individually.

▶ The issue is so large and so many potential reporters and news organizations are involved that a news conference is the only economical means of communicating with the media and your audiences, at least initially.

▶ You have considered both the strengths, weaknesses and strategy of using the news conference as an effective communication strategy.

There are pluses and minuses to news conferences. Here are some of the more important pros and cons:

1. *News Conference Negatives:*

   ▶ Reporters practice but complain about pack journalism.

   ▶ There is no assurance that reporters will ask useful questions.

   ▶ Follow-up questions can dominate the conference.

   ▶ Print and broadcast reporters have different needs, methods, goals, and objectives.

   ▶ Reporters will not be satisfied and will continue to push for individual interviews.

   ▶ Your event may be broadcast simultaneously by many reporters present.

2. *News Conference Positives:*

   ▶ You do exercise some message control, if you are really ready.

   ▶ You gather all interested reporters in one room at the same time.

   ▶ Your responses saturate rather than trickle out.

   ▶ Your story is told more closely to the way that you want it told.

   ▶ You control the lines of inquiry because of the number of reporters. No other situation allows this kind of coverage control.

   ▶ You may meet reporters you might never meet otherwise.

6.1.2 Types of Crisis News Conferences

There are three formats for dealing with many news media – *news conferences, briefings,* and *backgrounders.*

News Conference

A news conference is a structured meeting in which many news media are represented. In very dramatic cases dozens to hundreds of media representatives can be present. The goal of the news conference is to answer questions and get messages across to many different media at the same time.

The standard format of the news conference is pretty recognizable. Usually there are one or two spokespersons. They may or may not have prepared statements that define the scope of the topics the news conference will cover. The basic format after opening comments is Q&A.

News Briefing

A news briefing is a structured open meeting where complex information is presented, explained, and provided to the media verbally and in writing. Many individuals from the organization may be available and prepared to talk with the news media – either by making presentations or simply by answering reporters' questions. T here usually is an opening statement or summation. Virtually anything said at the briefing is on-the-record and available for use by the news media.

News Backgrounder

A media backgrounder is a fairly structured meeting to which only specific media are invited to attend and participate. The information presented at such meetings is given on the promise by the media that it will neither be used in a story nor attributed to the source of the information. The purpose of the backgrounder is to give reporters proprietary or crucial information that must be kept confidential but that they need in order to cover a specific story, problem, or issue.

> If it is a secret that matters, it will get out... The best briefings are those that are on-the-record. If it truly is a secret, keep still.

The backgrounder is the most difficult mass media encounter to execute successfully because security is difficult. The media may or may not actually agree to keep the information shared in total confidence. Most of all, news managers are frustrated by having information they cannot use. Be very careful with this format. The reporter's first impulse is to get what they hear on the record, somehow, promptly.

Avoid off-the-record backgrounders. If it is a secret that matters, it will get out even if reporters have to attribute comments – that you thought were private – to an anonymous source. The best briefings are those that are on-the-record. If it truly is a secret, keep still.

6.1.3 News Conference Techniques

Telephone/Skype

The telephone is used increasingly because of its instant availability, convenience, and real-time value. Limitless ports are available through dozens of service providers. Telephone-type conferences are usually one-way where the reporter e-mails or texts questions, which are responded to, hopefully, in real time as well.

The "analyst call" technique can also be used. In this format, an operator assists the person who convenes the teleconference by serving as the contact point during the call for listeners who want to be put in a queue from which they can ask a question in real time. All parties to the call hear participant questions along with the spokesperson's response.

Mass call providers today offer three kinds of teleconferencing services:

1. **Hosted, one-way, listen-only call** in which participants simply dial a designated number, are greeted by an operator, and placed in a queue until the conference call begins.
2. **Fully automated conference call** in which no operators are involved, the host notifies participants of the call-in numbers (which have been selected by a computer), and time of the call by e-mail or another convenient means. The call proceeds without any telephone company intervention.
3. **Operator-assisted call** in which an operator notifies participants, starts the call, stays on the line, and takes question requests from participants. The operator either queues questioners on a first-come basis or queues callers in the order suggested by the teleconference convener. Using this format you can control which questions get asked and in which order.

> The goal is twofold: a better-educated reporter and a better chance of the news conference resulting in the stories that reflect your desired messages.

e-Conferences

The Internet has become a useful tool for news conferences. So-called e-conferences have revolutionized the news conference. This format not only permits excellent back-and-forth between reporters and subjects, but also allows the use of a variety of media, examples, and prepared material. Reporters may make specific requests, and responses can be e-mailed back immediately, even while the e-conference is in progress.

What sets the e-conference apart is that reporters not only can "attend" from their desks or another convenient location of their choice, but they can also be transported electronically to other locations and sites to look at and ask questions about what is happening on that scene, or to get information from other resources. The goal is twofold: a better-educated reporter and a better chance of the news conference resulting in the stories that reflect your desired messages.

Webcast/Webstreaming

Streaming technology is improving and is becoming a dominant crisis response methodology. For example, most investment houses now have literally non-stop telecasting from their broker floors – either to various news outlets or to networks of their own viewers, listeners, and customers. The content is edited and broadcast to traditional television channels.

6.1.4 News Conference Planning Checklists

Setting Communications Objectives

Here is a procedure for identifying your communication objective and defining the messages that you need to convey.

Step 1: Write out your communication objective for the news conference in up to 150 words (about one minute of speaking time) each.

Step 2: Try to state, in a sentence or two each, up to three really important messages or themes about the topic or subject of your news conference.

Step 3: Say your communication objective and your messages out loud (rehearse) and refine the language so that you can say them comfortably and often.

Step 4: Draft your second or third communication objective as described in step 1 and develop messages as described in steps 2 and 3.

Achieving a single communication objective supported by a handful of messages is a major accomplishment in the brief time you will have available in the crisis news conference. The purpose for constructing the language and the words in the way described here is that they become a script. No matter what happens during the news conference in terms of questions or answers, you will always be able to come back to your scripted communication objective and messages.

The Opening Statement

Once you have completed the development of your communication objective, drafting your opening statement becomes relatively easy. Nevertheless, here are the attributes of a good opening statement:

▶ Up to 150 words in length (one minute of speaking time).

▶ Positive words and language.

▶ Packaged or bundled key ideas in groupings of three facts, five ideas, four key thoughts, etc.

▶ Constructed to generate specific and positive follow-up questions first.

▶ Stands on its own and gives complete information (who, what, why, where, when, and how).

▶ Creates the positive perception you seek from reporters and, therefore, from their readers, viewers, and listeners.

▶ Contains benefits to the reporters and their audiences beyond the features of the topic or reason for which you are having the news conference.

Preparation

Learn to relax in intense circumstances. Focused preparation, proper diaphragmatic breathing, and tension releasing exercises can reduce stress. Before you move into the news conference area, try some sequential isometric exercises beginning in the lower part of your body and then moving upward to your neck muscles, loosening or tightening muscle groups in sequence.

Use a voice or video recorder to rehearse your statements, ideas, and messages out loud. Listen to yourself. Be self-critical. Edit the language. Make it sound like you. The more time you truly rehearse out loud, the better you're likely to be in-person in front of the microphone.

Set Ground Rules

Ground rules outline what will be permitted and what will not be permitted along with what is expected of the presenter(s) and of the reporters who attend the news conference. Typical examples of ground rules relate to the:

▶ Time the news conference starts.

▶ Time the news conference ends.

▶ Location of the news conference.

▶ Topics to be covered (without having to state the topics that cannot be covered).

▶ Availability of other spokespersons to clarify issues and topics raised during the news conference.

▶ Media who will be admitted.

▶ Admission of other interested individuals including opponents or competitors.

▶ Time when information from the news conference can be released (so long as the timing is reasonable).

▶ Number of questions and follow-up questions each reporter can ask.

▶ Order in which reporters will be permitted to ask questions and their follow-up questions.

▶ Availability of presenters for follow-up interaction with reporters at the conclusion of the news conference.

▶ Granting of individual interviews by telephone or in person following the news conference.

> **Lay down the rule immediately that you will deal with only one reporter or one contact person on all issues until things settle down and you can be more accommodating.**

6.2 Guidelines for Calling andConducting News Conferences

Here are guidelines for assembling an effective news conference.

Step 1: *Notification*

▶ Notify the media you want to attend.

  ❏ Identify and notify the right media representatives.

  ❏ Communicate the logistics for the news conference (time, day, place, people involved).

  ❏ Accomplish the notification by:

    ◆ E-mail electronic invitation tools, like C-vent

    ◆ In-person

    ◆ Internet

    ◆ News advisory

    ◆ News release

    ◆ Telephone

  ❏ Note responses, e.g., will attend, might attend, want to attend but can't, won't attend, not interested in your organization or your story.

  ❏ Follow up systematically. For example: For "want to attend but can't," provide for getting the story to that person either by going to them, supplying printed or recorded material, or otherwise identifying and responding to his/her needs.

❑ Advise the media of your accommodations:
- ◆ Lighting availability (should they bring their own?)
- ◆ Parking for trucks and other vehicles
- ◆ Telephone/audio feed availability/technology

❑ Update and refine your notification list and system throughout the process.

In the crisis situation it's essential to notify each news medium that it may send only a single reporter or crew. Often in serious situations – multiple homicides, fires, riots, explosions – coverage will be via team. Team coverage means that more than one reporter will be assigned to the same story, which means major media outlets will require enormous amounts of your time. Lay down the rule immediately that you will deal with only one reporter or one contact person on all issues until things settle down and you can be more accommodating.

Step 2: *The News Conference Setting*

If you choose to hold a news conference the minimum requirements are:

▶ Facility or room large enough to comfortably accommodate everyone who will be invited or is expected and their equipment. If the room is on an upper floor, make certain there is an elevator.

▶ Electrical power sufficient to accommodate television lights and other AC-powered broadcast equipment.

▶ Sound system appropriately placed and tested so that attendees can hear, but so that there is no feedback (that annoying high-pitched squeal).

▶ Printed handout material (a necessity), also available on the web.

▶ Video handout material (optional), also available on the web.

▶ Audio handout material (optional), also available on the web.

▶ Proper visual background that identifies your organization and supports your messages.

▶ Contact names, locations, and telephone numbers for facility staff should problems arise.

▶ Directions/maps to the news conference location.

▶ Website for back-up information; place to review the news conference. List of questions and your answers to them on the web as soon as possible.

Step 3:　*Location and Physical Requirements*

▶ Choose a location advantageous to your message and near the site of the crisis situation.

▶ Select a carpeted room. Carpeting eliminates extraneous foot noise and also makes for better acoustics. A room with carpeting, draperies, and other fabrics produces better sound for radio and television crews, and live blog feeds.

▶ Draperies should be closed to eliminate glare.

▶ Plenty of chairs should be easily available and positioned in such a manner as to provide a center aisle. Depending on the market, a good rule of thumb for determining the number of chairs is:

　❐ Television: up to three chairs – one for the reporter, one for the cameraperson, and perhaps one for the audio person.

　❐ Print: up to two chairs – one for the reporter and one for a photographer.

　❐ Radio: generally one chair for the reporter.

▶ Test the public address system to make sure everyone can hear. (Bring your own.)

▶ Get a multi-box unit to distribute input to multiple microphone outputs for equipment to be plugged in. Increasingly reporters and/or news conferences have local hot spots in the news conference so people can connect easily and wirelessly.

▶ A lectern should be positioned at the front of the room.

▶ A water container and glasses should be placed near the podium.

▶ The company or organization's name or logo should either be high on the podium or on the wall to one side of the speaker.

▶ A table for handout information should be located near the door.

▶ A table for light refreshments should be positioned in the back of the room.

▶ Make arrangements with facility management to have maintenance and catering staff available in case of problems (audio problems, blown fuses, too few chairs, empty coffee urns, etc.)

▶ If the event is in a building with a paging system, have it turned off or down during the news conference.

Step 4: *Placement of Reporters*

▶ The site should accommodate special needs of the electronic media. A room with built-in television lights is preferable. If one is not available, check with maintenance staff to make certain that the electrical service will handle at least a 3000-watt draw. Make sure the room has plenty of electrical outlets.

▶ While television crews generally like to place their cameras near the front of the room (but far enough back so they can get a wide shot of the participants), it is usually advisable to position all TV cameras on risers at the back of the room. Television reporters like to sit next to their cameraperson so that when a reporter's question is answered, the respondent is looking at that station's camera.

▶ Radio reporters (unless there is a central multi-box) like to be near the front of the room so they can be near their recorders. However, they are generally satisfied as long as they are allowed to get good audio.

▶ Print reporters may use electronic equipment and can be seated almost anywhere.

▶ Avoid favoritism. Be professional. Offer people whatever help they need.

Step 5: *Handout Materials*

One single person must *read thoroughly* all materials for content, duplication, and errors before they are given to the media.

▶ Opening statement(s) and other relevant materials. Offer to e–mail versions to media newsrooms.

▶ E-news packet (as opposed to a "press kit"). All available on flash drive. These four items:

  ❏ Suggested questions and answers. Also available on the website.

❐ Fact sheet about company or organization. Also available on the website.

❐ Bio or other pertinent info about participants. Also available on the website.

❐ Appropriate photographs and B-roll availability. Also available on the website.

▶ Post all handouts on your website as the news conference begins or as early as feasible.

> Television and radio crews will most likely arrive early so they can set up their equipment. Use this setup time to get to know what is driving their news coverage.

Step 6: *Accommodations/Site Logistics*

▶ Expect reporters to arrive early, on time, or late. Television and radio crews will most likely arrive early so they can set up their equipment. Use this setup time to get to know what is driving their news coverage.

▶ Be prepared for reporters who ask if they can speak privately with the participants following the news conference. Generally, all they want is more detailed information on a specific point.

▶ On occasion a radio or television station may arrive late, or there may be an equipment malfunction. If either of these happens, you may be asked to repeat the opening statement or to answer a question again. Accommodate these requests if at all possible.

Step 7: *Accommodations Appreciated When Provided but Not Necessary*

▶ **Lights:** A lighting system is cumbersome for TV people to carry. Meeting facilities that cater to the news conference business have built-in lights or have portable lights available. Provide lights, if possible. Television crews will be grateful.

▶ **Multi-box:** This electronic unit allows for a central feed of the audio. The microphone on the podium is plugged into the multi-box. No other microphone is placed on the podium. Both television and radio stations then plug into the box. It is advantageous because everyone gets high quality audio, and microphone clutter on the podium is eliminated, thereby allowing a clear picture of the news conference presenter(s).

Most companies that rent sound equipment have multiplex audio systems available, as do most larger hotels.

▶ **Telephone audio feed system:** These systems, available from telephone companies, allow radio people to assemble their story on the spot and feed broadcast quality sound to their newsroom or direct to the world.

Step 8: *News Conference Details*

▶ The optimal time for a news conference is the moment there is news to be conveyed.

▶ Check with the local wire services (the AP and/or UPI daybooks) for competing news events.

▶ During crises the scheduling of news conferences is always a strategic communications decision. Schedule more and conduct them frequently in the beginning. As the crisis eases, you can begin to let more time elapse between news conferences. The greater the catastrophe, the greater the number of news conferences you are going to have to do because the media will make it look like a catastrophe anyway.

6.3 Conducting the News Conference

Step 1: *Determining Who Should Represent Your Company at the News Conference*

Some companies or organizations make the mistake of having too many people available, while others have too few. We recommend a maximum of three speakers at a news conference. You can use more if there is adequate time to carefully rehearse each participant.

▶ One should be a generalist. Someone who can answer companywide questions and can begin the news conference.

▶ The other one or two should be experts on the product or situation so that every question receives at least a partial answer.

▶ When there will be more than one spokesperson extra rehearsals are mandatory.

Step 2: *Setting the Scene*

A designated individual should begin the news conference process by introducing him/herself along with those involved in the news conference, and explaining which areas each will talk about. Reporters should be told how long the news conference will last, what the handouts are and what they mean, what additional information will be available at a later time, and exactly how the news conference is going to proceed – including who is going to say what and which individuals are going to answer questions on specific topics.

News conferences should last only 30 minutes. Usually by that time all the questions of importance will have been asked. Very few reporters will object to this limitation. If more time is needed, you might take a 15-minute break, then go on for another 15 or 20 minutes.

The mechanism for ending the news conference should also be explained and adhered to. Ask radio and television reporters if they are ready for the news conference to begin. Brief delays are common because of the time needed to set up electronic equipment. However, we recommend that you not delay the start of the news conference for more than five minutes. Introduce each principal involved in the news conference. You can assure latecomers that they will be given an opportunity to retake opening statements at the end of the news conference.

Step 3: *Making the Opening Statement*

The opening statement at the news conference should be done in a concise, simple manner. It should be no longer than 30 seconds (75 words) so that broadcasters can use it in its entirety.

The prepared spokesperson organizes facts in a pyramid style, starting with the most important information, the way reporters do. He/she puts the event in context (for example, that only three of 400 employees were involved) and casts a positive light on the company's safety practices. He/she speaks in terms that newspaper readers and television viewers can understand. This controls at least the opening portion of the news conference.

The opening statement should be available to everyone prior to the beginning of the news conference, and posted on your crisis website as the news conference begins. Also post other useful information and the handout that will be provided at the news conference. When it's as newsy as this one is, reporters will probably opt to video or audio tape it and even if the rest of the news conference produces nothing, at least they will have this tight, useful statement to use immediately.

Step 4: *Handling the Question and Answer Period*

After the opening statement ask for questions. Be sure that you have written the statement in a way that will elicit the questions you want to be asked.

The speakers should stand behind a lectern. Ideally, there should be two public address system microphones, one on each side of the speaker, so that no matter which way he/she turns, he/she is always on microphone. If the speaker gives way to a second or third speaker, the original participant should move away from the lectern so the next person can be on microphone. It is very important that anyone addressing the media speak into the microphones.

Step 5: *Closing the News Conference*

After principals have finished their statements and reporters have finished their questions, or the time announced for the end of the news conference arrives, the person who opened the news conference should stand up and thank the media for coming and remind them about handout materials, follow up, the next briefing, etc.

Offer to remain behind to handle news media questions on an individual basis. If news conference principals can't stay behind following the conclusion of the news conference, the reporters should be so informed at the start of the news conference and be given information on how to contact principals later – at work or at home.

6.4 The Questions You Can Expect

6.4.1 Question Types

In my experience, reporter questions can be categorized into three types:

1. *Killer questions* – those you never, ever really want to respond to but may be forced to, questions that irritate, agitate, or humiliate.

2. ***Questions you would love to respond to, if only someone would ask them*** – questions that would illustrate, illuminate, or otherwise demonstrate the truths you are attempting to get across.

3. *Google questions* – a crucial part of your preparation will involve searching for your name, the company, the issue, and related information that is now so readily available on the Web.

The value of gathering information to respond to common questions is the ease with which it can be translated immediately into the interview preparation process. The preparation process itself has four principal phases, each one revolving around the types of questions that are likely to be asked by the reporter or likely to emerge based on the directions the interview may follow. Let's take a look at each component one at a time.

> Simply listening to what you say in meetings, on the telephone, or in rehearsals for presentations and interviews helps you self-coach in ways that demonstrate immediate and constant improvement in your technique.

Killer Questions

Preparing for killer questions requires four preparation steps:

Step 1: *List the killer questions*, those questions that are humiliating, embarrassing, frightening, or that make you angry. Write them out in aggressively negative language. Remember, the last time you want to hear these questions asked this way for the first time is during the news interview itself. Most organizations can identify probably a dozen or fewer of these truly killer questions. But every organization, every issue, every product, every individual circumstance has its killer questions.

Step 2: *Write out answers to these questions in 75 to150 words.* Keep in mind that not everything you'll say will be used in the news story, but if you want to achieve communications objectives and get information across that is useful, you will have to say more than just "yes" or "no" or other very brief responses. A 75-word response is approximately 30 seconds speaking time in English-speaking cultures; 150 words are about a minute.

Step 3: *Say the answers out loud.* This is as crucial a step as the first two. We have all been taught to write for reading, not for speaking. Therefore, it is difficult to "say" these answers out loud; they don't sound like us or convey our information in the way we would like them to. So, change them and then speak them. Translate them so that they are written for the ear rather than for the eye.

Step 4: *Use an audio recorder, or occasionally a video camera, to record and analyze your rehearsal.* Play it back and analyze your performance. Ask yourself if you have achieved your communication objectives, if what you're saying sounds like you, and if the answers convey what it is you're attempting to get across. If not, go back and work on your answers some more.

One very important lesson I've learned in years of coaching senior executives is that an audio or video playback is one of the most powerful personal coaching tools anyone can use. While it's wonderful to have a personal coach, someone who can help you through the process, every executive should learn this important self-coaching technique. Simply listening to what you say in meetings, on the telephone, or in rehearsals for presentations and interviews helps you self-coach in ways that demonstrate immediate and constant improvement in your technique.

Common Killer Questions

1. Aren't you embarrassed by this?
2. Couldn't it have been prevented?
3. Doesn't that make you angry?
4. Doesn't this situation make you uneasy?
5. Do you care as much as they do?
6. How could this have been avoided?
7. Isn't that just a cheap shot?
8. Should you have done it?
9. They are furious. Aren't you at least angry or resentful?
10. What about the accusations?
11. What about the allegations?
12. What did you know and when did you know it?
13. What do you do?
14. What does your company do?
15. What does your company give back to the communities in which it operates?
16. What is your company doing to advance the interests of minorities and women?
17. Who is to blame?
18. Whose fault is it?
19. Why are you being blamed?
20. Who is really responsible for this mess?
21. Why didn't you act faster?
22. Why didn't you plan for this contingency?

The Questions You Would Love to Respond to If Only Someone Would Ask You

Reporters rarely know much about business or about much of anything in great detail. They simply can't. They also readily admit this. This is one of the secrets to their objectivity, at least in theory. The interviewee is the expert, the resource, the source. The reporter is the observer, the interpreter, the chronicler.

To be properly in control and provide information that is truly of benefit to the audience being reached by the reporter, the interviewee must accept responsibility for voluntarily providing information that is powerful, well-packaged, and obviously meaningful.

This technique is a two-step process:

▶ The first is moving from the reporter's area of questioning or a specific question to a question you would rather respond to. The technique is called *bridging*.

▶ The second step, once having bridged, is to provide information that is well packaged, useful, and more attractive, perhaps, than the information the reporter thought he/she would get through the use of the original question.

Like the previous process, preparation for answering questions you would love to respond to if only someone would ask involves four similar steps:

1. Make lists of the kinds of questions to which you would like to respond, probably organized by issue, by product, by audience, by technology – in whatever logical groupings will help illustrate what you will be interviewed about. You may develop 6 to 12 questions in each category. After all, this is the heart of the information you want to convey should you decide to take the time to be interviewed.
2. Write out answers to these questions in 75 to 150 words. For the same reasons mentioned previously, you're moving toward the sound bite you want to see in the story. The more information you give the reporter, the less likely it is that the most important information you want in the story will actually get there. This is because reporters – who do not know your information and cannot know your company – will be making the choice of what to include unless you make it for them. In my experience, it's always better if you make the decision for the reporter.
3. Say the answers out loud. As mentioned previously, this is a critical step in being completely ready.
4. Practice with audio or video equipment if you want to sharpen your skills and be truly as good as you think you are.

Using Google to Prepare for Questions

Studies demonstrate that all reporters use the Web on almost every story. That means you and the reporter have the exact same sources, the difference being skill in searching the Web and the willingness to go to the effort.

If you are involved in media relations activities, even if you are not the spokesperson, you should Google yourself anyway, as well as key products, services, locations, and circumstances.

The purpose for the Google question search is to find additional killer questions that might turn up in an interview (so you can develop answers for them) and to find more questions you would love to respond to if only someone would ask you.

Rather than make a third list of questions, integrate new questions into the previous two lists. Every day, millions of items are added to the Web and the searchability of the data on the Web gets easier and, at the same time, has more depth.

> Questions, for the most part, come from the reporter's view of what news is.

6.4.2 Where Do Questions Come From?

The Reporter's View of the News

Questions, for the most part, come from the reporter's view of what news is. News from the reporter's perspective has some or many of these 15 attributes:

1. **It's an event, situation, or product that affects people, animals, or the environment.**

2. **What the effect is** (death, damage, threats, risk, danger).

3. **Change.** Often approached by reporters as mistake repair, i.e., Who is responsible? What is the cost? Why is it necessary?

4. **Conflict:**

    ❱ From outside (competition, regulation, prosecution);

    ❱ From inside (whistle-blowers, union organizing, disgruntled employees); or,

    ❱ From organized opposition (environmentalists, activists, government attack).

5. **Confrontation.**

6. **Danger.**

7. **Editorial perspective** (what the editor believes and assigns the reporter to look for).

8. **Extremes** (the proposition or problem, skip the middle, and go right to the solution, indictment, or answer).

9. **Failure.**

10. **Mistakes.**

11. **Reporter's interests** (meaning what the reporter may already know through life or professional experiences about the subject).

12. **Secrets.**

13. **Unusual.**

14. **Vulnerabilities.**

15. **Weaknesses.**

The more of these elements that are a part of your news event or story, the more newsworthy you and your topic are going to be. Count on it.

Anticipating the Questions

In emergencies, the source of questions is quite predictable. As Alan Bernstein (1986) points out in his classic questions, the media will always ask:

1. What happened?

2. When did it happen?

3. Who is affected by it?

4. What was the cause?

5. Why did it happen?

6. Where did it happen?

7. How could it have happened?

8. Who, if anyone, was injured?

9. How much damage has been caused?

10. What's the potential for continued damage or danger?

11. Who was responsible?

12. What went wrong?

13. What do you plan to do about it?

14. When will more information be available?

In specific emergency situations the media may also ask about specific issues and subjects.

6.5 Giving Good Answers – Even to Bad Questions

After going through one of my coaching sessions, a wise old newspaper editor told me: "Interview subjects focus too much on the reporter, the reporter's behavior, and the questions. The fact is we rarely print the questions. But, we do print something from the interviewee's answers."

One could argue that his comments fail to apply to radio or television, but the thrust of his observation surely does. The crucial aspects of interviews are the answers provided and the information and communication objectives those answers contain. This section explores the attributes and characteristics that make answers successful, powerful, persuasive, interesting, and newsworthy.

Throughout the process described in this book, we have maintained that you control the interview. Because you are the resource and you have the information, how you present that information is critical to the reporter's ability to achieve his/her objective.

> **Effective answers rely on identifiable attributes or components, which make them powerful, clear, communicative, and useful to the audiences they are intended to reach.**

Your goal is to work on strategies and structures for answering that are totally focused on achieving your communication objectives while at the same time being responsive to the concerns of the media and those of the public affected by what you do, how you behave, and what you say.

Effective answers rely on identifiable attributes or components, which make them powerful, clear, communicative, and useful to the audiences they are intended to reach. Attributes are techniques – often very simple and direct verbal approaches – that when used, make the spokesperson very powerful. Some attributes are important control techniques, which tend to help the spokesperson manage the course of the interview, the direction of the answers, and, quite often, the nature of the story.

The more of these attributes that are built into answers, the more likely it is that the content of an answer will survive intact, even in the face of the toughest reporter and the most grizzled editor. These attributes help the spokesperson talk from the point of view of the audience. The section that follows contains an alphabetic list of these attributes.

6.5.1 Attributes of Good Answers

> Bridging... is invaluable for moving from the reporter questions that are uninformed, unknowledgeable, or confrontational to the question to which you would love to respond to in order to stay on message.

1. **About people.** Remember where reporters come from. Stories are about people, animals, and living systems. Answers should be as well. Those that are only about facts, data, and factoids make the source appear arrogant, cold, and heartless.

2. **Benefits versus features.** In sales, saying that something is red, short, high-powered, fast, or comes in seven sizes merely describes that product's features. We like to talk about features; they're all about us. Benefits, on the other hand, are about someone else. Customers buy products and ideas based on the WIIFM factor – *what's in it for me.* Effective answers come from the perspective of the viewer, listener, and reader rather than from the self-centered corporate or organizational interest. Benefits help the customer buy. Features only bore or anger the customer.

3. **Bridges.** Bridges are verbal phrases that save an enormous amount of time in verbally moving from one subject to another. Bridging is one of the most critical skills successful interviewees learn. Bridging allows you to verbally move from topic to topic quickly with very little explanation but in a seamless fashion. It is invaluable for moving from the reporter questions that are uninformed, unknowledgeable, or confrontational to the question to which you would love to respond to in order to stay on message. Here are some of the more common bridging phrases designed to take you in one lightning-quick move from territory laid down by the reporter or questioner to verbal territory that will get your messages across.

   ▶ *...But the facts are...*

   ▶ *...Here's an even tougher question...*

   ▶ *...I have heard that too, but the real focus should be...*

   ▶ *...I would describe it differently...*

   ▶ *...If I may, let me pick a more important point...*

   ▶ *...Let's deal in reality...*

▶ *...Let's talk about something I'm even more familiar with...*

▶ *...Let's use another perspective...*

▶ *...Opinions can differ, but I believe...*

▶ *...That's one view, mine is...*

▶ *...The critical issue is...*

▶ *...What concerns me even more...*

▶ *...Yes, but...*

4. **Compassionate language.** In emergencies, perhaps the single most damaging behavior is the lack of compassion – the lack of verbalized empathy and sympathy. If you don't express your compassion in your words and actions, it will not be assumed. Keep in mind that you have to behave compassionately, with empathy and sympathy, as well. It takes more than the right words, but the words are crucial because no one may describe your acts of compassion or empathy unless you do. Use words like:

▶ Ashamed

▶ Concerned

▶ Disappointed

▶ Embarrassed

▶ Empathize

▶ Failed/failure

▶ Humiliated

▶ Let you down

▶ Mortified

▶ Regret/regrettable

▶ Sad/saddened

▶ Shocked/surprised

▶ Sorrowful/sorry

▶ Sympathy/sympathetic

▶ Tragic

▶ Unfortunate

▶ Unhappy

▶ Unintended/unintentional

▶ Unnecessary

▶ Unsatisfied

5. **Complexity-to-process.** Often business activities require very complicated explanations. For the majority of interviews, these complex explanations must be made intelligible by reducing their complexity to process. This simply means taking a complex subject and breaking its complexity into appropriate elements, parts, steps, phases, pieces, numbered sequences, or a chronology. The fewer and larger parts the complexity can be bulked into, the more powerful and clearer the story is likely to be.

6. **Contrast.** Reporters deal in extremes in stories, telling stories that have bright, attractive beginnings, very little in the middle, and devastating or climactic endings. Plan for this when answering questions. Remember the "Rule of 298" from the previous chapter – if your business already services 298 out of 300 possible customers, the story would not be how successful you were, but the problems you were having in securing those last two customers.

7. **Core value sensitivity.** Core values are personal, protective beliefs to which people, communities, societies, and cultures believe they are entitled, and these values cannot be changed, modified, or adapted without their permission. Understanding this concept of core values helps you to understand why victims and neighbors get angry and become involved aggressively. The reporter's story is about the core values you may be offending.

Here is a list of the core values generally attributable to individuals within a community, in the order of their emotional power:

Community Core Values
▶ Health and safety

▶ Value of possessions and property

▶ Environmental threats

▶ Quality of life:

  ❑ Peace of mind
  ❑ Pride in community
  ❑ Absence of conflict
  ❑ Freedom from fear

▶ Peer concern (pressure)

▶ Economic security

Employee Core Values
▶ Company survivability

▶ Personal job security

▶ Recognition (from supervisors)

▶ Safe and healthy tasks

▶ Truth (principally from supervisors)

▶ Quality of working life

◻ Freedom from fear

◆ Pain/injury

◆ Toxic substances

◆ Wacko fellow employees

◆ Peace of mind

◆ Fit into the work environment (quality/team/other management lingo)

◆ Sufficient warning if job status will change

◆ Peer/supervisor acceptance

◆ No politics

◆ Fair/just management

8. **Credibility.** Credibility is defined as today,s assessment of your behavior yesterday. For a spokesperson to be credible, a pattern of verbal description and behavior is required. A pattern of personal credibility involves several verbal steps:

▶ Admit shortcomings (and how they are being repaired)

▶ Be people specific

▶ Express concern

▶ Speak from the public's point of view

▶ Talk in positive bundles of information

▶ Talk in terms of results

▶ Tell success stories balanced by shortcomings

> **Empathetic and sympathetic behavior is at the root of coming across as a person or organization that cares, and therefore should be respected, understood and, in emergencies, often forgiven.**

9. **Direct analysis.** Many questions we are asked can be answered quite directly, and they should be. So long as the information provided is clearly more in the interest of the receiving audience than in that of the sender, answering questions directly is the most culturally acceptable and personally satisfying approach.

10. **Empathy and sympathy.** *Sympathy* involves the verbalization of regret, concern, and feelings of interest in what happens or is happening to other people. *Empathy* is taking action that specifically addresses their problems. Language without behavior will be viewed as spin and arrogance. Empathetic and sympathetic behavior is at the root of coming across as a person or organization that cares, and therefore should be respected, understood, and, in emergencies, often forgiven. Actions always speak louder than words.

11. **Be positive and declarative.** Most bad news initially comes from negative phrases habitually and carelessly used by the spokesperson, either to begin answers or to close out answers, or both. Here are the most common negative comments that cause news about us to be negative, and corresponding positive comments. Eradicate the use of these and the vast, vast majority of your bad news will be controllable.

Negatives	Positives
▶ I don't like that idea.	▶ Here's what I'd like...
▶ I don't see the connection.	▶ Here's what matters...
▶ I wouldn't say that.	▶ Here's what I would say...
▶ It can't be done.	▶ We can make it work.
▶ It didn't happen that way.	▶ Here's how it happened...
▶ It won't work.	▶ We can make most of it work.
▶ It's against company policy.	▶ The company policy is...
▶ It's never been done before.	▶ This is the first time...
▶ It's not my responsibility.	▶ My responsibilities are...
▶ It's too expensive.	▶ It's affordable.
▶ It's too much trouble.	▶ Happy to help.
▶ No comment.	▶ We'll comment when we can.
▶ No one is safe.	▶ There's some risk for everyone.
▶ No problem.	▶ My pleasure; Thank you; You're welcome.
▶ Not my job, unfortunately.	▶ My responsibilities are...
▶ Not on my watch.	▶ Stop it now.
▶ Not that again.	▶ Let's try something different.

▶ Our boss would never buy it.	▶ Here's what he's done in the past...
▶ Our customers wouldn't like it.	▶ Here's what our customers told us they like...
▶ Our people would never do that.	▶ We expect more of our people.
▶ That doesn't mean it won't happen.	▶ It could still happen.
▶ That isn't our problem.	▶ Here's what we're focused on..
▶ That would wreck our product.	▶ Selling the product would be more challenging.
▶ That's impossible.	▶ It's possible.
▶ That's not a good question.	▶ A better question might be...
▶ That's not impossible	▶ It's possible.
▶ That's not our fault.	▶ Our responsibilities are...
▶ We aren't a bad company.	▶ We're a good company.
▶ We can't change that fast.	▶ We'll change what we can as promptly as we can.
▶ We can't talk about it.	▶ The information is confidential.
▶ We couldn't have known.	▶ It was a surprise to everyone.
▶ We did all right without it.	▶ We succeeded with what we had.
▶ We didn't know.	▶ It was news to us.
▶ We don't care.	▶ We have other higher priorities.
▶ We don't have enough studies.	▶ We need more data and input.
▶ We don't have the resources.	▶ Our resources are limited.
▶ We don't have the time.	▶ Time is always at a premium.
▶ We won't have the money.	▶ We need more resources to get it done.
▶ We're just too busy, we can't.	▶ Here are our priorities...
▶ We're not ready for that.	▶ It will be some time before we're ready.
▶ Why won't you use everything I say?	▶ We carefully excerpt your comments.

12. **Few modifiers.** This is the tendency in language to use words and phrases that take away from the direct and definitive nature of our conversation. Here are some examples:

Right Way	Wrong Way
▶ We will answer all questions.	▶ We will answer all the questions that matter.
▶ We respect everyone involved, everyone in the process.	▶ We believe that only some of those involved in the process are sincere.
▶ We will eradicate this problem.	▶ We will do the best we can. Human beings aren't perfect.

13. **Few negative words.** Eliminating negative words and phrases is the crucial attribute of successful answers. The reasons are simple but powerful. Negative language makes you feel defensive, immediately.

Negative responses give the reporter immediate follow-up questions (why couldn't you, why shouldn't you, why didn't you, why won't you) without even having to think.

No matter how many positive things are said in an interview, it's all the negative things that will be used and quoted.

The interview will stay on a negative course because the spokesperson put it there and has lost control.

Stay positive. The most important reasons for avoiding negatives are in the interests of the audience. For example, when we say, "That's wrong," what's right? What have we learned from the answer? When we say, "We don't do it that way," well how do you do it? Where is the useful information that might counter negative allegations against you?

14. **"For example."** In virtually every culture, any language, any circumstance, these are two of the most powerful words. No matter how dull, boring, irritating, or bland your answers, when you say, "For example," the audience or reporter will perk up to see if you can actually make what you have to say interesting and useful.

15. **Forecast future answers.** If you can't answer something now, make a forecast about when you will be able to do so.

16. **Goals for answers need to be clearly in mind:**

    ▶ Brief (75 to 150 words)

    ▶ Plain language (so a 13-year-old can understand)

    ▶ Positive (avoid defensiveness)

    ▶ Single topic (focuses the reporter)

    ▶ Time sensitive (stick to the important things; forget the rest)

17. **Influence others.** One of the major reasons we do interviews is to influence other individuals, groups, and constituencies. The attributes of influential language and ideas are:

    ▶ Accommodate

    ▶ Acknowledge

    ▶ Ask for agreement and participation

    ▶ Hear

    ▶ Listen

    ▶ Re-describe

    ▶ Recommend

    ▶ Re-interpret

    ▶ Understand

18. **Meaningful specificity.** Be specific. Avoid the often-used generalizations like, "We are a great company," or "We care about our people," or "We know how to solve these problems." Give two or three examples of what you mean immediately. Otherwise, what you say will be considered stonewalling and will not be believed.

19. **Memorability.** These techniques clearly group information in the listener's mind and help get more of your information into stories:

    ▶ Alphabetize

    ▶ Chronology

    ▶ Dramatic examples

    ▶ Packaging and bundling

    ▶ Power words. Repetition

▶ Tell 'em. (If it should be in the story, tell them it should be in the story; if it's important to understanding what is going on, tell them it's important to understanding what is going on.)

▶ Verbal cueing. (This is a second conversation, which threads throughout the interview, that simply describes, interprets, and explains what you are talking about and why it's useful, important, or necessary. Assume that the reporter has to be instructed, taught, as well as informed, then do the teaching, educating, and informing as you go.)

20. **Newsworthiness.** Remember we said that something is newsworthy because the reporter considers it to be newsworthy. Then take a look at what news is from our perspective. The list is self-explanatory:

▶ About people

▶ Accessibility

▶ Ask the reporter

▶ Body count

▶ Chronological

▶ Predictable

▶ Reporter oriented

▶ Tells a story

▶ Timely

▶ Topical

▶ Understandable

▶ Interesting:

❐ Reports

❐ Success stories

❐ Analysis of key business issues:

◆ Business

◆ Defense

◆ Education

◆ Health

◆ Law

◆ Space

◆ Technology

21. **Non-disparaging.** In emergencies and problem situations, one of the most obvious verbal techniques that discredits you is shifting blame to someone else. This happens when the spokesperson says, "It's not our fault." If it's about fault, say whose fault it is, or say nothing. Remember that whomever you blame will be asked to respond – and that person's comments in his or her defense will appear in the story right next to your statement.

> Remember that whoever you blame will be asked to respond – and that person's comments in his or her defense will appear in the story right next to your statement.

22. **Non-technical language.** Keep the number 13 in mind. That is, would your explanation be immediately understandable to a 13-year-old? That does not mean to "talk down" to the audience. Pretend your mother, your sister, your brother, your daughter, your son, your aunt, your uncle, your grandmother, or your grandfather were listening and had to understand what it is you are talking about.

23. **Ownership.** Good answers always come from the right perspective. For example, you could say, "In our view, the problem should be resolved in this manner." A better way, a perspective reflecting ownership, would be to say, "Our shareholders and the American public expect us to resolve the problem in this manner." Good answers reflect the appropriate ownership of the information being shared.

24. **Pacing, not racing.** Let the reporter finish speaking before you respond. Pause slightly, and then go ahead. The interviewee is in charge of the pace of the interview unless they insist on interrupting and over-talking the reporter. Yes, it's alright for the reporter to interrupt you, but be patient. Stop, let the interruption occur, and then proceed to answer the question as you initially began.

25. **Packaging and bundling.** I consider this the most powerful concept in verbal communication. Simply stated, it is verbalizing a number as you give your answer, thus making the listener count as well as listen. For example, you can say, "There are a few important ways we manage this problem." Or, you can say, "We manage this problem using three important techniques." The use of the numeral immediately adds value to your answer. Do not give a long numbered list – the smaller the number, the more powerful the answer.

26. **Persuasiveness.** There is a pattern of language and behavior that determines just how persuasive an individual can be. The persuasive spokesperson:

- Admits mistakes or shortcomings – and explains how they will be repaired).
- Asks for help in solving the problem.
- Asks others to commit to specific ideas.
- Grants at least two aspects of the opposing point of view.
- Interprets the issue or situation from opposing perspective.
- Offers at least three alternatives or options.
- Shows the value (benefit) of their recommendation.

27. **Positive, declarative language.** Among the most powerful control techniques in interviews is the use of positive, declarative language. Virtually any negative, emotional, colorful circumstance can be managed to the benefit of the audiences affected by the spokesperson's use of positive, declarative language. Here are some examples of positive, declarative language:

Negative Approach	Positive Approach
I don't believe it... or you.	Here's what I believe. Here's what we believe.
It won't work; it never worked.	Let me make a suggestion that might make it work, or let me find someone who can make a suggestion that might make it a more useful idea.
It's not the place for everyone.	Here's the kind of person who will be successful here.
Not everyone is willing to pay the price to work here.	This is a tough, challenging, interesting place to work. The commitment is high and the work is often difficult. It requires serving others every minute of the day.
That's a lie.	What I believe is...
That's not our style.	We're known, even respected for...
We don't do that.	Here's what we actually do.
We don't invest in benefits our employees won't use.	We have three categories of employees in our company, each with different needs.
We've never done that.	This is what we did, specifically...
You're wrong.	The facts are...

28. **Power words, not color words.** Power words are the specific vocabulary spokespeople should use to neutralize the damage done by reporters using color words. Always counter emotional color words (i.e., embarrass, humiliation, anger, fear, stupidity, etc.) with positive language and power words.

29. **Pyramid-Like Answer:** This approach looks like a vertical pyramid, with the point pointing up. At the very top of the pyramid are three important ingredients of answers:

   ▶ The direct answer to the question asked, where possible.

   ▶ Your communication objective – the scripted information you are supposed to be delivering.

   ▶ An answer to the question we wish they had asked by bridging from the question asked to something you would rather talk about.

   Avoid the Inverted Pyramid Answer: Most of us are taught by our mothers to answer questions promptly. If we stall or pause too long, the implication is that we must be guilty of something, not prepared, or some condition that is negative. The result of this training is that many of us, even experienced spokespeople, begin answering a question before we actually know what we are trying to convey or talk about. Picture an inverted pyramid where the base of the triangle is at the top and the top is pointing down. I call this habit oral idling – we put the mouth in gear before the brain is fully engaged. Thus, the concept of the inverted pyramid, in that we are saying all kinds of things at the beginning of our answer, and as time passes (and our mouths continue to move) our brain helps us figure out what we are supposed to get to and talk about. We get to the point of our answer last, hence the inverted pyramid approach.

   Clearly, the desired answer structure is vertical pyramid-like answer, with the metaphor being to get to the point first and then embellish what you talk about rather than the reverse – giving the embellishment first, causing great confusion, and quite often losing your point once you finally get to it.

30. **Repetition.** Most important themes, ideas, and facts need to be repeated three times during the interview; more than three is even better. Reporters, audiences, and editors can absorb only a certain amount of information, but if you repeat it enough times, they have to believe it's important and will use it.

31. Story-like construction:

- Beginning, middle, end
- Brief
- People oriented
- Plain language
- Positive
- Purpose, lesson, moral, or self evident truths

Power communicators are powerful storytellers. Consult *Reader's Digest* as a great example of how effective brief stories can be. Look especially in the magazine's regular columns such as "Life in These United States" and "Humor in Uniform."

32. **Themes/key messages.** Wherever possible, those ideas, issues, problems, and situations should be represented by brief, descriptive phrases or verbal themes. If these themes and key ideas are quotable and usable, they can manage the direction of a story.

33. **Victim sensitivity.** One of the most important attributes of crisis is that crises tend to create both explosive visibility and *victims*. There are just a couple things to remember about victims.

- First, victimhood is self-designated. There are no outside criteria that can tell people when they are victims or when they cease being victims. This is self-determined.

- Second, communication with victims needs to be simple, direct, positive, and extremely frequent because one thing that sets victimhood apart from normal circumstances is the inability to hear and understand much of anything unless it bears directly on the victim's needs. (***Note:*** *For more about understanding the victim dimension of a crisis, see the discussion in Chapter 1, including the Victim Recovery Cycle.*)

Chapter 6 – Questions for Study and Discussion

1. When your superiors insist that they intend to give an "off-the-record" briefing to the press, or a member of the press, what is your argument that will convince them that it's a bad idea?

2. When is an in-person news conference preferable to one done via telephone or computer? What are some of the advantages of an e-conference?

3. Explain how best to prepare to respond effectively to "killer questions"?

4. How do you "bridge" from the question you don't want to answer to the question that you do want to answer?

5. When confronted by a challenging question, do you usually give a "pyramid-like" answer or do you avoid stalling by giving an "inverted pyramid-like answer"? What kind of preparation and practice does a speaker need in order to be prepared to give "pyramid-like" answers consistently?

References, Chapter 6

Bernstein, A. (1986). *Emergency Public Relations Manual* (3rd ed.). Highland Park, NJ: PASE, Inc. [Out of print.]

7

Crisis Communication Plan in Action: Social Media

Keywords: legacy media, social media, digital media, blogs, YouTube, Flickr, Twitter, Facebook, citizen journalist, micro-communities, social media monitoring, reputation management, search engine optimization, RSS feeds, tag cloud, hardball, take-downs, NGOs, Risk IT, COBIT, SMART team

Whatever your experience relating successfully with traditional media – newspapers, magazine, television, and radio – the challenges and the opportunities of the new media are rapidly eclipsing the reporting and predictability of legacy media behaviors. Readiness today requires that current crisis management plans include a good working knowledge of the new media, functioning digital communication platforms, including dashboards, as well as applying time-tested media tactics.

This chapter will help you to:

➤ Understand how social media can supersede media relations.
➤ Assess your "web readiness."
➤ See the growing influence of the "citizen journalist."
➤ Monitor social media, assess its impact.
➤ Consider the ways in which you could use social media to help your company's business.
➤ Identify the ways in which social media could be used to attack your company's reputation.

7.1 What Makes Social Media Different From Legacy Media

Two distinct categories of media have now evolved – traditional or legacy media (see Chapter 4 of this book) and social media. What makes social media differ from traditional media is that the social media employ readily available web-based technologies, such as popular networking sites, to allow ordinary users, acting independently, to generate content, to share content with other users, to integrate content across networking sites, and to disseminate the content to a large audience almost instantly. Social media have injected new intensity, urgency, and effectiveness into the media relations equation:

- ▶ The emergence of the "citizen journalist."

- ▶ Instant, sometimes astoundingly broad distribution of "news."

- ▶ Direct reporting from individuals to local, national, and sometimes international audiences through iReports and web portals at all national networks. Most TV station news websites allow direct uploading of video content from citizen contributors who have produced video reports, which are aired virtually as they are submitted. In 2011, 22% of video on CNN came from citizen-submitted content through ireport.cnn.com.

- ▶ Elimination of the professional journalist, along with the entire time-consuming news editing and vetting process.

- ▶ Permanent shattering of the journalist/legacy media trust relationship with audiences, especially newspapers.

7.1.1 Changing Trends in How People Get the News

Newspapers everywhere are failing or struggling to survive, literally coast to coast. The same condition is true for many weekly and monthly news magazines. Recent Pew research monitoring the relationship between the American public and the news media appears to indicate that the American public no longer depends on newspapers as it did in the past. With the exception of National Public Radio (NPR), reliance on radio as a source of news is in full decline. While radio news still remains a staple at drive times, it is mostly "rip and read" services using the Associated Press and other news services. National Public Radio seems to be the only truly functioning news radio network in America today, but it is reducing the "news hole" in favor of music and arts features, and its Federal funding by the US Congress remains an issue. Still, the statistics indicate that, on the whole, the public tends to rate radio as more valuable than newspapers (Pew, 2010).

Television, which used to be first to serve the news, is now a poor second to social media. Nevertheless, respondents in a Pew study rated television significantly ahead of radio as a reliable and trusted news source (Pew, 2010). The decline in reliance on television news reflects the real-time information source competition from social media, talk channels, other Internet sources, and the rise of smart phones and smart communication tools.

The big surprise to the journalism community in this study is the public response to social media. The two major trends identified by the Pew study are 1) social media, and 2) mobile connectivity. Pew statistics reflect extraordinary levels of public trust and interest in social media as a source of information (Pew, 2010).

The report states, "Beyond the chatter about news that takes place in email exchanges, a notable number of Internet users are beginning to treat news organizations, particular journalists, and other news mavens as nodes in their social networks. In this survey we found that 57% of online Americans use social networking sites such as Facebook, MySpace or LinkedIn – and 97% of them are online news consumers. Some 51% of the social networking users who are in the online-news population say that on a typical day they get news from people they follow on sites like Facebook. That amounts to 28% of all internet users who get news via social networking with friends" (Pew 2010).

The broad acceptance of new media has raised questions and issues about this news coverage:

- Who is a journalist?
- What is journalism? Does this matter anymore?
- Who answers these kinds of questions?
- How important is a journalistic approach when so many of their social media sources seem to be untrustworthy, uninteresting, or unnamed?

Whatever the current state of flux of media relations, communication in a crisis now has new strategic and valuable channels.

Whatever the current state of flux of media relations, communication in a crisis has new channels that are strategically valuable. The challenge for the communicator is to use both new and old channels strategically in order to effectively, promptly, and credibly get information out.

7.1.2 Coping With Crises in a New Media Environment

Digital and social media have changed the way we communicate, redefining the meaning of "crisis response." By the time a crisis winds down, how promptly and directly an organization has responded can determine both its reputation and its future viability. The problem is how to respond in the digital and social media age. When news "reporting" is instantaneous, anyone can take on and easily embarrass a major corporation, politician or organization, and every misstep is magnified.

BP / Deepwater Horizon

On the evening of April 20, 2010, the Deepwater Horizon, a drilling platform in the Gulf of Mexico leased by British Petroleum (BP) exploded and caught fire. Eleven workers died, and survivors floated in the cold seas waiting to be rescued, watching the platform burn and sink into the mile-deep waters. As untold quantities of crude oil began bubbling up from the damaged well threatening the Gulf region from Texas to Florida, the story spread via digital and social media to millions. By the following morning, newspapers had caught up with the digital media and the 24/7 news cycle, which had been reporting on the catastrophe throughout the night.

At the outset of the crisis, how did BP respond to the crisis and the communications challenges? It is important to be aware that the U.S. Oil Pollution Act of 1990 promulgated in the aftermath of the Exxon Valdez oil spill, requires that drilling platforms must adhere to the same guidelines as a ship. First, the parties involved activated their crisis plans, issuing notifications and launching their unified command protocol, under which the U.S. Coast Guard acts as the central command for disaster response and as the central voice for the rescue mission and clean-up.

To ensure that it had controlled communications from the company's perspective throughout the response to the disaster, BP immediately launched several communication platforms. Hourly posts included links to images, videos, and news updates. The Houston-based crisis center was staffed by communications professionals flown in from BP's offices around the world. The company also hired a Washington, D.C.-based PR and public affairs agency to interface with the many federal regulatory agencies and the legislative and executive branches of government.

Web-based communications enable companies and individuals to communicate vast quantities of information to multiple audiences at the same time. To be sure that the facts going to the traditional media and new media were accurate, BP launched a micro site with the latest postings from the company and its suppliers. In addition to press releases, fact sheets and other bulletins, the company posted photos, maps, diagrams and videos. Thirty days into the crisis, millions of viewers, including the media, were watching the oil leak and kill attempts in real time from a video feed at BP's website. Of course, BP communicated through conventional channels, as well, issuing press releases, news conferences and providing interviews by phone and in person. But the heavy lifting was taking place on the web and in Facebook, Twitter and YouTube.

Social Media Pushes Out the Message

▶ News travels in milliseconds, not minutes, hours, or days.

▶ More than one billion people – combined active Facebook and Twitter users (Bennett, 2012) – can discuss your organization or client, its products, and its competitors in just a few minutes.

▶ Participants all "rave" about matters – positive and negative, large and small.

▶ Micro-communities are formed online, populated by friends and fans, otherwise unrelated except by their likes or dislikes.

▶ Anyone communicating online becomes, in effect, a publisher, reporter, author, and a member of the media.

▶ Most professional journalists live online every day, many searching social channels for scoops.

▶ More and more reporters and bloggers are being compensated by page views, that is, the number of views the story generates – "pay per click."

> **Anyone communicating online becomes, in effect, a publisher, reporter, author, and a member of the media.**

7.1.3 Importance of Crisis Website and Web Readiness

When a crisis or seriously negative event occurs, in today's world, everyone heads to the web before they look for anything else. Failing to have a website in place is what often leads to mistaken stories, stories based on erroneous assumptions, things getting made up very quickly, including by reporters.

There is a mistaken belief that putting things on the web actually spreads information across the web. In practice, websites are destinations where people go intentionally, seeking specific information. Those expecting to benefit from websites need to lead or herd people to their sites. This is one of the great benefits of a website. It is electronic. You can urge and herd people to your site when important information resides there; you can gain information and valuable data from their visits, as well as getting a sense of what interests or concerns people most.

Start with initial review and analysis of website readiness to handle a serious situation. Examine the site for, among other things, the following:

1. Language use (positive and declarative, eliminate all negative words).
2. Current simple structure vs. ideal complex structure for exploring and dealing with the problems at hand.

3. Where a crisis page may ideally fit within your site structure, or whether a whole different site might be appropriate.

4. Compare your site to other crisis or urgent information type websites.

5. The placement of key lists on the homepage for ease of location and navigation.

6. Overall ease of navigation throughout the entire site.

7. Presence of tracking analytics.

8. Issues, problems, scenarios requiring various dark sites.

Identify some general rules to follow:

1. Crisis websites generally have little production value. Production values tend to reduce credibility and trust. Their appearance and their information must meet the test of being "simple, sensible, honest, and sincere."

2 General tone of the site needs to be positive and constructive, basically any and all comments need to be relatively brief (75 to 150 words) so that the visitor can read the materials, absorb and use them.

3. Content must be sensible and constructive.

> **Web-based communications enable companies and individuals to communicate vast quantities of information to multiple audiences at the same time.**

Optional / Additional Analysis

1. Search engine optimization (SEO) assessment.

2. Social media opportunities and vulnerabilities.

3. Contact mediation. What goes on the web stays on the web, forever. If you are angry, chill out before you post. Today's issue or criticism will come back to haunt you in the days ahead.

Typical Crisis Website Content

We recommend that your company have in place a **crisis website** or dark site. Put lots up, and leave it up for some time, even years. *(In Chapters 3, 4, and 5 of this book, you will find instructions for creating, populating, and maintaining these sites so that they will be in place when needed.)*

▶ Advertising

▶ Applications & filings

▶ Blogs

▶ Comparisons with other sites

▶ Corrections and clarifications

▶ Crucial timelines

▶ Dear So and So

▶ Downloads (audio/video)

▶ In the news

▶ Issues & policies index

▶ Letters

▶ Links

▶ News & views

▶ Our purpose

▶ Overview

▶ Podcasts

▶ Presentations

▶ Publications

▶ Public meeting transcripts/audio

▶ Q&A

▶ RSS

▶ Rumor corrections

▶ Site map

▶ What we propose to do

▶ What we need from the community

▶ Who we are

7.2 What Are the New Media and Social Media? Why Should Your Company Care?

Google, Bing, Yahoo, Twitter, Facebook, LinkedIn, Flickr, Foursquare, and now more than two dozen others enable everyone with Internet access to locate, relate, analyze, and comment on an infinite number of topics. And, the same information providers and communities offer automated search features and RSS (really simple syndication) feeds that send alerts and feeds to computers and mobile devices telling subscribers immediately when news on a topic of interest breaks. Ubiquitous blogs enable everyday people to become editors, reporters, and publishers on an equally infinite number of specialized subjects. Of course, journalists and bloggers are armed with the same news feeds and search engines. In fact, the majority of reporters begin their work on each and every article with an online search and have well-established RSS feeds keeping them informed around the clock. Companies and their crisis teams have to keep pace, both by monitoring news via alerts and feeds and pushing out their own online news updates through RSS feeds.

Social media can be your company's enemy or friend. The very same new media that can be your enemy in an embarrassing crisis can also be your friend in promoting your business. A study by Wetpaint and the Altimeter Group (Li, C., 2009) demonstrates that engaging with consumers through social media channels – such as blogs, Facebook, Twitter, wikis, and discussion forums – correlates to better financial performance. The study found that the most engaged companies grew revenues by 18% over 12 months, while those of the least engaged companies saw revenues drop 6% in the same time period. The companies that came out on top in the study were: Starbucks, Dell, eBay, Google, Microsoft, Thomson Reuters, Nike, Amazon, SAP, Yahoo!, and Intel.

Significant differences between platforms and user groups require new approaches to media relations, especially in a crisis. Digital news is propelled from person to group to networks based on interest.

Influence and growth vary by social media platform. In September 2011, according to Shea Bennett in *Mediabistro*, the number of active Twitter users reached 100 million, with 362 million registered profiles. It is estimated that the number will reach 250 million active users by the end of 2012. These figures are in contrast with the even greater numbers estimated for Facebook, which was expected to reach one billion active users by the end of 2012 (Bennett, 2012).

However, a Pew study (Purcell, et. al., 2010), revealed that while 93% of teens and young adults were online, the young adults were more likely to use Twitter than teens – with one-third of online 18-29-year-olds posting and reading status updates. That study also indicated that less than 20% of all accounts sent a "tweet" in December 2009, down from 70% two years earlier. The data suggests that while Twitter continues to evolve, its influence may be waning. Nevertheless, following an election in Iran, news tweets from everyday citizens played an invaluable role, keeping the world informed of the protests and deaths in Iran.

Twitter clearly can work against companies in a crisis, unless the target company is well-versed in how the social media communities behave. For example, during the BP Deepwater Horizon incident, a fake BP Twitter account provided a forum for satirical posts and jokes made at BP's expense. It could be observed easily that this profile generated twice as many followers as BP's authentic Twitter profile.

7.2.1 Exxon-Valdez vs. BP: How the New Media Have Changed Crisis Communication Response

To illustrate the way new and social media have changed the crisis communication response, look at the difference between BP's communications and the methods used a generation earlier by Exxon – before the emergence of Internet and social media – to manage the media in the aftermath of the 1989 Valdez oil spill in Alaska. Exxon's few terse press releases and statements, and the constant public whining of its chairman, reflecting the obvious arrogance of its leaders, contrast strikingly with the flood of information issued by BP and its suppliers.

Ironically, it was the Exxon-Valdez spill that triggered the huge media efforts to cover this man-made disaster. At the same time, this event globalized what had been up until that time, 1989, a very fractured, disorganized, and unfocused global environmental movement. Exxon's corporate behavior and that of some of its executives forged a new global alliance in support of tougher environmental standards and punishments for the perpetrating company, all without the help of the web or social media.

In 2010, BP's communication team and consultants knew that interested parties would search online for news. So they posted messages hourly on BP's Facebook page and used Twitter to send concisely worded (no more than 140 characters) "headline" updates and key facts. In addition to posting information on a static website and pushing out its key messages for the search engines to aggregate, it also pushed the free video hosting (and search) site YouTube, and posted photos and images to free photo-hosting site Flickr. These pages remain up on the BP website today. Visit them and learn.

BP recognized that if they took direct control of their messages and delivered them directly to millions of people on the web looking for it, they could out-pace and out-manage traditional legacy media.

> **Because of the explosive nature of social media, developing a monitoring strategy and putting it in place as part of a crisis plan is essential.**

Why did BP do all of this? In the face of an overwhelming tide of adverse publicity, and until the oil leak was stopped, BP had to keep its voice and messages in the mix and influence the flow – and coverage – of the facts and new developments to minimize speculation, factual errors, and malicious criticism. It could, through digital and social media platforms, provide direct, regular news updates, thus maintaining input into the coverage throughout the crisis. In other words, new media and social media, when managed correctly, can help to communicate the point of view of your company in very difficult situations. Blogs and online media can help you diffuse and respond to online attacks and crises. The opposite is also true – if you fail to monitor your news and conversations in the media and are slow to respond to emerging news stories in social media, you can experience a humiliating, self-imposed type of crisis.

Case Study: A CEO Flames Out on Facebook

The Company

Badger Coal Corporation in West Virginia is a U.S. subsidiary of the International Clean Coal Enterprises, a UK-based company that has operations in several Eastern U.S. states. Badger, which has not been in the news very much, ever, employs approximately 550 miners and mining staff. Its operation has maintained a good reputation among state regulators and public policy makers. The only problem is the outspoken nature of the CEO of Badger Coal.

The Crisis

Months of inappropriate rants culminated on Memorial Day, 2012, when Benson Carter, the CEO of Badger Coal, took to his Facebook site and, as he had done several times before, loosed a long and characteristic rant. It was racist, it was misogynistic, it was offensive, and it was incredibly stupid.

His posting was seen by hundreds of thousands of people, many of whom were familiar with his previous rants. Employees e-mailed Board members, demanding that they put a stop to this embarrassing, humiliating behavior.

The Board had already tried repeatedly to stop him. After a previous rant, Carter had been admonished officially by the general counsel, told his use of Facebook was prohibited, ordered to take the site down, and instructed to cease using that kind of attention-getting hate speech.

The Complexities

Company attorneys were rebuffed when they requested that Facebook suspend Carter's site and take down existing posts. Comments coming into his site were about 6-to-1 against what he was doing. However, he had literally thousands of supporters, many of whom actually complimented the company on allowing a senior executive to speak as freely and as candidly.

Women's groups, various ethnic groups, and religious groups provided their member organizations and local media with excerpts from these racist and inflammatory comments. One group asked all of the company's customers to cease purchasing from the company, even if it meant breaking current contracts. They stated that the company's union retirement fund should dump its stock or sue the directors.

Weekly demonstrations were being announced for the company's headquarters and at the homes and businesses of corporate directors. Angry pressure groups threatened not only to post the names of the corporate directors – a matter of public information – but also to provide their home addresses and other personal information, including the names of their children and where they went to school.

Even in spite of all the warnings – and the turmoil caused by his behavior – Benson Carter took advantage of a pleasant holiday weekend to post one more rant on Facebook. Thus, the whole situation came to a head on Memorial Day, 2012.

The Choices

The company basically had four options that made any sense:

1. Leave the matter alone, defend it as a freedom of speech issue, taking the stand that, whether Carter's speech was popular or not, he had the right to make whatever statements he wanted to make.

2. Take decisive action against Benson Carter to prohibit and prevent his use of racist, misogynistic, and other kinds of hate language on his Facebook site, such as imposing some kind of fine, suspension, or other sanctions.

3. Attempt to shut the site down, disavow it, and disavow what this CEO had been doing, and take some aggressive action against the Benson Carter, short of firing.

4. Fire the CEO; shut down his site; reach out to groups that had been offended and victimized; and begin an extensive public apology process. Take action to resolve the issues and recover some semblance of reputation, attempting to forestall the threatened hate speech litigation by the State Attorney General.

The Culmination

▶ Because the Board was paralyzed and bitterly undecided about what action to take, Badger Coal and the behavior of its CEO were being more frequently mentioned on radio and TV stations throughout the United States and Canada. Several online chat groups were following Benson Carter's behavior.

▶ Prominent individuals in the private and public sector began to speak out against Benson Carter and Badger Coal – the Board's silence was interpreted as support for the CEO's statements. The company's attempts to distance itself from the public controversy failed.

▶ In all of the company's mines, union members were signing petitions and making public statements saying that the behavior of the company leader was hurting the company and humiliating its employees.

The Conclusions

On the evening of Memorial Day, 2012, the Board met by telephone conference. After ousting a vocal inside director, the Board finally united to take the most extreme measures possible. Benson Carter was relieved of his duties and a new interim CEO was named. A public statement explained Benson Carter had been fired and removed from the Board, and that the company, from its most junior workers to its most senior executives, completely disavowed what the former CEO had been doing and saying.

The new CEO stated, "None of us wants to be associated with this type of individual or his beliefs."

The Board statement explained that if the CEO had not agreed to these terms, Badger Coal would have filed a lawsuit against him on its own, requesting that the Justice Department and local officials consider prosecuting him for his use of hate speech.

As a condition of receiving a multi-million dollar severance, Carter was required to sell all of his stock, donate his options to an appropriate charity, and sever all ties with Badger Coal for the rest of his life. Many employees remain outraged that the former CEO will receive an extraordinary bonus for departing. The Chairman of the Board's compensation committee told employees, "Our hands were tied. We had to pay him to get rid of him."

The State Attorney General is still considering pursuing both Benson Carter and Badger Coal for hate speech. It appears that this scenario is far from over.

7.3 Monitoring Social Media

7.3.1 Develop a Monitoring Strategy

Because of the explosive nature of social media, developing a monitoring strategy and putting it in place as part of a crisis plan is essential. Of course, you could attempt to handle this monitoring yourself or assign it to someone on your staff. Or you could take advantage of companies like BrandProtect, and Risdall.com/listen, which provide reputational monitoring services. In either case, the message is: Have a listening platform ready for something to explode in social media.

Today, your organization most likely markets itself via a website (and blog); email, social media (Facebook and Twitter); and traditional print, audio, and video media. These key channels to the consumer are also pathways for online activism that can:

- Block public or private actions.
- Bully and humiliate.
- Spread corporate disinformation or misinformation.
- Decrease or increase market capitalization.
- Air legitimate problems that activists cannot get solved by other means.
- Give voice to victims.

▶ Publish just because they can.

▶ Provide publicity for their cause.

▶ Retaliate and extort.

▶ Push social-political-religious-nongovernmental organization (NGO) agendas.

▶ Target organizations to stop certain behaviors.

▶ Empower whistle-blowers.

▶ Foment shareholder issues.

Attack strategies can work quickly to build huge diverse audiences. Attacks – both now and even those that may have occurred in the past – raise lingering questions among key base audiences that must be corrected, clarified, or answered. In most instances, failing to respond can exacerbate the problem. Even minor inaccurate information published by a third party should be corrected as quickly as possible (most bloggers generally take the accuracy of their posts seriously and will correct errors of fact and misinterpretation). Why make the corrections? Attack sites persistently remain accessible – and searchable – for a long time. It's your destiny. If you fail to manage it, someone will step forward and do it for you.

You stay ahead of instant news coverage by monitoring blogs and social media via searches using key words for your organization and senior management team on Google, Yahoo, Bing, Twitter, YouTube, and other social sites. These searches will provide the baseline of your digital and social media listening platform. Build a baseline of blog coverage using the searches provided by Blogpulse, Technorati, Ning, Getsatisfaction, uservoice, and blogsearch.google.com. Build a digital and social media matrix incorporating your baseline profile, and then create standing searches to monitor your key search terms, sending Google alerts via email or Real Simple Syndication (RSS) feeds to a Social Media Action Response Team (SMART) dedicated to monitoring your company 24/7.

RSS feeds enable websites to multiply the distribution of their content through free subscriptions, which push out content updates automatically by email, Web, and news readers. For example, keywords associated with a company and its business, products, and services at the feed site allow subscribers to select their topics and automate monitoring of news, blogs, and other items 24/7.

For a crisis, web monitoring services help you assess the intensity, depth, interest, and emotion that surround your situation. Geo-locating sites can pinpoint the greatest concentrations of interest in your problem by geographical region. Keyword searches on Facebook, Google blog, search.twitter.com, LinkedIn and Yahoo, can tell you a lot about the volume of interest and type of comments the situation is generating. In a crisis, in order to drive readers to your site, buy Google search keywords as soon after the initial incident as they can be determined.

Protect your site content by copyrighting your site. Establish, use, and enforce an online posting/email/social media policy within your organization and with your outside advisors. Employees mean well, but they can hurt by trying to help, causing the worst damage.

> A strong offensive tactic before a crisis is to use the most popular social media platforms to form your own communities around your news, products, services, innovations, and so forth.

Build a fan base. Social media sites consist of smaller communities of individuals, often linked by common likes or dislikes. A strong offensive tactic before a crisis is to use the most popular social media platforms to form your own communities around your news, products, services, innovations, and so forth. Develop a fan base and engage your fans in a regular dialog. Once you get involved in the discussion, you will become familiar with using the medium and comfortable discussing your business and news, as well as responding to issues and complaints.

Attach a blog to your website, and engage in similar dialogs with people who post comments or complaints. Become expert in responding to issues without "fanning the flames." Before posting announcements, bulletins, and other information, take care to have the content reviewed thoroughly by key functions in the organization, such as legal, human resources, marketing. Before executing a preemptive strategy, always apply the common sense test:

▶ Are your employees talking about it?

▶ Are your customers talking about it?

▶ Have you seen any activity profile that can't be explained easily?

▶ Is there other chatter (on various other platforms) that includes references to your situation.

Some recommend purchasing "suck sites" and negative urls (web addresses), which are variations on your company name and branded products and services to prevent online misappropriation and attacks. Try searching with terms like your company or product name with "die," "sucks," and "I hate." It's also a good idea to search for any suck sites related to your organization.

Have you or your organization been the target of online activism? Have you experienced activist/contentious attacks; bullying; customer complaints; or whiny, disgruntled people? Or, have you been lucky, with no attack... yet? In any case, it pays to monitor and review "gripe sites" that mention your organization or even your direct competitors. (**Note:** *For more about dealing with online activism, see Chapter 8 of this book.*)

7.3.2 Drill Deeper Before Deciding to Respond

Once you have the data around a crisis impacting your organization, you will need to do a reality check and analyze the data (and the sentiment behind it) to determine:

- How many people are talking?
- How credible are the main contributors?
- How mainstream are the board members? (who are these people?)
- How popular are the websites?
- How tired is the complaint?
- What are the palpable impacts on your business?
- Is inflaming the issues further (by responding) worth the risk?
- Who is talking: Employees, customers, shareholders, regulators, bloggers, and bloviators
- How explosive, insulting, damaging, or corrosive are the comments?

Digital and social media techniques often provide the means to control themselves. Branding and product researchers know that "tweets" seem to track well with traditional polling over the long term. In fact, a recent study suggests the network could be used to gather information about public opinion (Carnegie-Mellon, 2011). Facebook and LinkedIn have polling functions. IBM has developed software that analyzes consumer sentiment from e-mail and social media data. In addition, many social media sites have analysis features, such as YouTube's free analytics that are available from the "Insight" button on every uploaded video. You can collect viewing statistics, demographics, community, and discovery information to detail how viewers located the video along with the links they used to arrive at the site.

> In an emotionally charged situation, analyze the data to determine the extent of negative sentiment before making the decision regarding a response.

BrandProtect (Mississauga, Ontario, Canada) uses its systems to search websites, forums, blogs, social media sites and bulletin boards and identifies various discussion posts where significant sentiment is being expressed by customers, employees, investors, analysts and other stakeholders. Malicious or negative content such as defamatory discussion, erroneous rumors, inappropriate language, inaccurate information and even reaction to poor service or product quality are identified in a timely fashion to alert you of potential damages to your reputation and financial position. Positive comments are also identified to provide for a balanced view of relevant community discussion. An analytics dashboard provides graphs for sentiment, volume of discussion, sources and key influencers.

Taxonomy: Positive and Negative Proximity
Emotionally Charged Discussion

The Brand Protect Approach:
Automated Discussion Monitoring and Sentiment Analysis

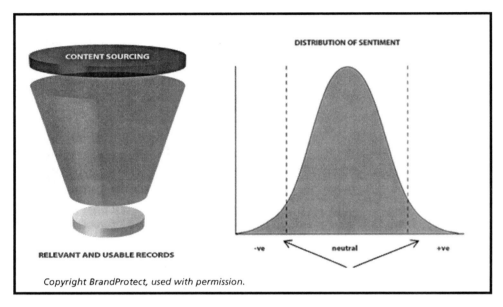

Copyright BrandProtect, used with permission.

7.3.3 Measure Commentary Sentiment

Even in digital and social media, the $1,000,000 question remains: To respond or not. Once you have a handle on the nature and magnitude of the crisis, it's time to examine your options. Now, it's time to decide whether to respond or to ignore online or other forms of criticism or negative sentiment. In an emotionally charged situation, analyze the data to determine the extent of negative sentiment before making the decision regarding a response. The normal distribution of sentiment among those interested in your situation is a bell curve, with vocal negative and vocal positive minorities. The majority of people, approximately 80%, will be in the category of neutral or don't care.

Sentiment measurement is a very sophisticated way of analyzing word and word patterns. Computer analysis of the taxonomy of emotional language produces transcripts and commentary that can determine the space between positive and negative comments, between negative and more negative comments, the degree to which the language being analyzed is contentious or emotionally charged. This method is extremely interesting and innovative in its attempt to use rational, computer-based means to determine some metrics in order to understand the level of emotion with which the issue is being discussed. In the aftermath of the oil spill from the BP Deepwater Horizon well, negative and positive sentiment could be measured easily with a Google keyword search. Both could be aggregated and charted to guide a response strategy and to measure the impact of executing it. Again, it's important to monitor and evaluate sentiment during and after a crisis to evaluate your response strategy and update your crisis plan in the aftermath of an incident. Digital and social media provide helpful tools to survey and measure sentiment that is not available in the more traditional media.

Tag Cloud

Over 200 tools and platforms are currently available to help you track and assess mentions of your business or brand in social media channels. A major service for social media monitoring is the Radian6 platform from Radian6 (Fredericton, New Brunswick , Canada). As part of a Radian6 report, users are able to view a high-level observation of what keywords and themes surround certain topics through online mentions, called a *tag cloud*. A tag cloud gives a visual depiction of words used most often on a certain topic. In the visual, the size and color of words indicate the number of mentions in the topic. The placement of the words correlates to how closely they appear within user-generated content to one another.

A tag cloud provides a nice, at-a-glance view of what the current online conversations and sentiment of a certain key term are, in that moment. But over time, the user can watch for change in the tag cloud to show engagement efforts having effect, creating changes in opinion and new user-generated conversations.

Below are three different tag clouds reflecting 30 days of user-generated mentions for the terms, "Barack Obama," "Geico" and "Jim Lukaszewski." To begin, let's start with the key terms "Barack Obama."

In this tag cloud, conversations in the past 30 days surrounding the current president reflect the news coverage of recent events, as well as the public's sentiment of the president. You can see terms such as "debt," "trillion," "job," "economic," "world," and "national," stemming from news coverage and commentary online. The terms "criticized," "unpatriotic," "irresponsible," and "good" are value words associated with web users' general sentiment of the president – they are emotionally charged and seem to be making judgments on the president's actions.

In the tag cloud the words, "past-president" "george," "bush," "ron," and "paul" tell us George Bush and Ron Paul are commonly associated with or compared to Barack Obama in online conversations. Over time, we'd like to see this tag cloud contain less negative terms and be replaced with more positive ones and making sure the comparisons to others are in favor of the current president, rather than negative.

save	buy	good	long	love	free	time	right
commercial	15%	work	information		think	california	
saved	companies	bad	switching	cost	insured		
better	company	auto	commercials	case	cheap	big	
insurance	home	**geico**		business	online	farm	
allstate	life	quote	money	motorcycle	best	pay	
bunch	music	progressive	news	rates	great	quotes	
coverage	high	claim					

In the second tag cloud, the key term "Geico," online conversations surround many industry specific key words, such as "insurance," "auto," "money," "coverage," and "claim." These words show people know who Geico is as a company, and what service they offer. But at the same time, there seems to be a lot of talk about their marketing efforts: "commercial," "music," "switching," and "15%." It seems they are remembered at times more for their interesting commercials, rather than their actual product.

The tag cloud also includes many value words, both positive and negative, such as "love," "good," "cheap," "best," "great," "bad," and "save." It would be interesting to look further into these words to see if they are associated more their marketing efforts or with their product. Either way, these words show mainly positive sentiment for the company, but could be improved by removing the negative terms and helping the positive words to grow in association with the key term.

managers　client　**impact**　**jim**　**seat**

facebook　slow　dead　**working**　work

information　**think**　releases　told

learn　**table**　difference　estimations

associated　planning　thinking　release

early　deserve　different

lukaszewski 　exercise

recommended　communicators　**reasons**

believe　business　**written**　tell

counsel　**listen**　talk　**communication**

marketing　matter　**boss**　coveted

strategy　gain　fact　**relations**　**book**

patience　**public**　**advice**

In the final tag cloud for the key terms "Jim Lukaszewski," online conversations mainly surround Lukaszewski's reputation and occupation. The terms "think," "learn," "strategy," "communication," and "advice" show what Lukaszewski is known for online. In addition, you can see many words from books by Lukaszewski, such as "boss," "listen," and "communication" showing interest in his writings. Finally there are many value words associated with the terms "Jim Lukaszewski," such as "deserve," "different," "gain," and "impact," showing the public's sentiment of Lukaszewski. It's interesting to note that the word crisis is not included in this tag cloud, which is one of the main areas of focus for Lukaszewski. Over time, it could be improved by bringing that word into the cloud, creating an online buzz about this impact area to represent Lukaszewski's services more completely.

7.4 Neutralizing an Internet Crisis

7.4.1 Traditional Behaviors and Strategies Work in New Media, Too

The basic rules of media relations still apply, whether you are dealing with traditional or social media. To neutralize an Internet crisis, it is essential to:

▶ Remain calm.
▶ Manage your assumptions.
▶ Investigate and verify the facts.
▶ Monitor exposure in all media.

Then, **diagnose the problem:**

- Identify complaint, problem, or issue.
- Identify the influence of the complaints on affected audiences:
  - ❒ Internet Network Information Center (InterNIC) database.
  - ❒ http://groups.google.com (old deja.com).
- Assess exposure in all media.
- Assess risks, especially legal and regulatory liabilities.
- Examine legal implications (if you have previously copyrighted or trademarked your intellectual property, including your website):
  - ❒ Copyright infringement.
  - ❒ Trademark infringement.
  - ❒ Libel and/or slander.

Conduct a **threat reality check,** which includes:

- How many people are talking?
- How credible are the main contributors, and what is their influence?
- How mainstream are the boards?
- How popular are the websites?
- How tired is the complaint?
- What are the palpable impacts on your business?
- Is inflaming the issues further (by responding) worth the risk?
- Who is talking: employees, customers, shareholders, regulators, bloggers, and bloviators?

Next, **examine your options:**

- Decide whether or not to respond.
  - ❒ What is your response threshold?
  - ❒ Will the Internet provide a workable position platform?
  - ❒ What other media will help resolve the problem?
  - ❒ Will visual media (photos, charts, diagrams, video) help explain your side of the argument?
- Solve the problem, if you can. Otherwise, put a solution into motion.
- Your response options include:
  - ❒ Do nothing.
  - ❒ Do something.

- ◆ Email.
- ◆ Bulletin boards.
- ◆ Website.
- ◆ Intranet.
- ◆ Blog postings.
- ◆ Social media responses.
- ◆ Communicate within communities.
- ❏ Do something more.
- ❏ Move beyond the medium.
- ❏ Direct action.
- ❏ Litigation.

In concert with your response strategy, it's important to **preempt, control, and contain** by the following methods:

- ❱ Response placement (notification to those most directly affected).
- ❱ Monitor specific issue in discussion groups, on activist sites, and in traditional media.
- ❱ Correct and clarify.
- ❱ Evaluate and if appropriate, take legal action.
- ❱ Remove false posts from search engines.

> **The traditional managerial arrogance that leads to less than optimal response strategies in traditional media settings is also at work when the media is digital.**

Common corporate **defense maneuvers** include:

- ❱ Get your message out as quickly as possible.
- ❱ Base your communications on facts, not opinions.
- ❱ Correct, clarify, and comment on what really happened.
- ❱ Make nice.
- ❱ Limit exposure – buy URL "sucks" sites.
- ❱ Litigate.
- ❱ Do take-downs or removals of offensive or fake posts.

7.4.2 Litigative Approaches (Which Can Lead to Take-Downs)

- File John Doe complaints.
- Subpoena the internet service provider (ISP).
- Action after identification.
- Using Computer Fraud and Abuse Act (CFAA)/Electronic Communication Privacy Act (ECPA).
- Trademark infringement.

The traditional managerial arrogance that leads to less than optimal response strategies in traditional media settings is also at work when the media is digital. There seems to always be the urge to "get these guys," rather than to focus on answering the allegations, questions, and bad information.

Hardball (that is, taking the tough, ruthless, confrontational actions to win at all costs) is the toughest course of action, because those on the defense rarely win and look increasingly defensive. For example, as the BP oil well continued to gush oil beneath the Gulf of Mexico, the company began to suggest that the platform operator, Transocean, had a part in causing the catastrophe. And, for its part, the Coast Guard's Deepwater Horizon Unified Command site published reports critical of the BP response, which were linked to the White House website and the White House's response. Should you be faced with a situation in which hardball may be an option:

- Establish an internal hardball team to activate promptly when needed.
- Get the facts, all the facts, continuously.
- Develop direct, conclusive evidence.
- Develop a drop dead accurate timeline of events.
- Decide what the ultimate purpose is and get agreement among all decision-makers.
- Act promptly.
- Test the process.
- Prepare to let the lawyers take the lead.

(**Note:** *For more about litigation-related challenges to crisis communications, see Chapter 9 in this book.*)

7.4.3 Questions to Ask the Boss When Hardball Is Considered

The desire to play hardball is often a symptom of the overconfidence that can occur in senior management in all crisis situations. Modern managers have been trained to believe that if you get the numbers right, if you make the right assumptions, and if you can model or simulate circumstances and situations, you can manage them. Crisis is largely a situation that has only one attribute – increasingly bad metrics; bills get larger, pools of victims grow, cost estimates skyrocket, anger and criticism grow by the day. Before you agree to choose the option for hardball, you need to ask some serious questions of the people in charge. Important: ask the people in charge *directly*, not just the people who work for them. Playing hardball is putting someone's career on the line. Here are some of the questions to ask:

- Is there conclusive evidence?
- Is there a solid legal basis?
- Will the organization devote the resources?
- What else may become public?
- Who wins?
- How many new critics, victims, or enemies will be created?
- Do we have equal or better alternatives?

7.5 Digital and Social Media vs. Traditional Media

Digital and social media are designed to ignore, or at the minimum, go around more traditional media. Their method is to establish a direct relationship between the authors of the content and the audience members benefiting from that content, virtually unrelated with the more traditional news media. Their success lies in their directness, their accessibility, their transferability among audience members and audiences, and the speed with which editorial material can reach consumers.

Radio, television, newspapers and other traditional or legacy media are all struggling and slowly failing. The audiences and those interested in gathering news and information, as consumers, have simply lost interest, or have relegated these media to ever lower levels of importance in their daily lives.

> Print media is shifting to the Internet. The demand for content to fill the digita news wells is extensive.

7.5.1 The Changing Value and Role of the News Release

Digital and social media are dialogues intentionally outside traditional legacy media. You and your opponents have become originators and publishers of information. When you issue a press release or other type of statement, image or video, it will reach traditional media and reporters, who will evaluate your announcement and interpret it. Print media is shifting to the Internet. The demand for content to fill the digital news wells is extensive. One of the effects, though experts agree it's temporary, is significant increases in newspaper websites which in first quarter 2009, recorded in 74.4 million individual visitors per month – more than one third of all Internet users (Falkow, 2010).

The problem is that traditional media still behaves as though they are the only media, while millions of their viewers and listeners flee to other information sources on the web or on social media platforms.

Your news releases will reach online media and other "aggregators," which will publish your unedited message or simply summarize it – in either case, without added interpretation. In these instances, your message appears unfiltered, making you, as the indirect publisher, fully responsible for its content. Take care to be sure the facts in your message are accurate and can be substantiated with data, reports, etc.

Post your statements and releases on your website immediately when issued. Be sure that your website is media-friendly. Here are some operational features that the media continues to expect from websites:

- A search-engine-optimized URL to enable an easy Google search.
- Clearly identified newsrooms with press releases and articles readily apparent and in chronological order. Maintain an archive for 3 to 5 years, since a clear history can support your arguments in a crisis.
- Links to your videos and photographs, "b-roll" (background, supplemental, or alternate footage), and captions.
- Links to your social media sites.
- Really Simple Syndication (RSS) feeds.
- Announce major news when posted on your website.

7.5.2 Consider Key Audiences

As you write and post your announcements, consider key audiences and what might impact most:

- **Bloggers:** Hot buttons and activist causes.
- **Brokers:** Misinformation, self-dealing, bad advice.
- **Colleagues, Partners, Allies:** Advance word wherever possible.

- **Critics:** They feed on everything you say and turn comments, data, and interpretations against you.

- **Customers:** Service complaints, product or service defects or failures.

- **Government Officials:** Offending them is pretty easy.

- **Reporters:** Breaking news, scandal, disaster, tragedy.

- **Shareholders:** Stock value manipulation.

- **Victims:** Almost everything you say to them will be mistaken, misinterpreted, and provoke even more intense anger.

- **Search Engines:** Always use the language that reinforces your messages and that search engines are primed to seek.

> **Asking for corrections in the legacy media is a waste of time, and you will get the last word anyway, because you're going to publish the last word yourself.**

Both reporters and bloggers who are interested in your statements have biases, whether they realize them or not. For example, the "honorable" goal of an investigative reporter to "defend the little guy" is a bias. Be mindful of a particular bias when you write your press releases and when you provide an interview. Review the discussion on dealing with the media that follows and apply the recommendations found there. Always stick to the facts and what you know. If your message gets garbled or your facts misstated publish your own correction, clarification, or commentary immediately. Your next step is to distribute your correction, clarification, and commentary to all of those having an interest or who care about your situation. Asking for corrections in the legacy media is a waste of time, and you will get the last word anyway, because you're going to publish the last word yourself.

Correction, Clarification, and Commentary: Your Most Effective Tools for Keeping the Record Straight and Managing Your Destiny

Giving interviews is necessary but can be risky. One of an interviewee's greatest frustrations, especially with print news stories, is what the reporter and editor may do with the answers the spokesperson gives. With broadcast stories, it's what the reporter leaves out that is of most concern. With critics, competitors, and complainers, it's how much confusion, emotion, and allegation they can get into a story about you.

- What if the reporter makes a mistake?
- What if the reporter leaves really important things out of the story?
- If the reporter does make errors and mistakes, how do you effectively correct them? Or should you?
- What do you do about unrelated, confusing, negative, sensational, or competitive ideas that creep into the story?
- What if the story is just plain wrong?

We advocate a Web-based technique we call "Corrections, Clarification and Commentary" where a print story or the transcript of a broadcast news story is laid out in such a way that it can be effectively corrected and clarified. These corrections and clarifications are then put on a website, and often also e-mailed to key stakeholders and stakeholder groups. This approach allows us to avoid the restrictions that letters to the editor, op-eds, and other media-dominated or controlled response mechanisms tend to place on our ability to have correct information on-the-record and available promptly to the publics we care about. This response technique works equally well with flyers, letters, news releases, video news releases, and white papers from those who oppose us in critical high-profile situations.

Why do this? As neat as this idea is, when first suggested, almost every client wants to know why anyone would put bad stuff, of any kind, up on the Web, for any reason. Their question is, "Won't this just make it available to lots more people and critics?" Here are five reasons why you should do this:

1. Your record is your responsibility. The public perception of your record is also your responsibility. This strategy manages both the public perception and the record.
2. Constructive approaches control the tone of debate, discussion, and differences of opinion.
3. Your constituents expect you to do this.
4. Honorable people can, and should, answer any and all questions.
5. The technique tends to script everyone, constituents, critics, the media, and commentators.

Face it, the media can use very little of what you give them, and they will choose what they want to use. Often the reporter or editor will leave the most important information out of the story. Control your own destiny.

Here's how we implement the technique.

Step One   Analyze the article, transcript, or document and highlight the words, phrases, or statements that need correction and clarification.

Step Two   Reformat the article, transcript, or document (if you can) so it will appear as a single column of text in paragraph format on the left side of the page or website screen.

Step Three Use a bold typeface to highlight the words, phrases, or statements on the left side of the page that you wish to correct, clarify or comment on.

Step Four   On the right side of the page, directly across from the words you highlighted on the left, insert approved, corrected, or clarified response language.

Step Five   As new issues arise or new subjects appear, develop approved language to clarify and continue the process.

The model that follows is taken from a real-life story and situation. Comparison of article text to the clarification will show you why this dispassionate technique, hammered home again and again, can be so successful in managing difficult, very public situations.

Always follow these general guidelines for all corrections and clarifications:

1   Use positive, declarative language. Avoid or eliminate all negative and emotional words and phrases.

2   Keep your cool. All statements should have a positive, declarative tone. The approach here is to correct and to clarify rather than to debate and counterpunch. This is where our real power comes from.

3   Categorize officially approved statements into specific topic areas. While time consuming and somewhat cumbersome at first, soon you will have more than enough pre-approved positive material to respond quickly to new articles or other information released by the media or those who hope to discredit you.

4. Constantly remember that the primary goal here is to script those who are interested in keeping the record straight with useful, helpful, and correct information.

Keep in mind that the groups most likely to visit your website frequently are reporters, opposing attorneys, your universe of audiences, and other self-appointed, self-anointed outsiders who have an interest in your issue or situation. The largest group of visitors, however, will be your employees and those directly affected by the situation at hand. Experience demonstrates that Web placement rarely enlarges an audience base, but does build trust and neutrality in the base audiences you care about.

Dakota Technology Enterprise Corporation (DTEC)
"Economic Development - Real Incentive"
The Dakota News
March 3, this year

Introductory Comments

Information, commentary, reports, and analysis developed and distributed by others about DTEC and our work often require additional amplification, correction, clarification, and sometimes commentary. DTEC provides analyses like these to ensure that an accurate, complete, and balanced perspective is available to those who are interested in, engaged in, and care about our work and purpose.

Text in bold in the left column is the subject of clarification, correction, or commentary in the right hand column.

Note: "Dakota" is a fictitious state, as are its leaders, quoted here.

	Article	Corrections, Clarifications, or Commentary
1.	By Bill Wilson, Business Editor Two of the top political leaders of the state Senate and House exemplify a major conflict encompassing government investment in economic development initiatives. Senate President Jack Slade, R-Anytown, believes spending tax dollars on business formation creates jobs that would otherwise not have materialized, while House Speaker Loren Smith, R-Anothertown, thinks advocates of these projects too often promise more than is delivered.	
2.	**"You can probably find lots of examples of how it's not been spent wisely,"** Smith said. Slade disagrees: "I don't see negatives from what we're doing." Contradictory views of these veteran lawmakers are at the core of a new study of economic development by the Legislative Auditor. The division's auditors are working to establish how much state and local governments in Dakota devoted to business promotion in the past five years and to quantify how well that investment paid off.	**An independent study of DTEC was conducted recently by Research Institute of America (RIA). RIA is a nationally respected tech-based economic development authority. RIA concluded that, "Overall, DTEC operates highly effective programs that generate positive outcomes for Dakota. This is accomplished through its collaborative network, on-target programs, institutional respect, and ability to provide strategic assistance to partners."**

| 3. | So far, the audit team reported that a minimum of $1.5 billion was expended on economic development activities by Dakota governmental units over the last ten years. In addition, a simultaneous evaluation of past research on publicly financed economic development produced a bleak diagnosis. Generally, auditors say, return on investment and job creation fell short of expectations. | To clarify, the Audit Report states that 70% of the $1.5 billion came from the Federal Government, 25% from the State of Dakota, and 5% from other sources. Note that approximately 5% of the $1.5 billion reported was allocated for DTEC programs during that period.

The articles referenced by the Audit staff analyze traditional economic development practices outside of Dakota.

A clear distinction should be made between the focused, technology-based economic development (TBED) that DTEC practices and general economic development activities.

DTEC provided the Audit staff a wealth of documents showing that technology-based economic development (TBED) is a wise state investment that often requires a different analysis process. Here is a partial list of resources supplied to the Audit staff to clarify the distinctions between technology investing and traditional economic development: |
| 4. | The audit also says Means County was the benefactor of $47.1 million in forgone revenue and direct payments from state agencies. Totals for other nearby counties: Shawnee, $2.5 million; Whippoorwill, $4.5 million; Thompson, $1.1 million; Laramie, $14.6 million. | It seems clear to us future economic growth will be strongly driven by technology based activity. This reality means that DTEC's programs will become increasingly important to Dakota' economy.

Our intent is to achieve all TBED objectives with transparency, disclosure, and real-time monitoring. The better understanding we have of the impacts, costs and effectiveness of the various economic development options, the better we serve the people of Dakota. |

Corrections, Clarifications, and Commentary
XYZ Corporation
Town Lashes Out at XYZ's Corporate Bullying
Response to Jack Wilson's Open Letter to XYZ's Chairman

Dear Mr. Wilson,

Thank you for your recent letter. We received it a couple of days after you published it in the newspaper. You seem very protective of "the small, local Thomasville Service District (TSD) Board" and "The sleepy little town," of Thomasville. I hope to clear up the questionable information some of your comments seem to reflect. My goal is that you gain a better understanding of the project's evolution and the project itself. I have responded as directly as I can to your questions, opinions, and assertions.

Note: I've put our response in the special format below as we find it a helpful way to offer our perspective and information directly toward the specific points raised. Analyses like these ensure that a more accurate, complete, and balanced perspective is available to those who are interested in, engaged in, and care about our work and purpose.

Text in bold in the left column is the subject of clarification, correction, or commentary in the right hand column.

	Your Letter	Corrections, Clarifications, or Commentary
1.	**Paragraph Two** **XYZ's process in Thomasville was consistently designed to stifle community involvement and bully the small, local Thomasville Service District Board into a ridiculously low annual fee.**	First, let's get the order of events correct: It was and is TSD's process: **1998:** The TSD contacted us to inquire if we were interested in locating a facility in Thomasville. Our Natural Resource Manager and regional Director both visited Thomasville at that time. We informed the TSD General Manager that while impressive, we were not considering locating a new facility in that geography at that time. **Late 2002:** We began consideration of a new facility in northern California and contacted the TSD General Manager to see if they were still seeking new businesses for the community. We were informed that TSD had spoken with a number of other prospects during the ensuing years but no projects successfully arose from those discussions. We were also informed that TSD was in negotiations at the time with a potential customer and that they were under a non-compete agreement which pro-

hibited further discussions with us until they were released from that agreement if negotiations failed.

In approximately early 2009, we learned that TSD's negotiations with the other company had indeed failed and that they were now able to discuss potential opportunities with our company. We entered into negotiations with TSD's designated representatives (two TSD Board Members and the General Manager) and successfully agreed on an apparoach.

Mid-September 2010, terms in the current contract were successfully negotiated. Our work within Thomasville and within the Thomasville area has been and is cooperative, inclusive, and collaborative. Some examples:

1. XYZ has been working with the TSD, the community of Thomasville and the greater community of Samson County for more than three years to develop and begin the environmental analysis for a local plant. Over this period, we have met numerous times with the community members and groups, seeking input and answering questions about our proposed project and anticipated operations within the community.

2. Separately, TSD provided multiple opportunities for the public to give input into their planning, both before and after XYZ became a District partner.

3. The progress of the XYZ-TSD contract negotiations was listed as an agenda item on the District's agenda for four meetings between June and September 2010.

4. An agenda and public notice were also provided six days prior to the September 29, 2010 public meeting at which the contract was discussed and approved.

5. The draft contract was also publicly distributed six days in advance of the meeting. The public was notified about this meeting through postings at the TSD office and a notice in the local.

6. Approximately 100 individuals attended this public meeting. newspaper. .

The revenue that TSD will receive from XYZ for this project was negotiated with TSD to reflect the anticipated customer-relationship XYZ requested to have with TSD. The pricing agreed to was judged to be fair by both parties. Let me lay out the facts, then you and anyone else who reads this can judge for themselves.

1. According to California Proposition 218, revenues received from its customers by TSD, may only be reinvested into improvements and maintenance for the town's infra-structure. Because of this, TSD and XYZ negotiated the payments from XYZ to TSD so that the majority of the XYZ-revenue to TSD could be placed into the General Fund and used for any TSD-related activities rather than be confined to infrastructure projects alone.

7.6 Digital and Social Media Crisis Management Recommendations

7.6.1 Establish a Useful, Helpful Social Media Policy to Moderate the Risks

> Text and figures in Section 7.6.1 are reprinted in their entirety from ISACA (2010). *Social media: business benefits and security, governance and assurance perspectives* (Emerging Technology White Paper), 6-10. Used with permission.

Since enterprise use of social media tools usually requires no additional technology to implement, an enterprise social media presence does not always begin with a project plan and risk assessment. To effectively control social media usage by both the enterprise and employees, a documented strategy (and associated policies and standards) should be developed with the involvement of all relevant stakeholders, including business leadership, risk management professionals, and human resource and legal representation. This holistic approach to integrating emerging technologies into the enterprise helps to ensure that risks are being considered in the context of broader business goals and objectives.

While the use of social media presents an additional entry point for technology risks such as malware and viruses, these risks are elevated primarily because more employees may be using social media sites without understanding the threats that exist. Therefore, any strategy to address the risks of social media usage should first focus on user behavior through the development of policies and supporting training and awareness programs that cover:

- *Personal Use in the Workplace:*
  - ❑ Whether it is allowed
  - ❑ The nondisclosure/posting of work-related content
  - ❑ The discussion of workplace-related topics
  - ❑ Inappropriate sites, content or conversations
  - ❑ Alignment with/part of the acceptable use policy
- *Personal Use Outside The Workplace:*
  - ❑ The nondisclosure/posting of work-related content
  - ❑ Standard disclaimers if identifying the employer
  - ❑ The dangers of posting too much personal information
- *Business Use:*
  - ❑ Whether it is allowed

❏ The process to gain approval for use

❏ The scope of topics or information permitted to flow through this channel

❏ Disallowed activities (installation of applications, playing games, etc.)

❏ The escalation process for customer issues

Training should be conducted on a regular basis and should focus on the benefits and opportunities as well as on the dangers related to use of social media. Emphasis should be placed on the specific dangers and methods of social engineering, common exploits, and the threats to privacy that social media present. Training should also ensure full understanding of the rules governing acceptable use and behavior while on social media sites.

Technical controls that exist for other e-commerce opportunities will benefit the enterprise when embracing a social media strategy. Technology can assist in policy enforcement as well as in blocking, preventing or identifying potential incidents. This strategic component should utilize a combination of web content filtering, which can block all access, allow limited access, and in some cases provide protection against malware downloads and end-user system anti-malware, antivirus and operating system security to counter such attacks. As with most security technology strategies, a layered approach is optimal.

Figure 1 - Risks of a Corporate Social Media Presence

Risk	Impact and Associated Risks	Risk Mitigation Techniques
Introduction of viruses and malware to the organizational network	▶ Data Leakage/Theft ▶ "Owned" systems (zombies) ▶ System downtime ▶ Resources required to clean systems	▶ Ensure that antivirus and anti-malware controls are installed on all systems and updated daily ▶ Use content filtering technology to restrict or limit access to social media sites ▶ Ensure that appropriate controls are also installed on mobile devices such as smartphones ▶ Establish or update policies and standards ▶ Develop and conduct awareness training and campaigns to inform employees of the risks ▶ Establish clear guidelines for corporate users that limit social media use to specific business-related communications
Exposure to customers and the enterprise through a fraudulent or hijacked corporate presence	▶ Customer backlash/ adverse legal actions ▶ Exposure of customer information ▶ Reputational damage ▶ Targeted phishing attacks on customers or employees	▶ Engage a brand protection firm that can scan the Internet and search out misuse of the enterprise brand ▶ Give periodic informational updates to consumers to maintain awareness of potential fraud and to establish clear guidelines regarding what information should be posted as part of the enterprise social media presence

Unclear or undefined content rights to information posted to social media sites	▶ Enterprise's loss of control/legal rights of information posted to the social media sites	▶ Ensure that legal and communications teams carefully review user agreements for social media sites that are being considered
		▶ Establish clear policies that dictate to employees and customers what information should be posted as part of the enterprise social media presence
		▶ If feasible and appropriate, ensure that there is a capability to capture and log all communications
In a digital business model, customer expectations to receive output in the form of communication or customer service more	▶ Customer dissatisfaction with the responsiveness received in this arena, leading to potential reputational damage for the enterprise and customer retention issues.	▶ Ensure that staffing is adequate to handle the amount of traffic that could be created from a social media presence
Mismanagement of electronic communications that may be impacted by retention regulations or e-discovery	▶ Regulatory sanctions and fines ▶ Adverse legal actions	▶ Establish appropriate policies, processes, and technologies to ensure that communications via social media that may be impacted by litigation or regulations are tracked and archived appropriately
		▶ **Note** that, depending on the social media site, maintaining an archive may not be a recommended approach

Figure 2 - Risks of Employee Personal Use of Social Media

Risk	Impact and Associated Risks	Risk Mitigation Techniques
Use of personal information to communicate work-related information	▶ Privacy violations ▶ Reputational damage ▶ Loss of competitive advantage	▶ Work with the HR department to establish new policies or ensure that existing policies address employee posting of work-related information ▶ Work with HR department to develop awareness training and campaigns that reinforce these policies
Employee posting of pictures or information that link them to the enterprise	▶ Brand damage ▶ Reputational damage	▶ Work with the HR department to develop a policy that specifies how employees may use enterprise-related images, uniforms, real estate, ideas, products, etc., in their online presence
Excessive employee use of social media in the workplace	▶ Network utilization issues ▶ Productivity loss ▶ Increased risk of exposure	▶ Manage accessibility to social media sites through content filtering or by limiting network throughput
Employee access to social media via enterprise-supplied mobile devices (smartphones, personal digital assistants [PDAs])	▶ Infection of mobile devices ▶ Data theft from mobile devices ▶ Circumvention of enterprise controls ▶ Data leakage	▶ If possible, route enterprise smartphones through corporate network filtering technology to restrict or limit access to social media sites ▶ Ensure that appropriate controls are also installed and continuously updated on mobile devices such as smartphones ▶ Establish or update policies and standards regarding the use of smartphones to access social media. ▶ Develop and conduct awareness training and campaigns to inform employees of the rest involved

Figures 1 and 2 provide risk mitigation techniques for both the risks of a corporate social media presence and the risks of employee personal use of social media.

Governance and Change Considerations

The introduction of social media use by an enterprise can produce significant shifts in both culture and process – particularly in the areas of communication, marketing, customer service and business development. The dynamic network of communication streams that are facilitated by social media can significantly alter the way an enterprise launches marketing campaigns, collects customer satisfaction data and provides customer support. Business processes in each of these areas may need to be altered to facilitate these changes.

The use of social media also introduces a new communication channel that must be monitored and managed. Depending on the nature of the use, and on the number and type of social media sites utilized, staffing and training requirements may be significant and should be taken into consideration during strategy development.

When considering new technologies, enterprises should look to established frameworks such as Risk IT and COBIT, which provide clear processes and controls to help answer key questions such as:

▶ What is the strategic benefit to leveraging this emerging technology?
▶ Are all appropriate stakeholders involved in social media strategy development?
▶ What are the risks associated with the technology and do the benefits outweigh the costs?
▶ What are the new legal issues associated with the use of social media?
▶ How will customer privacy issues be addressed?
▶ How can positive brand recognition be ensured?
▶ How will awareness training be communicated to employees and customers?
▶ How will inquiries and concerns from customers be handled?
▶ Does the enterprise have the resources to support such an initiative?
▶ What are the regulatory requirements that accompany the integration of the technology?

Assurance Considerations

Just as enterprises must develop an appropriate strategy and controls to manage their use of social media, it is the role of assurance professionals within the enterprise to validate and monitor these controls to ensure that they are, and remain, effective and that compliance with these controls is established and measurable. Assurance professionals should consider the following areas to provide assurance that risks associated with social media use are being managed appropriately:

1. Strategy and Governance
   ▶ Has a risk assessment been conducted to map the risks to the enterprise presented by the use of social media?
      ❏ The risk assessment should evaluate the planned business processes for leveraging social media and also the specific sites to be used.
      ❏ The risk assessment should be revisited whenever there are substantive changes to the social media resources in use, as well as when new social media resources are considered for adoption.
   ▶ Is there an established policy (and supporting standards) that addresses social media use?
      ❏ Policies and standards should be modified or created to define appropriate behavior in relation to the use of social media.
   ▶ Do the policies address all aspects of social media use in the workplace – both business and personal?
      ❏ Policies for social media should address four specific areas:
         ◆ Employee personal use of social media in the workplace
         ◆ Employee personal use of social media outside the workplace
         ◆ Employee use of media for business purposes (personally owned devices)
         ◆ Required monitoring and follow-up processes for brand protection

2. People
   ▶ Has effective training been conducted for all users, and do users (and customers) receive regular awareness communications regarding policies and risks?
      ❏ It is imperative that all users understand what is (and is not) appropriate and how to protect themselves and the enterprise while using social media.
      ❏ Customers who will be accessing an enterprise social media presence will need to understand what is considered an appropriate use of the communication channel and what information they should (and should not) share.

3. Business Processes

▷ Have business processes that utilize social media been reviewed to ensure that they are aligned with policies and standards of the enterprise?

▷ Unless business processes are aligned with social media policies, there cannot be assurance that they will not expose sensitive information or otherwise place the enterprise at risk.

❑ Change controls should be in place to ensure that changes or additions to processes that leverage social media are aligned with the policy prior to implementation.

4. Technology

▷ Does IT have a strategy and the supporting capabilities to manage technical risks presented by social media?

❑ The vast majority of technical risks presented by social media are also found in the use of malicious e-mail and standard websites. IT should have controls in place, both network-based and host-based, to mitigate the risks presented by malware.

❑ Suitable controls can include download restrictions, browser settings, data leak prevention products, content monitoring and filtering, and antivirus and anti-malware applications.

❑ Appropriate incident response plans should be in place to address any infection that does get through.

❑ Do technical controls and processes adequately support social media policies and standards?

❑ It should be verified that any required technical controls are present and functioning as expected, or that there are clear plans with timelines and a required budget to reach a specific capability.

▷ Does the enterprise have an established process to address the risk of unauthorized/fraudulent use of its brand on social media sites or other disparaging postings that could have a negative impact on the enterprise?

❑ While scanning for such material can be an onerous task, it is important that the enterprise have a strategy to address this risk. There are vendors that will provide this service, and this is generally the best option for enterprises that deem such monitoring a necessary activity.

❑ This risk exists regardless of the enterprise's active use of social media.

7.7 Accept That Social Media Is Becoming Ubiquitous

One among the many of the new paradigms of digital and social media is that they come in all shapes and flavors. For example, NBC's news anchor, Brian Williams, has one of the most popular blogs in the blogosphere and frequently breaks news and supplements on-air reports with more detail. Greenpeace also operates one of the most popular blogs. Be mindful that your messages to Brian Williams could be the same as your message to Greenpeace, or it could be radically different, depending on the issue.

Your employees will be bloggers, as well. Be sure that you cover blogging in your email/social media/online posting policy. As we have pointed out in earlier chapters of this book, the CEO of your organization or other senior leadership can also be problematic spokespersons. In an interview with the *Guardian* three weeks into the BP/Deepwater Horizon disaster, BP's CEO Tony Hayward said, "The Gulf of Mexico is a very big ocean. The amount of volume of oil and dispersant we are putting into it is tiny in relation to the total water volume." Meant to reassure, Hayward's mindless comment inspired a new discussion across the blogosphere within minutes and continued to resonate, as the quantity and toxicity of the dispersants became hot buttons within the states impacted by the spill. In another display of what was widely interpreted as insensitivity to the situation, a week later, Hayward attracted more criticism when he told someone, within earshot of a microphone, that he wanted his "life back."

Long a target of NGOs over its "sustainability" policies in manufacturing food products, Nestle, rather than whining or keeping up the contention, switched tactics and used its website to open a forum on deforestation, announcing an alliance with The Forest Trust, an NGO. The partnership enforced a set of guidelines posted on the website to guide the Nestle procurement process and assess suppliers performance, particularly in their managing or deforesting the plantation that produce palm oil.

Social media tools also are changing the way messages for public health and safety are communicated in a crisis, such as the important roles played by YouTube, Flickr, Twitter, and Facebook in the 2008 terrorist attacks in Mumbai and the 2009 salmonella-related peanut recall. Global social services agencies also are working to establish a set of guidelines to improve emergency communications.

Regulators monitor the social media. In the aftermath of the Pampers dust-up on Facebook, the U.S. Consumer Product Safety Commission launched an investigation into the complaints of rashes and chemical burns related to the Dry Max product, and P&G shares lost significant value. Train and involve your CMO and brand managers in your crisis procedures. Make sure they have appropriate plans to protect your valuable corporate reputation and brands in a crisis. Redouble product testing, and continually gather and monitor consumer input and complaints.

Case Study: Surviving a Personal Blog Attack – or Not

The Company

Gordon, an experienced state worker, had been appointed by Governor Green as department head in a large state agency. Almost immediately, the nomination was challenged via the Internet by one irritated and very vocal individual.

The Crisis

It was never clear what set this critic off. The attacks began on a private blog. At first it appeared that Governor Green was the focus of the attack. Soon, the blog postings began to focus on allegations of Gordon's incompetence, lack of political savvy, political cronyism, and friendships with large contributors.

The attacker continued to publicly demean Gordon, through dredging up information based on very few relevant facts supported by rumors, snippets from old editorials, and gossip – along with some fairly legitimate criticism of both Governor Green and his appointee, Gordon.

On the advice of staff members surrounding and protecting the governor, Gordon did his best to take the high road by simply ignoring the attacks. Then the allegations began to show up on other websites and blogs, with several new voices chiming in to confirm the original blogger's contentions. Finally, the attacks were so widespread that the governor was asked several pointed questions about Gordon and his qualifications at a news conference involving an unrelated but pet gubernatorial project.

The Complexities

At this point, Gordon's friends began to demand that he respond. His wife, Giselle, a public figure in her own right, was chomping at the bit to start protecting her husband's reputation. She disagreed strongly with the governor's advisors who were telling him to stay silent. Giselle was not about to take all of this lying down.

Meanwhile, a number of Gordon's longtime political friends volunteered to step forward, defend him, even taking a few shots onto themselves. Gordon's circumstances were now being described in several government-related trade publications.

The attacks began to speculate about what might be the real reasons why Gordon was likely not responding. Various legislative leaders were quoted, "off the record," as saying that they were very puzzled about why Governor Green had ever even considered appointing someone like Gordon to head a key state department to begin with.

Two of the allegations involved the handling of campaign contributions in previous elections. The blogger suggested that the state attorney general would likely open an investigation.

The Choices

Things were getting out of hand. Too much time had already passed, but some choices for remedying the situation were still available:

1. Begin responding by presenting some factual information in a friendly venue, such as Giselle's blog.

2. Attempt to determine the real identity of the blogger and his real problem, perhaps taking steps to discredit his information, allegations, and credibility.

3. Hire an attorney to begin preparation of libel and slander litigation.

4. Present a robust enough defense to Governor Green and his advisors to retain their support in keeping him in his newly appointed position.

5. Execute some outstanding agency program activities that would bolster his own credibility and change the subject.

The Culmination

Without waiting for guidance, Giselle launched a blistering attack on her own blog against her husband's attacker. It was a wild, angry, negative, accusatory rant which went on for about 1,000 words.

The blogger took the bait, immediately demanding that she justify her allegations. Why had she waited so long to say something? Why wasn't Gordon man enough to defend himself, rather than sending out his wife? What was he afraid of?

At this point, there was no stopping Giselle. Her fingers flew over the keyboard with even more vilification, accusation, and defensive excuses. The blogger countered by asking her why she maintained an automobile with an out-of-state license plate. Were they contemplating leaving the state? Were they, in fact, even legal residents of the state? And all this was just in the first three hours of the first day – Gordon had not yet said anything in any medium or venue!

It kept getting worse. Gordon remained confident he could ride it out, Giselle was still out for blood, Governor Green and his people were becoming more restless and uncomfortable – there seemed to be no way that any response, no matter how appropriate, would recover the situation. After 35 days of this, Gordon asked that his name be withdrawn from nomination, and Governor Green accepted "with regret."

The Conclusions

- Silence is always toxic to the perpetrator in these situations. Failure to speak is always interpreted as a sign of guilt, cover-up, or both.

- It is rarely the news media, the blogger, your toughest critic, or most aggressive competitor who will get you. When crises occur, your problems are more likely to be caused by arrogance and overconfidence at the highest levels, the false notion that the perpetrator is also somehow a victim, or it could be the misguided efforts of well-meaning friends or the defensive behavior and mistaken notions of relatives.

- Surviving attacks like these requires immediate, open, candid, responsive, positive, and constructive correction, clarification, or commentary.

- Truth is about 15% facts and data and 85% emotion and point of reference. Your simple recitation of the facts will have little effect on the attack or the attacker. Yes, facts and data do matter, but they need a constructive and conclusive context that will help counteract the impact of these negative attacks.

- Speedy responses always beat the "smart" more perfect response which takes longer – every time.

- Review my Attack Survival Manifesto. These simple, sensible, constructive, and positive reminders will keep you out of trouble, or get you out of trouble, if you should slide into harm's way.

- Remember, apologies are always on time; *thank yous* and *I'm sorrys* always arrive on time – but the sooner the better.

- Most contentious situations depend on the target responding angrily, defensively, combatively, and contentiously. If you're looking to energize your oposition, exhibit these behaviors and you'll get your wish, in spades.

7.7.1 Digital and Social Media Recommendations

- **Have a SMART (Social Media Action Response Team)** to deal with issues that arise:

  - Include representatives from all staff, HR, PR, legal, marketing, etc., and operating departments.

  - Determine types of issues of concern and priorities for response.

- **Protect your brands** by registering them across key sites; buy keywords.

- **Continually monitor and take action** where applicable.

▶ Develop in-house social media expertise.

▶ Always follow rules of conduct for each social media site – that is, learn how to blog before you launch your blog.

▶ Be transparent with intentions and your identity or you may alienate the very audiences with which you're trying to connect.

▶ Train executives and staff on social media engagement policies.

▶ Leverage social media within the context of broader strategy.

▶ Be aware that your response to a situation can and will be misinterpreted.

Chapter 7 – Questions for Study and Discussion

1. List at least three main differences between traditional (legacy) media and social media.

2. Why is the public more likely to believe information delivered via social media than it is to believe that same information from legacy media or the corporation itself?

3. Discuss how traditional corporate communications strategies may be ineffective in dealing with social media.

4. What are some of the tactics that can be used in the social media to damage the reputation of your company?

5. What can your company do to counteract these social media attacks?

References, Chapter 7

Bennett, S. (2012, January). Twitter on track for 500 million total users by March, 250 active users by end of 2012. *Mediabistro*. Retrieved from http://www.mediabistro.com/alltwitter/twitter-active-total-users_b17655

Carnegie Mellon University. (2011, May). *Carnegie-Mellon study of Twitter sentiments yields results similar to public opinion polls*. Retrieved from http://www.sciencenewsline.com/technology/2010051112000009.html

Falkow, S. (2010, May 6). Media relations in a web 2.0 world. *The Proactive Report*. Retrieved from http://www.proactivereport.com/c/pr/media-relations-in-a-web-2-0-world/

ISACA (2010). *Social media: business benefits and security, governance and assurance perspectives* (Emerging Technology White Paper), 6-10.

Li, C. (2009). *New study: deep brand engagement correlates with financial performance*. Retrieved from http://www.altimetergroup.com/2009/07/engagementdb.html

PEW Research Center. (2010, March 1). Understanding the participatory news consumer: the news environment in America. *PEW Project for Excellence in Journalism*. Retrieved from http://www.journalism.org/analysis_report/news_environment_america

Purcell, K., Smith, A., & Zickuhr, K. (2010, February 3). Social media and young adults. *PEW Internet and Association Life Project*. Retrieved from http://www.pewinternet.org/Reports/2010/Social-Media-and-Young-Adults/Summary-of-Findings.aspx

8

Crisis Communication
Plan in Action: The Activist Challenge

Keywords: viral, activist, radical, citizen journalist, fact-checking, reputation, counteraction communications, hostage, destiny management, laggership

*A*ctivist groups, as always, add interesting challenges to communications. Activists are emotionally committed to opposing and targeting you, and against traditional corporate behavior. To win, large organizations have to be as committed to victory as their critics are committed to defeating them. Fortunately, understanding the patterns of activist tactics puts you in a position to communicate effectively, sometimes even successfully.

This chapter will help you to:

> ➤ Recognize the tactics of activists.
> ➤ Correct the record effectively.
> ➤ Know the motivations and techniques of activists.
> ➤ Use websites and social media to succeed, even win, against the activists.
> ➤ Turn direct confrontation with activists into the chance to win.

8.1 Understanding Activists and Activism

8.1.1 Beginnings of 20ᵗʰ Century Community Activism

Much of today's activist behavior can be traced directly to Saul D. Alinsky (1909-1967), considered to be the father of modern American and even global anti-institutional activism. In the middle of the twentieth century, as a community organizer in Chicago, he developed strategies and tactics to convert the enormous emotional energy of grassroots groups and victims into effective anti-government, anti-corporate, and anti-elite activism. His ideas are widely taught around the world today as model behaviors, which – when combined with the enormous emotional commitment to victory (sometimes meaning "getting even") under any circumstances – can seem frustrating, humiliating, and unstoppable.

Study Alinsky's rules. They are the key models activists use and follow. We urge you to study these to be forewarned and to develop counteractive, counterintuitive strategies that level the playing field, especially during high profile public debate and decision-making. In many cases, his "rules for radicals" can become very effective counterintuitive rules for their corporate targets. Be creative. Think counterintuitively, and quite often these strategies can be used preemptively, with great success.

> **Notice how each of these rules takes advantage of the patterns of weakness, repeated mistakes, and false assumptions that large organizations and their leaders often make.**

Here are nine of Alinsky's "13 Rules for Radicals" as adapted from his 1971 book. Notice how each of these rules takes advantage of the patterns of weakness, repeated mistakes, and false assumptions that large organizations and their leaders often make.

8.1.2 Alinsky's *Rules for Radicals*

Alinsky suggests:

1. Power is not only what you have, but also what your enemy thinks you have.
2. Never go outside the expertise and interests of your people. Feeling secure stiffens the backbone; your people will work harder for you.
3. Whenever possible, go outside the expertise of your enemy. Look for ways to increase insecurity, anxiety, uncertainty, and paralysis.
4. Make the enemy live up to its own book of rules. If the rule is that every letter gets a reply, send 300,000. If the enemy has an 800-telephone number, make 30,000 phone calls each week.

5. Ridicule is man's most potent weapon. There's no defense. It's irrational. It's infuriating. It works as a key pressure process to force the enemy into concessions.

6. A good tactic is one your people enjoy. They'll keep doing it without urging and come back to do more. They'll even suggest better ones.

7. Keep the pressure on. Never let up. Vary the tactics and keep trying new tactics to keep the opposition off balance. Just as the enemy masters one approach, hit them with something new. Mislead them into thinking they are making progress, and then hit them again.

8. Go after people, not institutions. Pick a human target and freeze it, personalize it, polarize it. People hurt quickly. Besides, once you attack an individual, their own institution is likely to turn on them and help you. Isolate the target from sympathy.

9. The price of a good attack strategy is a doable alternative the enemy hates. The suggestion of rational alternatives confuses the enemy's arguments, saps their energy, and encourages defeatism.

8.2 Moving Out of the Target Zone

A renewed wave of anti-corporate activism began in the 1990s, particularly targeting the apparel industry and other areas of consumer manufacturing where the brand, usually American, uses offshore (that is, third world or lesser-developed) countries for sourcing. Activists succeeded in making these attacks reputation issues of the highest order. For some, the issue may be one of brand preservation. Here are some key facts and ideas to help move out of the bull's eye:

1. *Activist Organizations:*

   ▶ Often labor connected, but not always.

   ▶ Invariably networked with an array of non-government organizations (NGOs) created for the purpose of advocating, organizing, or attacking on behalf of some cause, country, or issue.

   ▶ Frequently religiously connected, even church affiliated.

   ▶ Brings a fervor and dedication that seems almost unreasonable due to an extraordinarily high level of zealotry.

   Lesson: Understand the power of activism and the activist mentality. Prepare to negotiate. Ignoring activism is toxic. Advancing the corporation as a victim is weak. These don't pass the straight faced test. Almost all corporate and government targets are considered to be guilty of something at first.

2. *Characteristic Patterns of Activist Action:*

▶ Attack the most well known brands, companies, or celebrities.

▶ Generate video of chain link fences topped with barbed wire and soldiers or "thugs" carrying automatic weapons.

▶ Use "testimony" from real workers who are "victims."

▶ Take one or two very young "victims," preferably women in their very early teens, tour them around the United States and other countries, and encourage them to make allegations against the target.

▶ Organize and recruit supporters through religious groups and labor unions to stage demonstrations and attention-getting events (but not boycotts).

▶ Humiliate the brand, company, or celebrity; then demand the target repair the damage and also take a much larger social role in their local communities with respect to the issues under attack.

Lesson: Anti-corporate actions can be anticipated both through aggressive enforcement of standards of conduct and compliance review, and by paying attention to the perceptions created by appearances. Be prepared to preempt these characteristic patterns of action aggressively. Avoid the obvious, the stupid, the callous, and the arrogant behavior. You will collaborate, or those who succeed you will.

3. *Activist Tactical Goals:*

▶ Alarm consumers. (Get supporters to avoid the brand, and ask questions.)

▶ Interpret situations. (Build fear or hate through slanted, emotionalized examples.)

▶ Intervene in the business. (Get control of the brand through demands and accusations.)

▶ Publicize allegations. (Virtually always taken uncritically by the media. Reporters feel good about helping with a "cause.")

▶ Speculate on motives. (Humiliate individuals within the target organization by emphasizing greed and insensitivity and questioning morals and ethics.)

▶ Allege terrible situations. (Death threats, harm, or harassment and discrimination against pregnant workers.)

Lesson: These tactical goals mirror what today's citizen journalists view as their daily mission: saving at least a part of the world from something bad (you) every day. These approaches are powerful and will have impact. It's virtually impossible to change these goals. Therefore, they must be anticipated, accommodated, and addressed.

> These tactical goals mirror what today's citizen journalists view as their daily mission: saving at least a part of the world from something bad (you) every day.

4. *Common Allegations Against Corporations Operating In Underdeveloped Countries Or Environments:*

   ▶ Child labor.

   ▶ Discrimination, especially against pregnant and younger women.

   ▶ Extraordinary forced over-time work.

   ▶ Greed

   ▶ Forced birth control.

   ▶ Forced labor.

   ▶ Inappropriate medical intervention (especially with young women).

   ▶ Intimidation.

   ▶ Less than subsistence level wages.

   ▶ Psychological coercion.

   ▶ Punitive employee relations.

   ▶ Slave or indentured labor.

   Lesson: While most codes of conduct accommodate and deal with these issues, too often there is no affirmative evidence of such abuses until after the allegations have been made and the damage to reputation done. Find ways, such as independent monitoring and effective internal enforcement, to ensure that abuses are prevented, detected, corrected, and deterred.

5. *The Great Irritations:*

   ▶ Emotional communication and action replace facts and reasonableness.

   ▶ Activism overshadows systematic information and evidence.

   ▶ Exaggeration overwhelms reality.

   ▶ Grassroots tactics and manipulation can mobilize customers and other constituencies.

Lesson: In this emotionally powerful environment, often there is very little in the way of concrete evidence on either side. The imperative is to respond or anticipate with a sense of energy, control and focus. Real on-the-ground facts and information can be controlling. Get some; get there first.

6. *The Good News:*

   ▶ Others are getting through this.

   ▶ You can succeed even though people might be angry, the government in opposition, and the news media attacking you.

   ▶ The results can seem underwhelming, but turn out to be significant.

   Lesson: The goal should be a better life for workers, stronger third world societies, better economic results, and therefore better lives for everyone while you are in-country. You may not always be in-country. These results are by definition very un-newsworthy and likely to be ignored by both the media and the activists.

7. *Allies and Critics:*

   ▶ You'll fight and win your battles largely by yourself.

   ▶ The agendas of your industry buddies will always come first. They may be happy that you are the target and they are not. Yet, they expect you to "hold the line."

   ▶ The media will never "take your side." They seem inclined to report even beyond activist exaggeration.

   Lesson: If you look for allies, chances are you'll find them outside your industry or by working collaboratively with those who are accusing you and their supporters. Industry "solutions" to activist attack are rarely successful and often cause only more controversy. Ironically, it's the opposition that tends to be more welcoming and helpful.

   > **Stay focused on the ultimate goal. Solve one or two problems at a time today because tomorrow will bring another set of issues.**

8. *Think Counterintuitively:*

   ▶ Your usual practices will be interpreted as corporate stalling and stonewalling.

   ▶ Your most factual analysis and statements will be considered biased, incomplete, and tainted.

   ▶ Your immediate involvement in the resolution process will be interpreted as manipulation and cover up.

▶ Your attempts to control the dialog, limit the damage, or impose a solution will be characterized as public relations tactics.

▶ Incremental progress will be challenged as unsatisfactory – a stalling tactic designed to save money.

▶ Be prepared for unexpected allegations. Act quickly.

▶ Learn to live with persistent, intentional misinterpretation:

    ❐ Progress is often described as mistake repair.

    ❐ Direct financial support or sponsorships are often interpreted as attempts to buy or bribe.

    ❐ Individual attempts to investigate or clarify are viewed as obstructionist or cover-ups.

    ❐ Economic arguments are interpreted as arrogant, insensitive, and anti-worker.

Lesson: Stay focused on the ultimate goal. Solve one or two problems at a time today because tomorrow will bring another set of issues. Leaping ahead will be difficult. Make incremental progress every day. Make certain that those who are affected, directly or indirectly, know progress is being made and what your next steps are. Avoid using the media as a forum or as a messenger. The media will never get it right and often, due to reporter's lack of understanding or overt sympathy, cause serious embarrassment and misinterpretation.

> **The more you interact directly with those whose lives, families, and future you affect, the less important what the media does or says becomes.**

9. *Reduce the Media's Power and Influence:*

▶ The more you interact directly with those whose lives, families, and future you affect, the less important what the media does or says becomes.

▶ Work in-country.

▶ Meet face-to-face.

▶ Talk with the critics directly.

▶ Reach out to communities at all levels.

▶ Keep public officials informed.

▶ If the most directly affected individuals and organizations know what's going on directly from you, what's printed, or said on radio and television, or even in social media will become less and less relevant.

▶ The opposition knows how sloppy you are about dealing with emtional issues and problems; get focused.

▶ It's always easy to challenge your credibility – thus making you defensive – rather than challenging the facts.

▶ Get your facts straight.

▶ The threat of some action to be taken against you, especially if amplified by the news media, seems more powerful than the action itself.

Lesson: Reducing the media's power is necessary and critical to truly helping workers. Failure to address the elements of activist action and media behavior confers credibility on the opposition and gives unnecessary additional power to the news media. The ultimate reality is that support among employees and other constituent groups is extremely fragile and difficult to maintain. Therefore, the most direct strategies and tactics are the most preferable and likely to moderate the attack and achieve real on-the-ground success.

10. *Ultimate Realities:*

▶ Timidity, hesitation and confusion (yours) cause embarrassment, humiliation and defeat.

▶ Activist attacks have impact and predictable consequences.

▶ Taking public credit often makes you a target.

▶ Each effective attack teaches activists success lessons for their next target.

▶ Getting it right, on the ground, is the ultimate priority.

Lesson: There are no end points, no clear victories. For each victory you attempt to declare, another set of allegations will surface.

11. *Credibility-building Communication Principles:*

▶ "When problems occur, we'll be prepared to talk openly about them and act quickly to respond to them operationally."

▶ "If key constituencies should know about an issue or problem that could affect them, we'll voluntarily talk about it as quickly and as completely as we can."

▶ "When problems or changes occur, we'll keep those key constituencies posted on a schedule they set until the problem or changes have been thoroughly explained or resolved."

▶ "We'll answer any questions those constituencies may have and suggest and volunteer additional information on matters they haven't yet asked questions about."

▶ "We'll be cooperative with the news media, but our primary responsibility is to communicate directly and as soon as possible with those most directly affected by our actions."

▶ "We'll respect and seek to work with those who oppose us."

12. *Break the Cycle:*

▶ Principles:

❐ Principle 1: Act credibly; build trust; wage peace.

❐ Principle 2: Drive the process by being outcome focused (avoid the past).

❐ Principle 3: Be satisfied with incremental progress.

❐ Principle 4: Avoid forecasts; stay focused; predict underwhelming results.

❐ Principle 5: Respect and appreciate each constituency's concerns and beliefs.

▶ Action Steps:

❐ Step 1: Create a communication environment that will support your goals from the community's/customer's perspective.

❐ Step 2: Act aggressively, with a positive attitude.

❐ Step 3: Focus on the process of resolution.

❐ Step 4: Prepare to manage (endure) unintended, constantly changing consequences.

❐ Step 5: Look ahead. What killer issues are on the horizon? Get ready.

Lesson: Take positive, aggressive action. Move quickly. Use common sense. Be inclusive rather than exclusive. Recognize that the language, beliefs, and thought processes of the opposition, while totally different from yours, are reconcilable.

Nine Tactics of Online Activists

Tactic One: Polarize the Issue

▶ No matter what, you're 120% in the wrong.	**Solution:** Solve problem if possible, point out exaggeration, admit errors, outline action steps

Tactic Two: Build a Support Base on the Web

▶ Set up a website devoted solely to attacking your company. ▶ Use mirror sites that look like your site or have a similar domain name, but contain negative information.	**Solution:** Assess actual damage or infringement, estimate potential damage, determine need for preemptive action.

Tactic Three: Trivialize, Emotionalize, Insult, Humiliate

▶ Pick domain names like "companysucks.com"	▶ Create neat, clean corporate response site; contrast your legitimacy with their juvenile tactics. ▶ Avoid pre-registering "anti-sites."

Tactic Four: Anger, Debilitate, Violate Trademarks, and Misinterpret Every Response

▶ Force your hand by provoking a legal response to showcase on their site. ▶ Vandalize your corporate site.	**Solution:** ▶ Choose battles carefully. ▶ Respond calmly; stay focused. ▶ Use appropriate language for medium. ❏ Everything shows up online.

Tactic Five: Use Ultimatums

▶ Bombard the company with "last chances" to correct allegations or charges, before "going live" and staging demonstrations.	**Solution:** Respond carefully, positively. ▶ If wrong, correct the problem. ▶ Ask for independent, unbiased proof. ▶ Stay cool.

Tactic Six: Register Their Site in Search Engines

▶ List in your company's section if possible.	**Solution:** Register your response site in same manner. ▶ Remove from search engine when issue is resolved.

Tactic Seven: Postings on Message Boards

▶ Promote their cause; promote their site. ▶ Locate others suffering from the same problems. ▶ Find disgruntled employees.	▶ Monitor the Internet; respond only if necessary. ▶ Remove libelous postings from search engines; implement postings policy.

Tactic Eight: Work the E-news Media	
▶ Target specific journalists who cover your industry or company. ▶ The media love David vs. Goliath stories. ▶ Reporters are now paid by website hits generated by their stories.	**Solution:** ▶ Direct journalists to your response site. ▶ Point out exaggeration. ▶ Admit errors. ▶ Outline action steps. ▶ Avoid whining.
Tactic Nine: Mis-Information	
▶ Post false news releases or wire stories. ▶ Seed message boards.	▶ Monitor adversarial websites and message boards. ▶ Trace information source, if possible. ▶ Evaluate legal options.

Case Study: Forest Management Company vs. Environmental Activists

Everybody everywhere loves trees. It is one of those issues that ordinary citizens, schoolchildren, and organizations like churches and service clubs participate in with great confidence and energy, even if the trees involved are on the other side of the world.

The Company

Green Acres Forest is a 250,000-acre forestry company located in the western United States. Several wealthy individuals had purchased the company and put it under new management; the announced purpose was to change the destiny of forestry by making Green Acres Forest a model company. They took over from previous owners, who had been constantly battling with protesters and critics in a war of deeds, words, and threats. Historically, under previous management, the company had been under fire from environmentalists, the state Department of Forestry, unions, and anti-corporate activists.

The Crisis

On the very day new management of Green Acres Forest took over, 12 individuals chained themselves to the main gate, and 13 individuals scaled 10 of the tallest trees, setting up encampments 150 feet overhead in the center of the forest. Protesters blockaded the parking lot at the company's small corporate headquarters building with two dozen large trucks.

The Complexities

Even before the new owners took over, major environmental organizations had begun to circulate a global online petition to shut Green Acres Forest down. A dozen anti-company organizations in the local area and around 50 neighbors participated in the campaign. The target of these petitions was the State Department of Forestry, the main regulatory body governing this company's operations.

The local public radio station committed to give three hours every Friday to the opponents and critics. Active recruiting of intruders was initiated at every local college campus.

Several nearby forests, operated by competitors, were subject to similar activist campaigns, each with its own collections of tree sitters, tree huggers, ecotage practitioners, and defense changers, all of whom had become local media stars as well as new media darlings.

The Approach

The new owners of Green Acres Forest adopted a very aggressive and constructive strategy. Owners and managers met with their foresters and managers and made it clear that:

▶ The mission of the new owners was to make Green Acres Forest a model for the forestry industry.

▶ Any forester having difficulty with the new approach — which included much greater openness, transparency, community collaboration, and engagement with critics — could count on the company's help in finding employment more to their liking in another company.

▶ The new approach would take time to be effective, and would require the enduring of insults and some threats mostly from the neighbors.

▶ All jobs with Green Acres Forest would be protected for at least three years.

▶ In the process, everyone in the company would be learning a lot more about the newest techniques in forestry.

Then the president of Green Acres Forest proceeded to take personal action. He offered a personal response to every single e-mail and petition that arrived at the State Department of Forestry. The company responded to 97% of the 75,000 e-mails. The remainder were sent via other channels to disguise their origin. The response was a simple one-page letter from the president of Green Acres Forest to the person or group sending the petition.

In the letter, the president offered to answer any questions directly and personally. He included his personal telephone number, encouraged petitioners to visit the new company website, which had a tremendous amount of detailed information including permits, permit applications, inspection reports, harvesting plans, and detailed reconstruction and rehabilitation proposals including the protection of endangered species, and new experimental harvesting techniques. The president further invited any interested person to take a personal tour of the 250,000-acre forest. In addition, he appeared regularly on the weekly public radio broadcast answering questions in studio and live call-ins.

The president promised that the company would undergo a certification regimen by outside, third-party forestry certification specialists.The entire process would be open to the public; all documents would be posted on their website.

The Culmination

This story actually began in 1997. Over the intervening years Green Acres Forest has been true to its word. Virtually all major environmental organizations hold this organization up as a model in forestry. Even so, a number of neighbors are still angry.

The entire forest was certified by two competing certification organizations. These forests maintain their certification to this day. Habitat for fish, birds, and dozens of animal species were rebuilt or reestablished. Roads were rebuilt or rerouted to minimize impact.

There never was another petition or successful media attack on Green Acres Forest. Of the 75,000 e-mails responded to early in the company life, more than half of the writers responded to the president's letter by apologizing for not having dug into the facts more deeply before sending the petition in.

In the seven years following the petition activity, Green Acres Forest honored more than 1000 requests for personal tours of the property, and the company remains a model forestry operation today.

Lessons Learned

Green Acres owners and managers experienced the rewards of sticking to their principles and following a positive and proactive approach to counteracting active and persistent activist challenges.

8.3 Coping With Activist Intrusions and Threats

> These threats are intensifying because current activist causes are frustrated by decreasing public and media interest.

Activism and terrorism are acts of communication. The aggressiveness of activism is intensifying in the twenty-first century. The threat of terrorism is growing in the United States and in other parts of the world; direct activist action against individuals and their families is becoming a routine tactical terrorist choice.

Targets for intrusion are key government officials, not-for-profit administrators, corporate chairmen and chief executive officers, as well as those with whom they associate, including members of boards of directors and family members, celebrities, and high-profile products.

These threats are intensifying because certain activist causes can be frustrated by decreasing public and media interest. In such cases, the tactics selected by activists must create ever larger disruptions to gain the leverage of fear and embarrassment necessary to attract media attention and to build groups of potential activist followers.

Learning to cope successfully with activist intrusion threats involves:

- Reducing or eliminating the news media component, which in turn reduces a target's attractiveness.

- Outsmarting and outmaneuvering activists, thus denying them the psychological, ceremonial, ritualistic, and public attention successes they need to achieve their objectives.

Even though activists usually alert the news media, the media will not call you in advance.

8.3.1 The Activist's Goals and Needs

Activists and terrorists have essential needs, which together achieve their audience impact objectives:

- Act or behavior of sufficient **magnitude** to gain audience and media attention.

- **Setting** for the act that facilitates communication (such as a major public event, i.e a news conference or public gathering) in a major city or at major events.

- **Timing** that suits their objective (coincident with live news broadcasts, or at major public events where communications are bound to be taking place, a major holiday).

- **Collaboration** or collaborators to carry out threats and demonstrations.

- **Demands or behavior sufficient to achieve their goal** yet retain some uncalculated flexibility. (Pushing a negative, endangering a popular figure needlessly, or demands that are too extreme may destroy the activist's credibility.)

- **Media access**, because that's the only way to reach the audiences the activist is trying to affect. Action is unlikely if no media can be present. (Even though activists always alert the news media, the media will not call you in advance. The media will, however, be there to cover the story and ask questions after you've been humiliated sufficiently.)

▶ **Suffering.** Although there are exceptions, the dedicated activist is almost always prepared to be arrested or to make the "ultimate sacrifice" if it will ensure that the message of the activist group gets through.

▶ **Newsworthiness.** All acts of terrorism and activism are first and foremost designed to make news, get attention, and reward the cause.

8.3.2 Common Myths About Activist Intrusion Activities

Look at these myths carefully. If you believe them or similar ideas from the past, you may very well suffer for your naïveté.

Myth #1: The media has reporters experienced in intrusion situations who understand enough to provide balanced coverage. Balance is the last concern of the media in a sensational story.

Myth #2: The media will take time to understand what you are going through. Reporters are generally under such enormous competitive and deadline pressure that they will believe and use almost any information acquired during a dynamic confrontational situation. They need to get the news out ahead of the competition. Sometimes the facts are sorted out later, but don't count on it. And don't count on the reporter's story being sympathetic to you or your family, except in connection with victims' deaths. Get ready to get your own story out.

Myth #3: If we explain everything to reporters, they will understand and help us out. Reporters just don't take time to learn about much of anything. They need the briefest, most appropriate, correct information as quickly as possible. If it is interesting, they will probably remember it.

Myth #4: If we avoid talking to the media until we get our facts together, the story will be better. Sadly, the media won't wait. They'll take whatever they get, put it out, and try to be in the front row when the chips fall.

Myth #5: Reporters work independently and verify facts vigorously during these situations – just as they do during regular reporting assignments. The truth is that there is almost no true checking of facts in these urgent, high-profile activist situations. Reporters go with whatever they have at the time. And, there is almost no fixing of their mistakes later. (In the past, you may have experienced and come to expect this type of research and fact-checking when dealing with experienced feature writers and editors, but these are not what you will be dealing with on the front line of a crisis.) Get ready to fix the facts yourself.

8.3.3 Preparation Errors (That Can Be Fatal)

Because of inexperience, disdain, and frustration in handling confrontations with individuals with the emotional commitment of activists and terrorists, targets make seriously false, sometimes very dangerous assumptions. Most commonly, they tend to:

> **Because of our inexperience in handling confrontations... with the emotional commitment of activists and terrorists, we make seriously false, sometimes very dangerous assumptions.**

▶ **Under-rate the activist's or terrorist's negative emotion.**

▶ **Assume that activists and terrorists are reasonable people** acting rationally when, in fact, they are emotional people acting with incomprehensible commitment.

▶ **Over-rate our own preparation.** Only specific preparation of the kind outlined here will truly prepare you to effectively move through the activist intrusion and threat.

▶ **Minimize the perceived danger.** Delay preparation.

▶ **Assume that the real danger is physical** when, in fact, it may be reputational. It may threaten your employment or relationships with others. Maximize your attention. Maximize your willingness to take the situation seriously.

▶ **Trivialize the risks.**

▶ **Assume we understand the full range of risks** involved when, in fact, until the situation ends or is resolved, or both, it's impossible to understand the full range of risks. It's much wiser to maximize, even exaggerate the potential risks and prepare for them than to minimize them for fear they might seem foolish to those around you.

▶ **Procrastinate.**

▶ **Delay getting ready** for responding to activist intrusions and threats until just after the phone rings and the demonstrators are at your door.

▶ **Ignore** issues and questions.

▶ **Assume that activists work suddenly.** Actually, the action is the end result of a careful process leading up to the action both to build media interest and sympathizers, and to get reaction from you for further energy and motivation. Every act, statement, and behavior is instructive and should be learned from. Pay attention. Think about preparing and acting should something happen.

▶ **Disparage your opposition.**

▶ **Speak foolishly** in an era of virtually instant communication. Thus, talking negatively, talking disparagingly, or acting pompously with respect to activist issues or purposes provides energy that encourages these individuals to go to further lengths to make their points when they threaten or intrude upon your activities.

> If you have a sense of activists' tactical approaches, you can then analyze your own operations and behavioral vulnerabilities and plan appropriately.

Remember:

▶ **Confrontation** is a strategy that can be modified, controlled, mitigated and anticipated.

▶ **Negotiation** face-to-face by a handful of people you trust is the only way resolution will be ultimately achieved. Remember reporters, editors, politicians, and activists don't sign treaties, agreements or contracts. They observe, speculate, move from allegation to allegation, and hope that whatever happens is interesting and furthers their search for saving the world and their world view.

▶ **Prepare, rehearse, anticipate, stay in touch, and avoid predictability.**

▶ Learn to **manage disappointment**; avoid taking things personally.

8.4 Coping With the Risk of Personal Attack

8.4.1 Tactical Advice

Avoid being or creating targets. If you have a sense of activists' tactical approaches, you can then analyze your own operations and behavioral vulnerabilities and plan appropriately. Activist tactical activities produce a visibility platform that allows them to dominate communication. Learn to preempt their tactical activities and, therefore, deny them a communication platform.

8.4.2 General Advice

1. **Think before you go somewhere.** Investigate your destination in advance so you know all your options (public entrances; public exits; secure, unobservable entrances and exits; pathways in and out; telephone locations; etc.).

2. **Avoid predictable patterns of movement and behaviors.** Activists watch, count, study, and practice.

3. **Use different doors and routes to routine places.**

4. **Avoid crowds.** When attending high-profile events, enter and leave from different entrances away from the main crowds.

5. **Avoid destinations with only one way in and out.**

6. **Always leave yourself a way out or around** – in meetings, crowds, and traffic.

7. **Be aware of what's going on around you.** Always move quickly away from unusual situations, such as accidents; incidents; noisy, attractive, unspecific activity; and problems.

8. **Arrange to be dropped off and picked up inside a building,** whenever possible, to reduce observation of your habits and avoid direct confrontation.

9. **Use escorts** – well-dressed, very big and muscular people whose mere presence can change the dynamic of a confrontational situation.

If Accosted

1. Be polite. Keep moving.

2. Respond to questions by verbally referring the questioner to someone specific in the company.

3. Move quickly toward your destination.

4. Avoid engaging in argument; be pleasant; keep moving.

5. Rehearse.

6. Always have a safe, secure destination.

Advance Preparations

1. **Cell phone:** Always carry a cell phone preset with at least a dozen critical telephone numbers (including 911) which can be dialed quickly using two-digit codes so that help can be summoned in the event something happens.

2. **Wallet card:** Always carry a wallet card with critical telephone numbers including early-hours numbers, after-hours numbers, cellular numbers, and private, unpublished numbers.

3. **Phone list:** Also carry a list of critical phone numbers for common destinations – the grocery store, department stores, gas stations, major public buildings, offices visited frequently, major event sites such as parks or stadiums. Being locatable is largely your responsibility.

4. **Contact person:** Always have someone who is in a position to make decisions know your whereabouts at all times.

5. **Avoid isolated places** that don't have easy linkages to the outside world.

6. **Communicate travel plans:** If you're going to be in a very isolated or remote site, plan in advance how you will communicate or arrange to be monitored by a trusted individual who is aware of your precise travel plans and schedule.

7. **Code phrase:** Develop a code phrase to indicate on the telephone or in a Tweet that you're in trouble. It might be a particular speaking mistake where you stumble over a common phrase, or a reference to an obscure relative or to a specific event in the past.

8. **Learn defensive driving:** Take a survival driving course – while scary, they can be fun and you'll know what to do and how to do it. Much of defensive driving is counterintuitive.

9. **Check in often** with your office or a trusted individual, or make certain someone monitors your movements and activities frequently.

> **Above all, avoid taking these situations personally however intense or emotional, or how direct and abusive the language and behavior. This is about their message, rather than you.**

Key Reminders

1. **Summon help** or alert the trusted people who monitor your movements the moment the situation looks unusual. There may be many false alarms. No matter. You should regularly make use of your preparations. If you don't, the one time you need help, you may not have it.

2. **Watch, learn, and listen.** Most activists have only a handful of arguments and points to make. Jot them down at the earliest possible opportunity after any confrontation. Alert the company's security people to the exact language used and the names of specific individuals.

3. **Pay attention.** The activist's power depends on simple, but powerful, emotional arguments or pictures.

4. **Remember it's not personal.** Above all, avoid taking these situations personally no matter how intense or emotional, or how direct or abusive the language and behavior. It's about creating a platform for making political statements by targeting the symbols of society – individuals and companies. It's your response that either provides or denies the platform. Maintain your perspective. Keep your wits about you.

8.4.3 Behavior in a Hostage Situation

In the event you are actually detained or held against your wishes, here are some important behaviors to remember:

1. **Remain calm.** You will be helped; the situation will end.
2. **Negotiate.** Ask for immediate contact with someone you have previously made arrangements with who can negotiate for you on terms you have previously approved.
3. **Listen carefully** to what is said and who says it.
4. **Ask good questions** which can help later if there are charges or prosecutions.
5. **Make only statements that will assist in your rescue.** It's okay to be sympathetic with your captors (it's called the Stockholm Syndrome), but refuse to offer statements or represent their interests unless you can use the occasion through code words or phrases to help others locate you or to communicate your condition.
6. **Remain optimistic.** Help is on the way to rescue you.

Additional Help and Information

1. In the United States, contact the local FBI Special Agent in Charge (SAC). In Canada, contact the Royal Canadian Mounted Police. They have literature and useful guides if more information is desired.

2. Contact the U.S. Department of State in Washington, D.C. Its Office of Counterterrorism has a series of pamphlets and web resources on security measures for individuals and businesses when working and travelling outside the United States.

3. Your security department can or probably does subscribe to special services that monitor various domestic and international activists and their organizations.

8.5 Coping With the Media for Victims and Targets

8.5.1 Frequently Asked Irrelevant Questions

There are certain questions targets and victims always ask, either as a part of the preparation process or after being humiliated. Sadly, given the nature of news media behavior, while these questions have become commonplace, both the question and the answer are irrelevant – there are simply no words or answers that would be satisfactory. For example:

1. **Question:** Why do the media cover these situations? Why can't the media simply ignore them so that the incentive is gone and activist action will stop? Doesn't the media care about my safety and peace of mind?

   Answer: These situations are covered because they are newsworthy, people's lives are at stake, or there is the potential for conflict. If it bleeds, or is about to bleed, or there are changes in bleeding, it's likely to lead the news.

2. **Question:** Why doesn't television stay away, or stay farther away, rather than incite violence?

   Answer: The public (you and me) wants good, clear close-ups of what's interesting and happening to somebody else. We all expect to be safely in the middle of the action regardless of the truthfulness, cost, or danger involved.

3. **Question:** Why do individuals without credibility, training, community standing, or credentials have credibility with the media, with government, and with many of our customers?

   Answer: Because... that's the way it is and that's the way it's going to stay. There is no other answer. Get ready.

4. **Question:** If we talk to the media and share with them our plans, fears, and goals, won't they cooperate in ways that might protect us in the event of an activist intrusion?

   Answer: No. The media will be very interested in your plans for negotiation, contingencies, security, and prevention or management of an intrusion incident. However, they'll then give the information to the activists in exchange for being able to be on the spot when you're attacked or taken, and to be in the middle if at all possible. Keep in mind, when it happens, they'll rush to cover it, let it happen, and report about it vigorously. The media often take credit for having "inside information," which they got from you and which allowed them to bring the audience even more extensive coverage of your public embarrassment or terror.

   > If it's important that your story be told accurately, clearly, and effectively, plan to do that yourself during and after the incident.

5. **Question:** Will the media call to get my view before reporting some story?

   Answer: Not a chance. Once they know an incident is planned, they'll want to be there to see what happens. Warning you might reduce the news value of the situation.

8.5.2 How the Legacy News Media Relates to Activism

Here are some very important factors to remember about the legacy news media:

1. Reporters are committed to saving the world from something every day.

2. Reporters' immediate sympathies lie with the activists and terrorists. Victims' concerns will come later and receive less coverage and interest than the opinions, attitudes, and actions of the activists and terrorists.

3. The reporter's training in aggression, hostility, and skepticism will make him or her question your motivations, your company's issues or problems before the reporter questions the motivations of the activists and terrorists.

4. Media coverage will be a combination of allegations, speculation, interpretation, forecasts, alarmism, and interventionism. As we see time and time again in every media crisis, neither the media nor the "peaceful" organizations have questioned the violence and destruction that occurred.

5. If it's important that your story be told accurately, clearly, and effectively, plan to do that yourself during and after the incident.

(**Note:** *For more about attitudes and mindsets in traditional or legacy media, see Chapter 5 of this book.*)

8.5.3 Counteracting Anti-Corporate Activism on the Internet

What do McDonald's, Tommy Hilfiger, Wendy's, Chrysler, General Electric, General Motors, Campbell's Soup Company, and Blockbuster Video have in common? These companies and hundreds of others have been or are the victims of highly visible, Internet-based boycotts, smear campaigns, online extortion, stock devaluation by short sellers, and other anti-corporate activism.

Responding involves specific steps, specific protocols, and specific rules, some of which may seem counterintuitive. Here are the more important response elements:

▶ **Remain calm.** Scope out the situation. Incidents most often begin with the actions of a single individual. Early observation is crucial. Use a professional Internet monitoring service – like eWatch (ewatch.prnewswire.com) – to monitor the Internet daily. Amateur monitoring misses a lot.

▶ **Assess the need to respond.** You may not need to respond. The Internet may take your position in responding. The exposure may be minimal or not affect critical discussion groups. Your business may not be affected after all.

▶ **Assume everything will come out.** Everything shows up on the web. If lawsuits are filed, it's likely that all legal correspondence, including discovery documents, will be placed on the web. So, be concise; be consistent. Expect to defend yourself beyond the courtroom. (**Note:** *For more about legal issues relating to crisis communication, see Chapter 9 of this book.*)

▶ **Shielding employee identities is impossible.** If you choose to participate in highly emotional situations in any of the social media formats, do it with full attribution to your organization or company. Avoid using pseudonyms; it always gets you into trouble later on.

▶ **Follow the "rules."** There are so-called rules of conduct such as staying in the medium and avoiding self-serving comments when posting information, etc.

▶ **Delete errors.** Work aggressively to have erroneous posts removed from Internet search engines. When confronted with proof that a post is libelous, not true, or otherwise incorrect, the major search engines will delete them from their databases.

▶ **Step out promptly.** Address obvious high-profile situations on your website. Failure to acknowledge or respond may make your company appear to be hiding something. The web is a very public medium; it exposes everything.

(**Note:** *For Internet and social networking tactics, see Chapter 7 of this book.*)

> **Companies lose to activists primarily because they are less committed to managing their own destiny.**

Companies lose to activists primarily because they are less committed to managing their own destiny. Activists are committed to defeating those they attack. Know what the activist knows. Understand the pattern of activist attack; go outside the pattern. Keep your cool. Stay focused. Remain relentless, but positive. Assess the actual damage; forecast potential damage.

Internet activism is a permanent fact of business life. Get used to it; get ready for it. Act decisively. There may be momentary damage, embarrassment, and humiliation, but activists rarely win against honorable organizations.

8.6 Guidelines for Communication When Under Attack Summed Up

The confrontational character of present day activism is designed to create a negative perception of the target, or of management's postures and attitudes. To counter these perceptions, management must communicate much more aggressively during activist attack. Here are some common-sense guidelines for organizations under attack to keep in mind:

1. Use disciplined, focused, responsive, positive communication:
   - Keep the focus on getting a positive result.
   - Get and keep negotiations out of the ditch.
   - Reduce wild goose chases (avoid taking so much so personally).
   - Control visceral response to emotional language (media focus will be inherently negative).
2. Responsive communication recognizes the emotional nature of activist communication. It means understanding the emotional vocabulary of the conversation and responding in relentlessly positive, constructive ways.
3. Only sticks and stones really break bones – words shouldn't, but negative words just about always do.
4. Even the most benevolent management, when challenged, usually tries to shoot the messenger – communicators need to wear bulletproof underwear.
5. We erroneously assume our allies know how vulnerable and weak our resolve is, and how to help us. Talk to them privately. Tell them what to do and not do. Tell them how to be of help, even if it means doing nothing. Avoid putting them in harm's way.
6. Your opponents assume you are as committed to winning as they are. Your ineptness is a surprise. Like bullies everywhere, when they detect your ineptitude, then they will count on it to allow them to escalate emotional intensity.
7. Your silence is toxic to your cause.

One of the great lessons in activist counteraction communications is that if you talk about war, if you act like you're going to war, and then you get ready for war, there will be war. Avoid getting sucked into war. *Plan for peace*. Peace is dull, uninteresting, but, ironically, it will force early, more positive resolution.

Here is a brief *destiny-management* strategy to counteract predictable patterns of activist attack.

Their Attack Will:

1. Polarize the issue. No matter what, you're 120% in the wrong.

2. Build a base on the web; use email lists; post to bulletin boards to create support for their cause.

3. Trivialize, emotionalize, insult, and humiliate; pick a web address like "companysucks.com."

4. Anger, irritate, debilitate, violate trademarks, and misinterpret every response; force your hand by intentionally provoking a legal response to showcase on their site.

5. Use ultimatums; bombard the company with last chances to correct allegations, charges, and "testimony" before "going live" and staging demonstrations.

6. Register their site on search engines – in your corporate section, if possible.

7. Post messages on electronic bulletin boards to promote their cause; promote their site; locate others suffering from the same problems; find disgruntled employees willing to help.

8. Work the news media; target specific journalists who cover your company or industry. The media never tire of finding ways to attack business.

Your Response Will Be To:

1. Explain exaggerations; admit errors; outline action steps.

2. Assess the actual damage; estimate potential damage; determine need for preemptive action, correct and clarify.

3. Create a neat, clean, corporate looking response site; contrast your legitimacy with their juvenile, trivial approach.

4. Choose your battles carefully; respond calmly, deliberately, succinctly, competently, incrementally. Stay focused; use appropriate language for the medium and key themes.

5. Respond carefully, positively, candidly, politely. If in the wrong, correct the problem. Point out errors; point out emotionalism; insist on independent proof. Be cool.

6. Register your response site in the same manner; when resolved, remove listings.

7. Monitor the Internet using a service provider such as eWatch; assess actual impact. Discourage loyal employees from responding on your behalf; respond only if necessary. Have erroneous posts removed from search engines.

8. Direct journalists to your response site. Point out the exaggeration; admit errors; outline action steps. Avoid whining. positive, declarative language.

Lukaszewski's Contention Survival Manifesto
Keeping Yourself and the Things That Matter Under Control

This manifesto is a personal and often publicly declared set of principles, policies, and intentions for addressing contentious public circumstances and situations, and behaving with integrity, honesty, and even good humor. If your mother could teach you the rules for winning in the irritating, aggravating, agitating environment of being under attack in the news media — personally, politically, or professionally — these are the 27 techniques and practices she (or most moms) would share. You can succeed even in the face of contentious people, angry neighbors, negative media coverage, and irritated public officials.

1. **Speak only for yourself.** Say less, write less, but make these communications truly important.

2. **Answer every question.** Aim for 75-150 word responses; this is 30-60 seconds reading or speaking time. Honorable organizations, people, programs, and initiatives can answer any question.

3. **Always let others speak for themselves.** When you try to speak for others, you will always be wrong, and attacked or humiliated for being wrong.

4. **Avoid claiming that you agree with your opponents** on anything, unless they say so first. Once opponents say it, you may quote them saying it, but always say what you believe to be true and back that up.

5. **Avoid saying that you work closely with public agencies,** other organizations, or even individuals related to your situation (even if you believe you do), unless they say so first and you then quote them. Otherwise, they can deny it (especially if controversy arises) or point out, as some may quite quickly, that whatever links exist are rather weak. They will then describe those weaknesses or deny that you have any real influence. Those who can and may support you in the future (public or private) must have their status preserved for the long run. Drawing them into your discussion could needlessly make them targets of attack. They will have to abandon or, perhaps, denounce or distance themselves from you.

6. **Assume that everyone in the discussion has more credibility than you do.** Your job is to validate your credibility, every time, rather than to discredit others.

7. **Be relentlessly positive** (avoid all negative words) and constructive (avoid criticizing and criticism). Both provide the fuel opponents thrive on.

8. **Focus on the truly important 5%;** forget the rest. Respond to and develop what truly matters.

9. **Let attackers discredit themselves.** Their emotional words and negative, destructive language equals less truth and trustworthiness. Avoid "friends" who suggest this approach. It will always backfire.

10. **Practice laggership.** Speak second but always have the last word.

11. **Remain calm.** Critics, agitators, and bullies are energized by anger, emotionalism, whininess, and negative counterattacks.

12. **Silence is always toxic to the accused.** After a while, even your friends will sacrifice or question you.

13. **Apologies are always in order,** provided they contain all of the crucial ingredients of an effective apology. The most constructive structures for apology are in *The Five Languages of Apology* (2008) by Gary Chapman and Jennifer Thomas. Here, with some paraphrasing and modification based on my experiences, are the ingredients of the perfect apology.

    ▶ **Regret (acknowledgment):** A verbal acknowledgement by the perpetrators that their wrongful behavior caused unnecessary pain, suffering, and hurt that identifies, specifically, what action or behavior is responsible for the pain.

    ▶ **Accepting Responsibility (declaration):** An unconditional declarative statement by the perpetrators recognizing their wrongful behavior and acknowledging that there is no excuse for the behavior.

    ▶ **Restitution (penance):** An offer of help or assistance to victims, by the perpetrator; action beyond the words "I'm sorry"; and conduct that assumes the responsibility to make the situation right.

    ▶ **Repentance (humility):** Language by the perpetrator acknowledging that this behavior caused pain and suffering for which he/she is genuinely sorry; language by the perpetrator recognizing that serious, unnecessary harm and emotional damage was caused.

    ▶ **Direct Forgiveness Request:** "I was wrong, I hurt you, and I ask you to forgive me."

    The most difficult and challenging aspects of apologizing are the admission of having done something hurtful, damaging, or wrong, and to request forgiveness. Skip even one step and you fail.

14. **Have courage, and refuse to be distracted by negativity, friendly pressure, or the agendas of others.** You are in the spotlight. They are in the shadows. Be especially wary of those who feel that responding empowers others, or that you might look like a sissy for having done it. Either of these outcomes is better than being considered boorish, bullyish, arrogant, or callous.

15. **Discourage others from explaining your situation.** They will get it wrong. You will be blamed, and they will be attacked. They will then have to abandon you altogether, keep some distance, or attack you to preserve their own credibility.

16. **Everything that goes around comes back around.** Avoid verbal "vegetables," the words phrases, arguments, assertions, and statements you write or say that you know you will have to eat some time in the future.

17. **Remember the math of truth:** Truth is 15% facts and data, and 85% emotion and perception; 65% of truth is point of reference (my backyard or neighborhood). Facts do matter, but addressing the emotional component of issues and questions immediately, continuously, and constructively is essential for success.

18. **Be strategic.** Say, act, plan, and write with future impact in mind.

19. **Prepare to work alone** and to be abandoned by just about everyone.

20. **Stay at altitude,** keep a distance, avoid taking events or actions personally, and be reasoned, appropriate, and direct. Positive and constructive responses tend to disempower those making the attacks.

21. **Keep the testosterosis under control.** Every bit of negative energy you throw in their direction will multiply by a factor of 5 to 10, and they will throw it right back at you.

22. **Be preemptive.** Work in real time. Do it now, fix it now, ask it now, correct it now, challenge it now, and answer it now.

23. **Write and speak simply, sensibly, positively, empathetically, and constructively.**

24. **Avoid trying to discredit anyone, any argument, any evidence, or any movement.** Such actions stimulate the creation of critics and adversaries, who accumulate, hang around, live forever, and search relentlessly to exploit your weaknesses, vulnerabilities, and susceptibilities. Prove your position with positive, declarative language.

25. **Get accustomed to accommodating the long-term, relentlessly negative nature of contentious situations.**

26. **Correct and clarify what matters promptly,** but do it all on your own website. Avoid joining blogs or conversations outside your site. The latter strategy will suck all of your energy into responding to the agendas of others who are having fun and sleeping well, while you are doing neither.

27. **It is your destiny.** Fail to manage it, and someone else is waiting in the wings to do it for you.

Chapter 8 – Questions for Study and Discussion

1. What is one positive step an organization can take when it becomes the target of activist criticism, bringing with it negative publicity?

2. What are the characteristics of an effective apology? Imagine that you work for a company that has been involved in a recent crisis involving damage to victims and stockholders, BP for example. Compose an apology that contains all the requirements recommended in the "contention survival" part of this chapter. Practice it with another person for effectiveness.

3. Why are the "rules" suggested by Alinsky so attractive to people who consider themselves ill-used, unheard, or under-rewarded? What makes the approach work so well? What are three steps you would advise management to take in the face of radicals who might "go public" regarding your company and its actions?

References, Chapter 8

Alinsky, S.D. (1971). *Rules for radicals: a pragmatic primer for realistic radicals* (reprint 1989). New York: Vintage Books.

Chapman, G. & Thomas, J. (2008). *The five languages of apology: how to experience healing in all your relationships*. Chicago: Northfield Publishing.

9

Crisis Communication Plan in Action: Litigation and Legal Issues

Keywords: visibility, compliance, legal risk analysis, legal management, civil litigation, criminal litigation, RICO, compliance, trial communication manager (TCM), privileged communication, legal risk analysis, litigation communications strategy, mediation, alternative dispute resolution (ADR), work product doctrine (WPD), apology

We talked about "unplanned visibility" at the beginning of this book. Lawsuits and indictments against your company and its principals are guaranteed to result in a level of visibility that you want to avoid. We recommend that you get ready by preparing for anticipated crises, making sure that management is aware of the legal ramifications of any lax compliance, and developing for yourself a knowledge of how law and lawyers operate and how best to handle the media in the event of high-visibility litigation.

This chapter will help you to:

> Act responsibly as a communicator in the face of litigation.
> Understand the difference between the civil and criminal court litigation processes.
> Manage lawyers.
> Avoid bad trial publicity.

9.1 Basic Advice: Avoid Litigation by Avoiding Trouble

Trust me on this: you want to avoid the criminal justice system at all costs. Corporate behavior patterns that predict trouble are easily recognized but often ignored. If you keep an eye on your company's approaches to regulated activity, you can easily detect operational facts and behaviors that reveal either the existence of or potential for troublesome, perhaps criminal, corporate behavior.

9.1.1 Institutionalizing Corporate Compliance Practices:
Seven Critical Steps

Effective compliance programs and practices help organizations to diligently prevent unlawful, even criminal, behavior. They also help an organization to take action capably and to defend itself when unwanted behavior is detected. The following seven steps are adapted from the due diligence process contained in the *2010 Federal Sentencing Guidelines Manual*.

Step 1: **Establish a centralized compliance function.** This corporate function and department are mandated by the Board of Directors, with access to the resources of the CEO, COO, and chief legal counsel. This function oversees compliance and adherence to standards for the entire organization.

Step 2: **Appoint a senior-level manager as senior VP, compliance.** As a member of the company's top management team, this individual has overall responsibility for establishing an effective compliance program, developing working standards, conducting annual training on compliance principles and standards, and establishing reporting processes to detect and disclose violations.

Step 3: **Train all employees, agents, vendors, and customers.** Conduct mandatory annual seminars, prepare and distribute written guidelines, produce videos that demonstrate the right way and the wrong way, and require compliance agreements from agents, vendors, and customers.

Step 4: **Establish a reporting process.** Set up an "800" telephone number, confidential e-mail system, or direct contact mechanism with the senior compliance officer through whom employees, agents, vendors, and customers can anonymously report compliance violations or inappropriate behavior.

Step 5: **When violations are found, take appropriate, consistent, prompt disciplinary action.** Standards without enforcement do not work. Non-enforcement looks like complicity or the condoning of non-compliance.

Step 6:   **Communicate immediately and conclusively about compliance violations.** Employees, agents, vendors, and customers need to know when compliance standards have been violated. Public acknowledgement is a powerful deterrent. No one wants his or her name in a violation report document.

Step 7:   **Commit to constant improvement.** Expect to detect incidents of non-compliance; good compliance programs will detect occasional non-compliance. While embarrassing, these situations are opportunities to review standards and procedures, to eradicate weaknesses in the organization's ethics and compliance processes, and to educate.

Measure the effectiveness of your ethics program against these seven steps. If you do not have an existing program, use these seven steps as a foundation.

9.1.2 Preventing Problems Through Legal Risk Analysis

Legal risk assessment must be added to your scope of issue investigation and problem prevention. Reputation-threatening legal risks arise from several corporate behaviors, all of which can be avoided:

▶ **Arrogance.** Example: A large multi-national petroleum company spills millions of gallons of oil in an environmentally pristine area, appears to respond slowly and not really care what outsiders think, and uses its financial and economic muscle to keep neighbors, outsiders, activists, and the government from investigating the spill and taking action.

▶ **Selective disclosure.** Example: A consumer product manufacturing company that sells a critical component used in millions of customer-owned machines discovers a defect, which has only the remotest possibility of causing user problems. This defect is disclosed to a select group of individuals who "understand" the situation and will not make a big issue out of it. No thought is given to what will happen when other owners discover the situation (which they inevitably will).

▶ **Deception.** Example: A large national retailer, one of the finest companies in the U.S., provides a standard of service backed up by one of the most powerfully positive guarantees in American business. The company is discovered to be falsifying repair reports, not replacing parts correctly, and in many cases billing for but not making the indicated repairs. The company initially discounts published reports calling it an "isolated incident," but within weeks, operations in 45 states are involved.

▶ **Ignorance.** Example: A medical products manufacturer, without notifying or receiving permission from the U.S. Food and Drug Administration, modifies crucial medical devices designed for use during life-saving surgical procedures. When, due to a patient death, the company is confronted with the alterations, it relies initially solely on its contacts with medical specialists, ignoring the concerns of hundreds of thousands of patients affected annually by their products and these surgical procedures.

▶ **Insensitivity.** Example: Following published reports of problems with implantable devices in women, the seven manufacturers band together to "get the facts" out. In the information campaign, they focus on selected scientific facts, ignoring the emotional distress suffered by millions of women with these medical devices. The manufacturers persist in using this "factual" approach until public outrage reaches Congressional proportions.

▶ **Intolerance.** Example: A national restaurant chain, following one embarrassing situation after another related to discrimination on the basis of color and sexual orientation, announces a complete reorganization of its company, approach, and, to some extent, its management. However, instances of intolerance and discrimination continue to be reported.

▶ **Regulation.** Example: Allegations are made that the company used undue influence on the rule-making process through the use of highly paid lobbyists, experts, and research. Subsequent investigation, including information provided by a whistle-blower, reveals a pattern of kick-backs, bawdy parties in remote locations for the benefit of government officials, and collusion with other industries.

▶ **Reputation.** Example: A large regional restaurant chain experiences an incident in which a number of customers, including several small children, become seriously ill. One child dies. The restaurant chain immediately announces that the food purveyor is at fault and attempts to shift public interest to that company.

▶ **Requirements.** Example: An internationally known, up-scale boutique specialty store that sells both a high-profile food product, and the equipment to process it, refuses to help a disgruntled customer with a product problem in an efficient and timely manner. The individual hires a lawyer and goes to the news media. The company, whose slogan is, "Your satisfaction at any cost," still refuses to help the customer. Stories about the problem continue to appear in major market newspapers.

▶ **Secrecy.** Example: The XYZ Corporation shuts down operations on a rather beautiful island location, announcing that the plant will be torn down and the site turned into a park and donated to the city. As the opening of the park approaches and after $7 million has been spent to develop the site, a black, smelly liquid is found oozing into the center of the main parking lot. The U.S. Environmental Protection Agency announces a criminal investigation of the company for non-disclosure of the existence of the contamination.

▶ **Stinginess.** Example: A national retail chain with more than 15 million credit card customers mistakenly over-bills 3,000 customers by amounts ranging from $2.50 to $65. After much discussion with the lawyers and in fear of many lawsuits, the company sends out a form letter, issuing each over-charged customer a precise credit for the amount accidentally billed. Two major class action lawsuits are instituted, mostly on behalf of those who were overcharged less than $10.

▶ **Stupidity.** Example: A large consumer food products chain, after having settled many cases related to burns caused by the spillage of hot beverages, decides that it will no longer settle these cases, but instead will pursue the next one to the bitter end.

▶ **Tardiness.** Example: A manufacturing plant suffers a major malfunction causing a noxious smelling gas to escape in large quantities. The emission forces the evacuation of hundreds of neighbors. Only after the public disclosure of the nature of the incident did residents learn that they had been exposed to very low levels of this same chemical for several years.

▶ **Testosterosis.** Example: The lending practices of a major bank are attacked publicly by a public interest research group. The bank labels the group as a "bunch of radical activists" and refuses to talk about the dispute or meet with representatives of the group. The bank's public comment is, "We can't afford to set this kind of precedent."

9.1.3 Litigation Volume Reduction Techniques
Today's corporations are so gun-shy of "responsibility" that very poor judgment is exercised when it comes to caring for victims.

Strategic approaches that reduce litigation include the following:

1. **Speak with compassion, even if you can conclusively prove that it was "the other guy's fault."** Every day we see settlements in which it's simply easier to pay something than to go through the course of lengthy, embarrassing, and costly litigation. The earlier you write the check, the smaller that check will be. The more compassionately you talk, the more sympathetic your approach, the smaller the check is likely to be.

> **Today's corporations are so gun-shy of "responsibility" that very poor judgment is exercised when it comes to caring for victims.**

2. **Act quickly to help the victims.** Today's corporations are so gun-shy of "responsibility" that very poor judgment is exercised when it comes to caring for victims. Better to pay for emergency room charges, rent hotel rooms, and provide temporary assistance immediately than to let victims suffer and to allow the media to aggravate the situation on the nightly news as attorneys for the plaintiff build a better case or attract a class action.

3. **Be neighborly.** Acting neighborly is what the public expects of large organizations in adverse situations. Remember that juries are made up of neighbors. Be nice.

4. **Measure carefully the unintended consequences.** While many legal issues are worth fighting for, they are rarely won in court. One reason is that large organizations are usually guilty of something. And that something always seems to come to light at the worst possible time. Are the visibility price, the relationship price, the cost of constituent irritation, and the lack of truth worth fighting to the death?

5. **Communicate strategically.** For example, here are strategies, priorities, and internal and external communication goals for a model visibility management communication approach to litigation:

   ▶ *Strategy*

   ❏ To activate, when necessary, an appropriately restrained public communications approach that preempts or neutralizes potentially negative news coverage.

   ❏ To be prepared to address and communicate externally and internally about the findings and the impact.

   ❏ To bring management together as necessary to coordinate communication objectives.

   ▶ *Priorities*

   ❏ To focus initially on audiences directly affected; then on audiences less directly affected, i.e., management, employees, sales force, customers, shareholders; then on the media and others.

▶ *Internal Communication Goals*

☐ To conduct communication between management and employees that is prompt, preemptive, candid, effective, and informative – from the perspective of the employees.

☐ To communicate the company's progress in areas where improvements have been made.

▶ *External Communication Goals*

☐ To respond positively in ways supportive of the company's litigation visibility goals.

☐ To communicate a limited number of very focused, specific, and useful messages.

The climate of litigation visibility is going to get more combative. In fact, it is getting easier to sue and indict corporations and large organizations. Litigation has become part of the American agenda, beyond politics and party. The lesson here is that much litigation is within the corporation's ability to manage – if the corporation and the people who run it so choose.

CASE STUDY: The Knock on the Door – A CEO Faces Criminal Indictment

It was George's last day on the job. He had been CEO for 20 years and had worked for the company 20 years before that. The company was in the Fortune 500 and it had pioneered many interesting and unusual medical devices. Now the Department of Justice had issued sweeping indictments of the corporation, its officers, and a number of employees on hundreds of felony counts. I was in his office to help him clean out his desk and take his stuff down to the car. His new office was located about two miles away in a nondescript suburban office building. His indictment had occurred a few days before, in Boston, and he was due to take his last flight on the corporate jet in the morning to surrender himself to Federal authorities. He flew up alone. The flight took about an hour and a half. He was greeted by his attorneys at the private aircraft facility at Boston Logan and was driven to the Federal facility where he surrendered himself and was taken into custody. He was subsequently photographed, fingerprinted, strip searched, and given a bright orange jumpsuit to wear with the words "Prisoner" in eight-inch letters across the back. He was escorted to a cell where he waited from approximately 9:15 a.m. until 4:10 p.m., when he was manacled and attached to a chain of 25 other prisoners and moved down the hall, chain-gang style to his arraignment.

The arraignment was scheduled to occur between 4:20 and 5:00 p.m. He was to be the last arraigned. However, in a surprisingly pleasant turn of events, the arraignment of almost everyone in the room ahead of him took place in about four minutes. They left the room, and he found himself alone with the judge, the attorneys, and a few onlookers. Nevertheless, the message was clearly sent: if you are a corporate criminal, especially of a significant company – guilty or innocent – you will be on display as part of a message being sent by the criminal justice system.

He pled not guilty and was released on his own recognizance. After a brief meeting with his attorneys, he was returned to the airport and took a commercial aircraft back to his home. When he and I spoke a few days later, he expressed his relief at getting the indictment out of the way. He could stop worrying about it and could finally begin doing some things he had wanted to do with his life.

My question to him was, "George, what could that possibly be besides preparing for your criminal trial?"

His response was, "Well, for so many years I was only involved in important causes in an honorary fashion. People used my name and title on the checks we sent. Now, I can actually spend some time with these endeavors and make the contribution I've always wanted to make."

"George," I said, "tomorrow morning, you, your wife, and I are meeting in your new offices to call all of these organizations, and you are going to resign. None of these organizations wants to have an indicted potential felon in any position of responsibility or visibility."

There was silence at the other end of the line. I thought I heard a very sad sigh.

Conclusion

As the parade of the prosecuted CEOs, CFOs, General Counsels, and other corporate executives (including some PR executives) continues, communicators need to know much more about the legal system, especially the unusual nature of criminal prosecution. Of all of the things that can happen to a company and an individual in that company, among the most devastating is criminal prosecution, or the threat of criminal prosecution. Any advisor working in a large-to-medium-sized company, not-for-profit agency, or public company has an obligation to understand and be conversant with the sequence of events and pattern of behaviors in a criminal prosecution scenario.

9.2 Challenges for Business in Today's Legalistic Environment

Primarily in Western democracies, but increasingly in all cultures, large organizations operate in more legalistic environments, requiring strict compliance. Such environments have a number of important attributes:

▶ **Rules and regulations:** The promulgation of rules and regulations has been refined to a maddening level of detail. Governments worldwide at every level are still attempting to define behaviors, outcomes, and even specific process steps at the most micro of levels, backing them up with stiff civil and, often, criminal penalties. The difference between these conditions in other parts of the world and those within the US is that even without the presence of relevant rules and regulations, stiff civil and criminal penalties are already in place. There is no more frightening prospect than running afoul of the law in a country where bail bond procedures have yet to be established.

▶ **Aggressive government enforcement:** In every regulated area, the government seems more inclined to investigate, take the initiative, and act on allegations with less evidence with the overwhelming support of the public.

▶ **Zero tolerance:** In a variety of areas, the public no longer accepts even small accidents or infractions, applying a standard of zero tolerance to environmental and health and safety issues. Most publics, including employees, are expecting near-perfect performance.

▶ **Public expectations:** In the US, expectations of business have always been high. Products are expected to work and not cause injuries. Corporations are expected to act, at the very least, in the public interest, and certainly not against it. When negative events threaten or occur, public and legal responses result.

▶ **Employee expectations:** A primary source of information used in anti-corporate legal action and prosecution comes from those within the organization. Information comes from disappointed or disgruntled employees; a far larger number of these employee informers or "whistle-blowers" are credible, honorable people who have witnessed wrong, stupid, or unlawful behaviors and feel they must bypass management to go to the authorities. The internal risks for whistle-blowers: in its biannual report on ethics in American business, the Ethics Resource Center in Washington, D.C., has documented a consistent increase in both the observance of unethical or perhaps criminal behavior in organizations, and an even greater increase in punishment meted out internally to those who report such behavior.

▶ **Personal exposure and liability:** Increasingly statutes, rules, and regulations are written to pierce the corporate barrier, making individuals personally responsible for regulatory infractions against laws involving health and safety, environment, and hazardous waste or disposal. In some cases personal liability and additional liability for the organization are highly probable, frequently prosecuted for conspiracy – when two or more people knowingly cooperate in an illegal activity.

▶ **Legal concerns dominate:** A study of 35 representative crisis situations (Fitzpatrick & Rubin, 1995) reveals that PR advice and participation (and by extension, PR concerns) were non-existent or clearly secondary to legal advice and counsel. The communications consultant is often left "outside the room" when issues have legal overtones. This is the result of perceived ineffectiveness of PR and communications, which need to repair their own reputation rather than whine about outside legal counsel or the executives who trust attorneys and seek their assistance.

> **Your challenge is to understand this matrix of outside legal consultants and to be ready to work through it when something happens.**

9.3 Corporate Issues and Legal Issues

9.3.1 Understanding the Categories of Law in a Business

No matter what your role in a corporation, you would do well to attain a higher level of sensitivity to legal issues. From your perspective, the legal issues of a business organization fall into four general categories: legal management, litigation, lobbying, and negotiation/conciliation.

Legal management, broadly defined, involves as many as 20 important categories – everything from personnel law, health and welfare law, unemployment law, workers' compensation law, and interstate commerce law, to laws that focus on specific industries. The job of inside corporate counsel is to understand how the law relates to the corporation and to quickly provide the skill-set necessary to handle legal problems requiring expertise beyond the general. However, because your in-house corporate lawyers need to preserve privilege, they hire specialist firms to manage special problems. Even when substantial in-house expertise is available, outside legal expertise is still hired. The larger the organization, the more likely it is that such outside assistance is already in place. Your challenge is to understand this matrix of outside legal consultants and to be ready to work through it when something happens.

Litigation is, of course, the business of suing others or being sued. Usually, two types of lawyers are involved in litigation.

▶ One group is made up of those who understand the issues and develop the legal framework the organization will use to take the offense or manage its defense.

▶ The other group is the litigators whose job it is to be out front either taking action, usually accomplished by filing a complaint and becoming the plaintiff, or responding to the legal actions of others and becoming a defendant.

Lobbying is included because so many lobbyists – those who influence legislation – also happen to be attorneys.

Negotiation/conciliation, also called mediation or alternative dispute resolution (ADR), involves lawyers in an environment in which both parties agree to bargain to accommodate each others' concerns to the point at which the problem can be resolved more or less amicably.

9.3.2 Differences Between Corporate and Legal Values

If you are not accustomed to the world of the law, you may find some aspects to be different than you expect. The five most readily identifiable differences between your corporate communication operations and the law are:

1. **Process.** Law is a process. An individual called a judge helps or makes everyone understand the rules of the game and has the power to intervene from time to time to ensure that the process moves in the correct direction. Standard procedures, rules, and approaches apply, no matter the situation or the kind of law. Serious legal consequences result when the process is not followed.

2. **Most aspects are known.** General familiarity with the law is both a function of the process itself and the existence of an entire branch of government structured to make certain that the legal process works from beginning to end – from initial filing of a complaint to appeals directed to the U.S. Supreme Court. Each aspect, each step, each variance, each procedure can be identified, defined, and positioned appropriately within the spectrum of legal activity.

3. **Automatic management respect.** Clearly, a strong desire to avoid the consequences of punishment, damages, humiliation, or other actions of a punitive or public nature causes management to respect the legal process and its representatives. Management knows it must listen very carefully when lawyers speak – even when lawyers talk about things that are outside of their expertise or for which they have little respect, such as corporate communications and other in-house matters.

4. **Words in the law have very specific meanings.** One example is the word *evidence*. In the law, evidence is a body of facts, assembled

and presented in court as a part of the legal process in an attempt to prove or disprove an issue, including such items as oral testimony, documents, and public records. Even the extent to which evidence can be admitted to be considered in court is governed by a set of rigorous rules and standards. On the other hand, in the corporate world, you find a broader definition of evidence, which often includes almost any document, newspaper clip, comment, or idea that seems relevant. Not so in the law. The meanings of most words in the law are far more exact than in general usage, making the business of legal communication one of precision and care.

> **Because an attorney may often regard the intuitive nature of corporate thinking as unintelligible and of little value, important ideas may seem to be dismissed out of hand.**

5. The **legal thinking process** is more logical, systematic, and strategic. Perhaps one of the most crucial differences is in the area of thinking and reasoning. The law is principally a process created to develop evidence. Evidence can be direct, that is, observed first-hand by someone, or indirect, that is, validated by other means. Because an attorney may regard the intuitive nature of corporate thinking as unintelligible and often of little value, important ideas may seem to be dismissed out of hand. To be successful in communicating with the attorney, you need to become aware of what the legal system accepts as factual evidence and learn to propose your company's ideas and concepts in more systematic, structured, well-reasoned ways.

9.3.3 Similarities Between Corporate and Legal Values

There is some good news. Corporate life has already given you experiences and skills that will assist you in the legal arena. The four most readily identifiable similarities between your corporate expertise and the law are:

1. **Writing and speaking skills.** Law is very much a verbal process. While many, many documents are produced and developed in the course of litigation or a legal situation, they are generally not the persuading factor. They play only a supportive role, a factual role, and, to some extent, a bureaucratic role. It's the lawyer's arguing of a case, position, or perspective that becomes the deciding factor – along with the evidence, which becomes part of any legal proceeding. Even during the appeals process – when lawyers receive only a very limited time to argue their cases and where appeals judges genuinely study and examine the records provided – it can be the lawyer's oral argument that focuses the court on the essential issues in the case.

2. **Novel approaches can win.** Despite all the process, the structure, the bureaucracy, and the enormous burden of litigation-generated content, the lawyer who is sought after is the lawyer who can apply all of these pieces in client-friendly, strategically effective ways. New law is made outside of the legislative process by how lawyers interpret and how they get courts and other legal jurisdictions to agree with their interpretations. In law, just as in corporate communications, the novel interpretation of a seemingly mundane set of facts can make a simple subject electrifying and exciting in the hands of the right individual and intellect.

> **In law as in corporate life, the individual who can focus on the needs and problems of the people... is the individual with the winning strategy.**

3. **People-focus.** In the law as in corporate life, the individual who can focus on the needs and problems of the people, legitimately putting himself or herself in the people's shoes and working from the people's perspective, is the individual with the winning strategy. In law, there's nothing worse than what's called an "expert's case," which features almost no testimony from a people perspective, but instead offers very technical testimony from academics, economists, scientists, technologists, and subject matter experts. The lawyer with the people focus, especially when that focus is demonstrated in front of a jury, can win. The same is clearly true for corporations that are striving to preserve their reputations and deal effectively with the issues that affect their important constituencies. Arguing an issue with a people focus helps to overcome the daunting, often arrogant image of large organizations.

4. **Personality dominates.** Law is often a personality-dominated profession, especially among high-profile specialists such as attorneys specializing in defense, criminal law, class action, and public advocacy. While nobody at your company may have a personality that has achieved the national fame of some attorneys, corporations also have their share of compelling personalities. Your company will need to put forward similar charismatic personalities to motivate and aggressively dominate the crucial communications issues that the company faces.

9.3.4 Understanding the Types of Litigation
Civil Litigation
In civil litigation, the individual or organization that sues is called the *plaintiff.* The action is usually for money, but it can also be for a variety of other claims involving injury or damages such as libel, loss of entitlements, loss of property,

or contract enforcement. The individual or organization being sued is the *defendant*. The result is generally the award of damages, or property, or ownership, or custody, or additional rights, or other remedies to repair or redress an "injured" plaintiff. Anyone can be a plaintiff, whether it is individuals, companies, the government, or lawyers acting on their own. Virtually anyone can file a civil suit.

Keep in mind that the government can and often does file civil lawsuits from which it is awarded and receives damages or is convicted and pays damages. Practically speaking, in civil litigation, both the plaintiffs and defendants have access to the same information, the same data, and each others' witnesses and evidence. Civil litigation can be frustrating, irritating, maddening, and time consuming, but victory usually goes to the side that is best prepared in terms of evidence and case presentation.

> **The principal difference between civil law and criminal litigation is the concept of punishment.**

Criminal Litigation

In criminal litigation, the *plaintiff* – now called the prosecution - is always an agency of government. It could be a county government, state government, the U.S. federal government, or an agency of government such as the FDA, EPA, or OSHA. The defendant can be virtually anyone: another government agency, a foreign government, a corporation, an individual, or a private organization.

A corporation, organization, or individual cannot face a more frightening or seriously debilitating situation than criminal prosecution. Criminal law is established for the purpose of "preventing harm to society." It declares what conduct is criminal and prescribes the punishment to be imposed for such conduct. The principal difference between civil law and criminal litigation is the concept of punishment, which, in criminal law can mean incarceration and fines. Because criminal laws are designed to protect society and individuals from harm, the government has great latitude in how it conducts its investigations and when it informs the defendants of the information it has collected. Government also has the ability to search and seize information using a variety of lawful – but secret – information collection processing methods.

Some criminal statutes have been adapted for use in non-criminal circumstances, for example the RICO statutes (Racketeer Influenced and Corrupt Organizations Act). Enacted by Congress in 1970, this act aims to combat the influence of organized crime in interstate and foreign commerce, making it unlawful to use a pattern of racketeering activity or the proceeds from such activities to control, conduct, or manage the affairs of a business operating interstate. Both civil and criminal penalties can be imposed. While RICO is a bit beyond the scope of this chapter, corporations and their PR/issues managers are well advised to study civil RICO statutes with respect to how they might apply to specific kinds of corporate activity.

Due to increasing government prosecution of corporate executives, a solid knowledge of law, particularly criminal litigation, has become mandatory for those who advise senior management. Many governments, at many levels, are either beginning to focus on and emphasize criminal prosecution of statutes and laws, or are criminalizing laws, rules, and regulations that in the past involved only civil penalties. This trend of toughened enforcement continues and, despite much public policy rhetoric to the contrary, the public's increasing demand for punishment will strengthen the government's use and enhancement of punitive measures that serve to satisfy the public's expectations.

Case Study: A Sexual Harassment Lawsuit

Abusive, coercive, bullying behavior needs to be dealt with conclusively, constructively, and very quickly. The more promptly the company acts with directness, compassion, and common sense, the more manageable this problem will become. Sexual harassment involves serial predator behavior. The perpetrator benefits because almost every victim remains silent and suffers alone – and there are always multiple victims. The higher these behaviors occur in an organization, the more witnesses there actually are – most if not all generally remaining silent, thus becoming complicit with the perpetrator.

The Company

Dependable Insurance is a 140,000-employee company with offices throughout the US and Canada and in many foreign countries, selling a full line of business and private insurance products. It has advertising and public relations budgets exceeding $10 million per year.

The Crisis

Dependable's legal department was notified that Karen, a former employee, was to file a sexual harassment complaint against Mark, the current CEO, within the next 48 hours. Karen alleged that she had been forced to travel and cohabit with Mark in order to keep her job. While Mark's interest in Karen and overt inappropriate behavior toward her in the presence of others was far from a secret, senior management banter was, "She must like it if she keeps going along with it."

The Complexities

According to a draft complaint of the civil suit, Karen was seeking restitution and damages. The graphic illustrations and allegations of her humiliation in the workplace promised adverse publicity in many company cities and in the trade press. Considering that the insurance industry already has dozens of watchdog organizations, critics, and ongoing commentators, this had the potential to develop into a very explosive situation.

The Approach:

To respond, the company had essentially three options.

Option one: Do nothing other than prepare for the litigation. In response to outside inquiries, the communication approach would be to deny all charges with little comment.

▶ "We believe these charges to be groundless and the emotions of a disgruntled former employee. We will prevail at trial."

▶ "We don't know what she's talking about; we cannot comment further because the matter is in litigation."

Option two: Prepare for trial and its attendant publicity, work to discover the facts, avoid making any statements, and suppress information through pretrial motions. Prepare to discredit the plaintiff if need be, but especially for the trial.

Option three: Immediately split the legal team in two task groups: litigation and settlement. Have the settlement team approach the plaintiff, if possible, before filing occurs. Attempt to achieve a negotiated settlement at the earliest possible time. Courts generally support any serious efforts at settlement at any time during the litigation process.

The Culmination

The company sought my advice too late, already having chosen option two, an aggressive anti-victim strategy to discredit Karen. Once a lawyer was chosen as a spokesperson, the company said very little. Company litigators argued vigorously against any settlement, claiming it would make Mark look weak. When I disagreed, I was excluded from company litigation strategy meetings. I advised that Mark be terminated, but he was kept on as CEO, finally suspended at the last minute, just before the trial began.

The trial went badly for Dependable Insurance. Karen was a credible, empathetic witness. Badgering by defense attorneys only made things worse. Throughout, Mark maintained his innocence, supported by his peers and colleagues. He was ultimately separated from the company with a significant payout, eventually taking a job with a startup company in Silicon Valley.

As for Karen, she had been assaulted repeatedly by Mark, who abused his position of power to take advantage of an employee, while his buddies stood around and watched. I doubt that even a good day in court will help Karen heal, but it may be a start.

Lessons Learned

Dependable Insurance appears to have learned little from the experience, and the corporate culture of insensitivity to women has continued. Lawsuits and accusations of wrongdoing are treated as one of the costs of doing business.

The Conclusions

While the insurance company appears to have learned little, this scenario offers powerful lessons to learn for companies that choose to heed them:

▶ Except in the rarest of circumstances, an effort to settle should be initiated immediately. My philosophy of settlement is the check you write today is the smallest check you'll ever write.

▶ Individuals accused of these behaviors, at whatever level, need to be suspended from their jobs, preferably terminated. Termination sends an extraordinarily powerful signal to the victim, other employees, and the public that you are serious about preventing such abuse. The argument against is that it will lead to wrongful termination litigation. However, it pays to remember that a litigation stemming from this termination will fully discuss and explore why the termination occurred, and most perpetrators will shy away from that.

9.4 Creating the Management Structure to Prepare for Litigation

The law department model of operational behavior is an excellent model for the corporate communications operation to follow.

Build your knowledge of the organization's legal environment and then identify specific legal, paralegal, and non-legal resources that can be marshaled on a moment's notice for specific areas of potential threat. In other words, the law department model of operational behavior is an excellent model for the corporate communications operation to follow.

The recommended model for applying legal knowledge and identifying areas of required preparation is based on proactive steps and approaches that build management confidence. The model effectively contributes to resolving issues beyond simple legal questions and involves seven active areas:

1. **Pay attention.** To become more legally sensitive, the current issue monitoring, identification, and analysis process must be augmented with some additional tasks related to potential legal exposure. Typically in the issue identification process, any given issue is broken down into a predictable group of categories such as a description, the current status, company impact, the stakeholders,

advocacy opportunities, current company position, unresolved questions, recommendations, related issues, and the potential unintended consequences of key actions. From a litigation perspective, a new series of evaluative standards should be applied to the legal questions at issue and the victims/stakeholders affected. Specific areas for evaluation include:

> The nature of the effect on each;

> Settlement options;

> Inclination to settle;

> Likely opposing issues;

> Anticipatable repercussions beyond the litigation;

> Adverse consequences of settling; and

> Adverse consequences of litigating.

> **Victory in decision-making often goes to the individual who can be brief, pragmatic, and positive, both verbally and in writing.**

2. **Have some specific approaches ready.** Fortunately, most approaches to corporate communications issues have useful direct application to the litigation process. They do tend to go beyond where the lawyer might go in developing information. In practice, because litigation requires the review of so many documents and discussion with so many people, you will need to be more succinct, more direct, and more pragmatic than in most other circumstances. A direct, five-step, problem-solving format is useful and effective for introducing your corporate perspectives into the mix of recommendations and decisions that need to be made:

   > **Step #1 - Situation Analysis:** Briefly describe the nature of the issue, problem, or situation.

   > **Step #2 - Situation Interpretation:** Briefly describe what the situation means, what its implications are, and how it threatens the organization.

   > **Step #3 - Options Available:** Develop at least three response options for the situation presented. You can suggest more, but three is an optimal number for management consideration.

   > **Step #4 - Most Recommended Option:** Select the option you would choose if you were in the boss' shoes. Provide an explanation of why you selected it.

   > **Step #5 - Unintended Consequences Forecast:** Explain those events or problems that could arise due to the options you suggested, or that could arise from doing nothing.

This is a straightforward problem-solving model. While similar constructs using as few as four or as many as 11 steps can be employed, this five-step model seems to work well and can be accomplished on one-side of one piece of paper. Victory in decisionmaking often goes to the individual who can be brief, pragmatic, and positive, both verbally and in writing.

3. **Use a "process" approach.** Have a structured, step-by-step approach ready for the different kinds of decisions that arise as a part of your corporate litigation process. Two key elements of a good process approach are;

    ▶ **First, work from a timeline.** Trials, litigation, and other events happen over time. Develop a timeline or "calendar" approach beginning with today and working through the various milestone events and circumstances that can be forecast through the resolution of the problem. In civil litigation, a calendar may begin today but move out six or seven years into the future. In criminal litigation, however, the timeline is often shorter – usually one year for the investigation, one year for grand jury deliberations, one year for development of evidence, and one year for trial conclusions and appeals.

    For the most part, the legal process is predictable and schedulable. Aside from developing a calendar of events that extends through the start of the trial, the corporation may require specific messages and constituency management plans during the trial. Typical trial segments include:

▶ Pre-trial period	▶ Motions
▶ Jury selection	▶ Summations
▶ Opening arguments	▶ Jury deliberation
▶ Special witnesses	▶ The verdict
▶ Initial rebuttal/arguments	▶ Post-verdict commentary
	▶ Appeals

Having an understanding of the flow of the process and major milestones helps your internal corporate team play a far more useful role in the overall communications litigation strategy approach.

▶ **Second, have simple, standard formats.** A well-structured communications/litigation management plan might have four components: a contacts list; situation description; communication/issues management objectives; and a tactical approach.

The tactical approach can be broken into six sections:

Tab 1:   Constituency issues

Tab 2:   Scenarios: Actions/Statements/Q&A

Tab 3:   Internal constituencies

Tab 4:   External constituencies

Tab 5:   Weekly assignments/action checklists

Tab 6:   Follow-up scenarios: Actions/Statements/Q&A

The message here is that an organized and focused communications plan will have more momentum. Using a process approach will also give your knowledge and opinion more weight.

4. **Anticipate carefully.** Your usual process may be charmingly intuitive and delightfully broad ranging in its acceptance of plausible potential scenarios. However, the lawyer is far more focused, far less inclined to speculate, and often antagonistic to the idea of extensive public communication preparation.

You may very well be asked why it's important to get ready for things that will never happen, or be told that it really doesn't take any preparation to manage the problems suggested. Therefore, be very selective and pragmatic about the issues, concerns, problems, or constituency issues you choose to introduce into the legal preparation process.

In many ways, attorneys practice the art of not communicating while maintaining constituency relationships. Once attorneys see a timeline-based, pragmatic approach, one not totally focused on external communications, they will participate in the process necessary to develop and maintain constituency relationship programs.

5. **Build relationships with the lawyers.** Building relationships means:

⬗ Identifying today those law firms and specialists your organization has on standby or retainer to deal with various issues and finding a way to introduce yourself and your function.

⬗ Including key attorneys in your reporting and private issue-related communications network and preparing them for your approach and the differences in style that will occur when something happens.

⬗ Asking advice ahead of time in areas where there may be legal consequences. (This can often be done with little or no charge to your organization, primarily because these individuals are probably already on retainer.)

6. **Prepare for rejection.** Attorneys have enormous clout when legal issues are at stake. Attorneys are used to working with consultants, but they're also used to having the last word. Providing fewer options increases the likelihood that those you present will be rejected, questioned, or modified in some respect. Provide more options. No scenario, litigation, or problem ever unfolds in a totally predictable fashion. Therefore, any expectation that your recommendations, no matter how well organized and presented, will survive as a whole, is unrealistic. If the focus is on the client's best interests and if the approaches taken make sense, it's time to move on graciously to the next issue.

7. **Be unchallengeable.** Build your credibility at every step, with every decision, with every action. To be unchallengeable:

   ▶ **Search for, find, and insist upon the truth.** Sooner or later, the organization will be forced to deal directly with whatever the truth is. The sooner, the better.

   ▶ **Know there is more than one truth.** Truth is defined by the point of reference of each individual constituency. Victims will never see it your way. Angry neighbors will never see it your way. Government regulations will never see it your way. Opposing counsel will never see it your way.

   > All litigation involves victims... Think, plan, talk, and act with the victim's perspective in mind.

   ▶ **All litigation involves victims.** In civil litigation, we create victims through the actions of our company or organization. In criminal litigation, the victim is society as a whole, certain groups within society, individual government agencies, or government as a whole. The function of the judge in the trial is to protect the rights of the victim. In an environment based on the presumption of innocence, it is the rights of the defendant that will be protected by the court. It's the plaintiff or the prosecution who must provide the proof. Think, plan, talk, and act with the victim's perspective in mind. (**Note:** *For a detailed discussion of victim issues in a crisis, see Chapter 1 of this book.*)

   ▶ **Be a pragmatist.** Settle what you can't win well. Settle quickly to avoid creating permanent enemies, even when you're right. A legal victory that creates permanent, generational enemies is worse than losing a war.

▶ Understand your own belief system, your values, and explain and act on them constantly.

The techniques suggested here will not be done automatically by management. The legal arena is one in which the non-lawyer needs to be proactive, making the assumption that for a limited but appropriate range of scenarios, management, corporate communications, and legal affairs will be teamed up in the interest of the corporation's reputation and constituent relationships.

9.5 Guidelines for Working With Attorneys

9.5.1 Some General Rules

1. **Prohibit all attorneys from talking to reporters**, even to take messages, unless specifically authorized and trained to do so. Reporter calls should be forwarded automatically to the appropriate communications source for the case. Reporters always call the attorneys. They know attorneys love to talk about the law. The problem with any other strategy is that, whatever information the reporters gather from the attorneys only gives them a significant tool to get information from others.

2. **If you are the defendant, the attorneys work for you.** You tell them what to do. You take their advice and listen carefully, but follow your bellybutton, experience, and instincts on how to get things done, and what the priorities really are. The lawyer, who is your advisor, must work within the parameters you set. It is your bus. There is no need to apologize for anything you do, even if it's really stupid. Rank has its privileges (RHIP), and clients have these same privileges.

> **Attorneys tend to think they have expertise in all areas, including communications.**

3. **Attorneys tend to think they have expertise in all areas**, including communications. They are required to be generally knowledgeable. Here are some examples from a recent conversation in which the lawyers mentioned topics they felt they needed to control, when, in fact, these topics were far more in communication territory:

   ▶ Activist issues: They are largely communications problems.

   ▶ Customer concerns: They are client problems far more than lawyer problems.

   ▶ Educating the community is mainly a communication concern.

▶ Public opinion and the court of public opinion are in the domain of communications.

4. **Listen carefully and push back.** Attorneys are expert questioners, something that is implicit to their nature. Some questions need answering; lots are less relevant to the situation at hand or can be set aside to a later time. Sometimes this questioning is just a controlling behavior. Questions can be extremely helpful and penetrating, but they can also be a tool used to keep the herd moving in a given direction or to override other voices. Listen carefully and push back when it is appropriate to let other voices get through.

5. **The goal remains settlement** (my non-legal opinion only). Unless fraud, deceit, or some other shenanigans on the part of the plaintiffs (which does happen) can be proven, the case is going to settle long before it is litigated. One ongoing question to ask the lawyers as the case proceeds is: "What's your assessment of the real chances of litigation success versus going for settlement right now?" If you prepare only for trial, the case can drag on for a long, long time and you may indeed end up going to trial, whether or not a trial will be the best result for your case.

> Settlement talks can start at any time... hire a separate law firm to manage the settlement, since litigation does have to proceed until the matter is resolved... There is an inherent conflict between the litigator and the negotiator.

6. **Settlement talks can start at any time.** Settlement talks are always supported by the court. My recommendation is always to hire a separate law firm to manage the settlement, since litigation does have to proceed until the matter is resolved. I always have contended that the two strategies are incompatible in the same law firm, no matter how large that firm happens to be. There is an inherent conflict between the litigator and the negotiator.

7. **Remember the power of victims.** The longer you wait to contact the victims directly to find out what they really want – or, worse yet, if we attack them – the tougher settlement becomes. The way to work this situation is to move ahead quickly rather than delay, hold back, and over-lawyer the situation. When you have a 20-day deadline, meet it in ten. When you have the option to short-circuit the process in a way that might benefit the victims, move quickly. Moving fast simply denies the plaintiffs the hang time they might use to ruminate, to think things up that are negative, or to give the lawyers and their media contacts time to dream up more questions.

With increased time, the visibility opportunity for the plaintiffs tends to expand while the defendant may begin to look desperate. None of this matters, of course – it's the settlement that matters.

8. **When you are given a time estimate by your law firm to get work done, press to make things happen faster.** If the attorneys forecast one or two months to accomplish something, it will more likely take two or three extra weeks past that deadline estimate. You have to keep the pressure on to get work done. If you are familiar with Parkinson's Law (Cyril Northcote Parkinson's cynical observation that work will expand so as to fill the time available for its completion), you may understand why I say that Parkinson may have been an attorney. Beyond the legal issues, you are going to be faced with a number of circumstances in which speed will be of the essence, e.g., activist action, bad news, employee or community concerns, explosive visibility. For these situations, turning on a dime is essential. Most "turning on a dime" situations start as communications issues. Settlement activity can cause this urgent "turn on a dime" atmosphere as well.

The Litigation Process, a Roadmap

These two flowcharts work together. The civil litigation court procedure map is designed to illustrate how the case gets started and the general steps in a civil trial.

The criminal court procedures map, which follows, fills in much of the detail about the trial itself. Each is quite helpful in assisting a novice in understanding what the next steps are in a trial setting. The most important elements to remember about the trial setting are these:

1. *The judge is privy to all information relevant to the trial, whether or not the information is ultimately introduced into the case.*

2. *Many of the motions that occur before the trial have to do with admitting or denying admittance of evidence and information related to the prosecution, plaintiffs' or defendants' cases. It's a very interesting process to see how information or knowledge is included or excluded from the deliberations of the judge or jury.*

3. *Generally, the entire trial is planned out from beginning to end before the trial ever begins.*

4. *Even jury instructions are largely completed before the trial itself begins.*

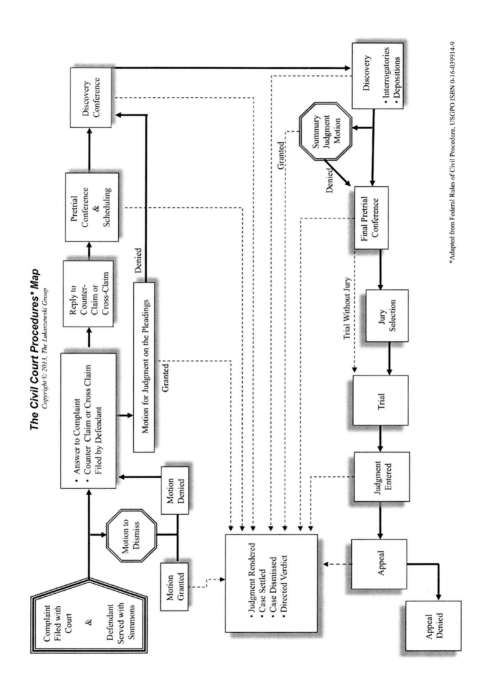

The Civil Court Procedures* Map
Copyright © 2013, The Lukaszewski Group

*Adapted from Federal Rules of Civil Procedure, USGPO ISBN 0-16-039914-9

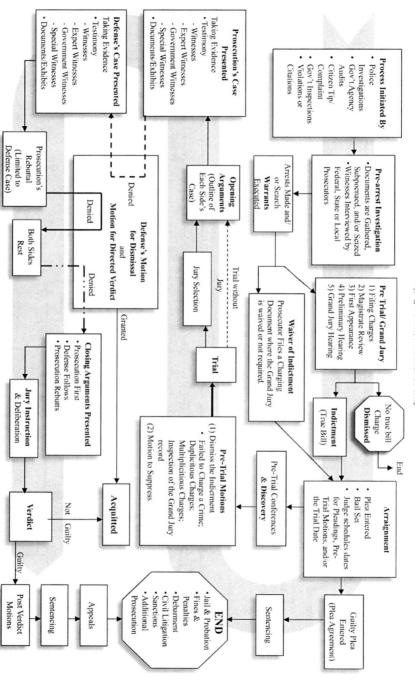

The *Criminal Court Procedures* Map
Copyright © 2013, The Lukaszewski Group

* Adapted from *Federal Rules of Criminal Procedure*, USGPO ISBN 0-16-039934-3

9.5.2 Control Attorneys to Prevent Press Leaks

In my judgment, if lawyers didn't talk to reporters, many cases would be significantly shortened and attract significantly less publicity. The question the attorneys have to ask themselves is whether justice is about maximum publicity or whether it's about maximum trajectory toward the courtroom to get the case settled, arbitrated, negotiated, abandoned, dropped or tossed out. Every time you see, hear, or view an in-depth analysis of some legal situation, it's likely that one of the participating attorneys is involved. Lawyers often call reporters to trigger stories about their cases. As sources for leaks, lawyers are second only to the top bosses and board members, who get to do this because it is their enterprise. Leaks of substance come from the corner office, the board room, or an attorney rather than the mail room.

Most attorneys fancy themselves to be excellent and strategic communicators and, in many cases, because the law is what it is, that they are the only ones capable of explaining the nuances of cases to journalists. Very frequently, the attorney's conversation with a reporter is done "off the record" without the client's knowledge. Lawyers are influenced to leak the information because reporters have always understood the vanity of attorneys. (**Note:** *For more about handling reporters and the media, see Chapters 5 and 6 of this book.*)

A reporter calls a lawyer whose client is muzzled and explains that, "I'm not an attorney and this is very complicated. I need your help to understand the case so I can report it more accurately and fairly." Then the deception begins, "I will protect you as a source and not connect you with the information you give me." The attorney, presumably with the best of motives (love of the law and eagerness to explain legal complexities to the reporter), agrees to speak to the reporter. Perhaps more often than not, the attorney doesn't bother to consult the client, thinking that the client will probably never find out and, who knows, something good might come of it.

A few years ago, I attended the retirement gathering for a long-serving CNN reporter. With the room full of journalists, the reporter being honored was asked a series of questions in front of the group. One of the questions he was asked most was, "What would you miss least as you leave journalism?" His answer was immediate: "Lawyers." When questioned further, he talked about the very situation I referred to above – that he was frequently called by attorneys who really felt the need, without being exposed, to talk about the legal issues in the case, and often to torpedo or otherwise develop interpretations for the reporter of the other side's strategy, weaknesses, and mistakes. Lawyers love to push other lawyer's buttons.

▶ Reporters learn quickly that lawyers love to talk about the law.

▶ Reporters really don't know this stuff, and they find lawyers to be easy sources.

▶ Like corporate communications people – who should inherently know better because 70% of them are former reporters – lawyers delude themselves that they can have special "relationships" with reporters.

▶ Like reporters, lawyers also love the negative, the contentious, the controversial.

▶ Most comments lawyers make to the press are to push the buttons of other lawyers.

Press Policies for Lawyers

I recommend that corporate clients issue specific policies to their lawyers.

1. All contact with the press will be handled, approved, or denied, through a designated spokesperson or trial communication manager (TCM).
2. All phone calls, questions, messages from reporters should be shifted instantly to the designated spokesperson or TCM.
3. In face-to-face meetings with reporters (such as those in and outside the courthouse or other venues created by the trial), all requests and casual conversations shall be directed to the designated spokesperson or TCM for disposition. In every case.
4. If an attorney has a burning desire to phone or e-mail a reporter, such urges will first be shared with the designated spokesperson or TCM, and the decision of the TCM will be final.

> I'd advise against much, if any, publishing of legal information. The only audience for legal discussions is the attorneys for the other side, and we have a place to talk to them – it's called a court room.

The behavior of a rogue lawyer is disruptive to good message strategy and delivery. This disciplined approach will help reduce distractions, shorten time-wasting meetings, and prevent dozens of off-the-wall questions and collateral distractions. This strategy keeps participants focused on their real roles and on-message. If you want to put out legal information, do it openly, on the record, on your own website or blog. But generally I'd advise against much, if any, publishing of legal information. The only audience for legal discussions is the attorneys for the other side, and we have a place to talk to them – it's called a court room.

9.5.3 Communications Behaviors Lawyers Need to Avoid

1. **Avoid Negative Confrontational Language and Behavior.** Yes, I know, our system is designed to be adversarial. But that's predominantly meant to occur in the courtroom where the issue is proof, and the jury, who hears every word and argument, gets to determine what is the truth. What is said outside the courtroom can have an influence on those who will be selected for juries. Attorneys must leave these conversations to the non-lawyers in the group, who usually hold these conversations out of earshot of the attorneys themselves.

   Negative confrontation prolongs litigation; angers the people with whom we want to settle and resolve issues; creates more victims; and fails to address the real problem or issue, or what is at stake. Negative language just causes more contention, clouds issues, and prolongs confrontation.

   Use positive, declarative language whenever possible. Say what you mean. Say less but say something. Positive, declarative language is quite often truthful language – certainly more truthful than negative outbursts and attacks. Positive language tends to cause calmness and detoxify arguments.

   > Bad news, bad behavior, and bad language have a tendency to cause very serious and expensive problems.

   My approach is to subject all statements, scripts, legal documents, and explanations to a three-step **strategic communications analysis:**

   ▶ All negative language is removed.

   ▶ Superfluous words, phrases, and unproductive language are aggressively removed. I generally shoot for a 20% reduction on copy – about every fifth word.

   ▶ The remaining remarks, writings, or comments, which are now tighter and more positive, are analyzed for the questions those comments generate so that the comments can be revised to answer questions and improve the power of the information presented.

   Bad news, bad behavior, and bad language have a tendency to cause very serious and expensive problems. Simple, sensitive, sensible, sincere, and positive language is the strategy to choose when you write or speak, even if you're dealing with your greatest adversary. The power to control, manage, and win, while avoiding negative career-defining moments, is the approach taken by honorable, trustworthy, and credible organizations interested in preserving their reputation, credibility, and trustworthiness.

2. Lawyers Must Avoid Encouraging Negative Behavior Among Operating Executives

Look at these unwise attempts by attorneys to verbally deter the media, strategies that always fail and cause more problems:

"Once again, your rag has chosen the 'path of least resistance' by printing a biased, unbalanced report of a small meeting held this week in support of shutting down our operation. Your source is a professional witness and anti-corporate activist, who criss-crosses the globe looking for opportunities to shut down the world's global companies. You have given his 'road show of fear' an unopposed, undeserved spotlight."

"The article did not include a quote from anyone else other than Mr. 'Fear Monger.' It listed him as an 'expert,' but did not include any data. There are outlandish and unsubstantiated assertions as well as several unrectified typographical errors. Yet, when you write articles about us, including the recently published corporate profile on the company, you sought out opposing opinions, even on subjects that didn't call for any criticism."

"This is a double standard you apply only to our company and those who support us. You do a tremendous disservice to your readers by denying them access to arguments based upon facts. As your coverage continues on this issue, this bias is becoming more apparent and blatant."

This approach in the quotes above – to "intimidate" the media – will serve only to antagonize the media and make your friends wonder why you are being so defensive. Those who are targeting you online will take your aggressive, negative comments, and make you eat them for lunch. These statements come across as a direct affront, inspire every critic and commentator to prove you wrong, and make you look like an idiot. Starting a conversation out this way gives them an enormous advantage. Why do such defensive attacks give the opposition an advantage? Look at the wording again and you will see that these statements are full of errors, assumptions, mistakes, and emotional allegations of the very type that the lawyer and the executive criticized in the news article and the coverage.

3. Avoid Talking to Reporters Behind the Client's Back

As we pointed out earlier, one of the most damaging errors is the lawyer's self-appointment as an "off-the-record" or "on background" explainer of the circumstances to reporters. I recommend that attorneys be instructed affirmatively that only the official spokesperson of the company, such as the TCM, is authorized to talk to any reporter for any reason. Further, any attorneys authorized to speak to reporters are required to take instruction from a communications expert, before such an interview. The better strategy is to ensure that all such conversations take place between the communicator and the reporter as opposed to the lawyer and the reporter. I strongly suggest that these attorneys be trained by a competent communication professional who is experienced in legal settings and that these attorneys be given rules and guidelines to follow. This is in the best interest of the lawyer's client.

4. Avoid Silence

As I've written previously in this book, *silence is a toxic strategy*. After a while even your friends and supporters will question you and then sell you out. Silence is a form of arrogance. Silence sends a signal of guilt. Silence attracts more attention than almost any other technique one could conceive of using. If there's anything a communicator understands and learns quickly, it's that on issues that matter, a communication vacuum is followed by an explosion of communication. People – whether the media, friends, or neighbors – just make things up to fill this vacuum. People magnify things beyond imagining. This is an enormously exciting arena for the media, the rumormongers, the bellyachers, and those with their own agendas. It is probably the most corrosive environment when it comes to maintaining trust, understanding, and credibility in tough litigative times.

5. Manage the Communication Product Rigorously

When it comes to litigation communication, I submit each communication idea to four tests:

▶ Will this communication inform those we care about most, those in our base and those who are related to us (in one way or another), helping them to understand the case or their environment?

▶ Will communications provide some assistance or help to employees, to allow them to tolerate time periods of little communication when under attack?

▶ Will communication inform those whom we'd like to know more about us, who might be confused about us, or who need to know more about what we're doing?

▶ Will communication move the knowledge base about the circumstances forward in some incrementally positive way?

6. Avoid Self-delusion

Some examples of **self-deluding talk** and concepts follow. These behaviors and excuses work against what you are trying to achieve. The self-deluded person may say:

▶ Not talking reduces risk.

▶ The lawyer's job is to reduce collateral litigation and risk.

▶ A strong negative denial is an effective communication tactic: *"It wasn't my client," "We couldn't possibly have done it," "Your facts are wrong," "You don't know what you're talking about," "We weren't there," "We wouldn't know how," "We wouldn't ever do that," "We can't believe you would think that," "I am not a crook," "I did not have sex with that woman."*

▶ What works in the courtroom, works on the street.

▶ Anyone who claims to be a victim must be denigrated, discredited, and treated with suspicion.

▶ Never be the first one to say yes.

Let me reinforce that the approaches listed above do not work.

7. Avoid Testosterosis (slapping people around as a reflex)

The adversarial nature of legal training coupled with the concept of zealous representation has created a style of communication and behavior that is needlessly confrontational, always negative, is intentionally insulting, and is done mostly for show. In fact, most legal communication during litigation is vacuous, self-serving, and legally insignificant. This combative tendency is true for the female lawyers, just as much as for the males. Apparently they are taught that you have to be nasty, cynical, negative, abrasive, and confrontational to win, especially if you have a telegenic, highly emotional victim you can put on cameras, on Facebook, and other public display.

Winning is such a powerful motivation that many attorneys, I believe, are afraid that if they don't act tough, their colleagues will think they're sissies and pushovers. I call it the "The Sissy Factor" – and it's a really powerful motivator of bad behavior. The other negative outcome of testosterosis is that lawyers can reinforce for an already defensive CEO or senior management that this type of behavior is acceptable and even contagious among managers.

> **In most litigation that matters, the first law firm is not around at the conclusion of the litigation.**

Over the years I've noticed an interesting pattern of legal representation in high-profile, highly emotional cases. The first law firm hired exhibits an extraordinary level of testosterosis, as does the head of the firm being sued. Together they conspire to beat the opposition into a bloody legal pulp. But after a couple of years, a couple million dollars, or more, the only group that's bloody is the defendant. Then, when they lose their summary judgment motion, a second firm is hired. The assignment for the new firm is to preserve whatever it was that seemed important to that first legal effort, but now the goal is to work for settlement but also a day in court. After another couple of years, and board members begin to notice footnotes in the annual report due to cost of litigation, a third firm is hired to settle the matter in 90 days. Testosterosis is a powerful and hugely costly affliction.

Hiring an emotional warrior may feel good at the time, but in most litigation that matters, the first law firm is not around at the conclusion of the litigation (except to be on the sidelines as a consultant because testosterosis never generates successful litigation strategies). Testosterosis, in fact, frightens juries, distorts the image of an organization and its leadership, and is, perhaps, the single most important behavior that makes the general public and others detest attorneys.

8. **Avoid Underestimating /Overconfidence**

Attorneys have trained their clients to make decisions based on percentages. It's almost like betting. What are the odds of a certain procedure working... 50/50, 60/40, whatever? It would be nice to hear, from the opening of the engagement, a realistic assessment of how cases would proceed. For example, far too much litigation occurs because the lawyers think they can win when they know according to the statistics, and in their hearts, that they're never going to win. Yet the process to go to trial can last many months, sometimes a number of years, even on a case that, at best, the lawyers would have to give a 50/50 shot of winning. As a result of so few criminal cases actually getting to trial, there appears to be a shortage of opportunities for young attorneys going into litigation to get criminal courtroom practice and instruction.

This underestimating/overconfidence approach always prompts me to try to understand which law firm I'm dealing with when I'm brought into a case, which is often well after it's undertaken and when the larger issues of trust, confidence, credibility, and reputation have seriously deteriorated. The pattern I often see goes like this: if it's the first law firm, they're generally working towards summary judgment because they're confident that they are going to win the case, hands down, throw everything out, and be done with it after a couple of years or so, a whole squad of attorneys, generating all kinds of stuff.

If the *second* law firm is working with the client, it means that summary judgment failed, the client looked at the bills, brought in a second firm to try to make sense of what's happened and devise a strategy to win this thing or put it away – and the first firm is retained as a consultant to the second law firm. Quite often the second firm, which is careful to preserve the work of the first law firm, spends another couple of years and maybe another bunch of dollars to develop an inconclusive approach through motions and other activities.

At this point the client, now looking (along with the Board and maybe some shareholders), at nearly five years of litigation activity and a host of different lawyers and attorneys, decides they need to hire a firm to get this matter settled. This leads to law firm number three, whose assignment is to get the matter put to bed within the next 90 to 100 days, and they do. Lawyers need to make more honest, candid assessments of where they are and where they're going.

> **The check you write today for the settlement may well be the smallest check you'll ever write in this matter.**

9. Avoid Failing to Settle Sooner Rather than Later

Settlement activity often eliminates or substantially reduces litigation visibility. Courts take the settlement with great seriousness. It is pretty difficult to be conciliatory in private and combative in front of the television cameras. Settlement happens privately, is sanctioned by the court, and much of what is discussed cannot enter the records of the actual case. Courts want fewer cases on the docket. If you are wrong – or the perception is that you are – acknowledge it, settle, and move on. It's only money. No one who matters is really counting anyway. The check you write today for the settlement may well be the smallest check you'll ever write in this matter.

9.5.4 Privileged Communication: The Work Product Doctrine

Work product is created when unique information and special expertise are required as a lawyer prepares for trial. Work product can be materials, reports, notes, or data developed by the attorney, or collected, developed, or prepared by outside specialists, investigators, consultants like PR practitioners, accountants, engineers, etc. at the direction and under the supervision of an attorney preparing for or in anticipation of litigation. Great caution is required of non-lawyers preparing information.

Attorney-client privilege protects certain confidential communication between lawyer and client from discovery in civil, criminal, or administrative proceedings and work that directly reflects the mental processes and legal strategy of the attorney. In addition, in US Federal Rules of Civil Procedure, Rule 26(b)(3), the work product doctrine (WPD) protects materials prepared in advance of litigation from discovery by opposing counsel. Unlike attorney-client privilege, WPD applies to all materials being prepared for the case, such as those from a consultant, not just communication between lawyer and client. However, WPD protection for consultant working materials is at risk of being overcome in various ways, such as the other side showing the court a compelling need for the information.

1. To obtain WPD protection, you must:
   - Work at the direction and under the supervision of an attorney;
   - Work in confidence; and
   - Have a strategic legal purpose (usually trial preparation) that is stated explicitly and understood.

2. To preserve WPD protection, you must:
   - Set up separate "Legal Matters" files, which are usually locked.
   - Limit access and distribution only to those who are authorized by counsel.

3. To maintain protection for specific documents you prepare, you should:
   - Address or copy them to the attorney who requested the work.
   - Mark them appropriately, i.e., *Privileged & Confidential, Attorney/Work Product*.

Waiver of WPD protection can occur very easily. Here are just a few of the ways:

▶ Give or expose documents to unauthorized third parties.

▶ Verbalize privileged instructions or material from protected documents to unauthorized individuals.

▶ Give protected material to a witness to refresh his/her memory in preparation for testimony.

▶ Communicate privileged material to other attorneys who are not a part of the litigation.

▶ Make indiscriminate use of "Privileged & Confidential, Attorney/Work Product" markings on inconsequential documents, or use without specific legal direction to do so.

Virtually any unauthorized disclosure of information to parties without specific direction or authorization by counsel (ask for and follow the attorney's direction) can waive WPD protection.

9.6 Litigation Communications Strategy

9.6.1 Prepare for Trial

First, everyone needs to come up to speed on the legal communication process step-by-step, including logical opportunities for visibility. I usually conduct a seminar for corporate staff on what the litigation process involves, both civil and criminal.

> **Judges, the court, juries, prosecutors, virtually the entire legal system is designed to protect the public and advocate for victims.**

Perhaps the most crucial concept that the accused needs to understand – related directly to the legal process – is that judges, the court, juries, prosecutors – virtually the entire legal system – is designed to protect the public and advocate for **victims**. If the defendant is not a victim – and, in public perception, most companies and large organizations are not – winning the public's hearts and minds can be very very difficult.

The first reality that needs to be recognized and overcome is that the courts, some judges, other participants in the process, and the news media tend to look at them as suspects. That's not the way corporations like to be viewed. That corporations can be regarded as suspects may not sound like news, but within the corporate environment, this perception is a revelation barrier that is impossible to overcome at first. An automatic, mistaken assumption is that if "we can just get the facts out, the public, the media, and everyone else will understand and go about their own business." I refer to this mentality as *advanced denial*.

You are courting disaster without a litigation communications strategy. When you expect significant notoriety in connection with a trial or non-trial legal proceeding, you'll need to create this strategy.

Step 1: Familiarize yourself with the American Bar Association's Fair Trial and Free Press Standards and local disciplinary rules. They will help you know how the judge will approach reporter access. During high-profile cases the court is likely to have its own media relations and visibility management plan. Contacting the Court may reveal some insight you can use in your visibility strategy.

Step 2: Develop a message strategy for each phase of the trial. Keep in mind that each trial phase may require message revision depending on public reaction, facts as they develop, news coverage, opposition commentary, employee reaction, and other foreseeable but not precisely predictable factors.

Typical litigation message development segments used for planning are:

- The pre-trial period.
- Jury selection.
- Special witnesses.
- Other rebuttal.
- Jury deliberation.
- Post-verdict assessment.

- Initial rebuttal/arguments.
- Opening arguments.
- Evidentiary motions.
- Summations by both sides.
- The verdict.
- Appeals.

Several high-profile variables may impact your strategy:

- The use of trial consultants (jury selection, celebrities, subject matter experts).
- Television in the courtroom.
- Public demonstrations during the trial (organized opposition/support).
- Daily visibility of your company's representatives.
- Someone else's notorious verdict in a similar case.

Take advantage of the litigation process. Its predictable steps, phases, and events also control opposing actions and help predict when news events will occur (thereby helping you develop a counteractive or counterintuitive strategy). It's this aggressive flexibility that can remove much of the corporation's defensiveness when attacked. Being unwilling, unable, or unprepared to respond is a strategy for failure.

9.6.2 Understanding the Patterns of High-Profile Cases

It is possible to forecast the patterns of high-profile cases – that is, the handful of truisms the defendant will have to live with and work against for the length of the process. I call them the *Axioms of High-profile Cases*.

1. **It doesn't have to be true; it just has to have been reported by a journalist.** Nowhere in the communication process is there more bewilderment than when the media gets the story wrong in key respects. With today's media, everyone is a potential journalist. (**Note:** *For more about social media, see Chapter 7.*)

2. **The victims are where the story is.** Even the best corporations in America, with the best reputations in their industries or in the commercial world, are no match for the intense interest the media and public display in the victims of their corporate actions.

3. **The victim is where the judge and jury are.** This perhaps is the most forgotten fact in litigation today. Judges, juries, prosecutors, and the entire legal system are really about protecting, compensating, and recognizing the suffering of victims.

4. **Acquittal, verdict for the defendant, and private settlements are not news.** Yes, your corporation's name may appear in a story about the case being dismissed or a verdict on your behalf, but only rarely are the details of a story complete enough to satisfy your organization or to repair the damage of negative publicity.

5. **Your reputation is only as good as the last negative allegation.** One of the great frustrations of managing litigation visibility is that the moment you feel progress is being made with various audiences and constituencies, some negative fact or allegation will surface to return you invariably to ground zero. Plan for it, anticipate the negative allegations, and be ready to respond.

6. **Much guessing and speculating surround the outcome and the process.** Because today's civil trials can last for many years and criminal trials can last two-to-three years, there's a tendency for everyone, not just the news media, to leap to the end of the process in an attempt to define what closure will be. Only a well-thought-out strategic communication approach can help counteract this constant tendency to short-circuit the process by guessing.

7. **The end result often satisfies no one.** After seven years of on-again-off-again court action, the end result is often anticlimactic, coming too late to help those who ran the organization at the time

the incidents occurred and causing much embarrassment to the new managers who are now on the scene and must deal with it.

9.6.3 Eight Ways to Assure Lousy Trial Publicity

The unfortunate reality is that lousy trial publicity begins with defendants and the bad things they do or are alleged to have done. This reality, combined with the combative nature of today's business litigation, often yields a public perception of insensitivity, arrogance, carelessness, and inhumanity. The defensive behaviors (that you should avoid) are predictable:

1. Talk arrogantly, talk tough, and talk a lot. Avoid saying anything that might make you look like a sissy. Words like "ashamed," "concerned," "disappointed," "regret," "sad," "tragic," "unfortunate," "unintended," and "unnecessary" don't seem to come easily to the lips of corporate executives or spokespeople.

2. Ignore the values filters through which society evaluates threats and other critical information:

   ▶ Health and safety;

   ▶ Quality of life concerns;

   ▶ Freedom from fear;

   ▶ Peace of mind; and

   ▶ Economic security.

3. Make your complaint or responses to a complaint as blatant, snotty, and insulting as possible. The defendant in a civil case sometimes forgets that the documents provided to the court – either as a complaint or in response to a complaint – belong to the public and are a part of the public record.

4. Blame the victims. In cases of injury, death, or substantial public threat, using the argument that it's the fault of the person who is dead, injured, or threatened is guaranteed to get you off on the wrong foot with just about everybody.

5. Refuse to negotiate; hold out as long as possible. Never, never, never give in. The refusal to negotiate is a combination of fear, adrenaline, machismo and confusion. This fear causes stalling, a search to find who's really guilty. All offers of settlement, mediation, or negotiation are refused.

6. Belittle, disparage, and minimize the opposition's words, actions, and goals. Those who live by arrogance and insensitivity will see their reputations die the same way.

7. Use lots of business and technical lingo, like "competition," "quality," "customer-driven," and "corporate policy," and then threaten to shut the business down or take jobs away.

8. Work to discredit or demean the integrity or intent of your opponent. Embarrass them publicly and challenge their thinking. Get critics to talk about them and discredit them.

9.6.4 Seven Keys to Manage Your Litigation Visibility

All prosecutions of major companies and executives have a pattern of intensely negative, high-profile visibility triggered by the prosecution, usually in collaboration with the news media. Targeted individuals, collaborating with the media, help to bring extraordinary public pressure on the company to cooperate, often through humiliation. Trade press, e-trade press, and specialized new media have the opportunity for an immediate and painful feeding frenzy. The beginning of this public play is orchestrated by the complaint or indictment, public documents filed by the prosecuting authority.

In the best of all possible worlds, we would begin by implementing a positive litigation visibility strategy immediately. But the reality is that defendants try just about anything else first.

> If you feel like a warrior, act like you're preparing for war, and forecast war, there's going to be war.

1. **Learn the process.** While it seems self-explanatory, it is helpful when everyone understands the road map and anticipates the milestones and major events ahead.

2. **Develop a message strategy for each phase of the trial.** Because trials often have interruptions and a variety of predictable phases, it is useful to think about and plan for what might be said or pointed out at each stage. The last time to do this for the first time is not, of course, when a particular legal milestone is upon you.

3. **Settle fast.** As unsatisfactory as settlements seem to be at first, settlement is probably the most potent litigation visibility management tool available. The faster the settlement, the less litigation visibility there is likely to be.

4. **Anticipate high-profile variables.** The concept here is to either take advantage of or prepare to appropriately characterize those things that can go wrong as litigation proceeds.

5. **Keep the focus positive.** Ultimately, it's a positive, productive attitude that leads to effective negotiations, a relationship with the jury, or a plea agreement.

6. **Try settling again.** This ought to be the primary litigation visibility management strategy.

7. **Fight nicely.**

   ▶ Be relentlessly positive.

   ▶ If you feel like a warrior, act like you're preparing for war, and forecast war, there's going to be war.

   ▶ Wars are very messy, very expensive, and your side will take the heaviest casualties.

   ▶ If you hire only warriors as lawyers, you will always be at war.

   ▶ Wars have a way of never ending.

   ▶ You will regret wars; they leave lousy legacies.

   ▶ Fire the warriors; hire the peacemakers.

   ▶ Avoid war and you avoid a lot of crummy trial visibility.

9.7 The Aftermath: Regaining Public Credibility Following a Damaging Situation

The three critical legal objectives are: 1) calm those most directly affected and reduce their likelihood to sue or pursue litigation; 2) reduce the news media's interest by behaving in the most appropriate peaceful, positive way possible; and 3) act promptly in constructive, cooperative ways to diminish the political attractiveness the authorities need to justify public litigation as a result of something a company does or causes, whether real or alleged. These three objectives are achieved through implementing seven critical communication intentions.

9.7.1 The Seven Communication Intentions

Step 1: **Candor:** The outward recognition, through promptly verbalized public acknowledgement or outright apology, that a problem exists; that people or groups of people, the environment, or the public trust is affected; and that something will be done to remediate the situation.

Step 2: **Explanation** (no matter how silly, stupid, or embarrassing the problem-causing error was): Promptly and briefly explain why the problem occurred and the known underlying reasons or behaviors that led to the situation, even if only partial early information is available. Also talk about what you learned from the situation and how it will influence your future behavior.

Step 3: **Declaration:** A public commitment and discussion of specific, positive steps that will be taken to address the issues conclusively and to resolve the situation.

Step 4:   **Contrition:** Continually verbalize regret, empathy, sympathy, and even embarrassment. Take appropriate responsibility for having allowed the situation to occur in the first place, whether by omission, commission, accident, or negligence.

Step 5:   **Consultation:** Promptly ask for help and counsel from "victims," government, and from the community of origin – even from your opponents.

Step 6:   **Commitment:** Publicly set or reset your goals at zero. Zero errors, zero defects, zero dumb decisions, zero problems. Promise publicly that, to the best of your ability, situations like this will never occur again.

Step 7:   **Restitution:** Find a way to pay the price quickly. Make or require restitution. Go beyond community and victim expectations and what would be required under normal circumstances to remediate the problem. Adverse situations remediated quickly cost a lot less and remain controversial for much shorter periods of time.

Step 8:   (Optional): **Apologize:** Apology is the atomic energy of empathy. The evidence is overwhelming that apology reduces and in many cases eliminates litigation. In 33 states, laws have been enacted that *exclude* voluntary apologies at car accidents from consideration by juries in damage awards. They have afforded the same protection to healthcare personnel in the course of their work. Insurance companies are driving both these efforts because they have learned that apologies dramatically stop litigation. In fact, insurance claims may actually rise, for apologies are used frequently. But paying claims is far cheaper than years in court. (**Note:** *For more about apology, see Section 9.7.4 below.*)

9.7.2 Anticipating Highly Visible Threats to Reputation

Certain image and reputational threats can be planned for and anticipated the moment the criminal prosecution process begins. Trials are powerful public events and a fundamental part of the democratic process. Consequently, powerful collateral interests have arisen to clutter up the process and dramatically shape and reshape public and courtroom perceptions of the case.

1. **Media/prosecutor alliances drive criminal case visibility.** We see this every day. Even grand jury processes, which are suppose to be secret, somehow find their way into the public's view. This cannot happen without the cooperation of the prosecutor and the prosecuting authorities. Usually it happens when a major organization with a good reputation seems to be getting the

benefit of the doubt in public discussion and coverage. One hopeful sign is that in recent years there has been an increased frequency of prosecution and disciplinary actions taken for prosecutorial misconduct – it's just a hopeful sign.

2. **Plaintiff's lawyers/news media alliances drive visibility in civil suits and class action suits.** The vast majority of news stories about civil litigation begin with a plaintiff's lawyer contacting the media with a story angle about the plaintiff's case. Generally, the cost of doing investigative reporting is so high and so unproductive that the media increasingly find the research and information developed by plaintiff's lawyers useful. The new wrinkle is, of course, new media. Based on rumor, news story or blog – or simply fabricated – these unguided, undisciplined, and unedited communicators can stir up more incredible but believable problems than any mainline, legacy media. And, the reality is, the public in ever-increasing numbers is believing what it reads, sees, and hears from the web far more than from the traditional legacy media sources such as radio, television, newspapers.

3. **Judges have a point of view.** Judges have real power, which can affect any participant in the process at anytime. The smart reporter calls the judge. No one knows the conversation took place because neither the judge nor the reporter will talk about it.

4. **Media/celebrity combinations.** Celebrity witnesses can have a dramatic, though temporary, impact on the public perception of the case. Receptivity of celebrities by juries is mixed. Consultants, trial commentators, jury selection experts, psychologists, and subject matter experts swarm around high-profile cases. The significant amounts of outside expertise and talent assembled by the corporate defendant in today's high-profile cases can have a very negative influence on public perception.

5. **People close to the case say the darndest things** – when asked. No matter how well we prepare executives, attorneys, and others for what they're going to say to the media, employees interviewed by the media in the parking lot may say something like, "Did they tell you about the stuff they spilled last year?" "No they haven't." "Does the prosecutor know about the stuff they spilled last year?" "No he doesn't." Suddenly, we now have an entirely new story, one more likely to happen if you choose a strategy of silence. Your friends will first speak because they know you can't. Then they will sell you out because you won't speak.

6. **Keeping crucial audiences informed, especially in criminal cases, is essential.** Having a place to refer media calls is essential.

7. **Media coverage will rehash everything with the underlying perception that the company is guilty.** The prosecutor writes his or her news release day by day as the process proceeds.

8. **If there is an agreement,** it will be followed by a self-imposed compliance program, which your own lawyers will design. Media coverage will rehash everything.

9. **If there is a compliance program,** it will contain an integrity and standards-of-conduct component. Media coverage will rehash everything.

10. **Collateral damage is also likely** – civil litigation, debarment, additional criminal prosecution, the defection of key executives, and government-imposed supervision on certain operations for a number of years, perhaps even negative legislation at various levels of government. Media coverage will rehash everything.

9.7.3 Plan to Live With the Result

When the case is over and the result is a plea or conviction, employees, friends, and associates – even after a highly visible case or prosecution - still believe that, "It can't be true; there must be another version or explanation of this story." If the company pleads it out, that's their story forever. And further, everyone in your company has to tell the story the same way. Numerous cases are on record of executives who in private conversations verbally denied what was agreed to in the official plea agreement and had their words come back later to cause additional sanctions, prosecution, or monitoring. Focus on the goal: getting through the situation of multiple, simultaneous prosecutions with as much dignity, control, and candor as possible, as quickly as possible. In other words, be responsive, but humble; be reticent to comment, but scripted in your approach; be brief and positive.

> **Building relationships with reporters must be done with full knowledge of the environment in which news organizations operate.**

Building relationships with reporters must be done with full knowledge of the environment in which news organizations operate. You need to understand two remaining concepts before you begin the process of establishing relationships with reporters. These concepts are *off-the-record* and *not-for-attribution*. The bottom line recommendation is still to stay on-the-record. It will save a great deal of time, trouble, effort, energy, and worry. (**Note:** *For in-depth information about dealing with the media, see Chapters 5 and 6 of this book.*)

9.7.4 Master the Art of Apology
Apology in Victim Management

Two great barriers to managing victim attitudes and actions are management's fear of liability, embarrassment, and humiliation, fostered by well meaning but misguided traditions, legal counsel, and peers; and, the traditional reluctance to simply say, "I'm sorry." We are learning systematically of the costly damage this strategy causes.

One lawyer interviewed for a landmark article in *JAMA* (Hickson, Clayton, Githens, & Sloan, 1992) put it this way: "In over 25 years of representing both physicians and patients, it became apparent that a large percentage of patient dissatisfaction was generated by physician attitude and denial, rather than the negligence itself. In fact, my experience has been that close to half of malpractice cases could have been avoided through disclosure or apology but instead were relegated to litigation. What the majority of patients really wanted was simply an honest explanation of what happened, and if appropriate, an apology. Unfortunately, when they were not only offered neither but were rejected as well, they felt doubly wronged and then sought legal counsel."

The "I'm Sorry" Movement

The healthcare industry's transformation in attitude about apology is being driven by the insurance industry. Insurers have finally recognized that early, sincere apologies can significantly reduce litigation risk. There may be an elevation of claims costs, but the beginning of substantial reduction in litigation risks is far more significant and important. Harvard is spearheading an effort to install an apology first strategy in all of its healthcare facilities. Harvard's effort has been joined by other major academic and private healthcare organizations in the Boston region.

> The reality is that honorable people, companies, and agencies will answer any question asked of them, respond to any rumors, issues or concerns about themselves, and apologize immediately.

The Metrics of Apology

So far, if you're interested in learning how to apologize, you'll have to look outside management and business schools. They don't teach this in management school. This is a sensational gap in the already skimpy ethics programs in America's management and business education. One public place to start is *The One Minute Apology* (Blanchard & McBride, 2003). Or, go to www.perfectapology.com. In fact, there are literally dozens of apology sites. Just insert the word apology in your browser and push the button. You can even access a very interesting free web newsletter www.sorryworks.net. Let me warn you, however, that these books and sites use words like *surrender*, *integrity*, *humility*, and *empathy*. These are concepts too infrequently seen in executive country, and even more rarely in our nation's business schools.

The plain truth is, as Blanchard and McBride (2003) say, "The longer you wait to apologize, the more wicked you begin to look." The reality is that honorable people, companies, and agencies will answer any question asked of them, respond to any rumors, issues or concerns about themselves, and apologize immediately. The evidence is mounting that an apology strategy is prudent, risk-reducing, and litigation-limiting, as well as the first step to forgiveness.

Invariably, the media are conflicted as they report on the growing apology movement. Detractors alternatively ridicule other's apologies as being too little too late and their own inability to apologize for media mistakes and negligence to retain public trust and confidence when errors occur. It's fair to say that promptly apologizing is good common sense, a trend that is here to stay, and is growing stronger every day.

Future Trends

The most obvious trend in litigation is the relentless movement away from the courtroom towards the conference room to mediate and arbitrate as opposed to litigate and settle.

Most American business contracts today require that each party agree to subject themselves to binding arbitration rather than litigation. In addition, judges and courts are pushing toward mediation as an interim step to forestall litigation. Both of these activities are between the parties, independent of the court system.

Whether it is the threat of litigation, or the initiation of litigation, the settlement strategy is also available. I always recommend to clients involved in potential or actual litigation that they propose settlement talks immediately, managed by an independent law firm that specializes in settlement (keep in mind that in this context my clients are always defendants). I generally recommend that clients retain counsel independent from their litigation forum. This may cause an argument, but those experienced in settlement have little or no need of contact with the litigators. Once a case has been filed, litigators need to proceed to put their cases together, gather evidence and information, go through the process of protecting what needs to be protected, and limiting the amount of information and evidence that can go into their trial. Settlement attorneys can immediately go to work toward achieving a resolution independent of the litigator's preparations.

Settlement is always interesting because courts support it and a settlement is a special forum where virtually anything can be discussed, and whatever is discussed remains generally out of the trial and out of the litigation strategy of both sides. Trial rate statistics indicate that for every 150 civil cases filed, only about 5% actually get to trial and verdict. The remaining cases are tossed out, shifted to mediation or arbitration, or dropped by the plaintiff. In short, the odds of successfully getting a civil case to court are about 100 to 1 against.

The numbers are roughly similar in criminal cases but for different reasons. Most cases in criminal cases go away because the defendant pleads out. The lesson here reflects what I've said earlier, that you really want to stay out of the U.S. criminal justice system. It is relentless, it is powerful, and it would appear that many defendants plead to something just to get the Department of Justice attorneys, or local prosecutors, off their backs. To coin a phrase, our criminal justice system is criminal within and of itself. This is a matter of great and growing controversy in the justice system. As this material goes to press, prosecutors are more routinely being cited for malicious or overzealous prosecution, and some defendants are winning their freedom or their cases are being dismissed.

Chapter 9 - Questions for Study and Discussion

1. What is the advantage of bringing in an outside lawyer rather than relying on corporate counsel?

2. Name three ways that lawyers think differently from corporate management and staff. What is the advantage?

3. Explain the chief differences between civil law and criminal law.

4. What is the most important factor to keep in mind when you are setting up a Litigation Communication Strategy?

5. Name and explain three mistakes you or the lawyer can make dealing with the media – how do these become worse when a "victim" is involved?

6. Why do "ethics" and "compliance" become important after a legal case involving the company has been concluded?

7. Consider crisis situations you have observed in the workplace or seen in the news. Now that you have read this chapter, how do you see that management could have handled the situation differently? On the other hand, in what ways did they handle it well? If you had been in charge of crisis communication, what would have been your first actions?

References, Chapter 9

Blanchard, K. & McBride, M. (2003). *The one minute apology*. New York: Harper Collins.

Federal sentencing guidelines manual (2010), chapter 8, part B.

Fitzpatrick, K. R. & Rubin, M.R. (1995). PR vs. legal strategies in organizational crisis decisions. *PR Review*. 21 (1), 21 – 33.

Hickson, G., Clayton, E.W., Githens, P.B., & Sloan, F.A. (1992). Factors that prompted families to file medical malpractice claims following perinatal injuries. *JAMA*, (267), 1359-63.

10

Crisis Communication:
Summing Up and Looking Ahead

Key words: crisis, victim, spokesperson, scenario, media relations, crisis response plan, crisis prevention, exposure management, crisis survival

As I travel across the United States, Canada, and other venues, teaching, talking, and consulting, most of my public appearances involve people asking me questions. Many questions relate to the future of crisis management and organizational readiness. The same questions are asked time and time again. As you review the development of your crisis communication readiness and strategies, consider these important questions. Then use the answers to help move your organization's management thinking toward the future.

This chapter will help you to:

> ➢ Sum up the main insights, methods, and strategies to apply to your readiness plans.

> ➢ Understand why crisis communication and victim management are core competencies for business.

> ➢ Determine the best role for top management in handling crisis communication.

> ➢ See the importance of preparing for a constructive outcome.

> ➢ Apply the lessons and wisdom of today to the crisis communication and leadership challenges in the future.

10.1 Answers to Some Essential Questions

10.1.1 How Do We Know If the Problem Is Really a Crisis?

If the visibility and victims have the potential to challenge the way a person, company, or entity conducts itself or even survives, it is probably a crisis. In evaluating the situation, consider the following:

▶ To determine if a scenario will become a communications crisis, estimate its chance of occurrence and relate that to the impact should the situation occur. Estimate the potential for collateral damage.

▶ Your crisis planning should reduce risk and eliminate some crisis threats.

▶ Every crisis scenario should provide for an "opportunity" component, having ready a strategy for getting out information and stories that the media would be less likely to cover under normal circumstances.

> Crisis media relations remains a core competency but has become very sophisticated... crisis management has become a cross-functional, multi-discipline competency.

10.1.2 What Is Readiness?

Crisis management has always been a multi-disciplined process, at least in the 30 years I've been practicing.

The concept of readiness is really designed to productively and contructively describe that period before the crisis actually occurs. Up to this point in time, comunicators and others have used the phrase "crisis management" as a kind of all-encompassing description, when, in fact, the phrase irritates management and sets up needless barriers between comunicators and other staff and operating functions.

Readiness actually does include the issues and concerns involving crisis management. This new term, made more essential after 9/11/01, is much of a management and leadership concept. Readiness has the added benefit of preparing managers and leaders to respond better questions about your organization when emergencies occur. Most managers assume that they are smart people, and can handle emerging situations intuitively, quickly, and successfully. These same managers also need to realize that when we're talking about readiness, that there are valid questions that can be raised that can lead to better preparation for crisis response. Wherever the term readiness can be substituted crisis management, it should be.

An organization that is ready has a series of baseline functions already in place and understood coming from a cross-section of staff and operational functions within the organization, including:

▶ A communications policy and crisis response plan endorsed by senior leadership.

▶ Readiness to make strategic use of appropriate technologies.

▶ Scenario-specific crisis response teams fully prepared with action plans, key messages, and pre-authorized instructions.

▶ A communication strategy accross all corporate disciplines involved in any given scenario. These include dark sites, preparation to interact with all stakeholders and employees, first, as well as those media, legacy and social media, who should be informed, need to be informed, or who request information.

10.1.3 What About the Crisis Communication Plan?

Crisis communication plans and many, if not most, aspects of operational response plans have a shelf life of approximately three years, even if consistently updated. Personnel changes, procedure and policy changes, ownership changes, and other disruptions make what you develop today less useful tomorrow. When leadership changes, response plans and their leadership also will change.

10.1.4 How Do We Win and Maintain Management Support and Participation?

Two greatest weaknesses frequently seen in response plans are failure to know exactly what to do first and have a grand strategy for the rest; and second, a lack of defined leadership roles for top management and the people whom top management trusts. You need to:

▶ Create a management briefing process that anticipates all surprises.

▶ Demonstrate simple, sensible, constructive, and productive approaches.

▶ Share two or three specific, positive recommendations or action options as the process of response unfolds.

▶ Avoid negative approaches and concepts. In virtually all cases negative approaches cause confusion, sometimes contention, and rarely offer constructive ways to move ahead to resolve upcoming and anticipatable problems.

10.1.5 What About Crisis Prevention?

There are generally three strategies for crisis prevention: aggressive readiness activities which reduce risk and expose weaknesses, well structured and well supported ethics and compliance programs, and scenario-based planning.

Readiness involves predominately preparing for those highly emotional, victim-producing, non-operational problems – the ones managers and leaders are least likely to be prepared for by education or experience. It is these incidents that cause the most explosive and devastating reputational damage.

A rigorous and comprehensive ethics and compliance program, fully supported by top management, will generally go a long way toward preventing the kinds of behaviors that only may seem unethical at first, but when allowed to proceed, or even succeed, serious reputational and legal problems can result.

Scenario planning is critical to response success because it focuses on specific vulnerabilities and risks. Scenarios then used for drills and exercises assure that a higher quality, more appropriate response can be achieved. Untested plans fail in most respects from the start.

> **Finding truth has become extraordinarily complicated in today's voracious media environment... The answer is, there is always more than one truth.**

10.1.6 How Do We Control the Media Environment of a Crisis?

The obvious answer is by responding properly, and behaving with sincerity, compassion, speed, and sensitivity, your crisis automatically becomes less and less interesting to those who are watching, reporting, Twittering about it, blogging or bloviating about it. If there is some corporate stupidity, inappropriate behavior, indefensible positions, or a smoking gun provided by your organizations, there will be bad news, there will be bad stories, and the bad news you create will ripen badly, for a long time.

Remember the trifecta of failure: timidity, hesitation, and confusion. Even if you're able to launch what might be defined as a perfect operational response, if your communication appears to be stumbling, fumbling, mumbling, and bumbling, this is how your response in total will be remembered, forever. Your messaging must pass the laugh test, the raised eyebrow test, the raised shoulder test, and the nine-year-old simplistic question over the dinner table. All of these actions will diminish the media's and the bloviators' interest, and more quickly reestablish trust among your key stakeholders:

▶ Finding truth has become extraordinarily complicated in today's voracious media and social media environment. Each person interviewed is working from the same basic data, but each comes from an entirely unique point of reference. Every listener or viewer, participant or survivor, hears all this data, further interprets, simplifies, and analyzes it. Then they watch the news delivered by reporters who have done virtually the same thing, but who report an entirely different conclusion. The truth of the story emerges incrementally as more is known about what is going on in any given crisis over time. The company, organization, and spokesperson who understand the evolution of news and are ready to incrementally and constructively move the messages forward, will have much greater control over what is ultimately reported and ultimately remembered. The answer is that there is always more than one truth. Every victim may seem to believe something different.

▶ Media is one conduit for reaching audiences and stakeholders with crucial information using available technologies and platforms. Social media is incrementally providing this function with a growing credibility versus legacy media's continuing decline in credibility.

▶ Speaking with employees is an all-important third step in your grand response strategy. Remember the concept of the 75-to-100 word statement bursts. Release more of them earlier in the crisis, and then they can taper off as the crisis element recedes and the recovery activities take hold. The goal is to provide immediate, useful, helpful information that employees can use, if they choose. Experience indicates that once they receive these bursts of information, they are far less likely to talk to anyone except their colleagues and family members about what is going on. Use all the information-based tools that you can prepare. This includes dark sites by scenario, a question-and-answer, again based on scenarios, and be ready to have a scenario-based crisis website go live within minutes of a serious situation. In today's world, reporters have incredible amounts of information at their fingertips through their smartphones, and they're used to finding things extremely quickly. Use these tools to brief reporters and individuals who have an interest in what's going on in your crisis response. Most every conceivable crisis situation now has many websites that describe what organizations will do to respond and how they have failed in the past; often there are lists of crucial questions that reporters can ask based on the pattern of events associated with the scenario. Be ready. Do your homework. Have a simple, sensible, constructive and positive message strategy for each phase or circumstance as the crisis unfolds.

> Spokespersons should be chosen based on the scenario and its severity. This is done during your scenario preparation process. These individuals are selected for three reasons. First, they are comfortable dealing with the news media; they want to do it. Second, they are willing to accept training and coaching and apply that training and coaching to the delivery of messages in their representation of the company or organization. Third, they are trained to have a sense of the entire crisis scenario so that they can act and speak carefully and smartly as various crisis situations unfold.

> The major question in most serious situations is: When do we send the boss out to the cameras? This is a very important strategic decision that needs to be made early on and takes into account the three factors mentioned previously, but also the signal that sending in the CEO generally sends. Today's world is one of extraordinary, continuous deadlines, endless questioning from strangers, employees, public officials, actual reporters, academics, and anyone who wants to opt in. Many CEOs of major companies recognize they have to be able to speak on their feet, avoid the kinds of mistakes that make them look foolish and the company look careless. Get them ready. It goes with the territory.

> **The crucial goals of crisis communication management are to deal with problems conclusively, unassailably, and promptly.**

10.1.7 How Do We Prepare for a Constructive Outcome?

There are three ways to bungle a crisis noticeably: fail to manage the victims dimension effectively; stumble, fumble and bumble your response; and to act arrogantly, callously, push back, and discredit those around you. As Stephen Covey would say, you want to plan with the end in mind. It begins with the communication strategy embedded in your crisis response plan. Or, in Lukaszewski language, let's plan with a constructive conclusion in mind. I refer to them as communication intentions, and they are: candor, openness, truthfulness, responsiveness, empathy, engagement, apology, and managing your own destiny. The public memory is extraordinarily short, often measured in hours. Victim and survivor memories can last a lifetime. The crucial goal of crisis communication management is to deal with every aspect of a crisis promptly, constructively, and conclusively. By establishing an important set of communication intentions, and carrying them out, whatever the temperature of media coverage or the bloviators, or the behavior of public officials, victims or survivors, it's these intentions that will get you through in the best possible shape, having better relationships with everyone concerned – employees, communities, neighbors, survivors alike – and allowing victims and survivors to come to personal terms with their situations. If you want good media coverage, it begins on the ground with everyone directly and indirectly affected by the crisis situation you're managing. It is important that you talk about your communication intentions so everyone knows what to expect of you and those who represent you, and can hold you to account.

Being remembered badly is relatively easy; all it takes is a series of avoidable mistakes, dumb decisions, and feeling and talking more like a victim than the victims your crisis created. In crisis communication management, it's crucially important to focus on the outcome you would like to see. From the earliest possible time, the vast majority of communication activities and executive actions must be directed to that goal. Forecast follow-up processes as part of ongoing media relations efforts. Let others know in advance what to expect. Then deliver more than they expected.

10.2 Looking to the Future of Crisis Survival

Occasionally, I am also asked a bigger picture question, such as "Mr. Lukaszewski, have your experiences over the years helped you foresee and forecast new and unusual or particularly dangerous future threat possibilities?" My general expectation is for future problems, issues, and behaviors that have been crises in the past to remain high potential candidates for crisis situations in the future. It is likely that we can look forward to increasingly successful cyber attacks, self-inflicted crises created by ineffective crisis readiness and preparation, amoral/immoral business decisions, media-fabricated crises, and incidents caused by negative web-based events and stunts.

> **It is the perpetrators themselves... especially over-confident leaders, who sabotage the competence of responses in crisis.**

Remember that Lukaszewski's first law of crisis survival is to recognize that forces like the government, new media, old media, your toughest critic, or your most aggressive competitor are rarely successful in bringing you down. After-action analysis nearly always reveals that it is the perpetrators themselves, through their statements, actions, and/or the statements of well-meaning employees, friends, even relatives, and especially over-confident leaders, who sabotage the competence of responses in crisis.

Finally, you can be confident that the lessons you have learned about effective crisis communication will serve you in good stead whatever the future brings. The single most powerful, strategic approach to succeeding in crisis response involves extraordinarily positive language combined with behaviors that support contention reduction and resolution of the issues, such as remediating victim circumstances and taking actions that prevent the types of criticism that prolong negative crisis coverage and perceptions.

If you pay attention to victim treatment and management; express regret, empathy, and apology; expedite compensation; do 120% in every direction on every issue in question; and answer every question; these behaviors will help reduce, even mitigate, crisis impact.

Throughout this book, as I have done across my career, I have stressed that the best approaches to crisis response are victim-focused, sensible, simple, positive, constructive and sincere.

At the same time, another set of commitments has impressed me, which I have found to hold extraordinary power to calm, remediate, resolve and remedy urgent circumstances. These are based on my adaptation of Rotary International's Four-Way Test[1]. As you find yourself responding to even the most urgent, devastating circumstances ask yourself these questions about what you think, say and do:

1. Is it the TRUTH?

2. Is it FAIR?

3. Will it build GOODWILL?

4. Will it be BENEFICIAL to all concerned?

As I said at the very beginning of this book, *the unplanned visibility that a crisis creates builds expectations of your honorable behavior among your most critical audiences and stakeholders – including your own employees, the community, the government, and the victims.*

In the end it is up to you, guided by your personal values, concerns and empathetic sense of rightness. I call it the *yo-yo* factor – if you are a CEO, senior official, or senior advisor working through a crisis, at the most critical times, when the decision are the toughest, *"You're On Your Own."*

My central goal in developing this book has been to help you be ready to powerfully and conclusively answer this crucial question: *"How ready are you?"*

---

[1] http://www.rotary.org/en/aboutus/rotaryinternational/GuidingPrinciples/Pages/ridefault.aspx

Glossary

abuse The intentional harming, verbally, physically, or emotionally, of another individual, intentionally causing pain and suffering.

activist An individual aggressively pursuing and advocating a cause, personal belief, political, religious, or highly emotional issues.

Alinsky's *Rules for Radicals* A book by Saul Alinsky, first published in 1967, outlining the specific anti-corporate, anti-government, anti-social strategies for developing public pressure for change.

alternative dispute resolution (ADR) A process outside the legal system for resolving disputes, differences of opinion, and contentious circumstances, often conducted or supervised by a third party acceptable to both sides of a disagreement. Results often wind up being sanctioned by an appropriate court or legal authority.

ambush opportunity Usually occurs when a potential news subject avoids contact with the media, forcing some kind of surprise confrontation, conducted by a news organization.

apology A specific series of behaviors, language, and written communication designed to alleviate the pain and suffering of victims. Effective apologies have six basic components: Admission, Explanation, Behavior Change, Victim Engagement, Request for Forgiveness, Compensation.

arbitration One form of alternative dispute resolution, usually conducted by a skilled arbitrator who negotiates a resolution of disputes and/or contentious circumstances.

arrogance Making decisions for others without their participation or permission.

assault A personal attack on another individual, group, or organization. It can be verbal, physical, in writing, or through other means of communication. It creates victims every time.

attack sites Websites designed to specifically target brands, individuals, ideas, concepts, products, companies. The URLs for these sites are often quite pejorative, indicating that they are attack sites, e.g. McDonaldsSucks.com. For a list of attack sites, simply insert this phrase in your browser and literally thousands will come up for your review.

berserk employee A pejorative label management uses to describe someone management doesn't like, or, for someone who doesn't like management, and management knows it.

bridging A verbal technique involving language shortcuts through the use of short, positive phrases a spokesperson will use to go from one topic to another very quickly. The technique is used to conserve language and time in answering questions and steering conversations.

bullying The use of abusive language or abusive behaviors that cause harm, pain, and suffering to others.

business continuity plan "A documented collection of procedures and information that is developed, compiled, and maintained in readiness for use in an incident to enable an organization to continue to operate its critical activites at an acceptable pre-defined level" (BS25999:2006, British Standards Institution).

callousness Intentionally ignoring the fears, concerns, and emotions of victims.

candor Truth, with an attitude, delivered very quickly. Candor is the basis of trust.

citizen journalist A person who plays a role in news reporting and commentary through posting information on various social media.

civil litigation Branch of law dealing with disputes between individuals or organizations, brought to court with the goal of redressing wrongs – generally, compensation or some other action is sought.

color words Emotionally charged words that elicit a strong response, usually negative, from the listener or reader. Often used by reporters and bullies to surprise and elicit an emotional, angry, negative reply from the person being questioned or attacked. Examples include: angry, ugly, stupid, worried, sad, fault. Best countered by the use of power words (*See* power words).

Command Center approach Very popular and important crisis response strategy, usually involving a formal facility to house a command center. The process is driven by an incident commander and it is generally established for very complex emergencies and crises.

commission In crisis work, meaning intentional, negative actions, decisions, and behaviors. The opposite of omission.

community core values These are universally held, personal, protected beliefs that are so powerful that if a company, organization, issue, or decision affects any of these values, people will become emotionally engaged and involved in opposing whatever decision has been made. These core values, which are universal across most Western cultures, are health and safety, the value of possessions and property, environmental threats, quality of life concerns, and peer pressure.

community involvement audit A process for understanding how an organization's members are engaged with their community. It's a structured questionnaire to determine how connected an organization is to the community on an ongoing basis.

community relations Increasingly known as stakeholder relations. The community represents one group of stakeholders with which organizations, companies, and agencies need to have ongoing relationships. Community relations is that portion of the stakeholder spectrum where intentional planning activities and engagement are undertaken on a regular basis.

compassionate language Language consisting of emotionally charged words which help others understand another person's concerns about his or her wellbeing. Compassionate words include: concerned, sorry, sad, regretful.

complete thinker A systematic approach to decisionmaking that can help those affected make better decisions. The usual steps in this process are: introducing a topic, explaining the importance of a topic, forecasting some possible end points, providing options for decision making, making a recommendation, and justifying that recommendation.

complexity-to-process These are oral or written techniques using numbers and adjectives to simplify or make complicated subjects more intense. The theory is that the use of small numbers and a variety of adjectives helps people understand, decide, or take action more quickly. The numbers would be from 1-3, preceded or succeeded by adjectives such as: parts, elements, pieces, ingredients, phases, stages.

compliance The continuous obedience and observance of laws, rules, regulations, restrictions, imposed by bona fide authorities for the protection of others, or quality assurance, or safety.

compliance programs Sets of controls within companies to ensure strict conformance to legal and industry rules, regulations, standards, and requirements (such as the Sarbanes-Oxley Act, for example). An effective compliance plan has been defined in Chapter 8 of the Federal Sentencing Guidelines.

confrontation In activism, the open intentional staging of contentious opposing themes, ideas, visions, and strategies. Usually occurs to generate visibility in the media, intimidate, and to demonstrate power and strength over an opponent.

consultation In the context of community relations, stakeholder and victim management, the intentional solicitation of outside views, sometimes even outside oversight, to help assure that appropriate steps are being taken, and promises and commitments are accomplished.

contention The negative emotional response to conflicting views, ideas, and recommendation. The feeling of emotional friction created by opposing or contested views and ideas.

contrition The ongoing expression of remorse, concern, even sorrow for having done something adverse to the health and safety, well being, goals, aspirations, or intentions of others.

core values *See* community core values

Corporate Crisis Communication Response Officer (CCCRO) A first response trigger strategy involving empowering a very select number of individuals to authorize and declare a crisis to start appropriate response activities and provide resources, as well as pre-authorize important decisions in crisis response.

corrections, clarification & commentary A unique approach for responding to erroneous, mistake-laden, or simply fabricated information.

counteraction communications Handling the intensity of activists and their allegations and accusations by controlling confrontation and negotiation such that you reduce contention, mitigate negativity, and detoxify the drama.

criminal litigation Branch of law dealing with criminal offenses that violate statutory law – the goal is the legal punishment of the wrongdoer and the satisfaction of the public's sense of justice. In criminal law, the plaintiff is always an agency of the state on behalf of the public.

crisis People-stopping, product-stopping, show-stopping, reputationally defining, trust-busting event that creates victims and/or explosive visibility. May cause death or significant injury to people, animals, and/or living systems, i.e. employees, customers, or the public. May close your business, disrupt operations, cause physical or environmental damage, or threaten the firm's financial standing or public image.

crisis management The deliberate and systematic preparation of leaders and management to be ready when significantly adverse situations occur.

crisis preparedness More often now called readiness, a term that is beginning to replace the phrase crisis management as a more constructive, positive approach to being ready when bad things happen. Readiness facilitates response.

crisis prevention The intentional reduction of risk through a systematic analysis of the vulnerabilities of an organization combined, where possible, with rigorously structured compliance programs, codes of conduct, and required ethical behavior, and the systematic detection of infractions.

crisis response plan Usually a collection of scenarios which represent the most likely threats or most devastating outcomes to an organization together with response action steps, pre-authorized decisions, and a pattern of urgent, prompt behavior, that reduces the reputational threat, damage, and the production of victims in responding to crisis situations.

crisis simulation exercise, drill, or test An exercise in which as many conditions as possible of an actual, foreseeable crisis in the organization are realistically created. People at all levels of the company will be expected to carry out, as realistically as possible, the exact tasks that would be required in a real emergency, such as evacuating people, moving to an alternate worksite, etc. The results are analyzed to determine what works in the existing plan and where improvement needs to be made.

crisis website A publically available website where those interested can find information about whatever an organization chooses to put there, which could involve a specific scenario, readiness activities in the event of a crisis, but most often begins as a dark site in readiness for a crisis to occur.

dark site A special page on your company web server activated only in emergency (thus, it remains fully ready but "dark" until it is needed). Contains previously prepared emergency information and contact lists. Source of accurate information for the media, victims, survivors, and others curious about an event. Frequently updated to keep fast-breaking events and information in perspective.

dashboards A section of the crisis website containing information that is actively changing and being updated continuously. Can include illustrations, animations, charts, graphs, data tables, progress reports, and incident and recovery timelines.

decapitation The loss of a group of senior executives or leaders during a crisis or emergency circumstance.

deception The intentional misleading of others through communications.

declarative language A method of communicating that avoids or eliminates all negative words, phrases, and descriptions. The techniques are used to settle people down, reduce contention, make people comfortable with what's going on.

defendant The party being sued or charged in a criminal or civil legal action or crime.

deranged employee *See* berserk employee

destiny-management A strategy of being prepared in advance with a program to act decisively, empathetically, and ethically to counteract the predictable patterns of activist attacks and allegations, thus influencing the long-range outcome. A key element of the strategy is using correction, clarification, and commentary approaches to keeping the record straight and interpreted accurately, from your perspective.

digital media The components include everything from cell phones and text messaging, to blogs, to various communication platforms in the general category called social media. New platforms and techniques are being invented continuously.

disaster An emergency event that disrupts normal lives and business activities; such an event can occur from natural causes, such as a flood, hurricane, or fire; or it can be man-made, such as an oil spill, computer crash, or accident. Typically, disasters are caused by forces beyond the control of humans, and if responded to promptly and competently, generally fall outside of the definition of a crisis. A disaster can become a crisis when it is mishandled in some respects, especially the treatment of victims, by those responding.

disaster recovery This is the time period following the explosive occurrence of a crisis. Crisis management actually is the first and most powerful ingredient of disaster recovery.

disclosure Promptly revealing information about crises tends to reduce public surprise and help appropriate response and readiness activities get underway more promptly.

discovery A procedure prior to a trial in which one party can require the opposing party to make available information known only to the opposing party that will be useful in preparing a case.

discrediting The intentional denigration of an individual, product or reputation to reduce his or her credibility, influence, and ability to respond or survive.

disgruntled employee A management term used to describe employees whommanagement doesn't like. *See* berserk employee, deranged employee.

dismissiveness An attitude that trivializes things that are very important to other people, organizations, or causes, and especially to victims.

disparagement The verbal or written denigration of people, ideas, products, companies, causes, to destroy or disturb reputations and public perceptions.

DOJ An acronym for the United States Department of Justice, the chief law enforcement agency of the U.S. Federal Government.

due diligence Organization-wide procedures based on standards of conduct and internal controls that prevent and detect criminal actions. An organizational culture that fosters ethical conduct and a commitment to comply with the law.

emergency A surprise event with the potential of unanticipated serious consequences, giving the organization little time to think or make decisions, causing the risk of uncertainty, stress, and bureaucratic confusion, and creating victims.

employee core values A set of personal, protective beliefs, very similar to those values held in communities, these being more directed toward retention of employment, protection of employability, working conditions that are safe and healthy, and similar concerns. See community core values.

evidence A body of facts, assembled and presented in court as a part of the legal process in an attempt to prove or disprove an issue, including such items as oral testimony, documents, and public records. There are two kinds of evidence: direct evidence (you saw the snow coming down the previous evening and there is snow on the ground) and circumstantial evidence (if you wake up in the morning and see snow on the ground you can infer or assume that it did snow the night before).

exposure management and issue surveillance An early warning system designed to inform management very promptly of potential risks in its environment. A systematic approach to monitoring activities, and events, circumstances created by an organziation on its own behalf, or by others and government that may have some impact on an organization, individual, or a product reputation or value.**extortion** Legally, a crime of obtaining money, valuables, actions, and decisions adverse to the victims' interest by virtue of the extortionist's power, position, authority, or especially adverse knowledge.

fair disclosure Regulation FD (fair disclosure) of the U.S. Securities and Exchange Commission (SEC), August 2000, mandates that all publicly traded companies disclose material information to all investors at the same time – at the risk of penalties and sanctions that the SEC has now gotten quite accustomed to imposing. Further, FD says that all company spokespersons, regardless of title or level, are regarded as equal company representatives. When a spokesperson intentionally discloses nonpublic information to a person covered by the regulation, the information must be disclosed publicly rather than selectively. If selective disclosure of nonpublic information was not intentional, the company must act swiftly to rectify the situation by disclosing the information publicly.

FD fair disclosure

fear The absence of trust (trust = the absence of fear).

forgiveness Seeking forgiveness is the essence of reconciling with the victims created by crisis situations. Obtaining forgiveness has nine distinct steps: candor, extreme empathy/apology, explanation, affirmation, declaration, contrition, consultation, commitment, restitution.

golden hour From military medicine, describing what happened after World War II when the Army began bringing highly trained surgical units to the front line, as opposed to having key hospital services in the rear areas. These hospitals were called MASHs (Mobile Army Surgical Hospitals). In war, one of the greatest causes of death to soldiers was blood loss after being wounded. Once the mobile surgical hospitals were fully operational, serviced by helicopters bringing in the wounded, the data showed that if a wounded soldier arrived alive at a MASH within an hour of being wounded, 97% left the MASH alive. The metaphor to crisis management is obvious.

hardball A method of communications behavior that is very aggressive and positive. However, to be successful, it requires having the facts, understanding the circumstances, and taking initiative to prevail in the public discussions and private debates. Usually directed by an attorney.

HIPAA Health Insurance Portability and Accountability Act of 1996. U.S. Government legislation that ensures a person's right to buy health insurance after losing a job, establishes standards for electronic medical records, and protects the privacy of a patient's health information (*From* dictionary.com).

holding statements A brief statement, usually less than 150 words (about 1 minute), used in response situations where little information may be known or information needs to be promptly shared.

hostile takeovers A technique for acquiring publicly held companies when the target company is adverse to being taken over or acquired.

I'm Sorry Movement This movement began back in 1991 at the Veterans Administration Hospital in Lexington, Kentucky. This VA Hospital undertook a study to determine how they might reduce litigation related to the adverse outcomes of medical procedures and medical care. They instituted a program called, "Extreme Honesty," which essentially required that when there was an adverse outcome of almost any kind, those on duty were obligated to organize themselves to notify the patient or those responsible for the patient, and as quickly as possible hold a meeting to describe to the patient or their responsible parties, the nature of the adverse event, to apologize, and to describe and discuss what will be done to remediate the problem or situation. In addition, if there were the possibility of claims or litigation against the hospital, the filing of those claims or lawsuits was facilitated by the hospital administrative staff.

Information collected over the ten year span of the test indicated that while claims against the hospital were up, litigation was steadily and dramatically dropping. The entire study was explained in the December 1999 issue of the journal, *Annals of Internal Medicine*, under the title, "Extreme Honesty."

From this study and related work, the insurance industry began noticing that if apologies and genuine regret were expressed to patients promptly following adverse or unexpected outcomes, patients were less likely to sue, although they were likely to file additional claims. This was a breakthrough in claims management thinking. Insurance companies now generally insist that health care givers, once an adverse event occurs, immediately organize to express empathy, sympathy, explain how claims can be filed, even lawsuits, so that the patient feels less like a victim and more like a patient. Be apologetic.

This approach, the "I'm Sorry" approach, reduces litigation. Apologies presented promptly tend to eliminate litigation, or at least expedite settlements. Go to the website www.sorryworks.net for ongoing discussion and examples of apology and extreme empathy expressed in the health care setting. The *National Law Journal* and several other health journals follow developments in the "I'm Sorry" movement every year, as well as producing data with respect to claims vs. litigation.

implied consent According to Wikipedia, consent which is not expressly granted by a person, but rather inferred from a person's actions and the facts and circumstances of a particular situation (or in some cases by a person's silence or inaction). The term is most commonly encountered in the context of United States drunk driving laws. Those operating a vehicle under the influence of drugs or alcohol must submit to a sobriety test or face arrest. When you undertake the privilege of driving you subject yourself to be subject to implied consent in these.

incident response approaches The most crucial response is the first response to crisis, and there are a number of accepted techniques depending on the circumstances, including incident command, chief response officer (CRO), crisis response committee (CRC), special operations response teams (SORT), help lines, and social media action response teams (SMART).

indemnity Legally, to compensate another party to a contract for any loss that such other party may suffer during the performance of a contract; a form of insurance related to contract performance.

installation/simulation The fifth step in the development of readiness response plans involving the training of response team members. A common technique is to use a specific scenario as the basic theme for the training. The more realistic the scenario, the more powerful the training tends to be.

intellectual property Content developed by an individual or organization that is owned and protected from use by others without specific permission.

inverted pyramid answer Those that start out in very complicated ways and wind up making a point or sending a message later in the process. Generally communications in this format cause us great confusion, misinterpretation, and context problems. *See* pyramid-like answer.

issues management The continuous and conscientious observation, interpretation, and management awareness of the changing circumstances within which an organization, product, service, individual, or reputation exists.

key audiences Generally those groups of individuals and organizations who are most important to be advised, briefed, and kept in touch with what is going on. Sometimes referred to as key stakeholders.

key issue Also known as key vulnerabilities or risks. That handful of situations that are so serious that, should they occur, the result could be catastrophic to an organization, product, or agency.

killer questions The kinds of questions that no one ever wants to be asked, those that agitate, humiliate, irritate, and embarrass. Nevertheless, if they exist, they need to be prepared for.

labor relations The process of encouraging productive interaction between management and labor, generally guided or controlled by a contrac.t

laggership A Lukaszewski word denoting extremely prompt action rather than instant, immediate response. In military terms, the shortest lifespan in a patrol is the patrol leader, since the patrol leader is generally at the point of the insurgency. The Lukaszewski philosophy is to be in that patrol, but two or three ranks back, so that an encounter is survivable and reportable. Actions and responses can be taken very, very quickly, but based on much better information.

leader Someone who moves other people toward goals through inspiration, motivation, verbalizing a vision, conducting strategic evaluations and questioning, and solving people problems; someone who tells us where we are going and moves us over the horizon.

leadership The ability of an individual to think outside the confines of existing management goals, to go over the horizon and determine new destinations and objectives, then to return and convince followers to move with the leader to these new destinations.

legacy media Generally what we consider in today's terms radio, television, newspapers, magazines. As opposed to new media or the so-called social media, which includes blogs, websites, various communications platforms, Twitter, etc.

legal management The job of inside corporate counsel, which is to understand how the law relates to the corporation, providing the expertise to handle legal problems within the organization and bring in specialist law firms to handle problems beyond the ordinary.

legal risk analysis Generally conducted by attorneys as a part of determining legal strategy, legal options, and litigation and settlement pathways to resolve legal matters.

lies Information, intentionally provided, which is at variance with factual or well-understood evidence and information. Sometimes lies turn out to be one individual's truth, but disbelieved by other individuals.

litigation Legal proceeding, the process of taking a case through court.

litigation communications strategy Recognition that in litigation there are a series of communication flash points that coincide with various milestones in each legal case. Some of these milestones include complaint filing, complaint responding, jury selection, jury verdicts, announcement of appeals, high-profile witnesses, surprises.

lobbying Strong advocacy of a position by a paid advocate with the intent to influence decisionmaking, in legislation, regulation, administrative proceedings, and public statements.

Lukaszewski's Contention Survival Manifesto A document that outlines 24 techniques for reducing contention and adversity.

Lukaszewski's validity/believability index test Using key questions and the behavior of various parties to news interviews and news gathering circumstances, as a methodology for determining the level of truth in a given report, story, or explanatory effort.

malevolence A deliberate human intent to cause harm, damage, and suffering. Sometimes used to describe negative events and outcomes that are the result of actions beyond understanding. Malevolence is constantly negative, constantly malicious behavior and thinking.

malfeasance The bad behaviors, misunderstandings, treacherous intent that lead to or are responsible for creating victims and suffering. Incompetent management or leadership.**manager** Someone who runs an organization, or part of it, by the numbers, focused primarily on producing tangible, expected results that achieve or exceed the targets as forecast.

media coaching/training A structured tutorial process designed to help individuals be effective spokespersons in a variety of circumstances, stressing mostly effective verbal communication, but also including non-verbal communication and testimony preparation.

media relations The professional skill and talent to work with members of the news media, and new media, for the benefit of a client.

media relations policy Approved management procedures and guidelines for having relationships with reporters and media organizations.

mediation A form of ADR (alternative dispute resolution) involving an intermediary who works with both sides to come to a mutually satisfactory result.

mindless verbiage A Lukaszewski concept, sometimes called "verbal vegetables." These are words, phrases, and information we provide in writing or through oral communication that we will have to take back or "eat" at some point in the future. These phrases, words, and ideas need to be avoided at all costs.

negative language and concepts Any ideas, instructions, or information that contain negative words, such as not, don't, can't, won't, shouldn't, and a host of other negative concepts. These are toxic additives to ideas and communication. Negative language breeds misunderstandings, is always inaccurate in some respects, often a flat out lie (any phrase with the word "can't" in it is perceived as a lie by the recipient). Negative language causes confusion, contention, and can create victims through persistent and careless use. Negative language, phrases, and concepts should be eradicated from all writing and speaking to ensure clarity, leadership, and the ability of those being instructed to know what to do.

negligence The willful failure to act with the reasonableness and prudence dictated by the circumstances. Failure to act with care. Acting with carelessness or callousness that results in harm, damage, or suffering of others.

negotiating/conciliation Reaching agreements using negotiators, arbitrators, lawyers, and intermediaries in which both parties agree to bargain and attempt to accommodate each other's concerns to the point at which the problem can be resolved more or less amicably, outside the legal system. Also called mediation or alternative dispute resolution (ADR).

news backgrounder Fairly structured meeting to which only specific media and others are invited. Attendees are given proprietary or crucial information they need in order to cover a specific story, problem, or issue – with the request that this information be kept confidential, a decision totally up to the honor of each attendee. The best briefings are those that are on-the-record.

news briefing A structured open meeting in which complex information is presented, explained, and provided to the media and others verbally and in writing. Many individuals from the organization may be available and prepared to talk with the news media – either by making presentations or simply by answering the questions of reporters. Virtually anything said at the briefing is on-the-record.

news cycle Traditional media maintain traditional news cycles. Magazines are long, weekly papers are shorter, daily papers are shorter yet, radio can be instantaneous, television is generally breakfast, lunch and dinner, plus late news segments, journalists and others have other deadline structures. However, nowadays, every one of these news organizations has a website, all of which are engaged in the 24-hour, instant news cycle. Far more news is release from traditional legacy media websites than is released in their traditional forms of communication. If you are working in the blogosphere or in other social media platforms, your reach is as broad as your ability to build followers, and the speed of contact is instantaneous, as is quite often the speed of response.

news magazine shows TV programs that offer a type of coverage similar to that of a print news magazine, covering several stories in the same program in the form of short, taped, and sometimes live-filmed documentaries. Topics can be either mainstream or offbeat stories. Stories are not covered in more depth than typical broadcast news, including profiles, interviews, and investigative coverage. Examples include *60 Minutes, 20/20, Nightline, Dateline,* and *The Fifth Estate* (in Canada).

news release A standard communication tool used to provide information to media outlets as well as other individuals, groups, and organizations requiring or interested in such information. The format is structured to include some kind of explanation, a quote or quotes from various individuals or organizations, some additional information perhaps about available spokespeople, a timeline of events, and other related information. The purpose of the news release is to invite coverage and generally does just that.

NGOs Non-Government Organizations. These are generally non-profit style organizations recognized, some officially, as bona fide representatives of various causes, issues, movements, and even individuals. Examples include the United Nations, the Public Relations Society of America, C.A.R.E., Oxfam, Save the Children, World Vision, Habitat for Humanity. There are hundreds and hundreds of these organizations throughout the world. Most operate internationally and domestically and are generally recognized as independent observers (even if they represent a known cause, issue, or movement).

not-for-attribution Information provided to the news media to be used in news stories but with identification of the news source withheld by the media. Caution: The rules vary by medium and by organization. Before you engage, be clear about the rules the medium you are speaking with or sending information to has in these matters.

off-the-record Information given to the reporter is mutually agreed to be confidential, not to be published or otherwise repeated to a third party – potentially, however, the information is likely to be published or otherwise revealed if the reporter can confirm the same information from another source. If it truly is a secret, keep still. Caution: The rules vary by medium and by organization. Before you engage, be clear about the rules the medium you are speaking with or sending information in these matters. Be sure the individual promising confidentiality has the authority to give such assurances.

omission In crisis work, omission is generally one potential factor contributing to the cause of a crisis or extremely urgent situation. Failure to take due care or precautions, failure to warn, failure to anticipate, and failure to predict and preempt are some examples of omission. Omissions, when there is serious damage, injury, and victimization, can become serious legal and litigation issues. Negligence is often connected to serious omissions.

on-the-record All that is said to the reporter can be quoted or attributed. The safest assumption is that if you are speaking in the presence a reporter or otherwise providing spoken or written information to the media, what you are revealing is on-the-record.

organizational barriers Typical barriers include those created by various urgent and crisis-like situations, such as resistance to change or the views of outside advisors; employees organizing against management; management organizing against employees; distance; language; cultural issues; any action, decision or behavior that needs to be overcome for success to be achieved; these would be considered organizational barriers. The finance department often becomes a barrier pretty quickly as they notice significant amount of money being required or purchased orders written. Crises do cause organizations to spend money foolishly, stupidly, but we don't know that until afterwards. One of the most important services leadership can provide in crisis is to keep the finance people in check so that unnecessary barriers can be avoided when decisions need to be made at lightening speed.

perception issues Perception issues arise when those who know about you and think about you do it in ways that you have trouble recognizing or reconciling. When your perception differs from the perception of those on whom you rely, you have perception issues. In crisis perception is reality.

plaintiff The party instituting a legal action in court, complainant. In civil cases, the plaintiff can be just about anyone. In criminal cases, the plaintiff is always the government.

plea agreement A negotiated settlement in a criminal case in which the defendant agrees to plead guilty to a lesser charge. The plea agreement clearly spells out the nature of the offense(s) as well as the various steps, sanctions, punishments, restrictions, and revised behaviors that will be imposed on the defendant in order to settle the case. Most plea agreements have a specific duration in time and involve supervision or oversight of the defendant or the defendant organization. Any deviation from what the plea agreement specifies can cause the agreement to be dissolved and the entire criminal matter returned to the court room, or additional sanctions and penalties or both.

Or, there may be automatic penalties assessed and imposed should the defendant disregard any elements of the plea agreement. In addition, most plea agreements have a clause which requires that should the defendant obtain new knowledge about the circumstances of the crime, that knowledge must be reported to the prosecution immediately or further sanctions may be imposed.

positive language The absolute absence of negative phrases, words, and concepts. Positive language is the most powerful contention-reducing tool humans have.

power words Attention-getting words that inspire or establish a positive framework or frame of mind response. Good to use when counteracting negative statements and emotional questions involving color words. (*See* color words.) Examples of power words are: critical, urgent, important, new, unique, interesting, essential. These words add positive energy and momentum to spoken and written information.

pre-authorization An alternate definition of readiness planning. Important decisions involving a known aspect of a scenerio are made ahead of time to empower responders to act more quickly.

privileged communication Always consult an attorney first before assuming exchange of information or protected or privileged. Protected by the Fifth Amendment of the U.S. Constitution, information exchanged between two individuals in what is recognized legally as a privileged protected confidential relationship (i.e., attorney/client, doctor/patient, husband/wife, clergy/individual, etc.). Protects information from being revealed in court. Privileged communication can also be created in a variety of circumstances, but virtually all must be under the supervision of an attorney.

Privilege is very fragile and can be waived very easily, even accidentally, for example by giving or exposing privileged information to unauthorized third parties; by verbalizing privileged instructions or material from protected documents to unauthorized individuals; communicating privileged materials to other attorneys who are not a part of the litigation or circumstance in which you seek privilege; virtually any unauthorized disclosure of privileged information to parties without specific direction or authorization by counsel. Again, seek legal advice and guidance. Cannot be used as evidence in court.

public relations (role/activities) The PRSA (Public Relations Society of America) defines public relations this way: "Public relations is a strategic communication process that builds mutually beneficial relationships between organizations and their publics." This definition was adopted in 2012. The process of public relations involves four fundamental steps: research, planning, execution, and measurement. Public relations activities are present in virtually every area of human endeavor; in the for-profit world, the not-for-profit world, government, corporate and business activities, religious and political activities, advocacy, military, academia, and more.

pyramid-like answers The preferred structure of answers is where a limited amount of critical information is given initially, then is further supported by additional commentary or language for the balance of the answer. *See inverted pyramid.*

readiness The state of being prepared to preempt, prevent, detect, deter, and identify the most threatening circumstances – both operational threats and non-operating circumstances – in advance and to prepare to manage or otherwise resolve these circumstances in a crisis. Readiness is a management term that should really replace "crisis management" in reference to being ready and being prepared to meet crisis circumstances.

reputation Conferred by others on an individual, product, service, company, organization, or agency by others based on past performance, reliability, behavior, actions, deeds, and behaviors. Reputation is the cumulative estimation by others of the various circumstances surrounding a product, person, organization, including ethical behavior.

reputation management The intention, planning, monitoring, maintenance, and readiness to repair adverse situations, as well as to capitalize on extraordinarily positive situations in order to establish, maintain, repair, and rehabilitate reputation.

reputational crisis Any negative circumstance that threatens the estimation of others of your reputation. Usually caused by non-operating kinds of circumstances which are highly emotional, victim producing, and extremely negative. A reputational crisis can also be caused by sudden, completely unexpected negative behaviors which take those who hold you in high esteem by surprise in a negative way.

response team Response teams come in a variety of designations – first response, issue response, reputational response, social media response. A group of individuals trained to follow specific response plans, guidelines, or directions. There can be as many response teams in and for an organization as there are adverse situations that need response.

restitution An essential ingredient in obtaining forgiveness from someone who has been harmed. Can take a variety of forms, judgments, cash and subsidies, reinstatement, generally a circumstance or situation where victims are being compensated in some way that they have requested or desire to reduce their victimization.

revitalization In crisis terms, this means removing contention, removing barriers, facilitating communication, and generally reinvigorating an organization through leadership, preparation, and risk reduction.

RICO Racketeer Influence and Corrupt Organizations Act. This is U.S. law, enacted in 1970, which allows victims of organized crime to sue those responsible for punitive damages, once an organization is identified as a Racketeer Influence and Corrupt Organization. There can also be civil RICO cases.

risk The possibility that a threat will exploit a vulnerability – risk assessment determines the likelihood of such an exploitation occurring, the extent of consequences that could result, and what it would take to recover from such an incident.

risk management The practice of management and leadership to identify risks and threats to an organization and to take steps necessary to mitigate, moderate, anticipate, or eliminate these risks and threats where possible. At a minimum, organizations of all sizes must have in place a management procedure for identifying and minimizing situations of risk.

RSS feeds This stands for, colloquially, Real Simple Syndication, an internet connection that disseminates, that is, syndicates, information at the request of recipients as well as senders.

SARA Superfund Amendments and Reauthorization Act, which amended the Comprehensive Environmental Response, Compensation and Liability Acts. This law was enacted to enable the U.S. Environmental Protection Agency (EPA) to administer the very complex superfund programs, which involve remediation of very seriously contaminated sites all across the United States and its territories.

Sarbanes-Oxley Act (SOX) A 2002 law providing mandates and requirements for financial reporting by publicly held companies. Important to corporate governance since it requires a standard data-entry system and because real-time reporting deters certain abuses, such as manipulating inventories and sales. Amendments to SOX adopted and initiated in 2004 set even more stringent requirements in terms of ethics and the behavior of corporate leaders, and the punishment they can experience should corporate governance laws be violated.

SOX has been subsequently amended and remains controversial: praised for restoring investor confidence and ensuring more reliable financial statements, and criticized as a costly act that has created an overly regulated environment.

sarcasm A verbal form of bullying and assault that generally humiliates, and embarrasses an individual. It can be seen as humor by some, but clearly damaging to the victim or target.

scenario A type of educational group planning exercise or drill that walks the group through a hypothetical incident with representatives of different functions in the company playing the roles they would play if this were an actual incident.

script/scripting A philosophy of oral and written communication which maximizes content, understandability, and relevance, with a minimum of complicated words and concepts, which everyone connected with a particular circumstance, situation, or problem is asked to utilize. Scripting is the goal of all crisis communication.

search engine optimization A digital technique that makes information on various digital platforms easily findable by search engines.

sentiment-measurement Methods of monitoring, evaluating, and measuring public response to a crisis and its critics. Determining the degree to which your communications efforts are helping to shift public feelings about the crisis and surrounding issues. Analysis of the volume and frequency of negative vs. positive conscepts and ideas in written and spoken communications.

settlement The preferred outcome for disputes, dissention, and damage.

shame Can be a form of verbal or written abuse and bullying; also an emotion felt by perpetrators once recognizing the damage they have caused to the victims.

short sale An investing technique that allows an investor to profit as the value of a stock declines.

silence The most toxic strategy in a crisis.

SMART team Social Media Action Response Team: a group of individuals trained to be ready for social media attacks, disruptions, or adverse circumstances.

social media Highly accessible interactive web-based and mobile technologies that allow ordinary individuals to become citizen journalists, to create and exchange content, disseminating it widely and rapidly.

social media monitoring Analogous to the old fashioned clipping services, except in this case social platforms are being monitored and often includes deeper analysis of the words, phrases, and content. An essential activity for individuals, products, services, and other actions visible in social media.

sound bite Generally a brief collection of words that make sense and is used orally and in writing to convey a lot of information in a very few words.

Special Response Unit (SRU) A group of individuals within an organization designated to respond to a variety of operating and non-operating problems with the authority to manage the response, the victims, and the outcomes.

spokesperson Someone who is designated, authorized, and trained to convey information through the media in forums, giving testimony, or directly, perhaps through social media and other circumstances on behalf of an organization, issue, victim family, etc.

stakeholder An individual with an interest in an issue, a product, a service, something affecting their lives or the lives of those they care about, other people, animals, living systems, whose interest is recognized and often monitored by others.

strategic counselor A consultant or advisor who coaches, counsels, and befriends those who have operating responsibilities, advising decisionmakers who do important work affecting the lives, lifestyles, and wellbeing of other people, organizations, cultures, even societies.

subject matter experts (SMEs) These are individuals who have recognized expertise in specific areas of knowledge, such as police, lawyers, architects, engineers, doctors, metallurgists; the list is almost as varied as there are activities, areas of knowledge and study, and intellectual activities on the planet.

"sucks" sites Attack sites generally using the name of a product, individual, or service along with the word "sucks" to attract attention as well as demean, minimize, and insult whoever the "sucks" target happens to be.

tabletop exercise A type of drill in which all the key members of the team gather in a room and go through all the steps of mock crisis response – to a real situation or a hypothetical scenario – each participant detailing what his or her next move in the process would be. Can reveal what is missing or incorrect in the current crisis management plans, while being less time-consuming and expensive than an actual drill.

tag cloud A digital analysis of web and social media site mentions of almost any subject topic, name, or idea. The resulting words appear in various sizes and colors depending on the intensity, emotion, positivity, and negativity of the mentions over a given period of time.

take-downs The technique of working with Internet service providers (ISPs) to take down offensive, inappropriate, embarrassing, humiliating, bullying, and highly negative posts by others. Generally take-down strategies are rarely successful, especially in the U.S. with its First Amendment freedom of speech.

terrorism An act of communication achieved through extraordinarily violent actions, usually in proximity to easy and large media coverage. The messages of these acts are designed to spread fear, uncertainty, doubt, and unease through the sheer audacity, extremeness of the action, and the vulnerability of the victims.

testosterosis A Lukaszewski word meaning: Aggressive, competitive, "smash-them-in-the-mouth" behavior, usually by executives and others whose organizations have been caught as perpetrators. Characterized by a stubborn refusal or denial of negative perpetrating acts, intentional failure to move ahead or to take petty, silly, meaningless issues and problems personally and lash out. Usually thought of as a "guy thing," but women in positions of responsibility and those who have to act tough often act this way as well.

The Help Line One of five First-Response strategies in an organization consisting of a single telephone number that anyone in an organization can call, text, or e-mail to alert the organization to some potential adversity, something out of wack, anything that might cause trouble. The line and the e-mail are monitored 24 hours/day, 7 days/week, and the person doing the monitoring is empowered to trigger a response immediately. Generally, organizations have information banks related to various adverse situations from pipes cracking to ceiling fixtures blinking to fire alarms not working to violence on the premises. Of all the first response triggering techniques in use today, the Help Line is the one that is organized to trigger a maximum level of prompt responsiveness.

themes/key messages In the crisis context, these are developed as a part of the planning and preparation process, usually based on the various scenarios for which the organization is preparing.

threat A possible danger. A risk to the organization that might be manageable or eliminatable. Adverse information or activities.

threat identification A systematic process for monitoring and surveilling those potential dangers, vulnerabilities, and adverse actions that are known or thought to be possible for which the organization may take steps to prevent, preempt, detect, and deter.

threat surveillance A strategic reporting system to key managers that alerts them to threats, risks, and potential adverse circumstances, either due to organizational operations or non-operating circumstances that seem likely to cause problems.

traditional media *See* legacy media.

unplanned visibility One of two kinds of visibility, planned or unplanned, that causes public exposure resulting from some operating process outcome or operating issues or outcomes that adversely affect people, animals, or the environment, create victims, and attract the attention of various news media, specific groups, social media, or government agencies.

validation This generally relates to the need of victims to assure themselves that they have truly been injured, wounded, or abused in some way that confirms the validity of their circumstances.

verbal speed The world tends to move at verbal velocity, that is at the speed people can talk or hear messages and information. In English-speaking cultures, we speak approximately 150 words per minute. That velocity presents the limit of information that people can absorb in any situation.

verbal vegetables Generally, this is language we use or write which we later are forced to deny, denounce, disparage, take back, or simply "eat," i.e. verbal vegetables.

verbal visionary An individual who, through the power of his or her intellect, thinking, rationality, and ultimately, speech and speaking, can get others to focus on meaningful, useful, positive goals, which these followers can willingly contribute, and then can move toward achieving important goals.

victim A person, animal, or living system considered to be physically, psychologically, emotionally, or financially injured as a result of an event caused by a perpetrator. The principal ingredient in a disaster or emergency escalating to the level of crisis is the creation of victims, who focus blame for their condition on the perpetrating organization and its leader or leadership, while going public with their dramatic and emotional "stories" to the detriment of the organization.

victim communication strategy The two elements in the crisis response strategy are, first, to stop the production of victims, and second, to manage the victim dimension, which will largely be done through communication, and action. Be ready.

victim confusion A state of management during crisis in which the managers often feel and express their emotion that they have been victimized just as much as those who are actually injured, lost, or killed. Perpetrators are never considered victims. Perpetrators feeling, talking, and acting like victims is a waste of time and energy, a diversion from stopping the production of victims and managing the real victim dimension.

victim recovery cycle A complex but predictable sequence of emotional responses and perpetrator actions toward those who consider themselves to be victims of the circumstance.

victimization Of the nearly twenty likely causes of victimization, only three are physical, the rest are communications related.

vindication The third step in the victim recovery process, after validation and visibility, wherein victims and survivors take credit for whatever modifications, changes, or improvements and prevention steps are taken by the perpetrators.

visibility The second step in the major recovery cycle of victims who need to talk about their pain, their suffering, and the causative individuals and factors. Being on television, being in the newspapers, speaking in front of groups, testifying before government bodies, are all ingredients of the visibility victims need to recover.

visibility analysis The systematic examination of the visibility of an organization, product, individual, issue or product for the purpose of readiness planning. There are two kinds of visibility, planned visibility and unplanned visibility (sometimes referred to as vulnerabilities).

vulnerability A weakness that leaves an organization or system open to any kind of threat, exploitation, or damage – natural or man-made disaster – bringing with it the risk of creating victims and of negative publicity and damage to reputation.

website readiness Generally the addition to existing websites of "dark pages" or "dark sites." These are template pages that are planned and predesigned, which reside on a server but remain dark until they are needed. The template is generally for early information that will be needed if various scenarios were to occur. Each page is for a single scenario allowing the organization to post useful, early information very, very promptly.

whistle-blowers These are individuals who have seen something adverse, unethical, illegal, immoral, or maybe just plain stupid in their organizational environment and report it to appropriate internal or outside authority. In the United States, there are a variety of laws that protect the identities and the persons who are whistle-blowers. In addition, in many circumstances the whistle-blower will receive a portion of the value of the recovery, or loss prevented for the circumstance that is reported. Generally considered "disgruntled employees" by management, being a whistle-blower can be a very personally, professionally, and socially risky behavior. Studies by the Ethics Resource Center and other creditable organizations demonstrate every year that whistle-blowers are abused, threatened, harassed, and are often at risk of being shunned by fellow employeees as well as company leaders.

wildcat strikes A Union action where workers unilaterally and generally without specific permission of any organized Union walk off the job or withhold their services.

work product Created when unique information and special expertise is required as a lawyer prepares for trial. Work product can be materials, reports, notes, or data developed by the attorney, or prepared by outside specialists, investigators, consultants like public relations practitioners, accountants, engineers, etc. at the direction and under the supervision of an attorney preparing for or in anticipation of litigation. Great caution is required of non-lawyers preparing information.

work product doctrine (WPD) As codified in the US Federal Rules of Civil Procedure, shields certain confidential pre-trial materials from "discovery" by opposing counsel. The specifics of work product doctrine (WPD) can vary from jurisdiction to jurisdiction; you must consult an attorney for specific guidance. In general, here are some useful information about WPD:

1. To obtain work product protection you must:

    •   Work at the direction and under the supervision of an attorney; work in confidence and have a legal purpose (usually trial preparation) that is explicitly stated and understood.

2. Under WPD protection, you must:

    •   Set up separate, legal files which are usually locked with access limited to the document preparers

    •   Limit access and distribution only to those who are authorized by counsel. There are other conditions you must meet to maintain the privilege circumstance under work product doctrine. *See* privilege above.

workplace violence An expanding problem in the American workplace. Employees who are having problems or causing problems, often for reasons never discovered, come to work and take their frustrations out through highly visible, violent acts. Despite decades of study and observation, there are no templates or model behaviors to predict who is a violent employee. In the more explosive cases, the employee often takes his or her own life, or may be slain as a part of the official response to the violent behavior. Even those few who do survive rarely can articulate in ways that are understandable what drove them to the violent behaviors they undertook. Prevention is extremely difficult and detection is virtually impossible. We do know, however, a lot about responding to situations involving threats of employee violence. These techniques can, and frequently do, reduce the extent of damage done by those executing violent behavior.

Index

Credits

Kristen Noakes-Fry, ABCI, is Editorial Director at Rothstein Associates Inc. Previously, she was a Research Director, Information Security and Risk Group, for Gartner, Inc.; Associate Editor at Datapro (McGraw-Hill); and Associate Professor of English at Atlantic Cape College in New Jersey. She holds an M.A. from New York University and a B.A. from Russell Sage College.

Cover Design and Graphics:	Sheila Kwiatek, Flower Grafix
Page Design and Typography:	Jean King
Cover Photography:	Steve Tiongson
Graphic Editing:	Tammy McCormick
Copy Editing:	Nancy Warner
Index:	Enid Zafran, Indexing Partners, LLC

Title Font:	Nueva STD
Body Fonts:	Sabon and Frutiger

Articles and Monographs

1. **Monograph: Influencing Public Attitudes: Direct Communication Strategies that Reduce the Media's Influence on Public Decision-Making**

http://qrs.ly/ii2qq4q

You will learn new concepts about audiences, The Theory of Mutual Inattention, the Six Myths of Communication, The Five Axioms of Influence, The Six Realities of Audience Behavior, and strategies to reduce the media's power and infuence.

2. **Monograph: The Ingredients of Leadership: Finding the Personal Power for Moving People and Organizations into the Future ©**

There are crucial behaviors important people, successful executives, and true leaders use to move processes and people forward. These behaviors are the key ingredients of leadership. The more of these ingredients leaders take to heart, teach and expect of others, the more power, and followers they will have to achieve their goals.

3. **Monograph: Becoming a Verbal Visionary: How to Have a Happy, Successful, Influential, and Important Life ©**

This monograph is about you, personally. It's about having a happy, successful, influential, and important professional life. It's about becoming a verbal visionary. This monograph will help you discover what you believe, the ingredience of your integrity and your personal values. It's about who you want to become.

4. **Monograph: Seven Dimensions of Crisis Communication Management: A Strategic Analysis and Planning Model ©**

True crises have several critical dimensions in common, any one of which, if handled poorly, can disrupt or perhaps destroy best efforts at managing any remaining opportunities to resolve the situation and recover, rehabilitate, or retain reputation. Failure to respond and communicate in ways that meet community standards and expectations will result in a series of negative outcomes. This article focuses on seven critical dimensions of crisis communication management.

5. Monograph: Building Quality Community Relationships: A Planning Model to Gain and Maintain Public Consent

This monograph is a road map to better community and stakeholder relationships, reconciling community differences, reducing contention, overcoming opposition, managing your critics, and constructing strong, positive, permanent communityand stakeholder relationships.

6. Strategy Newsletter: CEO Survival: The First 100 Days (Plus 1148 More)

If you're a new CEO, longevity indicators predict that you have about 41 months to accomplish your objectives. You need to take immediate action to assure your success as CEO. This monograph illustrates a strategy and framework for succeeding in those first 100 days; 13.32 weeks, 2,400 hours, 144,000 minutes, 8,640,000 seconds, and 1148 days that remain.

7. Strategic memo: Bad News Eradicator

The Bad News Eradicator was designed to help prevent and to eliminate defensive words and negative phrases from your speech and writing. Keep the document next your telephone. Take it with you when you travel. Collect and eradicate your own set of habitual negative phrases and words. List them on the sheet, then create their positive equivalent and get a whole new life. The goal is to create a positive, equivalent phrase that has the same or fewer words than the negative phrase.

With Special Thanks
From the Author

This book is the result of the confluence of many interesting circumstances over the years and the support, encouragement, collaboration and direct assistance of many people from all walks of life. Publicly thanking and recognizing them may take a little time. I hope you'll be interested in finding out who they are and what they did.

This book is focused on the five most crucial areas organizations, institutions, agencies, and businesses too often fail to manage effectively during urgent, crisis and victim-producing situations. Much of the content is empirical, derived from the adversity, embarrassing, even humiliating circumstances my clients have experienced. Let me express my gratitude to all of them here for having given me the opportunity to learn so much so quickly and so frequently.

However, their actual names will remain confidential. The lessons their experiences taught are far more valuable as learning opportunities than their identities.

Nevertheless, there are a number of individuals and organizations that deserve, and in fact, require recognition, and my public appreciation.

Rothstein Associates Inc.
Philip Jan Rothstein, FBCI, is the one person supremely responsible for this book coming to life. He has been a faithful promoter of my work and thinking, and surfaced the idea of a new book, inspired by the huge four volume crisis management technical manual I co-published with the Public Relations Society of America from 2000 to 2005. His editorial director, Kristen Noakes-Fry, piloted the effort. Together, they mined my material, examined my more recent writings, helped me create a fresh new approach to the most important organizational crisis response leadership challenges – and brought this book into the world.

The Risdall Marketing Group

At the end of 2009, my wife of 47 years, Barbara, decided to retire. We had operated our own businesses, except for four years, in New York, since 1978. Barbara loved running the businesses and I loved doing the business with her. Her decision to retire precipitated thinking how she would retire and how I could continue working.

We decided to close down all of our east coast business operations and, after 25 years in New York and Connecticut, return to Minnesota where she could be near her 96-year-old mother, Ruth, and our families.

At this point, I really didn't want to start a business of my own again and needed to find someone who would be willing to hire a 68-year-old National Crisis Consultant. Rose McKinney, at that time President of Risdall McKinney Public Relations, was among the people I called. We'd gotten to know each other through our work in the Public Relations Society of America (PRSA). We discussed various approaches for my relocating my operational base to the Twin Cities. She made truly valuable suggestions about what might work.

Ironically, when we started our first business in 1978 in the Minneapolis suburb of Fridley, Minnesota, one of my local vendors was a small new advertising firm run by John Risdall. He and I had only infrequent contact over the years. But, as my conversations with Rose progressed, it became increasingly clear, actually to my great relief, that they were quite interested in having me come aboard at Risdall.

On January 3, 2010, approaching age 69, I resumed my career, now as President of the Lukaszewski Group Division of the Risdall Marketing Group.

What an extraordinary gift and opportunity Rose and John provided. As this book comes to press in 2013, the troubles I am always seeking to fix for others continue to find me daily from all across America and beyond, at The Lukaszewski Group Division of Risdall Public Relations.

Chester Burger Co.

Shortly after starting our first public relations firm in the Twin Cities in 1978, I began publishing and speaking a great deal. After a while I began receiving lovely little encouraging notes in the mail from Chester Burger, a New York-based Management Communication Consultant.

It was Chester Burger who invited me to work at his firm in New York City when we sold our business to another Minneapolis firm. Barbara and I moved to New York City in July of 1986 with our youngest son James, a senior at Bloomington High School that year, and Chester Burger became a lifelong friend, mentor, disciple, and inspiration.

My national, even international career began the day I started work at

Chester Burger Company. My last conversation with Chet was in December of 2009. We both knew it was our last conversation; he was dying of cancer, and Barbara and I were moving to Minnesota. He had been on the phone that morning with commanders in the field in Afghanistan and Iraq providing strategic communications advice and counsel. He was a brilliant and committed American who had the habit of helping, guiding, and encouraging everyone he encountered, and his country.

His constant stream of comments, suggestions, ideas, analyses, and direct engagement over 30 years were powerful continuous energizers and oxygenators of my career.

Minnesota Metropolitan State University
Today Minnesota Metropolitan State University has more than 35,000 graduates. When I graduated in April 1974, I was graduate number 81, at age 32. This University has to be one of the most unique on the planet.

Its nontraditional approach, the use of active professionals, experts, and faculty from the community was the perfect home for my empirical style of learning, and working.

It has been a source of constant recognition and validation. Like the field of public relations itself, the life-long learning philosophy at Metropolitan State University is that every experience one has in life will be of value, perhaps again and again in life, but it may just not be immediately clear exactly when. This has certainly been the story of my life, and career.

New York University
Actually, these comments are more about Helio Fred Garcia than about New York University (NYU). It was Fred Garcia who recruited me to teach crisis management at the Management Institute, later named the Marketing & Management Institute, of the School of Continuing and Professional Studies. For 19 years, beginning in 1988, I taught a special 16-hour seminar on strategic thinking, crisis management, leadership recovery, and how to be a trusted strategic advisor. I spoke at several graduations, taught a variety of workshop topics all related to crisis management, leadership and reputation recovery.

It was at NYU that I first began working with practitioners in large numbers very directly. This experience culminated in my 2008 book, *Why Should the Boss Listen to You, the Seven Disciplines of the Trusted Strategic Advisor,* published by JosseyBass, an imprint of Wiley Books.

Fred Garcia has been another extraordinary influence and inspiring presence in my life and career. Teaching at NYU became my laboratory for exploring ideas, testing concepts, and thinking through vast amounts of information for the purpose of constructing sensible, helpful, unique tools and techniques to help clients, and practitioners.

NYU was also my first introduction to people from other cultures. Attendance in my courses averaged more than 60% students from outside the United States. This exposure combined with the globalization of business, education, even government activities, has given me a unique perspective on the cultural impact of crisis and victimization. It has also confirmed that regardless of cultural background, the fundamental causes and impacts of inappropriate behavior, decisions, and actions have very similar roots and remedies.

The United States Marine Corps

In 1986, just after joining the Chester Burger Company, I was asked to replace the retiring Chester Burger as a lecturer at the annual East Coast Commanders Media Training Symposium, held in New York City every October. This was my first introduction to any military service, and for almost 20 years, I conducted an important session on the responsibility of military leadership to engage with the news media.

Brigadier General Walter E. Boomer, now retired, who eventually became assistant commandant of the United State Marine Corps, invited me to become an instructor in the Brigadier General Selectees Orientation Conference (BGSOC) held at the Pentagon in the spring of each year. At one point, every active-duty Marine Corps General had gone through my two-day leadership and media training course. I was assisted by thirty USMC public affairs officers.

The Marines were very gracious. I lectured to senior noncommissioned officers, attended training exercises at various bases and locations, and have developed an extraordinary affection, admiration and respect for all Americans in uniform.

The Public Relations Society of America (PRSA)

Even before I went to New York, I was an active speaker, panelist, and presenter at professional conferences all across America for a wide variety of business organizations, trade associations, and individual businesses. In 2000, as an experiment, I piloted a series of monthly webinars for PRSA. The Executive Director at the time, Ray Gaulke, wanted to really give this new technology a test. Starting that year I began doing one webinar per month. These programs continued until December 2009. They resumed in 2012. This was another incredibly important intellectual laboratory for me to continue exploring, understanding, and testing those ideas and concepts I was learning every day, on the job. And, I was being exposed to thousands of practitioners in the Americas, Canada, and beyond.

In addition, the Society offered me many other opportunities to be visible, share my experience, present in larger forums, and associate with many extraordinary practitioners.

Over the years, PRSA has provided audiences in the thousands to hear me, challenge me, and sometimes cheer me. They publish my articles and ideas, including the four volume technical manual on crisis management for practitioners and leaders that I mentioned earlier. My most constant and helpful contact over the years has been Judy Voss, currently Director of Professional Development. Her professionalism and diplomacy combined with tenacity and efficiency maximized the value of my participation and activity to all PRSA members. Her colleague Colleen Seaver, has for many years provided the logistic support for the dozens of on-site programs I have done.

In 1991, I was appointed to the PRSA Board of Ethics and Professional Standards (BEPS). At this writing I am the longest-serving member. In 1996, BEPS, under the leadership of Bob Fraus, APR, Fellow PRSA, Seattle, undertook the redesign, reconstruction, and a new approach to public relations ethics, standards, and business practices. That code revision, introduced in 2000, has become the world standard for public relations practice. Many, if not most, of the group of practitioners who recreated the code, including Bob Frause, APR, Fellow PRSA, from Seattle; Kathy Fitzpatrick, APR, JD, of Quinnipiac University; Jeff Julin, APR, Fellow PRSA, from Denver; Roger Buehrer, APR, Fellow PRSA, from Las Vegas; Tom Duke, APR, Fellow PRSA, from Akron; Vivian Hamilton, APR, Fellow PRSA, from Anchorage; and Linda Cohen, APR, Fellow PRSA, from Tucson; have remained close friends and associates.

The International Association of Business Communicators (IABC)

In 2001, I approached the IABC about starting a series of webinars. By the end of that year, I was doing one program per month, which continued to the end of 2009.

Here was yet another laboratory for me to explore and share what my practice was teaching me. Former IABC president Julie Freeman, and especially professional development director Chris Corrigan, were always helpful in finding ways to leverage my knowledge and experience for the benefit of IABC members. They introduced me to Kathe Sweeney, Executive Editor, Professional Business, Nonprofit and Public Management, Jossey-Bass/A Wiley Brand, San Francisco, who became my publisher.

ASIS International

In 1999, at the insistence of Brian Hollstein, then head of Corporate Security at Xerox Corporation, I joined the organization formerly known as the American Society for Industrial Security. ASIS International now has chapters in more than 100 countries. I couldn't imagine, at the time, the impact that the September 11, 2001, attack would have on my career and on the field of industrial and corporate security.

ASIS provides platforms for me to share my views and test my thinking. I also am an active member of the Crisis Management and Business Continuity Council (CMBCC). This is a gathering of fascinating and important professionals who are security executives, teachers, leaders, educators, and authors from many countries.

ASIS helps me retain and expand my global perspective on a wide variety of issues related to the security, survival, and resumption of vital organizational and government services and activities affected by crisis situations.

Since 9/11/2001, these individuals and the security profession have taken on extraordinarily important responsibilities in the wartime conditions America finds itself in today.

Professional Colleagues

Kenneth Koprowski, a colleague and friend of many years read, edited and made extensive suggestions to the manuscript. He has taught portions of the book's content in various college courses. We collaborate on major crisis projects. Ken graciously contributed the introduction to this book.

Pamela Cardinale Koprowski, whom I've known longer than Ken, was, in 1986, the first corporate communications manager to hire me for what turned out to be a 20-year relationship with her company. In the process, she truly catalyzed the beginning of my national consulting career.

Kerrigan C. West came to our company in 2000 from the State University of New York at Buffalo (SUNY Buffalo). She became my Executive Assistant and, other than Barbara, knows more about our company than any one. For a decade, she produced my webinars, virtually everything I've written or spoke from 2000 to 2009, and handled the logistics of my rather complicated, episodic professional life. She told me that the only thing she couldn't do for me was move to Minnesota. And so we both moved on. We keep in touch and she has developed a wonderful new career for herself based near Stamford, Connecticut.

Mary Ann Nolan, who lives near Boston, worked for our firm for several years, beginning in the mid 1990's. We first met when she was working with Burson-

Marsteller on a large criminal case involving medical device tampering. She was truly the driver of all the staff work that was being done on the public relations side. We managed to hire her when she left Burson-Marsteller. She taught me about litigation, civil and criminal. She is an expert in pharmaceutical law and regulation. Best of all, she was a Burson-Marsteller trained account executive, and she taught me a great deal about improving both my professionalism and the approach our firm took to our clients, many of whom were Fortune companies. Every day she taught me something about how to serve our clients better. These are lessons I carry and teach others to this day.

Certain chapters in the book have had extensive outside scrutiny. Chapter 7 on Social Media was redrafted from my original writing by Kenneth Koprowski and subsequently contributed to by a number of key experts at Risdall Marketing Group, among them, Josh Dahmes, President of Risdall Online Marketing Group, and Joel Swanson, President of Risdall Public Relations.

Chapter 8 is about Activism, and probably the foremost influence on my knowledge about activism other than being in the trenches for so many years, began with Paul Ridgeway Sr., whom I met while serving as a Deputy Press Secretary to former Minnesota Governor Wendell R. Anderson. In his early 20s at the time, he had served as an advance man for President Jimmy Carter, and previously for Vice President Hubert H. Humphrey. Paul and I worked over the years on a variety of amazingly complicated, and high profile community relations and corporate community relations problems.

During that same time I met Terry Serie, another native Minnesotan who became a long-time colleague, who worked for Champion International Paper, then later for the leading Forest Industry Trade Association in Washington, D.C. His crucial insights and pragmatism had an enormous impact on how I learned to deal with settings involving communities, activists, activism, contention, confrontation, and corporate mistakes.

Another enormous influence was Stan Raggio, Senior Vice President for Sourcing at The Gap. He and I together worked through some of the toughest years of global anti-corporate activism against the clothing industry. Over the years, Stan demonstrated his extraordinary intellect in dealing with the various factions, opinions and attitudes of activists. He enjoyed engaging them with astonishing levels of philosophical and intellectual energy and sincerity. In the process, he completed his Master's in Catholic Theology at University of California, Berkley.

Others who helped me become nationally and internationally prominent in Crisis Management include Larry Kamer, who comes from San Francisco, California, a ceaseless booster of my work and activities, as well as a strong and important competitor.

The latest conscript to my entourage is Mrs. Carin Leonard-Gorrill who, when she accepted this job, essentially as Kerrigan's successor, probably had very little idea of my capacity to produce copy, and of the complexities of finishing a major publishing project. There were days when I'm sure she would rather have reverted to her previous life acting in commercials or on the stage somewhere. However, she has persevered, and has been the critical ingredient in actually making sure that this book, piece by piece, got to the publisher.

Family

As important as all these individuals were in my life, and career, the most important person has always been Barbara Bray Lukaszewski. We met when she was 16 and I was 18, and although Barbara is now retired, we continue to do most everything in life together. For 32 years of our 50 years together, she ran our businesses, raised our children, and managed much of my life so I could do our business. She is the sunshine girl.

Some years ago there was a wonderful movie called, "As Good As It Gets," starring Jack Nicholson and Helen Hunt. Jack plays an introverted weird guy falling in love with Helen Hunt's character. When he tries to describe her impact on him, his character says, essentially – when she smiles at you, you know you have a life. Lucky for me, after more than 50 years together, Barbara continues to smile at me every day.

Jim Lukaszewski

Bloomington, Minnesota
November, 2012

A Special Dedication to Chester A. Burger
1/10/21 – 3/22/11

Goodbye, Chet. The Remembrance of a Remarkable Man

From your first little note to me in 1975, complimenting something I'd said that was quoted in a PRSA publication, to our last conversation in December of 2010, the power of your friendship, the insight of your thinking, and the profoundly pragmatic advice you so freely offered have guided my career and much of my personal life.

Your sense of yourself was such an interesting part of knowing you. In November of 1990, you opened a presentation to the PRSA Foundation with the phrase, "In the afternoon of my own life..." During that presentation you predicted that if your computer was right you would live until approximately 2010. You did a little better than that.

Photo by Andre Burger, Chet's grandson and lifelong photography student

In a private note to me written last year, after I had asked you a question and for some guidance, your reply began, "Sure, especially in the evening of my life." Perhaps this is the most important lesson among the many I learned from you: The power of candor, which I have come to define as "Truth with an attitude, promptly given."

When Barbara and I came to work for Chester Burger Company in the summer of 1986 in New York, you became an indispensable counselor to both of us, and the stream of complementary notes and letters continued, despite the fact that you retired in 1987. I remember asking you at the time, "What did retirement really mean to Chester Burger?" Your response was so interesting. You said, "I will no longer work for money."

And so you spent the next 24 busy years as a key civilian advisor for the United States Air Force, the Central Intelligence Agency, various New York

City agencies, the Urban League, and countless other agencies, organizations and individuals who found their way to your door.

Whenever I made an important presentation in the New York area or received some recognition, you were in the audience. I've always felt that describing you as a management consultant, primarily in communications, words you chose, was so sterile and colorless. Your life and your work combined to be the very definition of friendship, of selflessness and graciousness.

A compliment seemed always to be on the tip of your tongue, or on the point of your pen. In 1992, I sent you a copy of the speech I was about to present. As always, you combined instructive and constructive advice with the motivation to get something important done.

You said, "Once again, you have written a solid and thoughtful analysis of the problem and what can be done about it. It is very good. As we discussed, I still believe your speeches will be improved by more anecdotes and company names when possible and appropriate (but always in a positive and sympathetic way). Over the years, I have read a lot of peoples' speeches. Yours consistently are among the very best because of the clarity of your content and your analyses of the problem."

Chet, you always had a useful suggestion tied to a compliment.

On another occasion, after having just arrived in New York, I discovered that because you walked to work every day to 171 Madison, you arrived about an hour before the rest of us. So, my wife Barbara and I would get up early, catch a train from Westchester to get to the office early enough to talk with you almost every day. I remember a great many of those conversations and have told stories about them and you for decades.

One of these early morning stories was about my attempts to get on the calendar of a very important New York City executive. I had prepared a letter of introduction which included part of my resume, part of what I wanted to talk to him about, and some lame language about the goals of the conversation, all in just under two pages, single spaced. You examined the draft, then looked thoughtfully at me and said, essentially the following:

"Why don't you tell him that I suggested that you and he could both benefit from having a brief discussion? Then, assure him that within the first 20 minutes he will be able to determine, from his own perspective, whether any further discussion might be useful."

That is exactly what I did. I got the appointment, and a new long-time client and friend.

Another one of my favorite stories is about you and one of your clients. You were invited in to analyze a set of issues and make recommendations for a company. In this particular case, you heard nothing from your client for a very long time. Your curiosity was getting the best of you, so you sent the CEO an amazingly short letter. The letter consisted of the salutation, a single question mark, and your signature. About one week later, as you told the story, you received a letter in response to yours. The letter opened, "Dear Chet," followed by a single exclamation point (meaning they had taken your advice) and the CEO's signature.

So much of your advice remains clearly in my mind. In the middle of a discussion of some problem you said, "Tacticians are a dime or less a dozen in any profession. If you truly want to provide value and have real influence, help others achieve their objectives from their perspectives. Think up, start your thinking as far above the tactics as you can."

Your rule for vivid expression, "Always say things and write things as simply as possible. Shorter sentences and colorful verbs always improve understanding and readership," has guided my own style from the earliest days of our relationship.

You made me a disciple of your devotion to positive, constructive, sensible language. You taught me the destructive and distractive power of "I," and you taught me the true power of being a strategic thinker, the key to be invited to counsel top management.

During the first Gulf War in 1991, long before I knew how deeply you were engaged in advising our military leaders, I drafted an article and submitted it to the New York Times, "News is the enemy's greatest weapon." At that time there was a great debate raging, as there has been during every war since, about secrecy, disinformation and delaying coverage of significant military events for security reasons. I sent it to you for comment and once again your insights were so powerful.

In May of 1991 you wrote me:

"Your piece for the Times is most thoughtful. You make many good points, specifically (among others) that truth delayed is not truth denied, the necessity for a commander to be able to communicate effectively, and your emphasis that war is not democracy (though war can be waged for preserving or establishing democracy)."

You continued, "There is no place where I disagree with you. But you make me wonder about two points: 1) Disinformation is an important military tool. General Schwarzkopf spread advance reports of plans to invade Kuwait from the sea. This deception worked. Disinformation is essential. I would like you to write and speak about the "dissonance" between the needs of the military to tell the truth and at the same time, the genuine need to lie."

You concluded, "2) In war, there will always be conflict between military organizations and democratic societies. America has had both for 200 years. It is an interesting point. I would like to see you discuss this."

It has been such a privilege to have this body of correspondence between friends for the last 30 years. It's even more remarkable, since most of it has occurred during your retirement.

During our last lengthy face-to-face conversation in November 2010, talking about your life, your career, and your accomplishments, you made the most interesting observation, "The only thing I truly planned for and did intentionally was to start Chester Burger & Co. in 1964. Everything else that has happened was beyond my control, fortunate coincidences, lucky breaks, or just being in the right place."

During this conversation you told some of your favorite stories. You observed that there is a statue of Nathan Hale, the famous American Revolutionary War patriot, located near City Hall in downtown Manhattan, although now inaccessible due to security precautions. This statue carries an inscription of Hale's famous statement as the British were about execute him for spying, "I regret that I have but one life to give for my country."

You went on to talk about the fact that there are two duplicates of this statute and its inscription, one in the lobby of CIA headquarters in Langley, Virginia and one on the Yale University campus in Connecticut. But then you mentioned there is actually a fourth lesser known version of this statue that resides in the Yale Club in the city of New York. "It's smaller, but a replica, and carries only the simple description, "Nathan Hale, Class of 1773," you said. You were always a master at identifying important, though seemingly inconsequential nuances of life, history and relationships.

Even last year, as you knew that your life was concluding, you managed to be on conference calls with Pentagon officials and commanders in Iraq and Afghanistan.

But perhaps the most profound thing you said to me, which has turned out to be true in my career, as it was in yours, is the reality in public relations that, "Anything you learn today will have some future value that you cannot foresee at the time." This to me is the definition of a life in public relations.

It's pretty lucky for all of us that you were so lucky in your life. You leave a legacy of civility, of intelligent discussions of issues and questions that matter beyond the tactical work of everyday communication, of helping two generations of leaders and aspiring leaders in the private sector, in government, and the military to lead with courage, integrity and conviction based on simple, sensible, constructive and positive principles.

We all have the legacy of friendship and accomplishment you shared throughout your remarkable life. Rest easy, dear friend. The evening of your life, as you forecasted 11 years earlier, has come to a close.

With enduring affection and admiration,

Jim Lukaszewski
New Brighton, MN
April 21, 2011

About Risdall Public Relations

Risdall Public Relations (RPR), a division of Risdall Marketing Group, LLC, is an integrated, marketing and executive/leadership-oriented PR agency headquartered in New Brighton, Minnesota. With 22 staff and 2011 billings of more than $4 million, the agency is the sixth largest PR firm in Minnesota and among the top 250 global firms ranked by the Holmes Report. Its client roster includes local, national and international work for business-to-business and consumer accounts, among others. In particular, the agency has specialized industry expertise in healthcare, education, technology, and B2B manufacturing.

RPR makes change real, embracing organizations to help transform them by first seeking understanding and strategic alignment of their brands and reputations. We work best with organizations seeking to change their organization and/or the external environment through leaders in their industry with a story to tell, needing insight and expression for telling it. RPR is uniquely positioned with industry-specific and practice experts spanning the public relations and marketing disciplines with a profound and always evolving understanding of the traditional and digital spaces. The PR agency is led by Joel Swanson, APR, and was founded by Twin Cities advertising legend John Risdall.

Crisis/Executive Leadership Issues
The Lukaszewski Group, a unique division of RPR, is led by Jim Lukaszewski, ABC, APR, Fellow PRSA. He is among America's leading crisis experts, managing and reducing contention, counteracting tough, touchy, sensitive corporate communications issues. Senior management retains him to directly intervene and manage the resolution of corporate problems and bad news. The situations he helps resolve often involve conflict, controversy, community action, or activist opposition.

Results that Matter
More than simply generating visibility and awareness for clients, Risdall helps organizations evolve their reputations, ultimately achieving results that matter to each one of them. Almost any firm can generate visibility and awareness,

but in the end, client satisfaction boils down to whether the visibility and awareness actually create a specific action, behavior or perception. At RPR, we call this Results that Matter, the tangible outcomes of our work.

Award-winning
Sometimes helping our clients succeed means that we earn recognition, too. In the past two years, we've won CLIO Healthcare Awards in the Innovative Media and Integrated Campaign categories. In the public relations universe, our work for GoGirl won a Sabre Award and a PRSA Bronze Anvil, among others.

Visit www.risdallpublicrelations.com for more information.

About the Lukaszewski Group
A Division of Risdall Public Relations

CRISIS MANAGEMENT, LEADERSHIP AND ORGANIZATIONAL RECOVERY

The Lukaszewski Group helps organizations manage tough, touchy, sensitive communication problems. We focus our energies on issues and situations with enormous organizational impact. Clients engage us to work across the spectrum of management communications and operational issues, reduce reputation risk, make things happen, move issues forward, provide second opinions, and resolve conflict and controversy.

Our work generally falls into four important areas – strategic guidance for senior management; hands-on direct action to resolve specific issues, problems, or conflicts on management's behalf; coaching for individual success and organizational leadership; leadership and organizational recovery.

Guiding management involves day-to-day advice, counsel and coaching. Typical services include developing specific strategies, plans and tactics; creating or analyzing corporate emergency communication plans; developing and executing intense, situation-specific exercises and simulations; providing confidential guidance in solving critical executive issues and problems; and first-response strategies.

Hands-on direct intervention on management's behalf may be required. Within hours we can activate situation-specific teams of experts and specialists. Typical direct action projects include directing community-based grassroots campaigns to influence public attitudes; preparing executives for appearances on *20/20*, *Nightline* and *60 Minutes*; and managing critical problems involving adverse government or community action, anti-corporate activism, business reversal/Chapter 11, environmental accidents, international disputes, high-profile civil and criminal litigation, labor negotiations, troublesome products, and extremely controversial public issues.

Coaching individual executives means, among other things, building their managerial and communication leadership skills and their ability to motivate and build commitment in employees, customers, shareholders and board members, and other key stakeholders, and to deal with angry, injured, fearful, or victimized constituencies.

Leadership/Organizational Recovery. The work life, professional life, even personal life of executives and leaders changes during and after a crisis, as does the organization. The process of experiencing a crisis is explosive and sudden; the process of repair and recovery is much longer term and incremental. Understanding ahead of time what the impact will be on organizations, individuals, communities, stakeholders, customers and others, as well as the organization is essential to organizational restoration and recovery. Management and leadership need guidance to anticipate the patterns of behavior and response that will occur, whatever the crisis is that initiates the circumstance.

We are prepared to make brief presentations about our work in more than 200 corporate issue areas.

OUR PRACTICE PHILOSOPHY

The Lukaszewski Group provides strategic guidance to the managements of major U.S. and international businesses and organizations on the most sensitive reputation and ethical problems, the kind that can redefine the reputation of an organization, executive, company, or brand.

Our style is to provide forthright, honest assessment and counseling. Whether we directly intervene to help companies promptly and conclusively manage reputationally defining situations, provide guidance and advice, or coach for individual success or organizational leadership, our goal is to build the fundamental management strengths of the organizations we serve. We strive to help client organizations solve problems, learn from mistakes and avoid future failures.

Clients describe our counsel and our actions as:

- Conclusive, timesaving and action oriented;
- Direct, positive, clear, do-able and pragmatic;
- Empathetic, useful and client oriented;
- Fair and humane;
- Honorable, ethical and morally sensitive;
- Open, prompt and highly focused;
- Principled and unassailable; and
- Simple, sensible, constructive, positive and sincere.

WHAT THE LUKASZEWSKI GROUP DOES EVERY DAY

▶ Strategic Thinking

▶ Managing Management Involvement

▶ Coaching

▶ Counseling

▶ Second Opinions

▶ Leadership & Organizational Recovery

Thinking and Acting Strategically

We are experts in developing conclusive, fundamentally sound communication strategies for companies with high-profile problems and issues ranging from activist demonstrations to civil, criminal, or class-action lawsuits; from environmental, health and safety risks to xenotransplantation. What makes us different is our ability to quickly and efficiently focus company management on the key decisions that need to be made and to structure an outcome-focused communication response. We often work with every critical operating function within the organization to get issues resolved, decisions made and actions taken.

The practical result is the immediate, responsive management of serious problems and appropriate, structured, focused communication. At the same time, while moving forward, the client organization learns more about resolving its own issues.

Managing Management Involvement

We are pragmatists. Our job is to tell it like it is, to forecast the unintended consequences of the organization's actions, and to make important, conclusive, and do-able recommendations.

Our style facilitates communication between different departments, divisions and individuals within the organization. The goals are to help managers and supervisors know what to say and when to say it; decide what to do and when to do it; and to recognize when it's time to say and do nothing.

Typically, we take these first steps to get a situation under control:

▶ Listen to senior management's most important concerns.

▶ Develop an action-based plan of attack.

▶ Build senior management confidence in the response team and the strategy.

▶ Focus the team and other consultants on getting it done.

▶ Reduce management anxiety through practical, do-able and useful recommendations.

- Manage senior management disappointment, irritation and impatience.
- Implement on-site programs; translate strategic assessment and program concepts into action steps.
- Work with and train mid-level managers on problem resolution approaches and strategy.
- Identify and plan participation exit strategies for senior management.

Coaching and Counseling
We only handle the toughest, touchiest, and most sensitive aspects of any problem. Much of our advice and counsel involves teaching and coaching executives, managers and supervisors to make fundamentally sound, results-oriented communication decisions and to effectively communicate those decisions to others.

Second Opinions
With more than 20 years on the front line of crisis communication management, one of our most important roles, aside from strategically directing response operations, is to provide second opinions. During a typical year, The Lukaszewski Group provides its opinions in situations involving activist attacks; angry communities; organized opposition; government investigations; high-profile litigation; network television news coverage; *60 Minutes*, *Primetime Live*, and other news magazine shows; media investigations, and the like. We are frequently called the "Consultant's Consultants" and the "Expert's Experts."

Leadership & Organizational Recovery
This is often the hardest part for organizations to accomplish, largely because of the immediate after effects of an emergency or crisis, frequently resulting in the termination of the CEO, along with other top officials and a new team is put in place. This replacement group often acts more to help forget what happened than to learn important lessons like detecting, deterring and preventing similar circumstances. It is a very challenging time and often, due to this initial approach of encouraging forgetfulness, this second team of leaders is temporary, to be replaced by a permanent team at some point in the future, and the reputation repair and organizational recovery process begin for real.

Three things are paramount in this first phase:

1. Preserving and retaining key leaders, producers, connections to the community, stakeholders and customers.
2. Maintaining and communicating with crucial stakeholders, the victims, survivors, and those who have opted into the conversation whether they appear to have any standing or not.

3. Establishing a constructive, sensible, positive sense of momentum, moving toward healing, resolution, and new goals and horizons, while learning to detect, deter and prevent a recurrence.

HOW WE WORK:
When The Lukaszewski Group Goes To Work For You...

The first thing we do is to put ourselves in your shoes and subject our ideas, proposals, project concepts, tactics, and strategies to the same tests and questions you would. That's how we're able to serve your needs best, no matter what the problem or situation. In addition:

1. **James E. Lukaszewski**, ABC, APR, Fellow PRSA, works directly with clients. He personally develops strategies, oversees project activities, serves as the principal coach/counselor for all training workshops, personally conducts all simulations, and guides and directs the support staff and related consultants.

2. **Joel Swanson**, APR, President, Risdall Public Relations. Joel and his group within Risdall provide a platform of effective public relations related services as required by situations responded to by The Lukaszewski Group. Risdall Public Relations, described elsewhere in the book, is a young, energetic and important ingredient in The Lukaszewski Group's successful client service. Professionals in the public relations group have a broad range of experience, ranging from consumer products to health care, to crisis response and readiness work.

3. **Kenneth Koprowski**, of counsel. Ken Koprowski is a strategic and crisis communication advisor, writer and educator. A highly regarded crisis communication consultant, Ken has extensive crisis communication and management experience. Currently advising both corporate and NGO management teams, he served as a GE crisis manager for four years and crisis communicator for 12 years at two GE financial businesses. He was the outside crisis communication counsel for Statoil North America for eight years, and led crisis communication efforts at PWC during the BCCI scandal and Standard Chartered savings and loan suit. He teaches crisis communication and reputation management in the MBA program at UConn, as well as communication strategy and practices, communications ethics and law, and advanced writing in NYU's Master's in Public Relations and Corporate Communication.

4. **Carin Leonard-Gorrill** coordinates with the Chairman for on- and off-site account services projects and helps set priorities and goals for client accounts and promotional and marketing materials. She maintains client relationships and correspondence and drafts client documents as directed by the Chairman. She also oversees the

production of the Chairman's teleseminars and monthly virtual web seminars, and the coordination of public appearance schedules, deadlines, and promotion materials.

5. **Only the most appropriate outside consultants are engaged** and then only for the specific time and tasks necessary to execute projects. This approach assures focus, expedited work and the tightest possible expense control.

6. **Whenever possible, we use client in-house resources first** – both to save money and to assure that what we learn is shared and made useful to your organization for the future.

7. **There are clear, mutually agreed upon goals** for each and every project, program, seminar, or simulation we undertake. The setting of goals is critical to our getting to the same place, at the same time, for the same reason. No surprises. Few mistakes.

8. **Concern for people – yours and ours –** is a top priority. We work to minimize the stress, fear, and fatigue these highly visible, critically important projects can cause.

9. **We focus on giving the most value** for the time invested in us. No one works harder or produces more than The Lukaszewski Group and its consultants.

10. **Organization, meticulous attention to detail and intensive hard work** builds our integrity and yours as we move through programs, projects, or problems.

11. **Originality and tactical ingenuity are hallmarks of our successful programs** because our tough, aggressively focused approach sparks positive, innovative ideas we can actually deliver.

Whenever there's another tough, touchy, sensitive communication problem... you'll call us back.

THE LUKASZEWSKI GROUP
www.e911.com
jel@e911.com
651-286-6788
Fax: 651-631-2561

About the Author

JAMES E. LUKASZEWSKI, ABC, APR, Fellow PRSA (loo-ka-SHEV-skee) advises, coaches, and counsels the men and women who run corporations and organizations through extraordinary problems and critical high-profile circumstances. The bulk of his practice is in the U.S. and Canada, although he has clients from many parts of the world.

He is an expert in managing and reducing contention, counteracting tough, touchy, sensitive corporate communications issues. He counsels companies facing the toughest internal and external problems. He is frequently retained by senior management to directly intervene and manage the resolution of corporate problems and bad news. The situations he helps resolve often involve conflict, controversy, community action, or activist opposition. Almost half of his practice involves civil and criminal litigation.

He is a teacher, thinker, coach, and trusted advisor with the unique ability to help executives look at problems from a variety of sensible, constructive, principled perspectives. He teaches clients how to take highly focused, ethically appropriate action. He has personally counseled, coached, and guided thousands of managers, executives in organizations large and small from many cultures representing government; the military and defense industry; the agriculture, banking, computer, financial, food processing, health care, insurance, paper, real estate development, and telecommunications industries; cooperatives; trade and professional associations; and non-profit agencies.

He is a coach to many CEOs, providing personal coaching for executives in trouble, or facing career-defining problems and succession issues.

He is a prolific author (six books, hundreds of articles and monographs), lecturer (corporate, college and university), trainer, counselor, and public speaker. He is an editorial board member of most of Public Relation's important Journals and serial Publications. His most recent book, *Why Should the Boss Listen to You?*, was published by Jossey-Bass in 2008.

An accredited member of the International Association of Business Communicators (ABC) and the Public Relations Society of America (APR), Mr. Lukaszewski is also a member of the PRSA's College of Fellows (Fellow PRSA); Board of Ethics & Professional Standards; a member of ASIS International, where he serves on the Crisis Management and Business Continuity Council. He lectured annually at the U.S. Marine Corp's East Coast Commander's Media Training Symposium from 1987 – 2009.

Lukaszewski received his BA in 1974 from Metropolitan State University in Minnesota. He is a former deputy commissioner of the Minnesota Department of Economic Development and assistant press secretary to former Minnesota Governor Wendell Anderson. He founded Minnesota-based Media Information Systems Corporation in 1978. Prior to founding The New York-based Lukaszewski Group Inc. in 1989 he was senior vice president and director of Executive Communication Programs for Georgeson & Company and a partner with Chester Burger Company, both in New York City. In 2011 he joined St. Paul Minnesota-based Risdall Public Relations as president of its Lukaszewski Group Division.

His biography is listed in 26 editions of various Marquis *Who's Who in America* (including the 2013, 67th edition), *The World* (including 2012, 30th edition), Finance and Government. The story of his career appears in *Living Legends of American Public Relations*, (2008) Grand Valley State University. His name was listed in Corporate Legal Times as one of "28 Experts to Call When All Hell Breaks Loose," and in PR Week as one of 22 "crunch-time counselors who should be on the speed dial in a crisis." Googling James E. Lukaszewski yields almost 34,000 entries.

CPSIA information can be obtained at www.ICGtesting.com
Printed in the USA
LVOW072217080313

323451LV00001B/5/P